THE WEALTH OF NATIONS IN THE TWENTIETH CENTURY

THE WEALTH OF NATIONS IN THE TWENTIETH CENTURY

The Policies and Institutional Determinants of Economic Development

Edited by
RAMON H. MYERS

HOOVER INSTITUTION PRESS
Stanford University
Stanford, California

Hoover Institution Press Publication No. 437

Copyright © 1996 by the Board of Trustees of the
    Leland Stanford Junior University

First printing, 1996
02   01   00   99   98   97   96   9   8   7   6   5   4   3   2   1
Simultaneous first paperback printing, 1996
02   01   00   99   98   9   8   7   6   5   4   3   2

Manufactured in the United States of America

The paper used in this publication meets the minimum requirements
of American National Standard for Information Sciences—Permanence
of Paper for Printed Library Materials, ANSI Z39.48–1984. ⊚

Library of Congress Cataloging-in-Publication Data

The wealth of nations in the twentieth century : the policies and
institutional determinants of economic development / edited by
Ramon H. Myers.
        p.   cm. — (Hoover Institution Press publication ; no. 437)
    Includes bibliographical references and index.
    ISBN 0-8179-9451-3 (alk. paper).
    ISBN 0-8179-9452-1 (paper : alk. paper)
    1. Wealth—Case studies.   2. Economic development—Case studies.
I. Myers, Ramon Hawley, 1929–   .   II. Series: Hoover Institution Press
publication ; 437.
HC79.W4W424   1996
330.1'6—dc20   96-35432
                                                                     CIP

Contents

PART II: EARLY DEVELOPERS OF WEALTH: THREE CASE STUDIES

PART III: WEALTH CREATION AND FAILURE IN THE TWENTIETH CENTURY: SEVEN CASE STUDIES

Tables

Figures

Contributors

DAVID BEVAN is deputy director of the Centre for the Study of African Economies, university lecturer in economics, and Fellow of Saint John's College, Oxford.

ROBERT CHRISTIANSEN is a senior economist at the World Bank. He currently works on agricultural issues in southern Africa.

PAUL COLLIER is director of the Centre for the Study of African Economies, reader in economics, and fellow of Saint Antony's College, Oxford.

NICHOLAS EBERSTADT is a researcher with the Harvard Center for Population and Development Studies in Cambridge, Mass., and with the American Enterprise Institute in Washington, D.C.

ALBERT FISHLOW is Class of 1959 Professor of Economics and dean of international and area studies. He has published extensively on issues of Latin American development.

JAN WILLEM GUNNING is director of the Economic and Social Institute and professor of economics at the Free University, Amsterdam.

ALAN HESTON is professor of economics and South Asia studies at the University of Pennsylvania. He has worked on the United Nations International Comparison Programme in India, Pakistan, and New York and was a consultant for the World Bank in Pakistan.

JAN HOGENDORN is Grossman Professor of Economics at Colby College.

VICTOR LAVY is a professor of economics at the Hebrew University of Jerusalem and the author of many journal articles on public policy and economic development issues of North Africa and the Middle East. His most recent publication, coauthored with E. Sheffer, is *Foreign Aid to the Middle East: Jordan, Egypt, and Syria* (Praeger, 1991).

ANGUS MADDISON is a professor of economics at the University of Groningen.

RAMON H. MYERS is a senior fellow at the Hoover Institution and curator-scholar of its East Asian Collection.

DOUGLASS C. NORTH is Luce Professor of Law and Liberty, Washington University, Saint Louis.

GUR OFER received his Ph.D. in economics at Harvard in 1969 under Abram Bergson and Simon Kuznets. He is the Harvey and Lyn Meyerhoff Professor of Soviet Economics at the Hebrew University of Jerusalem. He has published extensively on many aspects of the Soviet and socialist economies, including *The Service Sector in Soviet Economic Growth* (1973), *The Soviet Household under the Old Regime* (with Aaron Vinokur, 1992), "Soviet Economic Growth, 1928–1985," *Journal of Economic Literature* (1987), and *Reforming Planned Economies in an Integrated World Economy* (with Barry Bosworth, 1995). He was a visiting scholar at Harvard, the RAND Corporation, the Kennan Institute, the Brookings Institution, the Harriman Center at Columbia University, and the New Economic School in Moscow, where he currently serves as academic coordinator.

AMARTYA SEN is Lamont University Professor, Department of Economics, Harvard University.

KOZO YAMAMURA—Job and Gertrud Tamaki Professor and chair of the Japanese studies program, Henry M. Jackson School of International Studies, University of Washington—is the author of numerous works on Japanese economic policy and economic history.

Abbreviations

ACDA	Arms Control and Development Agency (U.S.)
ADMARC	Agricultural Development and Marketing Board (Malawi)
ASP	Arab Socialist Party (Syria)
ASPAC	Asian and Pacific Council
CEPAL	Comisión Económico para America Latina y el Caribe (U.N. Economic Commission for Latin America and the Caribbean)
CIA	Central Intelligence Agency (U.S.)
DGTG	Directorate General of Technical Development (India)
DPRK	Democratic People's Republic of Korea
DRC	Domestic resources cost
EC	European Community
ECU	European currency unit
EPB	Economic Planning Board (ROK)
ERP	Economic Recovery Plan (Ghana, 1983)
Eurostat	Statistical Office of the European Communities
FAO	Food and Agriculture Organization (U.N.)
FERA	Foreign Exchange Regulation Act (India)
FMB	Farmers Marketing Board (Malawi)
GDP	Gross domestic product
GM	General Motors (U.S.)
GNP	Gross national product
IBGE	Fundacão Instituto Brasileiro de Geografia e Estatistica (Brazil)

ICOR	Incremental capital-output ratio
IBRD	International Bank for Reconstruction and Development (World Bank)
IDB	Inter-American Development Bank
IDRA	Industries Development and Regulation Act (India, 1951)
IISS	International Institute for Strategic Studies (London)
IMF	International Monetary Fund
IPC	International Comparison Project (U.N.)
IRDP	Integrated Rural Development Program (India)
JETRO	Japan External Trade Organization
JCRR	Joint Commission on Rural Reconstruction (ROK-U.S.)
KCIA	Korean Central Intelligence Agency (ROK)
kWh	Kilowatt-hour
KMT	Kuomintang (Nationalist) Party (ROC)
LDC	Less-developed country
LDP	Liberal Democratic Party (Japan)
MITI	Ministry of International Trade and Industry (Japan)
MOF	Ministry of Finance (Japan)
MRTP	Monopolies and Restrictive Trade Practices Act (India)
NFC	Ninth Finance Commission (India)
NIC	Newly industrializing country
NMP	Net material product
NNP	Net national product
NTIS	National Technical Information Service (U.S. Dept. of Commerce)
NUB	National Unification Board (ROK)
NWRP	Northwest Frontier Province (Pakistan)
OECD	Organization for Economic Cooperation and Development
OPEC	Organization of Petroleum-Exporting Countries
PAMSCAD	Program of Actions to Mitigate the Social Costs of Adjustment (Ghana)
PPP	Purchasing power parity
PRC	People's Republic of China
R&D	Research and development
ROC	Republic of China
ROK	Republic of Korea
Rs.	Rupees (Indian)
SC	Scheduled castes (India)
SDP	State domestic product (India)
SEWA	Self-Employed Women's Association (India)
SIA	Secretariat for Industrial Approvals (India)
SME	Small-to-medium-scale enterprise

SOE	State-operated enterprise
ST	Scheduled tribes (India)
TFP	Total factor productivity
UAR	United Arab Republic
U.N.	United Nations
UNFPA	United Nations Fund for Population

Introduction

RAMON H. MYERS

The idea for these essays originated in a conversation many years ago between the editor and Thomas A. Metzger in Taipei, Taiwan. We pondered how the Republic of China (ROC) on Taiwan, after a stinging defeat by the Communists in mainland China, had overcome poverty, backwardness, and authoritarianism to become the first prosperous and democratic Chinese society in Chinese history. If that government and its people had raised living standards and democratized while shouldering an immense national security burden, why had countries with more abundant resources and having more advantages not done as well? We did not know. We believed that trying to understand why a few countries had become wealthy and democratized, while most had not, was a worthy task.

We conceived of undertaking a *tour d'horizon* of countries having different cultures, resource endowments, and economic and political systems to understand how they tried to develop wealth and democratize. After consulting with leading scholars Douglass C. North, S. Eisenstadt, and others to help us identify common themes and choose scholars to address them, we convened two conferences in the spring of 1990 at the Hoover Institution, the first organized by Myers to focus on economic development or wealth creation and the second organized by Metzger to examine political development or democratization.

This collection of essays focuses on how eighteen countries—England and Spain in the seventeenth century, Japan and the USSR in the twentieth century, and fourteen underdeveloped countries after 1950—tried to create wealth as defined by their gross domestic production of goods and services valued at market prices. Ever since Adam Smith argued that "the natural progress or opulence" of nations must be achieved by allocating a greater part of their capital "first, directed to agriculture, afterwards to manufactures, and last of all to foreign commerce," the leaders and elite of nation-states have tried to find the most appropriate means to create wealth for the purpose of enhancing their national power and prestige as well as the material well-being of their people.[1]

As we will see in the essays that follow, most twentieth-century states violated Adam Smith's first principle of economic development and intervened in the marketplace with policies and institutions that tended to impede the functions the marketplace could effectively perform to facilitate the key economic processes necessary for the creation of wealth. Although a worldwide pattern of growth acceleration of gross domestic product (GDP) can be observed from 1950 to around 1973 (for developing as well as advanced countries) that pattern, with only a few exceptions, changed to one of economic slowdown over the next two decades. By the mid-1990s, then, the worldwide pattern of economic growth had become complex, with more nation-states exercising prudence when intervening in the economic marketplace. Many governments were trying to promote private enterprise, protect private property rights, nurture free markets, and foster economic competition. Central planning as practiced in the Marxist-socialist states, in contrast, has been jettisoned, and the government regulations imposed by authoritarian states in the economic marketplace are being loosened.

Our *tour d'horizon* of how eighteen nation-states tried to create wealth describes, explains, and evaluates three general themes. First, these essays try to identify and describe the key economic processes that the authors believe explain why the creation of wealth was facilitated or impeded. The second theme addresses the policies and institutional changes that national leaders used to intervene in the economic market process. In most cases national leaders selected the wrong policies and initiated institutional changes that distorted or limited the role that organizations in the economic marketplace could play to create wealth. Therefore, these countries failed to realize their wealth-creating potential. Yet a small group of nations in East Asia after World War II did far better than many thought possible in accelerating economic growth and creating wealth. A second important conclusion, then, is that certain types of state policies and institutional changes can remove impediments and facilitate the role that organizations and the market can play to allocate resources efficiently and creatively for the purpose of realizing a nation's wealth-creating potential. In essence, this finding confirms Adam Smith's insight that removing impediments to vitalizing the market's role is an important function of government.[2]

The third theme applies this volume's findings to the current state of economic development knowledge, which, as summarized in the following normative patterns of economic change, describes how wealth can be created:

- An efficacious circle of four interacting activities—a more equitable distribution of income, a rising market demand for goods and services, an increasing share of savings of gross domestic product, and more investment in physical and human capital
- Avoiding large wage increases and inflation
- A gradual shift from relying on the domestic market to opening the domestic market and integrating with the international market economy

If government intervention and institutional change in the economic market process can produce these three patterns of economic change, national leaders and elite can transform their economies and create more wealth.

It seems clear that government can play a definite role in promoting national economic development. But, as this study shows, government failures have been far more numerous than successes during the twentieth century. Government has been far too eager to intervene, ignoring the lessons of the past. Recent scholarship is now addressing the issue of developing an adequate theory of government policy and institutional change to promote successful economic development.[3] Historical reality is not only complex but forever changing. Without a sensitive understanding of the complex nexus between organizations, market processes, and society (including society's political groups, culture, etc.), government policy and institutional change will produce more harm than good.

The conference that produced this study owes much to the vision and encouragement of Dr. Chang Ching-yü, former director of the Government Information Office of the Republic of China, former president of National Cheng Chih University, director of the Mainland Affairs Council, and a distinguished scholar. Finally, I want to acknowledge the support of the Hoover Institution's Sun Yat-sen Endowment for Advanced Chinese Research Studies and thank Dr. John Raisian, director of the Hoover Institution, for making this conference publication possible.

Notes

1. Adam Smith, *An Inquiry into the Nature and Causes of the Wealth of Nations* (Chicago: University of Chicago Press, 1976), p. 405.

2. Andrew S. Skinner, "Adam Smith," in John Eatwell, Murray Milgate, and Peter Newman, eds., *The New Palgrave: The Invisible Hand* (New York: W. W. Norton, 1989), p. 29.

3. For example, see Douglass C. North, *Institutions, Institutional Change and Economic Performance* (Cambridge: Cambridge University Press, 1990). See also the new series, the Political Economy of Institutions and Decisions, edited by James Alt and Douglass North and published by Cambridge University Press.

PART ONE

DEFINING AND MEASURING WEALTH EXPANSION IN THE TWENTIETH CENTURY

1

The Concept of Wealth

AMARTYA SEN

Science and Policy

The nature and causes of the wealth of nations have been a subject of systematic inquiry for a long time, going back at least to William Petty in the seventeenth century and to the diverse contributions of Gregory King, François Quesnay, Antoine Lavoisier, and Joseph Louis Lagrange, among many others. The inquiry took a particularly systematic form in the economic analysis of Adam Smith (1776).

Right from the beginning, two rather different concerns have characterized these inquiries, to wit: (1) scientific interest in the commodity basis of the well-being and prosperity of people and (2) political interest in the advocacy of public policies and support for appropriate social judgments. The study of wealth cannot be dissociated from its policy interests. In fact, even William Petty's pioneering work on the measurement of wealth, which was a part of his general enterprise of "political arithmetick" (Petty 1691), was directly motivated to show, among other things, that "the King's subjects are not in so bad a condition as discontented Men would make them."[1] Petty's characterizations of "the condition" of the "King's subjects," while concerned with commodities and their valuations, directly invoked the relevance of various different rules for appropriate assessments of the well-being of the people, including ideas of "the Common Safety" and "each Man's particular Happiness."

Similarly, Adam Smith's (1776) classic inquiry led to firm policy recommendations regarding what the government should and should not do. The force of Smith's policy advocacy greatly dependend on the broad and plausible way he saw the well-being of the people and the objectives that he took to be appropriate for policy analysis.[2] He used that view of wealth and welfare as the motivating basis of his investigation of the role of the government. The scientific interests merged well with the policy concerns. For example, Smith's critique of mercantilist barriers to trade and exchange was both powerfully political in content and thoroughly dependent on the nature of his economic cognizance. There is a similar mixture of scientific and political concerns in his analyses of policies to deal with poverty, in which he both acknowledged the need for public help to the indigent and investigated (and suggested reforms of) the counterproductive aspects of the contemporary Poor Laws.[3]

The policy motivation is particularly important to bear in mind in the context of the preparation of a series of studies on "the wealth of nations in the twentieth century," of which this chapter is a part. There are important scientific issues in determining how wealth may be understood, characterized, and explained, but such investigations must also be seen in the context of policies and judgments in the contemporary world that invoke the concept of wealth. Although "wealth" does have some widely acknowledged descriptive content (particularly its association with assets and resources), the concept cannot be adequately specified without also paying attention to its possible uses and their normative interests. The link with assets and resources, and generally the commodity basis of social well-being and prosperity, establishes certain limits that serve as "boundary conditions" for the characterization of wealth.[4] Within these limits, there remains considerable freedom to delineate wealth in different ways, and this is where the cogency of the possible policy interests becomes directly relevant.

To illustrate, the following questions are certainly admissible within the general framework of the concept of wealth: (1) Should wealth be seen as a *flow* or a *stock* in ascertaining the commodity basis of well-being? (2) Should the commodities be evaluated at *market prices* or at some *other* relative values? (3) Which commodities should be included in the list of things to be valued in the overall measure of wealth? (4) More foundationally, is it appropriate to characterize wealth as an objective in its own right? and so on. These and other questions have to be addressed bearing in mind the nature of the normative interests in the well- being of the people.

Importance and Instrumentality

The idea of wealth is closely related to the pursuit of well-being and other ends, but it is not identical with these ends. The boundary conditions referred to earlier would tend to rule out identifying wealth with welfare. Insofar as wealth relates to well-being, it belongs to the category of *means* to well-being rather than to the *content* of well-being as such. It can also serve as means to other (nonwelfarist) ends. But it is hard to see wealth as an end in itself.

Indeed, Aristotle's famous warning against the claims of wealth maximization as an objective dealt precisely with the point that wealth is not an end but a means:

> The Life of Money-making is a constrained kind of life, and clearly wealth is not the Good we are in search of, for it is only good as being useful, a means to something else. On this score indeed one might conceive the ends before mentioned to have a better claim, for they are approved for their own sakes.[5]

This distinction, while elementary, is an important one to invoke at the beginning of this study because the claim of "wealth maximization" as the ultimate objective of practical reasoning has received a certain amount of championship, particularly in the literature on jurisprudence.[6] The point at issue here is not necessarily the utilitarian or the welfarist one—that only individual welfare or utility can serve as the ultimate end (that is a claim that we may or may not accept)—but the broader affirmation that wealth is valued derivatively as a *means* to whatever our ends are (whether or not those ends are best seen in utilitarian terms).

In this sense, the idea of wealth belongs to the category of what John Rawls (1971) calls "primary goods," things that rational people want for the sake of pursuing their respective, possibly very diverse, ends. Indeed, Rawls includes wealth prominently in this list of primary goods.[7]

Implicit use is being made here of the conventional definition of wealth as the value of resources at our command. This general identification fixes the "subject matter" of wealth in a way that is hard to escape, even though many questions can be raised about the details of the valuational conventions and the items to be included in the commodity baskets that constitute wealth. The basic point is that wealth is identified as a commodity-based means to our ends, and in seeking an appropriate characterization of wealth we have to work toward refining this role of wealth as "means," rather than trying to move the concept of wealth from the category of means to that of ends. The operative question, then, is *How best might we characterize wealth, seeing it as a means, related to commodity command, for the pursuit of human ends?*

The means role of wealth also relates to John Hicks's (1981) affirmation of the "diminishing marginal significance" of wealth with increased prosperity. As Aristotle had discussed, the contingent variability of importance depending on the context is a characteristic of means as opposed to ultimate ends. Hicks puts his argument thus:

As wealth increases, wealth itself becomes (or should become) less important. At low levels of income, it is right to concentrate on economics; the first need of man is to fill his belly; politics are at best a distraction, at worst no better than communal drug-taking. But as wealth increases, there is room for other (and better) standards. . . . We are not so affluent that the need for more wealth has disappeared; but it has become *relatively* less urgent. The problems of combining security with freedom, equity with responsibility, come thereby more strongly to the fore.[8]

This Hicksian analysis not only affirms the view of wealth as means, but it also points toward seeing wealth specifically as a means to the pursuit of some ends rather than others—in particular the economic ends of "filling one's belly" and in other ways achieving a good economic basis of living well and being well. The categorization of ends is useful because we have many different types of ends (whether or not we establish priorities among them in the way Hicks does), and means can be correspondingly diverse. It is the general Hicksian perspective of seeing wealth as *the economic means to the pursuit of material well-being* that is particularly relevant in what follows.[9]

Stock or Flow?

The modern concept of wealth tends to see it as a stock rather than as a flow. It is taken to be some kind of concept of "capital." (The subject index of Simon Kuznets's *Modern Economic Growth* even identifies the two: "Wealth. See Capital.")[10] This tendency creates some difficulty for the modern reader in understanding what classical political economists such as Adam Smith were trying to say because they frequently saw wealth as a flow concept. Hicks presents the problem thus:

We are nowadays so accustomed to thinking of wealth as capital wealth that it may not be easy to realize that in Smith wealth is normally taken in a "flow" sense. Even in the first sentence of his book there is a snag which worries the modern reader. "The annual produce of every nation is the fund which originally supplies it with all the necessities and conveniences of life which it annually consumes. . . ." The repeated *annual* emphasizes flow; but what about *fund*? I suggest we get nearest to Smith's meaning if we interpret *fund* to mean *revolving fund*. This would square with what he says later (in Book II) about capital. The flow interpretation of the sentence, which is meant to set course for the whole work, and must therefore be coherent with the title, would then become clear.[11]

What would be the consequence of taking the flow view of wealth in the context of modern economic analysis? As Hicks rightly points out, the consequence would be to see wealth as *national product*. It would be also to establish a close relation between the concept of wealth as current production of goods and services and the resulting social welfare generated on the basis of that production. This view would, thus, take us toward the economic analysis presented by A. C. Pigou (1920) in his *The Economics of Welfare*. Hicks presents the connection thus:

> *The Economics of Welfare* is *The Wealth of Nations* in a new guise. For remember the exact title of Adam Smith's book—*An Inquiry into the Nature and Causes of the Wealth of Nations*. If we take that title, not as a mere label in the modern manner, but as a description which means what it says, it corresponds to what we have found in Pigou. Wealth is production; the Wealth of a Nation is what we now call the National Product. Adam Smith is to tell us what the Social Product of a Nation is; what is meant by its being large or small; what is meant by its growing. That is "nature" ([compare] Pigou [*Economics of Welfare*] Part I). Then he is to tell us why the Social Product is large or small, and why it grows. That is "causes" (Pigou Part II). There is a close correspondence.[12]

Combining this analysis with what was presented earlier in this chapter (drawing on the Aristotelian identification of wealth as a means rather than an end), we have in the flow view of wealth the flow of goods and services as the basis of contemporary social welfare.

This view might appear to be unduly narrow from the point of view of the long-run welfare of a nation. The advantage of a stock view would be to give us a better idea of a nation's ability to produce things in the future. It is not hard to see merit in this criticism, but there are, I believe, some good grounds for sticking to the Smith-Hicks view of wealth as a flow.

First, it is hard indeed to estimate the stock of capital of a nation from the point of view of its ability to produce goods and services in the future and valued in terms of relative values that would be appropriate in the future. The *market values* of capital are swayed by fluctuations of optimism and pessimism (as Pigou himself had analyzed in graphic terms in discussing business cycles). In contrast, the *historical cost* estimates of capital tell us little about what they could do in the future. Once again Hicks provides good grounds for skepticism (in a different paper, "Measurement of Capital—in Practice"):

> We reject the market value, as determined on the stock exchange, because it is too future-oriented; it is too much affected by hopes and fears for the future, by guesses which are not fact but at the best probability. We reject the "original cost" of the balance-sheets of businesses, because it is too much oriented towards the past. We are baffled in our pursuit of a "national balance-sheet," because it is impossible to reduce these forward-looking, and backward-looking, valuations into even a formal consistency. We may doctor them to make them appear consistent, but how much do we gain when we do so?[13]

Second, the problem is even more difficult when we bear in mind the need to evaluate future production potential not necessarily at market prices but at the valuations that would be appropriate in assessing commodity flows as the basis of social welfare (including problems of externalities, public goods, and distributional weighting).

Third, the evaluation of human resources (what we have learned to call, I fear rather grossly, "human capital") adds further difficulties because there are no stock exchanges for skills and dexterity. And yet, as the experiences of different countries in the world have clearly brought out, and as was altogether clear to Adam Smith, the stock of human resources often (perhaps always) has the profoundest influence on what a nation can or cannot produce. Indeed, Smith saw the human aspect as the prime determinant of the ratio of national produce to the population:

> But this proportion must in every nation be regulated by two different circumstances; first, by the skill, dexterity, and judgement with which "its" labour is generally applied; and, secondly, by the proportion between the number of those who are employed in useful labour, and that of those who are not so employed.[14]

Fourth, on the other side of the balance, it is not absurd to presume that the size and nature of current production levels can give us some reasonably good idea also about production possibilities in the proximate future. We can, for example, guess that Germany can produce more in the proximate future years than, say, Ethiopia by simply noting how much richer Germany *currently* is vis-à-vis Ethiopia, *without* having to do a detailed accounting of the stock of physical capital and human resources in the two countries. In this context, it is also important to note that the size of *national production*, which is the focus of attention in the Smith-Hicks flow view, is more of a basis for predicting future production than national *consumption* level would have been.

There is, of course, little doubt that the flow concept leaves out things that we would profit from knowing. It would be good to get some idea of how much production potential (appropriately valued) for the future there is in the existing stock of physical capital and human resources. But given the near impossibility of a reliable estimate of that, it makes sense to concentrate on taking a more careful look at the present national production, appropriately valued from the point of view of social welfare. It is the combination of these considerations that pushes us in the direction of taking the flow view of wealth and trying to do a good job of valuing current production at the appropriate weights than to opt for what would likely be a bad job of estimating the stock of wealth seen in terms of future production potentials.

Market Valuations and Corrections

In view of what has been discussed so far, it seems reasonable to see wealth as the flow of goods and services valued in terms of their ability to generate social welfare, in particular related to people's ability to live comfortably and well. We are, thus, concerned with valuing the national production but not necessarily as the "gross national product" (GNP) or the "net national product" (NNP) would be evaluated in standard economic accounting. This is because the market prices at which the weighting is done in the estimation of GNP or NNP may be misleading in terms of the contribution of the national product to any acceptable concept of social welfare.

The reasons for the failure of market prices to provide appropriate valuations are well-known in the literature of welfare economics, and I have tried to present an overall picture of the relevant correspondences elsewhere (in Sen 1979). I need not, therefore, belabor each point in detail here. But it may be useful to distinguish between different sources of failure of the market evaluation and to consider briefly the type of problems raised in each case.

First, evaluation at market prices does not distinguish between the rich and the poor and treats the welfare correlate of a millionaire's dollar in the same way as that of the pauper. I have discussed elsewhere (Sen 1976) how distributional corrections can be made, using the weight w_{ij} on a commodity j going to person i, a function that increases with the price of the commodity p_j and decreases with the income of the person y_i. This approach can be integrated into the standard theory of evaluation of "real national income," making use of analytic properties of convexity and partial orderings (Sen 1976, 1979).[15]

Furthermore, such a distribution-corrected evaluation can be done in an approximate way by adapting the standardly available statistics. For example, if m is the mean income and G the Gini coefficient of the distribution of income, then $m(1-G)$ can serve as the basis of distribution-corrected comparisons of real national income, using appropriate price weights.[16] There are other ways of doing such corrections, and it is possible to go considerably beyond the distributional blindness of the standard GNP or NNP measures.

Second, the market valuation of "public goods" tends to be deeply defective. Using market values can severely underestimate the contributions to social welfare made by national production in such fields as health and education.[17] This can be particularly important in valuing wealth in terms of people leading lives free from avoidable morbidity and escapable mortality, with opportunities to pursue their creative interests. As will be illustrated below, the conventionally measured GNP can give inadequate clues about the true opportunities that people actually have.

Third, some of the provisions of health, education, and social security are often organized outside the standard market system, and the prevalence of such arrangements can be seen in diverse forms, varying from national health services in Britain and Canada to socially organized cooperative enterprises in Costa Rica, Cuba, and China. Here again we cannot get any idea of the value of what is being provided by simply looking at what is being transacted within the confines of the market.[18]

Fourth, the extensive externalities in many fields can take a positive form (e.g., skill formation) as well as a negative shape (e.g., environmental degradation). Here again far-reaching corrections may be needed, in many cases.[19] The subject of externalities is a well discussed one in economic theory; the issue here is the powerful empirical relevance of some of these failures of market valuation. This subject also relates closely to some of the strongest concerns of the international community, particularly with the deterioration of the global environment and with such problems as intense urbanization and the creation of problematically large metropolitan cities in many developing countries of the world.

Fifth, market prices are often out of equilibrium, and treating them as having the standard "optimizing" properties can be a serious mistake. There is also the problem that the balance between work and leisure may not be determined in terms of marginal equilibration when there are indivisibilities in paid work.[20] There are also the related problems of unemployment and its negative effects on human will and enjoyment.

Sixth, in making international comparisons we may be misled by variations in relative prices.[21] Real income comparisons are meant to be performed at constant relative prices, not—as is frequently done in making quick statements on international living standards—at their own respective prices adjusted for exchange rates. Even when constant relative prices *are* used, the results may depend on *which* set of relative prices is employed. The use of real-income techniques with varying prices needs a careful integration of theory with practice.[22]

This is a long list of issues, but in principle there is nothing insurmountable in these evaluations and reassessments. The important thing to bear in mind is the motivation underlying all this, in particular the characterization of wealth as the commodity basis of social welfare, and to refer to the demands of that objective when faced with alternative procedures.[23]

Conversion Relations and Equivalent Wealth

The discussion in the last section invoked the ultimate ends of the pursuit of wealth to provide a more appropriate measure of the flow concept of wealth—and of the national product—than is provided by such figures as GNP or NNP. But that discussion did not explicitly bring in the Aristotelian distinction between wealth as a means to ends and the ends themselves. The distinction is important not only for foundational clarity but also for us to note that the relationship between wealth and our freedom to pursue our ends can vary greatly from person to person and between one community and another.

A variety of circumstances affect the functional relation between (1) a commodity bundle and (2) the capability to function that is achieved on the basis of that bundle.[24] For example, the food needed (and thus the "wealth" required to buy that food) to avoid undernourishment can vary greatly depending on a person's basal metabolic rate, the presence or absence of parasitic diseases, and proneness to wasting ailments, as well as on the epidemiological atmosphere in which we live and also on one's age, body size, gender, whether the person is pregnant, and so on. We must, therefore, distinguish between (1) the actual freedoms we enjoy to lead the life that we may really wish to live and (2) the means we possess that may contribute inter alia to our freedoms.[25]

It is possible to argue that the success of a society can be best judged by the freedoms enjoyed by the people in that society. This requires that attention be paid to the interpersonal and intercommunity variations in the conversion of wealth and other primary goods into the freedom to lead valuable lives.

What would be the practical differences in the evaluation of wealth if this approach is accepted? There are two major effects. First, in terms of achieving particular levels of functionings, the requirement of wealth would have to be assessed in each case by taking note of the respective conversion relation. To illustrate, let F^1 and F^2 stand for two functional relations, converting means M into achievements A for two persons, 1 and 2, respectively, with person 2 having a less favorable conversion relation than person 1. For the same level of means OA, person 1 achieves a functioning of AB, whereas person 2 achieves only AC (see figure 1.1). If the means M is revalued in terms of achievement (using the inverse function of F^1 and F^2), then OA amount of the means for person 1 is equivalent to the larger required amount OE for person 2 because each would yield AB level of achievement. There is, thus, an issue of establishing *equivalences* in terms of achievement (and, correspondingly, in terms of the freedom to achieve).

Second, the variations between one country and another may not only relate to immutable natural factors, such as climatic conditions, but also to physical and social environments that could be altered by economic and social policies. For example, health services could alter the epidemiological atmosphere in which people live, which could radically alter the achievements of nourishment and well-being from similar baskets of food and other purchasable commodities. Thus, aside from establishing *equivalences*, there is also a policy-related question involved here of taking note of the wealth-enhancing effects of particular policies when the enhancement is brought about through *improvements* in the conversion

Figure 1.1   Relationship between Achievement and Means

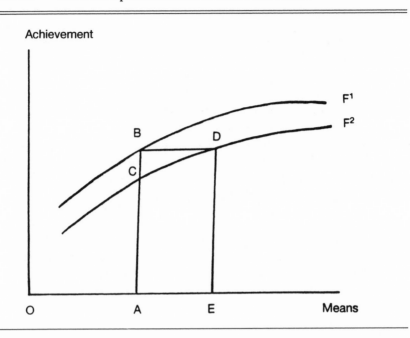

relations, rather than through increases in the purchasable bundle of commodities. For example, if a public health policy moves people from conversion relation
F^2 to F^1, then that is an increase in "equivalent wealth" (for example, for achievement AB, it is an increase of equivalent wealth to the extent of AE).

We must, however, distinguish between a temporary raising of achievement—for any given level of means—and a sustained enhancement, for there
have been rapid increases followed by a downward slide. The concept of equivalent wealth has to take note of this possibility of temporal variability. The policy
interest of the concept would depend on the sustainability of the relationship in
question.

Variations in conversion relations can indeed be important both for appropriate assessment of comparative wealth and for guiding public policy. It is true
that detailed quantitative calculations of differences in conversion relations
would often be difficult if not impossible. But that is not an argument for ignoring
this aspect of the problem and for assuming the same conversion rate everywhere.
On the contrary, given its descriptive and prescriptive importance, there is a
strong case for taking as much note as possible of this aspect of the problem, even
if it is informal and qualitative, rather than formal and exact. In this field, like

many others in economics, unattainable precision should not be made into an
enemy of sensible presumption.

Does It Make a Difference?

Does it make a significant difference whether these corrections
are (formally or informally) considered? It can. For example, ranking countries
according to the value of commodities produced or gross national product per
head (even after appropriate distributional corrections) may differ significantly
from ranking them according to some dimension of basic freedoms, such as the
ability to escape premature mortality.

To illustrate, figure 1.2 presents the GNP per head and life expectancy at
birth for five countries—China, Sri Lanka, Brazil, South Africa, and Oman—in
1985.[26] Although China and Sri Lanka have only a small fraction of the GNP per
head of Brazil, South Africa, and Oman (e.g., Oman's per capita income is about
twenty times that of China or Sri Lanka), those richer countries have substantially
lower longevity rates (e.g., a life expectancy of fifty-four years for Oman vis-à-vis
sixty-nine and seventy years, respectively, for China and Sri Lanka). Thus, for the
present exercise the contrast is important.

Similar contrasts can be found between other aspects of elementary freedoms (including political and social liberties), on the one hand, and commodity
opulence, on the other. The issue is of considerable generality.

The success stories of the Third World in raising GNP per capita come from
economies that have made pervasive use of markets and entrepreneurial capitalism (e.g., South Korea, Brazil, Hong Kong, Taiwan).[27] If GNP growth were all
we were concerned with, then there is homogeneity in the observed pattern of
successes. But if we turn our attention to enhancing life expectancy or reducing
child mortality or expanding literacy, the picture is more mixed. The same applies to the elimination of persistent undernourishment—a common characteristic of underdevelopment. These achievements are closely linked with the public provisioning of health, education, and social security. Even the problem of
endemic undernourishment cannot be dissociated from that of deprivation of
health care and basic education; undernourishment is often generated by parasitic disease and fostered by epidemics. In the delivery of public health care and
basic education, the state does have something substantial to offer. The picture
then is much more mixed.

Even in this mixed pattern, many of the market-reliant economies do very
well. For example, if we identify the top ten performers during 1960 to 1985 in
reducing infant and child mortality (the so-called under-five mortality rate)

Figure 1.2   GNP per Head and Life Expectancy at Birth for Five Countries, 1985

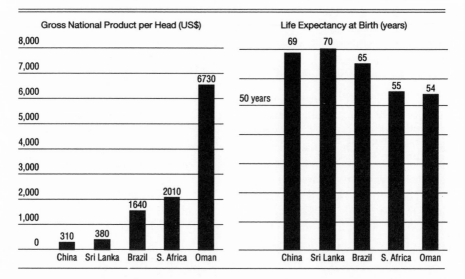

among all the developing countries, we find in our list such examples of successful capitalism as South Korea, Hong Kong, Singapore, Kuwait, and the United Arab Emirates.[28] It is, however, important to note that these countries have not only had high growth of real incomes—to a great extent through the market mechanism—but also plowed back a lot of the fruits of that growth in the public distribution of education and health care.[29] There is a striking contrast between these experiences[30] and those of, say, Brazil or Oman, with comparably high economic expansion but much less use of public intervention and correspondingly less achievement in mortality reduction.

A second and no less important issue concerns the *remaining* five countries in the list of the top ten in reducing infant and child mortality. They are all much poorer countries, but nevertheless they have all achieved tremendous reductions in under-five mortality and have reached very low absolute mortality rates. This has been achieved mainly through public programs of medical care, epidemiological control, and elementary education, through which the "equivalent wealth" has been much enhanced. That list includes socialist economies such as China and Cuba. Other countries are Costa Rica, Chile, and Jamaica, all relatively poor economies that have also been exceptionally active, for substantial parts of the period in question, in securing health care and basic education through public intervention.[31] The reaping in the form of enhancement of "equivalent wealth," related to improving the conversion rates, can be plausibly seen as being connected with the sowing in the form of widespread public provisioning of health, education, and social security.[32]

Another interesting case is Sri Lanka, which has had tremendous success in raising life expectancy and curtailing premature mortality (despite the contrary impact of the violence that has gripped the country in the last decade and spoiled that record of longevity increase to some extent). It did not make it in the list of the top ten in mortality reduction during 1960–1985 because the sharpest reduction of mortality rates in Sri Lanka occurred before 1960. Indeed, by 1960 Sri Lanka had already cut its death rate to 8.6 per thousand from 20.6 in 1940. This was largely because Sri Lanka, which was a pioneer in public provisioning, went into extensive state intervention earlier than other developing countries (including those in the list of top ten), with public distribution of free and subsidized food being introduced in 1942 and massive expansion of public health services in the mid-1940s.

Another substantial region not included in this list of top performers is the Indian state of Kerala, which has, in fact, also achieved rapid expansion of life expectancy and of other indicators of good living, using extensive public provisioning.[33] Kerala, which now has a life expectancy of about seventy-one years (as opposed to the Indian average of fifty-nine), is not included because it is a constitutive state in a federal country, not a country on its own, though in terms of population size it is much larger than a great many sovereign countries. In fact, the experiences of Kerala and Sri Lanka reinforce the pattern identified earlier — that public provisioning of health care and education can lead to substantial expansions of equivalent wealth judged in terms of mortality reduction.

It is legitimate to wonder how the government of a poor country can afford to spend so much on health and education even before its GNP is raised through simple economic growth. But a pragmatic economic analysis must include an adequate recognition of the highly labor-intensive nature of these activities, which makes them relatively cheap in poor countries because of the low wages.[34] This is important to bear in mind when comparing the high equivalent wealth advantages of public health and education vis-à-vis their low cost.

These illustrations bring out the fact that the empirical import of taking note of "equivalences" in wealth evaluation can be significant indeed. We are dealing here not just with a point of some theoretical relevance but also with a consideration that can substantially affect practical reasoning on what is to be done and how.

A Concluding Remark

The twentieth century, which is coming to an end soon, has seen some major organizational changes in economic, social, and political fields. The changes have not been all in the same direction, and right now a good deal of rearrangement is taking place. The political and economic reforms in the erstwhile Soviet Union, Eastern Europe, and China are perhaps the most prominent developments of recent years. But the century has seen many other radical changes as well, including the development of public health services and the welfare state in Western Europe and the emergence of a mixed system of dynamic capitalism with publicly funded social security in Japan and East Asia.

In analyzing and assessing these changes, an adequate understanding of the content, relevance, and reach of the concept of wealth can be quite central. In this chapter, I have tried to discuss some basic conceptual issues in the evaluation of wealth in studying "the wealth of nations in the twentieth century." The starting point was a recognition of the policy perspective in assessing wealth (section 1). Taking a lead from Aristotle, I have argued for seeing wealth as an important means but not as an end, and therefore I have resisted the claims of "wealth maximization" as an objective. The importance of wealth has to be seen in instrumental terms (i.e., as means to other ends), and thus the valuation of wealth is inescapably linked with the functional connection between wealth and the ends that wealth can help to promote (section 2).

Further, taking a lead from Adam Smith and John Hicks, I have argued for a flow characterization of wealth, even though the stock view is more common. Using the means characterization in the flow context, the notion of wealth ends up being an appropriately evaluated assessment of the national product (section 3).

In doing that assessment, the market values help to some extent, but they also have built-in biases, which are reflected in the figures of gross national product or net national product. There are, thus, good grounds for departing from mechanical use of measures such as the GNP and NNP, even though these measures are not without practical interest once their limitations are clearly recognized. The types of corrections needed relate to the respective sources of failure of these evaluations (e.g., distributional insensitivity, undervaluation of externalities, and public goods) and the practical exercise of going beyond the GNP or the NNP to be alive to the possibility of systematic corrections (section 4). In the studies that constitute this collection, various attempts have been made to take note at least of some of the problems identified here.

The assessment of wealth in instrumental terms calls for paying attention to the functional relation between the effective means and the relevant ends. This yields a notion of equivalent wealth that takes explicit note of the ends-means relations (section 5). It is easy to illustrate the pitfalls of treating GNP as a means with a *fixed* relation to ends by comparing international performances (section 6). The assessment of equivalent wealth is an attempt to judge the means in terms of their contingent effectiveness in promoting the ends.

It is important to take note of the underlying idea of the parametric variability of ends-means relationships, even when it is hard to accommodate the concept of equivalent wealth in all its complexity. Informal consideration of the contingent mutability of ends-means relationships can help qualify overhasty conclusions and point toward appropriate reassessments. The demands of evaluative sophistication need not take an all or none form.

Notes

For useful suggestions, I am most grateful to Sudhir Anand and Ramon Myers.

1. In C. H. Hull's (1899) edition of Petty's writings, vol. 1, p. 313.

2. See also Smith's broader study of human well-being in the context of analyzing moral sentiments, in Smith (1790).

3. In fact, Smith combined scientific commitment with a deep dedication to giving political priority to the interests of the poor. He was inclined to judge economic policies (including his promarket recommendations) to a great extent by their impact on the interests of the impoverished. On this and related matters, see Winch (1978) and Rothschild (1992).

4. The "commodity basis" includes services as well as material goods, which requires a broader view of wealth compared with some parts of standard practice.

5. Aristotle (Rackham 1934, 17) goes on to say that even ends that are approved of "for their own sakes" are not necessarily "the Supreme Good," which takes him on to a discriminating analysis of different ends.

6. For a forceful presentation of the case for "wealth maximization" as a basic principle of jurisprudence, see Richard Posner (1981). For a critique, see Ronald Dworkin (1985), chap. 12.

7. See Rawls (1971), pp. 60–65. See also Rawls (1982), p. 162.

8. Hicks (1981), chap. 6 ("A Manifesto"), pp. 138–39. I am not necessarily agreeing with Hicks that the claims of broader political concerns going beyond filling one's belly are necessarily weak in states of poverty (I have tried to argue against that stagewise view elsewhere). But the point is the Aristotelian one that the context-dependent variability of the importance of wealth indicates its status as a means rather than as an ultimate end.

9. Note that this use does not require us to accept Hicks's priorities in favor of economic ends over other ends that are seen as coming in less urgently and "later." We simply operate with the Hicksian distinction without necessarily accepting the Hicksian ordering in terms of urgency.

10. Kuznets (1966), p. 529.

11. Hicks (1981), chap. 10 ("The Scope and Status of Welfare Economics"), p. 224.

12. Ibid., pp. 223–24.

13. Hicks (1981), chap. 9 ("Measurement of Capital—in Practice"), p. 216.

14. Smith (1776), "Introduction"; in the Clarendon Press edition (1976), p. 10.

15. On related issues, see also Graaff (1977), Hammond (1978), Muellbauer (1978), Roberts (1980), and Atkinson and Bourguignon (1982), and Atkinson (1983), among others.

16. On this see Sen (1976), Dutta (1980), Kakwani (1980, 1986), Osmani (1982), Broder and Morris (1983), and Bhattacharya, Chatterjee, and Pal (1988), among others.

17. The classic presentation of the problem of the evaluation of "public goods" goes back to Samuelson (1954).

18. On this see Drèze and Sen (1989) and the literature cited there.

19. See, for example, Shinohara et al. (1973) in the context of such corrections for Japan.

20. On this and several other needs for correction of market valuations, see Nordhaus and Tobin (1972).

21. On this, see particularly Usher (1968).

22. Many of the difficult issues of international comparisons have been tackled with great skill and imagination by Kravis, Heston, and Summers (1978).

23. I have tried to present a critical survey of the analytic literature in Sen (1979).

24. For a discussion of the factors leading to variations of the functional relations, see Sen (1985) and Drèze and Sen (1989). See also Sen et al. (1987), including the contributions of Geoffrey Hawthorn, Ravi Kanbur, John Muellbauer, and Bernard Williams.

25. The focusing on means is part of John Rawls's (1971) powerful and path-breaking analysis of "justice as fairness," which includes judging individual advantage in terms of respective holdings of "primary goods." I have argued elsewhere, building on (but differing from) Rawls's approach, that the Rawlsian theory of justice is flawed by admitting the possibility of considerable inequities in *actual freedoms* enjoyed even when the means to freedoms are equitably shared. On the importance of the distinction between freedoms and *means* of freedoms, see Sen (1990).

26. On this and related matters, see Drèze and Sen (1989). See also Sen (1991). On related matters see also United Nations Development Programme (1990).

27. Some of these countries have also had extensive state planning, influencing the direction of private investment through well-coordinated government decisions. South Korea is an example of that, with a government that has been active in pushing industrial expansion in particular directions and that has used the nationalized banks among other institutions to do this influencing.

28. See Drèze and Sen (1989), chap. 10.

29. In South Korea the state was initially much more active in education than in public health, but later public health received a comparable priority

30. The list of "growth-mediated successes" would also definitely include Taiwan, which is not in the top ten list mainly because it is not in the basic list of "countries" at

all; the comparative data have been obtained from publications of the World Bank and the United Nations, and neither organization accommodates Taiwan in their category of existing countries. But Taiwan is, in fact, a model example of generating high economic growth and using the growth-generated resources for social support.

31. See Drèze and Sen (1989), chaps. 10 and 12, and the extensive literature cited there.

32. In China the mortality reduction took place well before the economic reforms of 1979 that brought in the market system in selected parts of the economy. Indeed, after the reforms, there was a reported *increase* in mortality rates. Some of the reported increase in mortality rates since the economic reforms may well be the result of better statistics rather than an actual rise in real death rates, but the comparative slowing down in the rapid progress in mortality reduction might well be connected, at least partly, with the problems faced, in the years immediately following the reforms, in the provision of public health care because of the decline in the real resources going into communal medical facilities in the rural areas. On these issues, see Judith Banister (1987), Hussain and Stern (1988), Baumgartner (1989), and Drèze and Sen (1989, chap, 11).

33. On this see Drèze and Sen (1989), chap. 11, and the literature on Kerala cited there.

34. Also, there can be substantial economies in large-scale public provisioning, which reinforce the "public goods" characteristics of these commodities and their labor-intensive resource requirements.

References

Aristotle. *Nicomachean Ethics*. Translated by H. Rackham. Loeb Classical Library series. Cambridge: Harvard University Press, 1934.

Atkinson, A. B. *Social Justice and Public Policy*. Brighton: Wheatsheaf; Cambridge: MIT Press, 1983.

Atkinson, A. B., and F. Bourguignon. "The Comparison of Multidimensional Distributions of Economic Status." *Review of Economic Studies*. 49 (1982).

Banister, Judith. *China's Changing Population*. Stanford: Stanford University Press, 1987.

Baumgartner, R. "China: Long-Term Issues in Options for the Health Sector." World Bank, 1989. Mimeographed.

Bhattacharya, N., G. S. Chatterjee, and P. Pal. "Variations in Levels of Living across Regions and Social Groups." In T. N. Srinivasan and P. Bardhan, eds., *Rural Poverty in South Asia*. New York: Columbia University Press, 1988.

Broder, I. E., and C. T. Morris. "Socially Weighted Real Income Comparisons: An Application to India." *World Development* 11 (1983).

Drèze, Jean, and Amartya Sen. *Hunger and Public Action*. Oxford: Clarendon Press, 1989.

Dutta, B. "Intersectoral Disparities and Income Distribution in India: 1960–61 to 1973–74." *Indian Economic Review* 15 (1980).

Dworkin, Ronald. *A Matter of Principle*. Cambridge: Harvard University Press, 1985.

Graaff, J. de v. "Equity and Efficiency as Components of General Welfare." *South African Journal of Economics* 45 (1977).

———. "Normative Measurement Theory." Manuscript. All Souls College, Oxford, 1985.

Hammond, P. J. "Economic Welfare with Rank Order Price Weighting." *Review of Economic Studies* 45 (1978).

Hicks, John. *Wealth and Welfare*. Oxford: Basil Blackwell, 1981.

Hull, C. H. *The Economic Writings of Sir William Petty*. Cambridge: Cambridge University Press, 1899.

Hussain, Athar, and Nicholas Stern. "On the Recent Increase in Death Rates in China." London School of Economics, 1988. Mimeographed.

Kakwani, N. *Income, Inequality and Poverty*. New York: Oxford University Press, 1980.

———. *Analysing Redistribution Policies*. Cambridge: Cambridge University Press, 1986.

Kravis, I. B., A. W. Heston, and R. Summers. *International Comparisons of Real Product and Purchasing Power*. Baltimore: John Hopkins University Press, 1978.

Kuznets, Simon. *Modern Economic Growth: Rate, Structure, and Spread*. New Haven, Conn.: Yale University Press, 1966.

Muellbauer, J. "Distributional Aspects of Price Comparisons." In R. Stone and W. Peterson, eds., *Economic Contributions to Public Policy*. London: Macmillan, 1978.

Nordhaus, W., and J. Tobin. "Is Growth Obsolete?" In National Bureau of Economic Research, ed., *Economic Growth: Fiftieth Anniversary Colloquium V*. New York: National Bureau of Economic Research, 1972.

Osmani, S. R. *Economic Inequality and Group Welfare*. Oxford: Clarendon Press, 1982.

Petty, William. *Political Arithmetick*. London: N.p., 1691. Republished in Hull (1899).

Pigou, A. C. *The Economics of Welfare*. London: Macmillan, 1920.

Posner, Richard A. *The Economics of Justice*. Cambridge: Harvard University Press, 1981.

Rackham, H. *Aristotle's Nicomachean Ethics*. Loeb Classical Library. Cambridge: Harvard University Press, 1934.

Rawls, John. *A Theory of Justice*. Cambridge: Harvard University Press, 1971.

Roberts, K. W. S. "Price Independent Welfare Prescriptions." *Journal of Public Economics* 13 (1980).

Rothschild, E. "Adam Smith and Conservative Economics." *Economic History Review*, 1992.

Samuelson, Paul A. "The Pure Theory of Public Expenditure." *Review of Economics and Statistics* 33 (1954).

Sen, Amartya. "Real National Income," *Review of Economic Studies* 43 (1976). Reprinted in Sen, *Choice, Welfare and Measurement*. Oxford: Blackwell; Cambridge: MIT Press, 1982.

———. "The Welfare Basis of Real Income Comparisons. *Journal of Economic Literature* 17 (1979). Reprinted in Sen, *Resources, Values and Development*. Oxford: Blackwell; Cambridge: Harvard University Press, 1984.

———. *Commodities and Capabilities*. Amsterdam: North-Holland, 1985.

———. "Justice: Means versus Freedoms." *Philosophy & Public Affairs* 19 (1990).

———. "What Did You Learn in the World Today?" *American Behavioural Scientist* 34 (1991).

Sen, Amartya, et al. *The Standard of Living*. Cambridge: Cambridge University Press, 1987.

Shinohara, M., et al. *Measuring Net National Welfare of Japan*. Tokyo: Economic Council of Japan, 1973.

Smith, Adam. *An Inquiry into the Nature and Causes of the Wealth of Nations*. 1776. Reprint, Oxford: Clarendon Press, 1976.

———. *The Theory of Moral Sentiments*. 1790. Reprint, Oxford: Clarendon Press, 1975.

United Nations Development Programme (UNDP). *Human Development Report 1990*. New York: UNDP, 1990.

Usher, Dan. *The Price Mechanism and the Meaning of National Income Statistics*. Oxford: Clarendon Press, 1968.

Winch, D. *Adam Smith's Politics*. Cambridge: Cambridge University Press, 1978.

2

Growth Acceleration and Slowdown

Postwar Experience in Historical and Comparative Perspective

ANGUS MADDISON

In the golden age after the Second World War, the period 1950–1973, per capita real income growth accelerated in all regions of the world and in virtually all countries. The slowdown after 1973 was also very general, affecting all areas significantly, except Asia. In analyzing the characteristics and causes of these unparalleled and generalized phenomena, it is useful to take a global view and assess the situation in rich, medium-income, and poor countries to see what the underlying causes have been.

This chapter analyzes both the ultimate and the proximate causality of growth. By *ultimate* I mean national institutions, policies, degree of sociopolitical harmony, and the impact of the international order. By *proximate* I mean the factor inputs and other quantifiable influences that one finds in conventional growth accounting. The opportunities also vary according to initial levels of real income and productivity; they are much less for the lead country, the United States, than for those lower-income countries that are able to mount a serious effort to catch up with the leader.

The following interpretation makes use of the tool kit of Kuznetsian analysis, placing heavy emphasis on national accounting aggregates to measure growth and levels of performance. The approach is not maximalist but selective, as it rejects figures for a number of countries where there are reasons to be skeptical about the validity of national measures of growth or levels. Nevertheless, my sample covers forty-eight countries, with a combined population of about 82 percent of the world total and a total gross domestic product (GDP) of about 87 percent of the world total. The national GDP figures are converted into dollars using 1990 purchasing power parities rather than exchange rates (see table 2.1).

Wherever possible, the estimates are carried back to 1820, but for the earlier years there are many gaps. The earlier estimates are generally shakier than those for more recent years. I have not given annual figures here but opted for benchmarks that seem to mark off significant phases in performance.

By dividing the world into seven groups of countries, we can examine the postwar acceleration and slowdown of each group from measures of GDP per capita or productivity. The analysis is rather aggregative, giving it a more stylized picture than if one were scrutinizing individual country experience closely. Virtually all the regions show a good deal of internal consistency with regard to postwar growth/slowdown experience; the first five regions now exhibit only a modest intercountry income variation. Asia is the region with the greatest heterogeneity of income levels and growth rates. It is also the continent where supergrowth has been most prevalent.

Advanced Capitalist Countries of Europe

"Modern economic growth," in Kuznets's sense of sustained rise in per capita product, clearly began in Western Europe. The twelve high-income European countries have an average per capita product that is about four-fifths that of the United States. They have experienced sustained and quite generalized growth since 1820. It is clear that their levels of income were higher in 1820 than those in most of Asia in 1950, due in all probability to the fact that these countries had experienced some modest degree of economic progress in the eighteenth century and earlier. Throughout the nineteenth century these countries had significant growth. There is no evidence for the staggered and differentiated takeoffs that were once suggested by Rostow and Gerschenkron. There has been a process of convergence, with the richer countries of 1820 (Netherlands and the United Kingdom) having the slowest growth. In 1992, the gap between the most and least prosperous was 1.4 : 1; in 1820 this gap was 2.3 : 1.

Western European countries were the first to experience "modern economic growth" because of their institutional sophistication, which was propitious for capital accumulation and technical change. Their legal arrangements put few constraints on markets for goods and services and factors of production. Contracts were not subject to arbitrary interference by the state, and ecclesiastical constraints on the development and diffusion of knowledge and new ideas were minimal. These countries' propinquity facilitated the growth of trade, and quite a few of them benefited from being imperial powers with wide-flung interna-

Table 2.1   Growth and Slowdown in Seven Major World Areas

Panel A: Indicators of Growth and Slowdown
(arithmetic average of country performance, average annual compound growth rate)

	GDP PER CAPITA		
	1913–50	*1950–73*	*1973–92*
Advanced capitalist Europe	1.2	3.8	1.8
Capitalist periphery of Europe	0.7	5.2	2.1
Eastern Europe and USSR	1.2	3.4	−0.5
North America and Australasia	1.3	2.4	1.2
Latin America	1.4	2.5	0.7
Africa	n.a.	1.8	−0.3
Asia	0.0	3.4	3.5

	POPULATION		
	1913–50	*1950–73*	*1973–92*
Advanced capitalist Europe	0.6	0.8	0.3
Capitalist periphery of Europe	0.7	0.5	0.7
Eastern Europe and USSR	0.1	1.0	0.5
North America and Australasia	1.4	1.9	1.1
Latin America	1.9	2.6	2.1
Africa	2.2	2.8	3.0
Asia	1.5	2.7	2.0

Panel B: Average per Capita Product
(in 1990 international dollars)

	1913	*1950*	*1973*	*1987*
Advanced capitalist Europe	$3,482	$5,513	$11,694	$17,412
Capitalist periphery of Europe	1,991	2,500	7,777	11,413
Eastern Europe and USSR	1,894	2,816	6,006	5,470
North America and Australasia	5,051	8,083	13,828	17,475
Latin America	1,838	2,821	4,765	5,414
Africa	n.a.	1,178	1,758	1,688
Asia	903	1,071	3,102	6,035

SOURCE: A. Maddison, *Monitoring the World Economy, 1820–1992* (Paris: OECD Development Centre, 1995)

tional markets and the opportunity to exploit the rest of the world through colonialism.

The post–World War II boom in the European core was to a large extent a catch-up phenomenon. Over several decades, European productivity had fallen behind that of the United States, which was the country closest to the frontiers of technology. With the stimulus of Marshall aid and new forms of international cooperation, liberal policies were reapplied to international trade and international capital markets were reopened. High levels of domestic demand promoted full employment, better internal resource allocation and led to an investment boom on an unparalleled scale. This European boom, together with enlightened international economic policy in the United States, the abandonment of colonialism, and its replacement by aid programs, was basically responsible for the worldwide diffusion of the postwar golden age.

To a considerable extent this long postwar boom in Europe was due to utilization of opportunities lost because of two world wars and the protectionist, dirigiste, and otherwise defensive policies of the interwar years. The boom was biggest in countries that had suffered most from these policies. By the end of the boom, the productivity gap between the advanced European countries and the United States had been considerably reduced. There was a convergence in levels of per capita income and productivity, which was normal between countries that had close cooperation, similar institutions, similar human capital, and convergent economic policies. If there had been a substantial postwar acceleration of technical progress, one would have expected this postwar supergrowth in the advanced European countries to continue. However, the fact that there was little acceleration from 1950 to 1973 in productivity in the United States (the frontier country) meant that eventually the advanced European countries would reach a stage where the payoff on such high levels of investment was bound to falter. This likelihood was considerably increased by the marked slowdown in U.S. productivity growth after 1973.

In fact, the slowdown after 1973 was not gradual but quite general and quite sharp. It did not simply reflect the gradual erosion of supergrowth possibilities. The sharpness of the slowdown was due to three closely clustered and interactive developments that forced major changes in policy. These were the acceleration of inflationary momentum that accompanied the prolonged boom, the collapse of the postwar monetary order (the dollar-based fixed exchange rate system), and the OPEC shocks. On any reasonable accounting, even the most sophisticated governments could be expected to lose output in dealing with these shocks in such very open economies because they involved new risks and transition problems in devising and learning to use new policy weapons, such as floating exchange rates. This was equally true of entrepreneurial and trade union decision makers whose reactions significantly affect macroeconomic outcomes.

A third influence that reinforced the sharpness of the slowdown was the basic change in the "establishment view" of economic policy objectives. A new consensus emerged as a response to events, but it also helped to mold them. The shock of inflation, the new wave of payments problems, and speculative possibilities brought a profound switch away from Keynesian-type attitudes with respect to demand management and full employment. In most countries, overriding priority was given to combating inflation and safeguarding the balance of payments. Unemployment was allowed to rise to prewar levels. Even when oil prices collapsed and the momentum of world inflation was broken in the early 1980s, the new orthodoxy continued to stress the dangers of expansionary policy, despite widespread unemployment and strong payments positions. It looked to self-starting recovery rather than one induced by policy.

Although there is evidence (in terms of high unemployment rates and poor capital productivity) that the European core has not exploited its growth potential fully since 1973, it should nevertheless be stressed that its labor productivity performance has been considerably better than it was in the eight decades before 1950 (see table 2.2). Average productivity growth was 2.3 percent a year from 1973 to 1992 compared with 1.8 percent for 1913–1950 and 1.6 for 1870–1913. Furthermore this was achieved at a time of sharp slowdown in growth in the United States, so the process of catch-up on the United States has certainly not come to a halt. The differential between rates of productivity growth in the European core and the United States has diminished but is still substantial.

The European "Capitalist" Periphery

The countries of the European capitalist periphery are clearly middle-level rather than poor countries. Real income in 1992 ranged from $10,314 in Greece to $12,498 in Spain, a gap of a bit more than a fifth.

It is sometimes alleged that these peripheral countries were poorer than the core in prewar years because of exploitation, discrimination, or quasi-colonial treatment. This is the argument of Paul Bairoch's *Commerce exterieur et developpement économique de l'Europe au XIX siècle* (Paris: Mouton, 1976).

I do not think this explanation is very plausible and would attribute poorer peripheral performance mainly to (a) longer persistence of ancien régime institutions (in land ownership, serfdom, local tolls, ecclesiastical constraints on knowledge); (b) more extreme class, social, regional, or ethnic differentiation/conflict, which impeded the orderly development of civil society and the widespread improvement in human capital that characterized Western Europe; and (c) less efficient economic policy and institutions (e.g., fiscal indiscipline, monetary imprudence, weaker financial institutions, protectionism, and less clearly established property rights).

Table 2.2   Growth of GDP per Man-Hour
            (annual average compound growth rates)

	1870–1913	1913–1950	1950–1973	1973–1992
Austria	1.7	0.9	5.9	2.5
Belgium	1.2	1.4	4.5	2.9
Denmark	1.9	1.5	4.5	1.7
Finland	1.8	2.2	5.4	2.2
France	1.7	1.9	5.1	3.7
Germany	1.9	0.6	6.0	2.7
Italy	1.7	2.0	5.8	2.4
Netherlands	1.3	1.3	4.8	2.2
Norway	1.6	2.5	4.2	3.2
Sweden	1.8	2.8	4.1	1.3
Switzerland	1.5	2.7	3.3	1.7
United Kingdom	1.2	1.6	3.1	2.2
AVERAGE	1.6	1.8	4.7	2.3
Portugal	n.a.	n.a.	6.0	1.9
Spain	n.a.	n.a.	6.4	3.3
AVERAGE	n.a.	n.a.	6.2	2.6
Australia	1.1	1.4	2.9	1.5
Canada	2.3	2.3	3.0	1.5
United States	1.9	2.5	2.7	1.1
AVERAGE	1.8	2.1	2.9	1.4
Japan	1.9	1.9	7.7	3.1
Korea	n.a.	n.a.	4.1	5.2
Taiwan	n.a.	n.a.	5.6	5.3
AVERAGE	n.a.	n.a.	5.8	4.5
Argentina	n.a.	n.a.	2.4	0.5
Brazil	n.a.	n.a.	3.7	0.9
Chile	n.a.	n.a.	2.9	1.0
Colombia	n.a.	n.a.	3.3	1.5
Mexico	n.a.	n.a.	4.0	0.5
AVERAGE	n.a.	n.a.	3.3	0.9

n.a. = not available

SOURCE: A. Maddison, *Monitoring the World Economy, 1820–1992* (Paris: OECD Development Centre, 1995).

The periphery experienced an even greater acceleration in economic performance in the postwar golden age (1950–73) than the core. In the core countries the average growth rate was 3.8 percent a year, about three times as fast as historical experience, but in the periphery the acceleration was sharper, with an average per capita growth of 5.2 percent per annum compared with 0.7 percent in prewar years (see table 2.3).

The postwar growth acceleration in the European periphery had much the same causes as in the European core, but the results were better, partly because the starting point was lower and partly because more institutional modernization took place. These economies benefited greatly by their proximity to the European core, which provided them with booming export markets and very large earnings from tourism and emigrants' remittances.

The sharp slowdown after 1973 was due to some of the same reasons as in the core, and the present close integration with the core meant that the periphery felt the full retarding influence of the slowdown in the core. The peripheral countries had even bigger problems in controlling inflation and dealing with payments disequilibria than did the core.

Communist Europe

Economic performance of the European communist countries accelerated a good deal in the postwar golden age, with average per capita growth of 3.4 percent a year compared with 1.1 percent for 1913–1950. This was slower than that of the rest of Europe.

The performance of these countries is not as well documented as that of OECD countries. Their yardsticks for measuring growth and levels of performance have hitherto differed from those in the West, and we have to rely on the skill of Kremlinologists for measures of performance that are comparable to those we use for OECD countries. The communist countries did not benefit from Marshall aid and were relatively isolated from the new liberalism in the world economy. The acceleration in their growth generally involved a more conscious government effort to mobilize high rates of investment, and their capital stocks probably grew more quickly than did those in the core. Poor results were due to less efficient resource allocation, greater diversion of resources to military spending, and the deleterious effect of censorship and thought control on processes of innovation.

Since 1973 the performance of these economies has deteriorated sharply. In origin, the slowdown was influenced to some extent by the slowdown in the capitalist countries but also reflected the increasing problems of running a command economy efficiently at increasingly sophisticated levels of demand. Since

Table 2.3   Rates of Growth of GDP per Capita in European Countries,
1820–1992 (annual average compound growth rates)

	1820–1870	1870–1913	1913–1950	1950–1973	1973–1992
Austria	0.7	1.5	0.2	4.9	2.2
Belgium	1.4	1.0	0.7	3.5	1.9
Denmark	0.9	1.6	1.6	3.1	1.6
Finland	0.8	1.4	1.9	4.3	1.6
France	0.8	1.5	1.1	4.0	1.7
Germany	1.1	1.6	0.3	5.0	2.1
Italy	0.6	1.3	0.8	5.0	2.4
Netherlands	1.1	0.9	1.1	3.4	1.4
Norway	0.5	1.3	2.1	3.2	2.9
Sweden	0.7	1.5	2.1	3.1	1.2
Switzerland	n.a.	1.5	2.1	3.1	0.8
United Kingdom	1.2	1.0	0.8	2.5	1.4
AVERAGE	0.9	1.3	1.2	3.8	1.8
Greece	n.a.	n.a.	0.5	6.2	1.5
Ireland	1.2	1.0	0.7	3.1	2.7
Portugal	n.a.	0.5	1.2	5.7	2.1
Spain	0.5	1.2	0.2	5.8	1.9
AVERAGE	n.a.	0.9	0.7	5.2	2.1
Czechoslovakia	0.6	1.4	1.4	3.1	−0.1
Hungary	n.a.	1.2	0.5	3.6	0.0
Poland	n.a.	n.a.	n.a.	3.4	−0.6
USSR	0.6	0.9	1.8	3.4	−1.4
AVERAGE	n.a.	1.2	1.2	3.4	−0.5

All figures are adjusted to eliminate the impact of territorial change. Averages for regions are arithmetic.
n.a. = not available.
SOURCE: A. Maddison, *Monitoring the World Economy, 1820–1992* (Paris: OECD Development Centre, 1995).

1990 they have fallen into a condition of deep crisis with the disintegration of the Soviet Union into fifteen countries, the collapse of communism, and the unprecedented problems of how to switch from a command to a market economy.

High-Income White Settler Countries

In this group there are four countries: Canada, the United States, Australia, and New Zealand. They are all British offshoots whose institutions from the beginning were characteristic of or went beyond the most advanced

European capitalist models, taking over vast territories previously occupied by hunter-gatherer indigenous populations that they exterminated or marginalized.

From their early settlement these were relatively prosperous countries benefiting greatly from very favorable natural resource endowments. More recently their remoteness saved them from the wartime destruction suffered by other countries. Their human resources were strengthened by high levels of education, and they also enjoyed a considerable inflow of immigrants and capital from Europe.

The outstanding performer in this group was the United States, which from the 1890s has been the world productivity leader because of its higher levels of education and research and its massive stock of physical capital. Its natural resource advantage is still relevant but not the dominant factor in its level of performance.

There is a bigger income range within this group than in the high-level European group, U.S. per capita income being $21,558 in 1992 compared with $13,947 in New Zealand. Australian and New Zealand levels of real income fall beneath the European average, despite their greater natural resources. The poorer performance in Australasia may be due to protectionism, smaller investment in education, greater distances, less accessible resources, or other influences with which I am not familiar. However, the four countries are reasonably homogenous institutionally, and none have had supergrowth in the twentieth century. Postwar growth performance was less brilliant than in Europe. There has been a general deceleration since 1973, and per capita growth rates have reverted to something like the prewar norm.

In the United States, the world leader in technology and productivity, there was little acceleration in productivity growth in the golden age, which leads one to believe that the postwar boom there and in the world economy generally was not due to an increase in the rate of technical progress. Since 1973, there has been a major and unprecedented slowdown in U.S. productivity.

Latin America

Latin American countries are culturally and institutionally the offspring of Spain and Portugal, with much higher levels of natural resources per head of population than their respective metropoles. Most became politically independent in the 1820s.

The quantitative evidence on Latin American performance in the nineteenth century is poor, but it seems clear that there was substantial economic growth before 1950, by which time per capita income levels were above those in the Iberian metropoles.

Latin America's shortfall below North America or Australasia is sometimes attributed to exploitation by the capitalist core or to bias in world economic development against primary producers (Prebisch; Gunder Frank). I think that this view is grossly exaggerated and that lower average real income in Latin America was due mainly to poor educational levels and extreme social divisions deriving from the heritage of slavery and peonage, which have adversely affected the nature of policy and its development impact. The abundant natural resources were engrossed by the rich, and popular access to land was more restricted than in North America or Australasia. The governmental tradition was also much more interventionist, regulatory, and protectionist. These greater policy-institutional obstacles to progress in Latin America relative to North America were clearly spelled out by Adam Smith in 1776 in *The Wealth of Nations* (book 4, chapter 7, part 2) and still have a great deal of validity.

In the period 1913–1950, Latin American countries performed very well compared with most of the rest of the world (see table 2.4). They did not suffer significantly from the two world wars, and they offset the effects of the 1930s depression by successful import substitution and industrialization. In the early postwar years they had advantageous terms of trade.

As they had no wartime backlogs to make good and chose to remain fairly isolated from the world economy for a considerable period after the war, they did not have a postwar golden age. Their experience in 1950–1973 was nevertheless better in per capita terms than before 1950, so one might call those years a silver age.

Latin American growth did not deteriorate sharply in 1973 as did that of the OECD countries. Latin America generally did not react with the same caution as did most of the world to the OPEC shocks. Governments felt they could accommodate high rates of inflation, and they were able to borrow on a large scale to cover payment deficits incurred as a result of expansionary policies in a world economy that had slowed down a good deal. The crunch came in the 1980s, after the Mexican debt moratorium, when their supply of new foreign funds dried up and service costs of existing debt soared because of rising interest rates.

The dramatic Latin American slowdown was not due to a sudden drying up of supply potential but to deep-seated macroeconomic disequilibria having these major characteristics: (1) large foreign debt, on which amortization payments have generally stopped and on which interest payments are a heavy burden for both the balance of payments and the govrnmental budgets (the bleak outlook here has led to major capital flight and undermined the domestic and international creditworthiness of government); (2) fiscal crises in which governments found it very difficult to maintain revenues or borrow; (3) hyperinflation and exhaustion of a whole menu of heterodox methods of dealing with it; and (4)

Table 2.4   Per Capita Real GDP Growth in Non-European Countries,
1870–1992 (annual average compound growth rates)

	1870–1913	1913–1950	1950–1973	1973–1992
High-Income Countries				
Australia	0.9	0.7	2.4	1.4
Canada	2.2	1.4	2.9	1.5
New Zealand	1.2	1.3	1.7	0.5
United States	1.8	1.6	2.4	1.4
AVERAGE	1.5	1.3	2.4	1.2
Latin America				
Argentina	2.5	0.7	2.1	−0.2
Brazil	0.3	1.9	3.8	0.9
Chile	n.a.	1.0	1.2	1.9
Colombia	n.a.	1.4	2.3	1.9
Mexico	1.7	1.0	3.1	1.1
Peru	n.a.	2.1	2.5	−1.7
AVERAGE	n.a.	1.4	2.5	0.7
Asia				
Bangladesh	n.a.	−0.3	−0.6	2.2
China	0.6	−0.3	2.9	5.2
India	0.4	−0.3	1.6	2.4
Indonesia	0.8	−0.1	2.5	3.1
Israel	n.a.	n.a.	5.4	1.3
Japan	1.4	0.9	8.0	3.0
Pakistan	n.a.	−0.3	1.8	2.7
Philippines	n.a.	−0.2	1.8	0.7
South Korea	n.a.	−0.2	5.2	6.9
Taiwan	n.a.	0.4	6.2	6.2
Thailand	0.4	0.0	3.2	5.3
Turkey	n.a.	0.8	3.3	2.6
AVERAGE	n.a.	0.0	3.4	3.5
Africa				
Côte d'Ivoire		n.a.	3.1	−2.2
Ghana		1.7	0.2	−1.2
Kenya		n.a.	1.9	0.6
Morocco		n.a.	0.1	1.8
Nigeria		n.a.	3.2	0.1
South Africa		1.2	2.4	−0.6
AVERAGE		n.a.	1.8	−0.3

All figures are adjusted to eliminate the impact of territorial change. Averages for regions are arithmetic.
n.a. = not available.
SOURCE: A. Maddison, *Monitoring the World Economy, 1820–1992* (Paris: OECD Development Centre, 1995).

distortion in resource allocation due initially to excessive government intervention and protectionism, then made worse by hyperinflation.

Africa

For Africa the measures of economic performance are statistically weakest of the seven groups, and estimates for prewar years are meager indeed. With the exception of middle-income South Africa, a resource-rich country controlled until recently by its white settler minority, Africa consists mostly of newly independent black countries with very low per capita incomes. The general level of education and health is poorer than in other continents, and experience in running nation-states efficiently is short. Africa had only a modest acceleration of growth in the golden age and has had significant declines in real income since 1973. It is also the continent with the fastest population growth.

Asia

Asia is the biggest continent in terms of population. Our twelve-country sample had a combined income of around 9 trillion dollars in 1992. From the limited evidence available it would seem that Asian per capita income levels were a good deal lower than in Europe when modern economic growth got under way; in 1820, the average was probably well under half the European level. Before 1950, economic growth in Asia was modest indeed. By 1950 average Asian incomes were about a sixth of those in Europe, a quarter of those in Latin America, and lower than in Africa.

Since 1950, there has been an enormous acceleration in Asian growth, with a sixfold increase in average per capita income by 1992. After 1973, when economic growth slowed down sharply in the rest of the world, most Asian countries bucked the general trend and continued to have high and, in some cases, supergrowth.

Asian countries are more heterogenous than those in most other regions, both in levels of achievement and in rates of growth. In 1913 the range in Asian per capita incomes was little more than 2:1; now the gap between Japan and Bangladesh is 27:1. Nevertheless, all but Bangladesh experienced significant acceleration in growth in the 1950–1973 golden age, and more than half our sample had even faster per capita growth after 1973 than before.

The reasons for Asia's initial low-income position relative to Europe are not entirely clear. It has been argued by Adam Smith and others that, as lands of ancient settlement, some of them had poorer ratios of natural resources to population than Europe, but this is certainly not true for all the countries. Their ancient civilizations were probably not as favorable to innovation or technical change as those of Europe, and their organizational and military capacities were certainly inferior to those of Europe at the time they were colonized.

To some extent these indigenous characteristics making for relatively low income may also explain the fact that (with the exception of Japan) they grew slowly until after the Second World War. However, the other major retarding influence was probably the colonial experience to which most of Asia was subjected.

Colonialism installed foreign elites in key positions who gave priority to their own interests and those of their home countries rather than to indigenous welfare. Colonialism tended to drain capital out of these countries, did virtually nothing to promote indigenous education, and involved the colonies in wars in which they might otherwise have been neutral. Of course, colonialism was not a uniform system; Japanese and U.S. colonies tended to do better in some respects than those of the Netherlands or the United Kingdom.

In much of the literature on development, the possible retarding influence of colonialism is given little weight. For instance, it is specifically repudiated by two major economists from developing countries—Arthur Lewis and Hla Myint. However, I think that Indian nationalists like Naoroji were nearer to the truth, certainly if one believes that the counterfactual was a modernizing bourgeois nationalist elite on Japanese lines.

In explaining the great postwar acceleration in Asian growth, at least up to 1973, there were seven types of causal influence at work:

1. The advent to power of new national elites whose legitimacy was generally stronger than those in other areas and development of an indigenous capitalist class who was willing to keep its savings at home and was free to pursue its own interests.

2. Virtually all the Asian countries followed the advice of development economists like Arthur Lewis, Walt Rostow, and Paul Rosenstein Rodan in mounting a big push in investment rates and an even bigger acceleration in growth of capital stock.

3. They also followed the advice of Theodore Schultz to improve human capital. In 1950 their educational stock was a quarter of that in Europe, but it has grown prodigiously; in some of the supergrowth countries it is now close to European levels.

4. The colonial drain was replaced by a net inflow of foreign capital and aid. In prewar years they used to have big trade surpluses, which have now become deficits.

5. The postwar period was one of buoyant world trade, thanks to the faster

growth in the OECD countries and their reduction of trade barriers. A good many Asian countries, and in particular those with supergrowth, took advantage of these new outlets by remaining competitive and aggressively seeking out new markets. The opening up of their economies improved their efficiency and and facilitated their growth.

6. In many Asian countries there have been high per capita labor inputs. Working years of 2,500 hours or more can be observed in Korea and Taiwan and more than 2,000 in Japan, compared with around 1,500 in European countries, North America, and Australasia.

7. Finally, Asian countries were able to get a large catch-up bonus because their starting levels of productivity were so low and they were so far from the productivity frontier.

However, their fast growth since 1973 makes one realize that there were other elements in their menu of progrowth policies whose importance was not obvious in the golden age. These Asian characteristics now stand out all the more clearly because they were so lacking in Latin America and Africa.

The seven supply-side characteristics we have already mentioned did not disappear in Asia after 1973. The world economy was of course less buoyant, but world trade did not collapse and continued to offer opportunities to vigorously competitive countries, and the world capital market did not collapse for creditworthy borrowers.

Except for Japan, most of the Asian countries were still rather far from the technical frontier and could still enjoy a catch-up bonus after 1973. What did differentiate Asia from Latin American and African countries was the quality of its macroeconomic policy:

1. Inflation was better controlled in Asian countries after 1973 than it had been in 1950–1973.

2. The fiscal and monetary policies of Asian countries were generally more prudent than those of Latin American countries.

3. Their foreign borrowing was more judicious. On a per capita basis it averaged only a third of that of Latin America; with the exception of the Philippines they remained creditworthy and did not face the crunch that hit Latin America in the 1980s. Furthermore, less of their debt was incurred on a floating-rate basis to commercial bank lenders.

4. They generally maintained their export competitiveness.

5. Most of them were economies with more flexible wages and prices than those of OECD countries or Latin America.

PART TWO

EARLY DEVELOPERS OF WEALTH: THREE CASE STUDIES

3

Economic Development in Historical Perspective

The Western World

DOUGLASS C. NORTH

The object of this essay is to account for the diverse performance patterns of economies in light of the experience of Western economies.[1] In this volume, Angus Maddison (chapter 2) provides not only a quantitative overview of past performance but also delves into the proximate causes of the differential performance. This chapter complements his analysis by exploring in depth some of the basic characteristics of Western development. Maddison, for example, contrasts the performance of the European core countries with those on the periphery (the United Kingdom is in the core, and Spain, in the periphery). But in the sixteenth century, when my analysis begins, their roles were reversed; Spain had the greatest empire in the Western world since the Roman Empire, and Britain was still a peripheral power. How their roles were reversed explains a good deal about long-run economic growth. Moreover, the institutions that they carried over to the new world basically shaped North and Latin American growth, and the path-dependent analysis I develop extends and elaborates on Maddison's comments about the underlying problems of Latin America. Finally, my analysis of United States economic development provides an explanation of the underlying forces that have made it the world leader since the late nineteenth century.

To evaluate modern economic development in light of Western economic history, I first develop a framework that highlights the critical factors in that development. In this essay I argue below that it is the way in which institutions evolve that shapes long-run economic performance: I illustrate my argument by contrasting English and Spanish economic developments and their extensions into the new world. In subsequent sections I examine (1) the difference between allocative and adaptive efficiency, (2) the relationship between institutions and economic performance, (3) the nature of institutional change, (4) the institutional evolution of the English and Spanish economies and the consequences, (5) nineteenth-century U.S. economic development in the light of analysis advanced in the foregoing sections, and, finally, (6) the implications of this historical analysis for modern economic growth.

Economic Efficiency

To explore the nature of long-run economic change, we need to think of the issue of economic efficiency in somewhat different terms than we do in standard economic theory, where we are examining allocation at an instant in time. The key to sustained economic growth is adaptive rather than allocative efficiency. Adaptive efficiency is the willingness of a society to acquire knowledge and learning, to induce innovation, to undertake risk and creative activity of all sorts, as well as to resolve problems and bottlenecks of the society over time. As Alchian reminds us, in a world of uncertainty no one knows the correct answer to the problems we confront.[2] Adaptive efficiency maximizes trials and eliminates errors. The society that permits the maximum generation of trials, as Hayek has persuasively argued, will have the best likelihood of solving problems over time. Adaptive efficiency, therefore, encourages the development of decentralized decision-making processes that will allow societies to explore alternative ways of solving problems. It is essential to learn from and eliminate failures, thereby generating organizational trials and eliminating organizational failures. This is a difficult process, in that organizational failure may be not only probabilistic but systematic, owing to ideological preferences that may give people, on the basis of imperfect knowledge, preferences for the kind of solutions that are not efficient.

Because institutions define the incentive structure of a society, different institutional rules not only determine the kinds of economic activity that will be profitable and viable but also shape the adaptive efficiency of the internal organization of firms and other organizations. This efficiency comes about as a result of rules that regulate entry, governance structures, and the flexibility of organizations. In particular, rules that encourage the development and utilization of tacit knowledge and therefore creative entrepreneurial talent are important. Obviously, competition, decentralized decision making, well-specified property rights, and bankruptcy laws are crucial. Rules not only eliminate failed economic organizations but also eliminate failed political organizations as well. The structure of rules, therefore, rewards successes but also vetoes the survival of maladapted parts of the organizational structure, which means there must be rules for dissolving unsuccessful efforts as well as rules for promoting successful ones.

The criteria for realizing the Paretian conditions involved in allocative efficiency are seldom if ever specified in terms of the institutional framework, but they assume secure property rights and enforcement of contracts. But how would the rules be balanced between the security of existing organizations and the encouragement of innovation and displacement—in effect the creative destruction in Schumpeter's vision? It is not obvious that the ideal rules for current allocation are the ideal rules to encourage the conditions for adaptive efficiency in a world of positive transaction costs. In terms of the political economy of institutional evolution, it is in the interest of existing firms, trade unions, farm groups, and the like to devise political and economic rules that protect their well-being. The resultant stagnation is the theme of Olson's *The Rise and Decline of Nations*; Olson's study, however, is devoid of political institutions and therefore does not analyze how this stagnation comes about.[3] We must understand the nature of institutions and how they change to explore meaningfully the dynamics of economic change.

Institutions and Economic Performance

Institutions—the constraints that human beings impose on themselves to structure human interaction—consist of formal rules, informal constraints, and their enforcement characteristics. Together they provide the rules of the game of human interaction. The cost of defining and enforcing agreements reflects the effectiveness of the institutions. To measure what is being exchanged and to enforce agreements across time and space at low cost requires complex institutional structures; conversely, the inability to measure and enforce agreements make it costly for institutions to transact (or produce). Successful economic growth is the story of the complex institutions making possible cooperative exchange relations over long periods of time, among individuals without personal knowledge of one another. Institutional reliability means we have confidence in outcomes increasingly remote from our personal knowledge. The combination of formal rules, informal constraints, and enforcement characteristics of institutions defines the humanly devised constraints and, together with the traditional constraints of standard theory, the choice set. To understand the choices available in an exchange, one must take into account all the dimensions that make up an institution.

Institutional Change

Understanding institutional change entails an understanding of the (1) stability characteristics of institutions, (2) sources of change, (3) agents of change, and (4) direction of change.

A basic function of institutions is to provide stability and continuity by dampening the effects of relative price changes, making possible complex exchanges across space and time. A necessary condition for efficient markets, which underlie high-income societies, is channels of exchange, both political and economic, that make possible credible agreements. This condition is accomplished by a complex set of constraints that constitute institutions and by rules nested in a hierarchy, each level more costly to change than the previous one. In the United States the hierarchy moves from constitutional rules to statute law to common law to individual contracts. Political rules are nested in a hierarchy even at the level of specific bills before Congress. Both the structure of committees and the control of the agenda ensure that the status quo is favored over change.

Informal constraints—the extensions, elaborations, and qualifications of rules that "solve" numerous exchange problems not completely covered by formal rules—are also important anchors of stability and hence have tenacious survival ability. They allow people to make everyday exchanges without thinking out at each point and in each instance the terms of exchange. *Routine, custom, tradition,* and *culture* are words denoting the persistence of informal constraints. The complex interaction of rules and informal constraints, together with the way they are enforced, shapes our daily living and directs our mundane activities. These stability features in no way guarantee that the institutions are efficient;[4] stability is a necessary condition for complex human interactions, but it is not a sufficient condition for efficiency.

Although one major source of institutional change has been fundamental changes in relative prices, another has been changes in preferences.[5] For instance, I know of no way to explain the demise of slavery in the nineteenth century in an interest-group model; rather, the growing abhorrence on the part of civilized human beings of one person owning another spawned the antislavery movements and, through the institutional mechanism of voting, eliminated slavery. Although interest groups *did* use the abolitionist movement to further their interests, their success entailed the ideological support of the voter. The voters only had to go to the polls to express their conviction; the slave owner had no feasible way to bribe or pay off voters to prevent them from expressing their beliefs. Institutions make ideas matter.

The agent of change is the entrepreneur—political or economic. Thus far I have left organizations—firms, trade unions, political parties, regulatory agencies, churches, and so forth— and their entrepreneurs, including human activities that result in altering constraints, out of the analysis. The definition of institutions has focused on the rules of the game rather than the players. Organizations and learning alter outcomes, but how?

Let me begin with organization. More than half a century ago, Coase argued that transaction costs are the basis for the existence of the firm.[6] That is, if information and enforcement were costless, it is hard to envision a significant role for organization. How do transaction costs lead to organization? The answers have ranged from the firm being a form of exploitation[7] to a response to asset specificity[8] to a response to measurement costs.[9] Whatever the merits of these alternatives (and they are not mutually exclusive), they all focus on the trees, not the forest. Organizations are a response to the institutional structure of societies and, in consequence, the major cause of the alteration of that institutional structure. Let me explain.

The institutional constraints together with the traditional constraints of economic theory define the potential wealth-maximizing opportunities of entrepreneurs (political or economic). If the constraints result in the highest payoffs in the economy being criminal activity, or if the payoff to the firm is highest from sabotaging or burning down a competitor or to a union from engaging in slowdowns and makework, then we can expect that the organization will be shaped to maximize at those margins. In contrast, if the payoffs come from productivity-enhancing activities, then economic growth will result. In either case, the entrepreneur and his or her organization will invest in acquiring knowledge, coordination, and "learning by doing skills" to enhance the profitable potential. As the organization evolves to capture the potential returns, it will gradually alter the institutional constraints either indirectly, via the interaction between maximizing behavior and its effect on gradually eroding or modifying informal constraints, or directly, via investing in altering the formal rules. The relative rate of return on investing within the formal constraints or devoting resources to altering the constraints will reflect the structure of the polity, the payoffs to altering the rules, and the costs of political investment.

But it is not just organizations altering the rules that shapes long-run economic performance. It is also the kinds of skills and knowledge that they induce the society to invest in. Investment in formal education, new technologies, and pure science has been a derived demand from the perceived payoff to such investment.

Institutional change, then, is an incremental process in which the short-run profitable opportunities cumulatively create the long-run path of change. The long-run consequences are often unintended for two reasons. First, entrepreneurs are seldom interested in the larger (external to them) consequences, but the direction of their investment influences the extent to which there is investment in adding to or disseminating the stock of knowledge, encouraging or discouraging factor mobility, and so forth. Second, there is frequently a significant difference between intended outcomes and actual outcomes because of the limited capabilities of the individuals and the complexity of the problems to be solved.

The Economic Evolution of England and Spain

In this section I briefly contrast the institutional evolution of England and Spain and the its consequences for North and Latin America.

THE BACKGROUND

By the beginning of the sixteenth century, it was clear that England and Spain were evolving very differently. England had developed a relatively centralized feudalism, as a result of the Norman conquest, and had, in 1485, established the Tudors with the Battle of Bosworth. Spain, in contrast, had just emerged from seven centuries of Moorish domination of the peninsula and was not a unified country. Although the marriage of Ferdinand and Isabella had brought Castile and Aragon together, they continued to maintain separate rules, Cortes, and policies.

Both England and Spain, however, along with the rest of the emerging European nation-states, faced a critical problem: the need to acquire additional revenue to survive as warfare became more expensive. The king traditionally lived on his own, that is, off the revenue from his estates together with the traditional feudal dues; but these resources were insufficient in the face of the new military technology—the crossbow, long bow, pike, and gunpowder. This fiscal crisis of the state, first described by Joseph Schumpeter,[10] forced rulers to make bargains with constituents. In both countries the consequence was the development of some form of representation on the part of constituents in return for revenue (Parliament in England and the Cortes in Spain). In both countries the wool trade became a major source of crown revenue. But the consequences of the common relative price change arising from the new military technology were radically different in the two countries. In England it led to the evolution of a polity and economy that solved the fiscal crisis and went on to dominate the Western world. In Spain, despite initially more favorable conditions, it led to unresolved fiscal crises, bankruptcies, confiscation of assets, insecure property rights, and three centuries of relative stagnation.

In England the tension between ruler and constituent (although the barons at Runnymede might have caviled at that term) surfaced with the Magna Carta in 1215. The fiscal crisis came later with the Hundred Years' War. Stubbs describes the consequence as follows: "The admission of the right of parliament to legislate, to enquire into abuses, and to share in the guidance of national policy, was practically purchased by the monies granted to Edward I and Edward III."[11] This led, as we know, to 1688 and the final triumph of Parliament.

In Spain the union of Aragon (made up of approximately Valencia, Aragon, and Catalonia) and Castile joined two very different regions. Aragon, which had been reconquered from the Arabs in the last half of the thirteenth century, had become a major commercial empire extending into Sardinia, Sicily, and parts of Greece. The Cortes, reflecting the interests of merchants, played a significant role in public affairs. In contrast, Castile was continually engaged in warfare, either against the Moors or in internal strife; although the Cortes existed, it was seldom summoned. In the fifteen years after the union, Isabella succeeded in gaining control not only over the unruly, warlike barons but over church policy in Castile as well. Although the role of the Castilian Cortes has, in recent scholarly work, been somewhat upgraded, it was the centralized monarchy and bureaucracy in Castile that defined the institutional evolution of both Spain and Latin America.

THE INSTITUTIONAL FRAMEWORK

Although a critical difference and symptomatic of the broad differences in both the polity and the economy, it was not simply centralization or decentralization in the polity that differentiated the two societies. Not only did the Parliament in England provide the beginning of representative government and a reduction in the rent-seeking behavior that had characterized the financially hard-pressed Stuart monarchs, but Parliament's triumph betokened increased security of property rights and a more effective, impartial judicial system.

Spain's polity, in contrast, consisted of a large centralized bureaucracy that "administered the ever growing body of decrees and juridical directives, which both legitimized the administrative machinery and laid down its course of action."[12] Every detail of the economy, as well as the polity, was organized with the objective of furthering the interests of the Crown in the creation of the most powerful empire since Rome. But with the revolt of the Netherlands and the decline in the inflow of new world treasure, fiscal demands far outstripped revenue; the result was bankruptcy, increased internal taxation, confiscations, and insecure property rights.

THE ORGANIZATIONAL IMPLICATIONS

In England, Parliament created the Bank of England and a fiscal system in which expenditures were tied to tax revenues. The consequent financial revolution not only put the government on a sound financial basis but laid the groundwork for the development of the private capital market. Secure property rights, the decline of mercantilist restrictions, and the escape of textile firms from urban guild restrictions all combined to provide expanding opportunities for firms in domestic and international markets. Both the growing markets and patent law encouraged the growth of innovative activity. In Spain, however, repeated bankruptcies between 1557 and 1647 were coupled with desperate measures to stave off disaster. War, the church, and administering the complex bureaucratic system provided the major organizational opportunities in Spain; in consequence the military, the priesthood, and the judiciary were the most rewarding occupations. The expulsion of Moors and Jews, rent ceilings on land and price ceilings on wheat, and confiscations of silver remittances to merchants in Seville (who were compensated with relatively worthless juros) were symptomatic of the disincentives to productive activity.

PATH DEPENDENCE

The term *path dependence* is associated with the increasing returns characteristic of an institutional matrix that locks in a particular institutional structure.[13] To make convincing illustrations of path dependence would entail an account of the political, economic, and judicial systems of each society as a web of interconnected formal rules and informal constraints that made up the institutional matrix and led the economies down different paths. To demonstrate the network externalities that made the actors' choices limited and prevented them from radically altering the institutional framework is an undertaking far beyond the kinds of existing empirical evidence with which I am familiar. I can only indirectly infer such implications from the evidence.

In a controversial study that examines the origins of individualism in England, Alan Macfarlane maintains that, beginning in the thirteenth century or earlier, the English were different from the traditional picture we possess of peasant societies.[14] The traditional characteristics—patriarchal domination, extended family, low status of women, tight-knit and closed peasant villages, self-sufficiency, and the family as the work unit—were conspicuously absent from England by the thirteenth century. Instead, Macfarlane paints a picture of a fluid, individualistically oriented set of attitudes involving the structure of the family, the organization of work, and the social relationships of the village community complemented by an array of formal rules dealing with property, inheritance, and the legal status of women. Macfarlane points out that England was different and that the difference went back in time; in doing so he makes clear the complex, interdependent network of formal and informal constraints that gave rise to the increasing returns characteristic of path dependence.

Telling evidence of the increasing returns feature of the Spanish institutional fabric was the Crown and its bureaucracy's inability to alter their direction despite the decay and decline overcoming the country. In a single century—the seventeenth—Spain declined from being the most powerful nation in the Western world since the Roman Empire to becoming a second-rate power. The depopulation of the countryside, the stagnation of industry, the collapse of Seville's trading system with the New World were paralleled in the political realm by the revolt of Catalonia and Portugal. The proximate cause was recurrent war and a fiscal crisis that led Olivares (1621–40) to pursue desperate measures—price controls, tax increases, and repeated confiscations—that only exacerbated the fundamental problems. As for the perceptions of the actors, Jan De Vries in his study of Europe in the "age of crisis" (1976) describes the effort to reverse the decline as follows:

> But this was not a society unaware of what was happening. A whole school of economic reformers . . . wrote mountains of tracts pleading for new measures. . . . Indeed, in 1623 a junta de Reformacion recommended to the new king, Philip IV, a series of measures including taxes to encourage early marriage (and hence, population growth), limitations on the number of servants, the establishment of a bank, prohibitions on the import of luxuries, the closing of brothels, and the prohibition of the teaching of Latin in small towns (to reduce the flight from agriculture of peasants who had acquired a smattering of education). But no willpower could be found to follow through on these recommendations. . . . It is said that the only accomplishment of the reform movement was the abolition of the ruff collar, a fashion which had imposed ruinous laundry bills on the aristocracy.[15]

Both England and Spain faced fiscal crises in the seventeenth century, but the contrasting paths that they took reflected deep, underlying institutional characteristics of the societies.

THE DOWNSTREAM CONSEQUENCES

American economic history—characterized by a federal political system, checks and balances, and a basic structure of property rights—encouraged the long-term contracting essential to the creation of capital markets and economic growth. Even one of the most costly civil wars in history failed to basically alter the institutional matrix. Latin American economic history, in contrast, has perpetuated the centralized, bureaucratic traditions carried over from its Spanish/Portuguese heritage. John Coatsworth characterizes the institutional environment of nineteenth-century Mexico as follows:

> The interventionist and pervasive arbitrary nature of the institutional environment forced every enterprise, urban or rural, to operate in a highly politicized manner, using kinship networks, political influence, and family prestige to gain privileged access to subsidized credit, to aid various stratagems for recruiting labor, to collect debts or enforce contracts, to evade taxes or circumvent the courts, and to defend or assert titles to lands. Success or failure in the economic arena always depended on

the relationship of the producer with political authorities—local officials for arranging matters close at hand, the central government of the colony for sympathetic interpretations of the law and intervention at the local level when conditions required it. Small enterprise, excluded from the system of corporate privilege and political favors, was forced to operate in a permanent state of semiclandestiny, always at the margin of the law, at the mercy of petty officials, never secure from arbitrary acts and never protected against the rights of those more powerful.[16]

The disparate paths established by England and Spain in the New World have not converged despite common ideological influences. In England, an institutional framework evolved that permitted the complex impersonal exchange necessary to political stability and the economic gains of modern technology. In Spain, personal relationships are still key to much political and economic exchange, giving rise to an institutional framework that produced neither political stability nor any consistent realization of the potential of modern technology.

U.S. Economic History Reconsidered

What is different about the institutional story as opposed to the traditional economic history that the cliometrician tells? After all, both accounts use neoclassical price theory and the quantitative techniques of cliometrics. The difference is that the institutional story abandons a crucial assumption of neoclassical theory (instrumental rationality) and incorporates a crucial feature about the characteristics of institutions (the increasing returns characteristic that produces path dependence).

By instrumental rationality we mean that actors have correct theories by which to interpret the world around them; if their theories are initially incorrect, the information feedback that they receive will lead them to correct these theories. Herbert Simon has accurately summarized the implications of such an assumption as follows:

> If we accept values as given and constant, if we postulate an objective description of the world as it really is, and if we assume that the decision-maker's computational powers are unlimited, then two important consequences follow. First, we do not need to distinguish between the real world and the decision-maker's perception of it: He or she perceives the world as it really is. Second, we can predict the choices that will be made by a rational decision-maker entirely from our knowledge of the real world and without a knowledge of the decision-maker's perceptions or modes of calculation (we do, of course, have to know his or her utility function).
>
> If, on the other hand, we accept the proposition that both the knowledge and computational ability of the decision-maker are severely limited, then we must

distinguish between the real world and the actor's perception of it. That is to say, we must construct a theory (and test it empirically) of the processes of decision. Our theory must include not only the reasoning processes but also the processes that generate the actor's subjective representation of the decision problem, his or her frame.

The rational person in neo-classical economics always reaches the decision that is objectively, or substantively, best in terms of the given utility function. The rational person of cognitive psychology goes about making his or her decisions in a way that is procedurally reasonable in the light of the available knowledge and means of computation.[17]

The implications of procedural rationality as opposed to instrumental rationality help us understand economics and economic history. Institutions are unnecessary in a world of instrumental rationality; ideas and ideologies do not matter; and efficient markets—both economic and political—characterize economies. Procedural rationality, in contrast, maintains that the actors have incomplete information, limited mental capacities by which to process such information and in consequence develop patterns to structure exchange. There is no implication that the consequent institutions are efficient. In such a world, ideas and ideologies play a major role in choices and transaction costs result in imperfect markets.

Institutional matrices are characterized by increasing returns as a result of the symbiotic relationship between institutions and organizations described above. The political and economic organizations have come into existence because of the opportunities created by institutional and other constraints. The result is a set of reinforcing mechanisms such as network externalities that bias incremental costs and benefits in favor of those that are broadly consistent with the institutional framework and correspondingly make choices unprofitable that would run counter to the institutional framework.

When I put the procedural rationality postulate together with the increasing returns characteristic of institutions, I get an economic history that appears to more closely fit the historical record than does the a-institutional, instrumental-rationality approach. I shall illustrate how different this economic history is by elaborating on the downstream consequences of the English story—that is, U.S. nineteenth-century economic history.

The English heritage of institutions and ideas together shaped a thriving colonial economy, providing the opportunities that produced plantations, merchants, shipping firms, family farms. The heritage was not just economic but political and intellectual as well—town meetings and self-government, colonial assemblies—intellectual traditions from Hobbes and Locke that are essential to make the events of 1763 to 1789 into an integrated story of political and economic organizations driven by subjective perceptions of the issues (such as the

Navigation Acts) that produced the institutional framework of the newly independent nation. The institutional path and the perceptions of the actors make sense of the story and account for the radical contrast with other contemporaneous revolutions and subsequent development (the Latin American experience, for example).

Just what made the nineteenth-century American economy a hospitable environment for economic growth has occupied the attention of scholars examining the consequences of the Constitution, the evolution of the law, the role of the frontier, the contribution of immigrants, and so forth. In fact, the adaptively efficient characteristics of the institutional matrix (both the formal rules and the informal constraints embodied in attitudes and values) rewarded productive activity, encouraged investment in knowledge and education, and provided the decentralized decision making that maximized trials and alternative choices.

Part of the costs entailed in that growth was the price paid for adaptive efficiency. The system wiped out losers, and there were lots of them—farmers who went bust on the frontier, shipping firms that failed as the United States lost its comparative advantage in shipping, laborers who suffered unemployment and declining wages from immigrant competition in the 1850s. Part of the costs, however, was a consequence of institutions that exploited individuals and groups—Indians, slaves, and not infrequently immigrants, workers, and farmers—for the benefit of those with superior bargaining power. Both the sources of growth and the costs entailed in that growth are a common derivative of the institutional framework.

The political framework resulted in the losers having access, albeit imperfect, to remedies for their perceived sources of misfortune, which consisted of immediate grievances filtered through ongoing intellectual currents and ideologies of the actors. The farmer could observe price discrimination by the railroad or the grain elevator, but the Populist Party platform reflected overall ideological views such as the perceived burden of the gold standard, widespread monopoly, and the pernicious consequence of bankers. We cannot make sense out of the protest movements and policy prescriptions of the period without understanding these intellectual currents.

Nor can we make sense out of the direction of change in the polity and economy that resulted from these movements without understanding them. Whatever were the underlying sources of the farmers' plight that produced discontent in the late nineteenth century, it was farmers' perceptions that mattered in changing the political and economic institutional framework.

But it was not just the farmers' perceptions that mattered. The evolving subjective models of other actors in other organizations could influence outcomes as a consequence of the institutional matrix. Whether the Supreme Court understood the implication of *Munn vs. Illinois* and the many other court decisions that gradually altered the legal framework depended on whether the information feedback on the consequences of existing laws was accurate and hence gave them true models. True or false, the models they acted on incrementally altered the judicial framework.

An overall contribution that institutional analysis can make to American economic history is to make it a truly historical story, something that has been lost with cliometrics. Much of that history is path dependent because constraints from the past impose limits on current choices and therefore make the current choice set intelligible. But much of it reflects path dependence as a consequence of the increasing returns characteristic of the institutional matrix. The reinforcing role that the political and economic organizations gave the institutional matrix via network externalities and the other sources of increasing returns provided the decisive stamp to American economic history. Meanwhile, the organizations were also inducing incremental change; it is that blend of underlying stability and incremental change that can give us a deeper and more satisfying account of that history.

Economic Growth Reconsidered

If economies were not characterized by institutions with increasing returns, and if instrumental rationality characterized human decision making, then the problem of modern economic growth would be reduced to a matter of preferences. Economies not only would know the political and economic policies that would take them on an adaptively efficient path but also could overnight transform the institutional framework to create the proper incentive structure. Because institutions do result in "lock in" and the actors proceed on the basis of limited information and use subjective models as guides to choices, economies diverge widely and persistent poor performance can continue.

But paths do get reversed (Spain from stagnation to growth in the 1960s or Argentina reversing directions in the 1940s), and economies sometimes do devise political/economic policies that result in improved performance (South Korea and Taiwan, for example). How come? The puzzle, I believe, can only be resolved by a deeper understanding than we now possess of the nature of institutions and political markets.

Institutions are composed of formal rules that can be altered by polities and informal constraints that can have remarkable staying power and do not automatically change when the formal rules change. Indeed, a radical change in formal rules will lead to a tension between the new rules and the persisting informal constraints that typically produce substantial political instability. The reason is that, in equilibrium, the informal constraints, which will complement the formal rules and solve innumerable exchange problems not covered by the formal rules, are a key part of the increasing returns characteristic of institutions. Conventions, norms of behavior, and self-imposed codes of conduct that make up informal constraints are culturally derived, however, and we know little about how they change. But I would venture that new political policies that produce rapid improvement in performance can only occur when there already exists an underlying set of informal constraints that will be complementary to the new formal rules.

Political markets are characterized by high transaction costs. The literature on efficient markets has not only blinded us to the fact that they are rare in economic markets and entail stringent information and institutional requirements but also prevented us from appreciating that they are far rarer in political markets precisely because the necessary conditions do not exist even in democratic polities—the most favorable political markets for such efficiency. Rational voter ignorance, substantial agency problems, and incomplete comprehension of the true consequences of political decisions make for high political transaction costs.

The consequent imperfection of political markets can result in reinforcing persistently poor economic performance, but, paradoxically enough, it can also result in political entrepreneurs, on occasion, having enough freedom to alter paths (by enacting rules that induce increased competition: tariff reductions, for example). Such reversals can only occur in periods of stress that reduce, at least in part, the bargaining power of those groups that stand to gain from the existing institutional framework. In such circumstances, political entrepreneurs may encourage the creation of, or foster the expansion of, organizations with different agendas. Although this conjecture is compatible with the kind of casual empirical observations we possess of the alteration or even reversal of institutional paths, it lacks theoretical grounding. To my knowledge, however, no existing body of political theory provides insight into such problems.

Notes

1. This essay is drawn from a book by the author entitled *Institutions, Institutional Change and Economic Performance* (Cambridge, Eng.: Cambridge University Press, 1990).

2. Armen A. Alchian, "Uncertainty, Evolution, and Economic Theory," *Journal of Political Economy* 58 (1950): 211–21.

3. Mancur Olson, *The Rise and Decline of Nations: Economic Growth, Stagflation, and Social Rigidities* (New Haven, Conn.: Yale University Press, 1982).

4. By efficiency I mean a set of constraints that will result in increasing real income per capita.

5. Douglass C. North and Robert P. Thomas, *The Rise of the Western World: A New Economic History* (Cambridge, Eng.: Cambridge University Press, 1973).

6. Ronald H. Coase, "The Nature of the Firm," *Economica* 17(1937):53–71 .

7. Stephen Marglin, "What Do Bosses Do?" *Review of Radical Political Economy* 6 (1977): 33–60.

8. Oliver E. Williamson, *Markets and Hierarchies: Analysis and Antitrust Implications* (New York: The Free Press, 1975); and Oliver E. Williamson, *The Economic Institutions of Capitalism* (New York: The Free Press, 1975).

9. Yoram Barzel, "Measurement Cost and the Organization of Markets," *Journal of Law and Economics* 25 (1982):27–48 .

10. Joseph A. Schumpeter, "The Crisis of the Tax State," *International Economic Papers*, no. 4(1954): 5–38.

11. William Stubbs, *The Constitutional History of England*, vol. 2 (Oxford, Eng.: Clarendon Press, 1896), p. 599.

12. William P. Glade, *The Latin American Economies: A Study of Their Institutional Evolution* (New York: American Book, 1969), p. 58.

13. Path dependence is a concept developed by Brian Arthur and Paul David to characterize the increasing returns characteristics of technological paths; see W. Brian Arthur, "Competing Technologies, Increasing Returns, and Lock-In by Historical Events," *Economic Journal* 99 (1989):116–31 .

14. Alan Macfarlane, *The Origins of English Individualism: The Family, Property, and Social Transition* (Oxford, Eng.: Blackwell, 1978).

15. Jan De Vries, *The Economy of Europe in an Age of Crisis, 1600–1750* (Cambridge, Eng.: Cambridge University Press, 1976), p. 28.

16. John H. Coatsworth, "Obstacles to Economic Growth in Nineteenth-Century Mexico," *American Historical Review* 83 (1978):80–100, especially p. 94.

17. Herbert Simon, "Rationality in Psychology and Economics," in Robin M. Hogarth and Melvin W. Reder, eds., *The Behavioral Foundations of Economic Theory*, supplement to *The Journal of Business* (1986).

4

Bridled Capitalism and the Economic Development of Japan, 1880–1980

KOZO YAMAMURA

Between the Meiji Restoration (1868) and the late 1930s, Japan was transformed from a backward agrarian economy into a major industrial power. Beginning with the onset of the Korean War in 1950, the transformation accelerated, achieving an average real growth rate of more than 9 percent a year, until the "oil shock" of 1973. Japan's economy thus accelerated between the early 1880s, when industrialization led by the textile industry commenced, and the early 1970s, when the technological capabilities of most Japanese industries had reached those of Western nations. Although the growth rate decelerated after 1973, the performance of Japan's economy continues to surpass those of many other industrialized nations.

This chapter argues that ideologies, policies, and institutions have substantively influenced the 1880–1970 century of Japanese economic growth. I first present definitions and brief discussions of those ideologies, policies, and institutions. Next, I review how those three factors shaped the patterns and rates of economic growth that Japan has achieved since the 1880s using four industries as examples, as well as improvements in the standard of living and quality of life. Finally, I present an analytic summary characterizing Japan's economy as "bridled capitalism," in which policies and institutions, reflecting a shared ideology of "catching up with the West," effectively performed the role of a bridle. That is, Japan did not follow the path of unbridled capitalism, in which unrestrained market forces were given free play, but chose the path of bridled capitalism, in which individuals and firms were motivated to save more, to acquire new knowledge, and to take risks and in which market forces, made vigorous through the incentives provided, made manufacturing firms more competitive. I also discuss briefly the "costs" that such a wealth-creating process produced.

Ideologies, Policies, and Institutions

Ideologies include the shared beliefs, perceptions, and values that affect the performance of an economy over time because they determine the political or economic preferences of a society. Because societal preferences also shape and change institutions and policies, they also determine economic performance over time.

Policies—the laws, regulations, and actions taken by the government to affect the allocation of resources and income—can be considered a part of broadly defined institutions (see below) because they determine the structure of incentives, transaction costs, and the stability of relative prices. It is, however, useful to view the effects of polices and institutions separately for two reasons: policies tend to be more short-lived than most institutions because, as a rule, they are adopted for a specific duration to meet specific goals; policies, unlike institutions, are made in the political arena and subject to the constraints of the policy-making process and the competing strengths of political power of interest groups.

Institutions, in the broad sense, include the social norms and patterns of behavior followed by most individuals and groups in ordinary circumstances and play crucial roles in determining the performance of an economy over time in three related ways: First, institutions constrain the behavior of individuals and groups and thereby determine the structure of incentives, that is, how much and with what probability they can capture economic gains by taking specific actions. Institutions also determine the structure of incentives within an economy, that is, whether and how effectively the largest possible number of individuals and groups is motivated to acquire new knowledge, adopt innovations, and take necessary risks.

Second, institutions determine the transaction costs of obtaining information, contracting, and enforcing contracts that are significantly affected not only by levels of technology in communication and education but also by traditions, social norms, laws and the legal system, intergroup institutional arrangements and practices, and other institutions. These costs of transactions can differ substantially from one economy to another, and economies with lower transaction costs are better able to achieve higher economic performance. Third, institutions provide formal and informal constraints on the exchange activities of individuals and groups; therefore, they can minimize uncertainty and reduce many types of economic dislocation that occur when relative prices change. Certain institutions help maintain the stability of relative prices that is essential for making complex economic transactions and decisions over time. With more-stable relative prices, individuals and groups are less exposed to changes in the structure of incentives and transaction costs and are thus better able to make decisions and engage in activities conducive to innovating and investing to sustain economic performance.

The preceding is a brief and broad description of the analytic characteristics of ideologies, policies, and institutions that will be discussed in the following sections. What I want to stress here is that the analytic underpinning just described differs from neoclassical studies of economic history in significant ways. For example, neoclassical economic historians typically attribute the growth of output to the adoption of new technology or increased use of productive factors or both. In so doing, they fail to consider how institutions and ideologies affect the adoption of new technology and the mobility of factors of production; instead, they tend to treat the effects of economic polices as exogenous variables, that is, on an ad hoc basis. Thus their studies assume that individuals and groups have "correct models" and all the necessary information to make decisions. In this study, no such assumptions are made. I argue instead that the path of an economy is determined by individuals and groups who possess neither "correct models" nor all the necessary information but who respond to the incentive structure shaped by ideologies, polices, and institutions.

Neoclassical economic history also does not deal with the cumulative effects that institutions and policies have on an economy's ability to perform over time by reducing transaction costs and improving the structure of incentives. These characteristics of "momentum," or "path-dependent" societal capabilities, suggest that today's structure of incentives and transaction costs determines current decisions, which in turn change the incentive structure and transaction costs likely to affect tomorrow's decisions. The historical path an economy takes depends on whether the momentum is performance enhancing or performance inhibiting. In the following sections, I offer examples of the performance-enhancing momentum of increasing returns that enabled Japan to achieve the acceleration of the past hundred years.[1]

Trend Acceleration and Sustained Growth

IDEOLOGIES AND "EXPORT-LED" GROWTH

The story of Japan's successful economic development, both before and after World War II, begins with ideology. In prewar Japan, political leaders and many others determining the course of the nation believed that Japan had to increase its economic capabilities as rapidly as possible to maintain its sovereignty in the "age of imperialism" and become an industrial power capable of participating in the international community.

A series of international developments forcefully reminded the Japanese of their "second-rate" status. In 1895, the major powers forced Japan to relinquish the Liaotung Peninsula, a spoil of the Sino-Japanese war. In 1905, the humiliating Portsmouth treaty ending the costly Russo-Japanese War gave Japan no war indemnity. The "unequal treaties" Japan signed with the Western powers early in the Meiji years could not be renegotiated until 1911 for Japan to be free of foreign extraterritoriality and restricted tariff autonomy. Further, at the 1919 Versailles peace conference, Japan gained little compared with its expectations and the Western powers showed no interest in the racial equality clause demanded by Japan. In several 1920s treaties that determined the relative size of naval forces, Japan had to accept a small force, which it regarded as not befitting a "first-rate nation." Finally, during the 1930s, Japan's efforts to achieve expansionist political and economic goals in China and Southeast Asia met strong resistance from the Western powers. For prewar Japan's political leaders and citizens, then, the only way to become a "rich nation with a strong army" was to become a "first-rate nation" through industrialization. Japan's national goal, thus ideology, was to catch up with the West in all industrial capabilities.

The desire to catch up with the West was no less strong in the post–World War II period. Defeated and demoralized, Japan's national goal was to wage a "total war" for rapid economic recovery and growth. "There was no politics in the sense of the competitive advocacy of the fundamental goal of society" because the goal of rapid growth was "a war to be won, the first total war in Japanese history for which all of the nation's resources were mobilized *voluntarily*."[2] Therefore, there was a national consensus throughout the 1950s and 1960s for adopting policies and creating institutions to help achieve rapid growth, despite the burdens that were brought on by such growth and those institutions. This consensus, which kept Japan's ruling party—the Liberal Democratic Party (LDP)—in power, weakened visibly by the late 1960s. Yet the nation's desire to become an efficient "factory to the world" showed little sign of wavering, even as late as the 1980s.

To pursue these goals, Japan's national strategy was to successively adopt, as rapidly as possible, new (Western) technology to increase the capabilities of manufacturing industries so that they could produce and export increasing quantities of technologically advanced products, which I refer to as *achieving dynamic technological efficiency*. The strategy of achieving dynamic technological efficiency and that of import substitution were the same: both meant long-term, sustained efforts to increase the output and productive efficiency of manufacturing industries. This strategy was called *bōeki rikkoku* (building an economy through international trade).

After World War II, Japan pursued dynamic technological efficiency vigorously; there was no longer a need for a strong army, and efforts could focus on becoming a "rich nation" by increasing the international competitiveness of its manufacturing industries. The strength and effectiveness of this strategy changed in the early 1970s, however, because there was much less technology to borrow once Japan had "caught up," because the former consensus for rapid growth had begun to weaken, and because industrial policies were increasingly criticized by trading partners. Yet the institutions created to implement this strategy still enabled Japan to expand its share in international markets for technologically advanced products.

To argue that Japan pursued the strategy of *bōeki rikkoku* is to argue that rapid growth was "export-led." Although this is a generally accepted argument in *prewar* Japanese economic history, many economists argue that the rapid economic growth of *postwar* Japan was "investment-led" rather than "export-led." Such a view is erroneous for several reasons. Many manufacturing industries tried to increase output by adopting new technology so as to produce larger quantities of more–internationally competitive manufactured products. Those industries able to invest and adopt new technology could export an increasing quantity of output, thus achieving high rates of productivity increase. Exports that rose rapidly further stimulated overall investment. These same industries helped the industrial sector grow because the rapid increase in productivity absorbed resources and raised the overall productivity of the economy. It should also be noted that, for a Japan heavily dependent on imported raw materials, rapid growth was unattainable if the exports needed to pay for the imports were not also rapidly increasing. One could criticize the view that Japanese growth was not export-led by citing various technical grounds,[3] but let us look at the data in table 4.1, which Shinohara argues are best relied on "in judging whether or not a country's economic growth was export-led."[4]

POLICIES

The Meiji government employed approximately six thousand Western engineers, technicians, and foremen in government pilot plants and on other projects adopting Western technology; it also imported and actively disseminated many types of machinery used in military ordnance, textile, iron-steel, and other industries. After World War I, large innovating private firms in the chemical, machinery, and other industries contracted with Western firms for their technology and managerial guidance. The government's principal policies consisted of providing low-cost capital and enabling private firms to minimize their investment risks. The government also created a dozen research institutions, some under its control and others affiliated with universities, and sharply increased funding for middle and high schools, especially for "practical learning and skills."[5]

Table 4.1   Value of Exports of Advanced Industrial Nations, 1950–1987 (US$ million)

	Japan	United States	United Kingdom	West Germany	France	Italy	RATIO OF EXPORT QUANTITY	
							Japan/ United States	Japan/ Five Western Nations
1950	$ 825	$ 10,282	$ 6,325	$ 1,993	$ 3,080	$ 1,206	8.0%	3.6%
1955	2,011	15,558	8,467	6,123	4,959	1,856	12.9	5.4
1960	4,054	20,601	9,953	11,415	6,866	3,654	19.7	7.7
1970	19,318	43,241	19,608	34,228	18,099	13,206	44.7	15.0
1980	130,441	220,786	110,155	192,861	116,016	77,679	59.1	18.2
1987	229,221	250,405	131,239	294,168	148,534	111,967	91.5	24.5

SOURCE: IMF, *International Financial Statistics.*

Policies to provide capital to industries took many forms. In both the Meiji period and the interwar years, the state granted subsidies directly and indirectly through grants; improved infrastructure to benefit industrial firms; sold pilot plants at a fraction of their cost; imposed modest taxes on corporate and individual incomes (while obtaining revenues from taxes on salt, tobacco, sake, imported consumer goods, and services); adopted monetary and fiscal policies to minimize the cost of capital (although at the cost of steady inflation); and limited wage increases by severely constraining labor union activities while allowing innovative, oligopolist firms to capture above-normal profits through cartels.

To minimize the risks of capital investment using new technology, the state purchased much industry output in areas such as iron-steel, machinery, automobiles, ships, woolen cloth, and Western paper. The state also promoted cartels when firms acquired excess production capacity because of expanded private investment or a sudden decline in demand. Additionally, the state passed laws to protect the chemical, iron-steel, and other industries by exempting them from corporate taxes and import duties on raw materials and machinery for an initial ten-year period.[6] To carry out a strategy of *bōeki rikkoku* by promoting dynamic technological efficiency, the Meiji (1868–1912) and Taisho (1912–1926) governments also implemented various policies that increased exports and limited imports that competed against Japanese infant industries. The most notable such policies were subsidies to the shipbuilding industry and shipping lines, tariff and tax measures to promote trade with Japan's colonies, tariffs and other policies to restrict the import of many consumer and producer goods, and an exchange-rate policy to boost exports and minimize the trade deficit.

Regarding the industrial policies of postwar Japan, which have been described by many in recent years, I would like to add a few salient points. Until the late 1960s the government adopted numerous policies and marshaled its resources to help Japanese firms acquire and make the most effective use of Western technology. The most important of these were several ministries' gathering and disseminating Western technology; government-owned or -sponsored agencies conducting research and experiments on that technology and disseminating it to firms at no cost; and direct subsidies to firms attempting to find ways to adopt or improve their imported technologies.

Firms, however, were the principal agents in seeking out new technology and adopting it. Therefore, the postwar government's principal contribution was to promote new technology by providing firms with large amounts of capital at low costs. The state did this during the rapid growth period (1950–1973) by implementing a "low interest rate disequilibrium policy" under which both loan and deposit rates were maintained at below-equilibrium rates; the Bank of Japan and private banks used credit rationing to direct funds to innovating firms needing rapid capital investment. Another policy was to provide preferential loans to innovating firms at below-market rates. The state's tax policies allowed generous deductions for R&D expenditures, rapid depreciation of capital investment and other reserves, and exempting capital gains and interest income from taxation (although interest income became taxable in the early 1960s, it continued to be taxed at a lower fixed rate separate from personal income). Finally, monetary and fiscal polices balanced the twin goals of providing capital to manufacturing firms at the lowest possible cost and minimizing inflation and trade deficits.

Since 1973, firms have relied less on these policies because of the economy's deceleration and the increased ability of large firms to finance their own capital needs. As a result, the low interest rate disequilibrium policy has been gradually abandoned, low-interest loans made by government-owned or -controlled banks have declined, and many provisions in the tax policy favoring capital accumulation and savings have been changed.[7]

The government also adopted other significant policies that further minimized the long-term risks of adopting new technology and increasing productive capacity. The substance of these polices differed little from those of the prewar period. Two major policies were industry-specific laws and the revision (as well as weak enforcement) of the Antimonopoly Act of 1947. Industry-specific laws in the rapid growth period were enacted for the machine tool industry, a key industry in increasing the productivity of all other industries. The first of these laws (a five-year, temporary law) was enacted in 1956 to provide low-cost loans to firms in the industry; the firms were in turn required to inform the Ministry of International Trade and Industry (MITI) of the specific character of their technological progress and to produce products observing various standards set by the ministry. The law also permitted firms to engage in "coordinated activities" in regard to prices, quantity, and types of machinery and machine tools produced. This law was renewed twice in the rapid growth era "to cope with liberalization of international trade and capital markets."[8] Further, new laws differing little in substance from those just described were enacted in 1971 and 1978; even in the late 1970s, thirty-six similar industry-specific laws helped various industries limit output or control prices or investment or both.[9]

Revisions of the Antimonopoly Act (in 1949 and 1953) and its lax enforcement helped reduce the risks of adopting new technology and expanding productive capacities. Although their numbers decreased by the late 1970s, two types of authorized cartels—"recession" and "rationalization"—enabled many firms in a large number of industries to invest in large-scale and more-efficient productive capacities. For example, in the manufacturing sector in late 1971 the total number of these cartels exempted from the Antimonopoly Act and the number authorized by industry-specific laws stood at thirty-six. Even today, Japan's enforcement of the Antimonopoly Act, compared with other industrialized economies, remains significantly more lax in prosecuting illegal retail price maintenance, exclusionary trade practices, and illegal (unsanctioned) cartels of many types.[10]

Other policies were adopted to increase exports and limit imports more directly. Most important for promoting exports were tax incentives, export cartels, and efforts to allow firms to obtain market information and overcome legal and other difficulties abroad. As for policies limiting imports, the most notable were stringent quota and tariff policies of the 1950s and early 1960s, policies limiting imports of capital through the late 1960s, and inspection and product standard polices that imposed high costs on foreign exports to Japan until the late 1970s. By the late 1970s most of these polices had been curtailed, and in the early 1980s Japan could claim one of the lowest average effective tariff rates among the major industrial economies and imposed no quota on the import of industrial products.[11]

INSTITUTIONS

To appraise the contribution made to Japan's economic performance by institutions, let us examine them at three levels: (1) those created by laws; (2) those evolved among firms, between the government and industry, and between management and labor; and (3) those that are better termed *social norms*, or *expected behavior patterns* of individuals or groups. As the following descriptions make evident, these levels overlap, and in many instances the distinctions among them are only for the convenience of exposition.

Starting with level 1, many laws were enacted to reduce transaction costs and provide a progrowth incentive structure. During the early Meiji years, some of the most important laws were often modeled after Western counterparts; in subsequent decades they were revised to meet the changing needs of the economy. These included laws recognizing private property ownership; commercial codes; laws establishing banks and other financial institutions, insurance companies, and accounting procedures; and patent laws. Except for the constitution imposed by the Allied occupation, postwar legal changes revised rather than fundamentally changed the legal basis of the economy.

No less important in explaining the performance of the Japanese economy are the many institutions at level 2 that evolved to aid Japan's rapid economic growth. Let us focus on four that arguably made the most substantive contributions in reducing transaction costs, determining the structure of incentives, and enabling Japan to realize the institution-based "increasing returns."

The first was the interfirm relationship maintained by enterprise groups of old and new *zaibatsu* in the prewar period and *keiretsu* in the postwar period. The old *zaibatsu* consisted of four firms, the Mitsui and Sumitomo groups of pre-Restoration origins and the Mitsubishi and Yasuda groups created shortly after the Meiji Restoration. Each of these four in turn consisted of a few dozen firms: a holding company that owned the majority or controlling shares in a large bank, other financial institutions, and a score of large manufacturing firms in rapidly innovating industries. Each manufacturing firm owned controlling shares in a dozen or more small and medium-sized firms that acted as divisions of their respective parent firms. The new *zaibatsu* groups were composed of five groups of firms that emerged in the early World War I years and rapidly grew in importance during the interwar years by focusing on industries that were quickly expanding because of accelerating technological change in the chemical, transportation equipment, machinery, and other industries.

Although the emergence of firms controlled by holding companies occurred in Western nations as well, the old and new *zaibatsu* were distinct from their counterparts in the West because they controlled the appointments of executives in each network of firms involving financial, technological, marketing, and other relations. Interfirm relations in each group were also long lasting, and terminating relationships was extremely rare. The collective presence of these *zaibatsu* was also much larger than that of analogous groups in Western industrial nations. For example, by the late 1930s, the paid-in capital of all financial institutions and manufacturing firms controlled by the four old *zaibatsu* amounted to 24.5 percent of total paid-in capital; if the paid-in capital of the new *zaibatsu* firms is added, the proportion reaches almost 30 percent.[12]

These *zaibatsu* firms contributed significantly to increasing Japan's technological capabilities by their ability to coordinate use of capital, to exchange information (regarding technology and markets) through interlocking directorates, to engage in joint development of new technology, and to share the risks of entering new ventures. Firms in the same industry belonging to different *zaibatsu* also competed fiercely to adopt new technology and increase market shares. This is why cartels, often "sponsored" by the government, frequently collapsed and why it was inconceivable for *zaibatsu* groups to combine to monopolize various markets. In short, these oligopolistic groups had the capital and managerial ability to coordinate their intragroup activities and facilitate Japan's pursuit of dynamic technological efficiency.

In the postwar period, *keiretsu* emerged in the early 1950s to replace *zaibatsu* disbanded by the Allied powers. The first type of *keiretsu* was horizontal: six groups of two to three dozen of the largest firms, built around major banks that acted as the principal supplier of capital within each group. Four of these were reconstituted from the old *zaibatsu*; the other two were the Sanwa and Daiichi-Kangyo groups that emerged around the largest banks. For the horizontal *keiretsu*, interlocking directorates and a presidents' club for each group closely resemble attributes of the prewar *zaibatsu* holding companies. They pool financial, managerial, and technological resources to engage in joint ventures and R&D activities and, recently, coordinate their efforts to enter markets abroad.

Another type of *keiretsu* is vertical: subcontracting relationships between a large parent firm in a manufacturing industry (that may or may not belong to or have only a loose relationship with a horizontal *keiretsu*) and a large number of small and medium-sized firms. Although subcontracting relationships existed in the prewar period, the postwar relationships were more extensive and intensive because the government encouraged such relationships during the 1930s and the war years to enhance productive efficiency. Also, as the pace of technological progress accelerated after the end of World War II, these close, multidimensional relationships became even more important because they significantly reduced the costs of transactions (as exemplified in the automobile industry case described later). Like prewar *zaibatsu*, the presence of *keiretsu* in the economy was enormous. In 1980, the six horizontal *keiretsu* earned approximately 18 percent of the total net profits of all Japanese business, had almost 17 percent of total sales, held more than 14 percent of total paid-up capital, and employed 5 percent of the Japanese workforce.[13]

The last type is the distribution *keiretsu*, created by large manufacturing firms in the rapid growth period. These represent distribution networks maintained between a large parent manufacturer and a few layers of distributors consisting of wholesalers and retailers. The networks maintained by the largest producers in automobiles, electronics products, and pharmaceuticals are extensive (as shown in the example below of television sets). The economic advantages of the distribution *keiretsu* for producers attempting to achieve dynamic technological efficiency lie in the fact that the *keiretsu*, to the extent that the parent firms were able to assure that their wholesalers and retailers maintained the sale prices the parent firm "suggested," effectively limited price competition, thus earning larger profits. This type of *keiretsu* was even more important for producers in that such a practice, which enabled them to earn large profits and reduce the risks of ever-larger investment, enhanced their ability to rapidly adopt new "lumpy" technology and realize the gains of scale economies and "learning by doing."

The second level-2 institution is that of the dual structure. The size distribution of firms, measured in terms of assets, employment, capital-labor ratios, and various measures of productivity, reveals that Japanese manufacturing industries maintained a two-tiered structure: a small number of large firms and a large number of small firms. This dual structure was most pronounced during the rapid growth period and, in such an exaggerated form, is not observable in other industrial nations.[14]

When Blumenthal examined the pertinent data, he found that the ratio of wages to rental cost of capital (costs of interest and depreciation) was much higher for large firms than for small and medium-sized firms because the cost of capital was lower for large firms. Although wage rates were higher for large firms than for smaller firms, the disparity in the cost of capital resulted in the difference in the ratio; this difference was more pronounced during the rapid growth period than in the early decades of the century. The difference in the ratio during the prewar period was a result of the ready access to capital (i.e., to the *zaibatsu* banks and other large banks) enjoyed by the large firms, such as the sale of pilot plants at bargain prices and direct subsidies. In the postwar period the large disparity in the ratio resulted from preferential loans to the largest firms by government-controlled and *keiretsu* banks, government subsidies in many forms, and tax exemptions and reductions that benefited the large innovating, investing firms.

In adopting policies to maintain this dual structure, Japan ignored the "correct model"—the static, neoclassical theory—which claims that

> as long as there is a marked discrepancy between factor endowment and factor utilization, given a particular state of the arts, innovations should be "biased" in a labor-using direction, as a learning effort in the use of the country's relative abundant resource (i.e., labor) and in conserving the relatively scarce resource (i.e., capital).[15]

Such a "correct model" was ignored because policy makers were convinced that Japan could become a "factory to the world" only if preferential access to capital was given to a small number of the largest firms. Blumenthal puts it best:

> The choice of technology is a long-range decision because changes in technology take a long time to be implemented. The reason lies in the need to disseminate information, train labor, overcome vested interests, change the attitude of management, and create the necessary physical capital in which new technology is embodied. An early introduction of capital-intensive techniques, though inefficient in the short run, prepares the economy for the time when changing factor proportions set in. Moreover, capital-intensive technology imported from more advanced countries may well have a quicker pace of technological improvement since such improvements, made in the exporting country, can also be introduced. The long-term dynamic advantage more than offsets the static disadvantage.[16]

The third level-2 institution is labor-management relations, which many argue have substantially contributed to Japan's economic performance since the 1920s and which differ from those found in other industrial nations. Neoclassical economic analysis explains such distinctively Japanese practices as the permanent employment system, the seniority wage system, and enterprise unions by saying that the permanent employment system was preferred by firms that found it profitable to retain employees whose "human capital" was increased by investment in employee training and by employees seeking job security. The seniority wage system was a way to minimize the loss of employees in whom the firms had made investment; enterprise unions came about in the 1950s and early 1960s because they miniized the risk of labor strife and motivated employee loyalty.

But such neoclassical explanations ignore the roles played by ideology and social norms. In prewar Japan, the ideology of catching up with the West enabled firms to justify their paternalistic labor-management relationships and to discourage unionism. The dual structure, a product of this same ideology, enabled large firms with more capital, advanced technology, and market power to use Japanese-style labor management to pursue dynamic technological efficiency.

The final level-2 institution, government-business relations, has received much attention in recent years. Chalmers Johnson concluded that post-1925 Japan was a "developmental state" in which "the government will give the greatest precedence to industrial policy, that is, to concern with the structure of domestic industry and with promoting the structure that enhances the nation's international competitiveness."[17] Johnson's observations hold true for the Meiji era as well: Meiji political leaders, who repeatedly argued the necessity of government exerting its power to industrialize Japan, worked closely with bankers, nascent *zaibatsu* firms, and many others eager to "cooperate" with the government. The Meiji ministers also facilitated the rise of major industrialists (and merchants) called "political merchants"; their shared ideology of catching up with the West justified such cooperation.

The substance of the relationship did not change in the interwar years. During this period, close government-business ties developed and effectively pursued the tasks of a "developmental state" as MITI and other ministries gained the necessary skills, knowledge, and administrative structure. Indeed, the government-business relationship in the 1920s and 1930s, unlike earlier decades, was one in which the *zaibatsu* were able to place their executives in cabinet posts and win many significant policy favors in exchange for sizable financial contributions to political parties. The largest firms in the dual structure had few disagreements with the government and ministries on policies related to taxes, money, finance, and exchange rates. The government and industries increased the international competitiveness of Japan's industries and suppressed labor unions and leftist political groups.

As *zaibatsu* reemerged to become *keiretsu*, the postwar government-business ties changed remarkably little. The postwar relationship, however, was more organized, systematic, and multifaceted than its prewar counterpart partly because of the changed domestic and international economies and partly because catching up with the West could be pursued without the distraction of building and maintaining a costly military force.

The government provided exactly what the industries, especially the large innovating manufacturing firms, wished. The government made "economic plans" and issued "administrative guidance" to aid industries in increasing productive capacity and efficiency and in so doing promoted economic growth. The economic plans, beginning with the first one (1955–60) to the eleventh (1988–92), consist of broadly stated economic goals and descriptions of how the plans could be achieved. As economic plans in a capitalist economy, these are "indicative," not "command," plans that present national economic goals to be attained within a few years or a decade. They justify policies and help banks and firms know what assistance will be forthcoming from the government when banks make loans to the industries targeted for rapid growth and to firms that adopt new technology or engage in prescribed new ventures. In short, these plans work because they articulate national goals and facilitate the efforts required to achieve dynamic technological efficiency.

Throughout the rapid growth period, MITI consulted with industry representatives and guided the largest firms to coordinate the pace of investment. The guidance of MITI, in virtually all cases, helped firms minimize the risks of excess capacity and price competition. When excess capacity did develop, MITI helped the firms form cartels to fix prices or limit output. This action helped firms focus on sustained competition to increase productive efficiency and adopt their new technology. Some of these cartels were legal recession and rationalization cartels permitted under the Antimonopoly Act, but many were not.

Although economic planning and administrative guidance continued, their importance in the 1980s declined substantially. Liberalization and internationalization of the economy had reduced the power of the ministries, whereas the largest firms, which now possessed more capital and technological capabilities, became less reliant on the government. Japan, having caught up with the West in most industries, now had fewer industries to be targeted for rapid growth. Japanese consumers and Japan's trading partners now opposed state guidance to fix prices, limit competition, and coordinate investments.

In level-3 institutions, "social norms," or the behavior of individuals and groups motivated by sociocultural traditions, were in many ways more important than the legal and economic institutions (levels 1 and 2) in enabling Japan to achieve its high economic performance. As many sociologists, anthropologists, and others have observed, the Japanese are more "group oriented," more inclined to maintain intensive, multidimensional, longer-term intergroup relationships than Westerners. This group orientation has been defined as follows:

> The Japanese concern for belonging relates to the tendency toward collectivism, which is expressed by an individual's identification with the collective goal of the group to which he belongs. Collectivism thus involves cooperation and solidarity, and the sentimental desire for the warm feeling of *ittaikan* ("feeling of oneness") with fellow members of one's group is widely shared by Japanese.[18]

As to why the Japanese maintain such intensive intergroup relations, Reischauer has made this observation:

> For these various [cultural and historical] reasons, Japanese do not develop new associations lightly. It may be easier for two people to continue to pass as strangers than to take on the burdens of a recognized relationship. Japanese on the whole are less inclined than Westerners to enter into casual contacts and are likely to seem forbiddingly formal in any new encounter.[19]

(Although no explanation of these Japanese behavioral characteristics is ventured here, the predominance of a functional and vertical organization, the Confucian tradition, and other cultural values surely important.) Thus the Japanese are more likely to maintain long-term relationships for sociocultural reasons than are Westerners, and their group orientedness and long-term orientation can reduce the costs of transactions and affect the structure of incentives in ways that enable them to maintain high economic performance over time.

Case Studies

I will now describe the roles policies and institutions played in promoting the growth of four important industries.

THE COTTON TEXTILE INDUSTRY

In 1880 the government, intent on reducing imports of cotton thread and increasing exports as rapidly as possible, imported ten sets of two thousand modern spindles and, by advancing long-term, low-cost government loans, sold them to ten firms. But nine of these firms either could not begin operation or failed soon after because of managerial inexperience. The Osaka Spinning Mill, however, begun in 1882, quickly prospered under the guidance of Takeo Yamabe, who had studied cotton textile machinery in England, and because it had obtained enough start-up capital by taking advantage of the newly enacted commercial code. Osaka was organized as a share-issuing corporation because banks, established in 1876, had loaned it the necessary operating funds. The Osaka Spinning Mill began its operations using ten thousand spindles, five times the number the government judged necessary to start a profitable cotton textile firm. Its success encouraged new firms to enter the industry; by 1890, their number had reached thirty-nine.[20]

By 1889 the total output of cotton thread exceeded imports, and in 1890 exports to China began. Aided by the abolition of export duties in 1894, exports sharply rose, while imports steadily declined. In 1897, exports exceeded imports, and, by the first decade of the twentieth century, imports had ended while exports were growing rapidly.[21] An important part of this success story is that cotton textile firms, which numbered seventy-four by 1897, joined cartels to cope with the periodic excess capacity created both by rapid expansion and by the recessions of the 1890s and 1900s. Although these cartels, which fixed prices and monitored output, enabled the young firms to weather such difficulties, they were short-lived, lasting for only several months at most, during which fierce competition was suspended.[22]

However one interprets the relative importance of the efforts made by the firms and the contributions made by institutions (the commercial codes, the banking system, cartels, and others), both were essential in transforming Japan's cotton textile industry from being that of an importer to that of a major exporter competing successfully against England within thirty years.

THE IRON AND STEEL INDUSTRY

This industry too received considerable state assistance in prewar and postwar Japan. In both periods, competition for technological progress and market share among oligopolistic firms enabled the iron and steel industry to take advantage of governmental assistance and cease being an infant industry. It is one of the best examples of successful dynamic technological efficiency.

The modern iron industry began in 1873 in northern Japan when the government began to build, with the aid of seventeen foreign engineers and foremen, large-scale Western furnaces and ancillary facilities (including railroads). This venture, however, ended in failure in 1882 because high-quality coke was unavailable. In 1886, Chobei Tanaka started up his iron venture with government bargain furnaces and with large government orders and orders from several industries that were rapidly adopting new technologies that required iron.[23] Productivity, however, failed to meet the rapidly increasing government, especially military, and industrial demand for more iron and steel. In 1896, a government foundry, Yawata Ironworks, was built in Kyushu that began to produce, after a few years of agonizing failures, both iron and steel in 1901. By 1904, the Yawata Ironworks produced 26 percent of the iron and 63 percent of the steel in Japan; these figures had risen to 75 and 89 percent, respectively, by 1912.

After this government venture had begun, Tanaka expanded his firm to produce steel as well as iron; four other large firms also entered the industry between 1901 and 1912, expanding capacity and using new technology. Even so, Japan in 1913 remained a large importer of iron, importing roughly as much as it produced, and steel, producing only about one-third of the required amount. The growth of the industry continued during World War I and throughout the interwar years with the help of preferential loans, low taxes, and state subsidies. Although the Yawata Ironworks' productivity was rapidly increasing, private firms' output was growing even more rapidly. By 1921, Yawata's share of iron production had dipped to 47 percent and steel, to 29.6 percent of total output.[24] The total output of iron and steel, which had accounted for only 1.7 percent of total industrial output before World War I, reached 10.8 percent by 1936, and *zaibatsu*-related firms produced more than half of the 1936 output.[25]

In the postwar period, the Occupation powers dissolved the Yawata Ironworks, and the iron and steel industry became an oligopolistic industry composed of private firms with prewar *zaibatsu* ties. Under the first and the second "rationalization" plans (1951–55 and 1955–60) for the iron and steel industry, the government provided preferential loans, tax exemptions, and other industry-specific inducements to help the industry recover and grow. During the rapid growth period, firms periodically formed cartels to maintain collusive "administered prices" in cooperation with major wholesalers.

Borrowing from their respective *keiretsu* banks, these firms fiercely competed, building large-scale furnaces and new strip mills as well as adopting new furnace technology. By the mid-1960s, the industry had become internationally competitive, and exports of steel products rose rapidly because of the steady increase in productivity. Although the total cost per ton of producing steel in Japan was $8.99 higher than that in the United States in 1956, by 1960 the Japanese cost was lower by $35.10 and by 1979 had fallen to $143.93. This difference was primarily due to the widening gap in labor costs (because of high Japanese labor productivity), not to a difference in the cost of materials.[26]

THE AUTOMOBILE INDUSTRY

During the 1920s and early 1930s, when Japan was rapidly importing Western technology, of the many contracts signed with American and other Western firms to obtain patents, know-how, and capital, the machine tool and automobile industries accounted for the largest number. Although Japan had attempted to produce automobiles before World War I and had enacted a law in 1918 to assist in automobile production for military use, auto production did not begin until the mid-1920s, when Ford and General Motors (GM) began to assemble automobiles in Japan, importing most of the parts from the United States. These firms were crucial for the growth of the Japanese industry because they trained manpower in the production, servicing, and marketing of automobiles and promoted the growth of the parts industry as both U.S. firms steadily increased the local content of their final products. But the growth of the industry was slow, and as late as 1929 there were only twenty-nine thousand automobiles in Japan.[27]

Because their technological capability was no match for that of Ford or GM, the few Japanese firms that attempted to enter the industry produced a very small number of what could best be characterized as experimental samples until 1932, when Nissan and Toyota entered the market on the strength of their technological competence in the machine tool industry and with government encouragement in the form of procurement orders and loans. What enabled these Japanese firms and others to establish large-scale and viable auto production was the Automobile Industry Act of 1936, enacted to build "national defense and the promotion of industry." Requiring at least 50 percent of management personnel and the capital of automobile firms to be Japanese, it also provided a five-year tax exemption from corporate income and import duties.[28] This law and many other restrictive measures forced U.S. firms to abandon their activities in Japan, leaving

Nissan, Toyota, and Tokyo Automobile to increase their output, greatly aided by military orders.

Although leaders of the financial community argued that Japan had little hope of successfully competing with Western auto producers and that it should use its resources for the growth of other industries, MITI and the Ministry of Finance (MOF) began heavily promoting the industry in 1951. They enacted a few major laws to help "rationalize" the industry as rapidly as possible (namely, laws that allowed rapid depreciation, generous tax deductions for R&D, defraying the costs of royalties paid to foreign firms, and other incentives) and issued plans about how the industry should develop. With MOF guidance, substantive low-cost loans were advanced well into the late 1960s.[29] But the Japanese auto industry's growth after 1950 was achieved not only because of government assistance but because of fierce competition among the oligopolist firms to produce better, lower-cost automobiles and their superior marketing and services. In the early 1950s, when Japan produced fewer than two thousand automobiles a year, no one thought it possible that automobiles would be exported to the United States by 1962. By the late 1970s, Japanese autos were being produced in the United States, and by the late 1980s Japanese producers had succeeded in gaining more than 20 percent of the U.S. market.

Television Sets and Semiconductors

The output and quality of Japanese television sets also rose rapidly in the early 1950s and soon attained the globally competitive position they enjoy today. Again, U.S. technology and progrowth tax benefits, loans, and other policies greatly helped firms producing television sets and other home electric appliances. The six largest producers were allowed to fix prices in the domestic market and to adopt aggressive—many argue, anticompetitive—strategies to increase their market shares abroad, especially in the United States.

The nonenforcement of the Antimonopoly Act into the late 1970s helped the producers of television sets increase their technological capabilities. By forming illegal cartels, these firms increased or maintained their profit levels in times of excess capacity or recessions or both. Being assured profits, firms competed to improve product quality, increase the variety of products, and offer better services. These firms thus gained a foothold the U.S. and other foreign markets. Simply put, exports of both monochrome and color TV sets rose rapidly because their quality improved as a result of technological competition at home and firms investing their profits in the home market to subsidize their exports. These firms also established extensive and tightly controlled distribution networks abroad. The number of television *keiretsu* distribution outlets in the early 1980s ranged from thirty-five hundred for Sharp (the smallest firm in the industry) to about twenty-five thousand for Matsushita (the largest firm).

The cartels of the 1950–75 period were replaced by government-sponsored joint research programs for semiconductors, computers, and other electronics products. The *keiretsu* distribution system is also gradually shifting from rebate and other incentive schemes to offering varied services demanded by consumers. Nonetheless, Japan's capabilities in high-technology industries continue to increase at a pace exceeding that of many firms in other industrial nations because capabilities are cumulative and the policies and institutions described above continue to evolve to serve the needs of these Japanese firms

Quantitative Evidence and the Roles of Institutions and Policies

The growth rates of both GNP and per capita GNP in Japan were not only rapid but also relatively more consistent than the growth performance of other major industrial economies (see tables 4.2 and 4.3). In the prewar period, "whether looking at three-year averages or annual GNE [gross national expenditure] data, it was only Japan's growth *rate* that rose and fell, there being almost no cases of recessions with negative growth. This contrasts remarkably with other countries where negative growth was not at all rare."[30] In the postwar period, Japan's sustained growth rate was marred only once, in 1974 with zero growth resulting from the oil crisis. Even the growth rate in the recession years (3.5 percent) was not appreciably lower than the mean growth rates most other industrialized nations were able to maintain during the 1950–80 period.

Additionally, I have observed some other noteworthy patterns: (1) because Japan's economic performance was achieved with fewer and smaller fluctuations than in other industrial economies, Japan limited the hardships that originate from significant and prolonged periods of recession or depression; (2) Japanese policies and institutions helped many to save, thus increasing the ability to adopt new technology and increase productivity; and (3) Japanese policies and institutions promoted the structural changes essential for sustaining this economic performance.

As to why Japan has had fewer prolonged recessions and depressions, we must remember the wars and militarism in its history. From the Sino-Japanese War of 1895 to the Vietnam War of the rapid growth period, wars helped sustain Japan's growth performance, as did the mobilization of resources for the war efforts during the 1930s. The Great Depression affected the Japanese economy far less than it did other industrial economies, partly because of debt-financed expansion of productive capacities to meet military needs.

Table 4.2   Economic Growth Rate, G(Y), Population Growth, G(N), and Growth of per Capita Gross National Expenditure, G(Y/N), in Japan, 1876–1980 (in percent)

	G(Y)	G(N)	G(Y/N)
1876–1890	—	0.82	—
1889–1890	3.53	0.85	2.68
1891–1895	3.12	0.92	2.19
1896–1900	2.25	1.10	1.15
1901–1905	1.84	1.18	0.66
1906–1910	2.29	1.14	1.16
1911–1915	3.35	1.36	1.99
1916–1920	4.77	1.11	3.66
1921–1925	1.93	1.26	0.67
1926–1930	2.53	1.50	1.03
1931–1935	4.98	1.36	3.62
1936–1938	5.07	0.95	4.12
(1889–1938)	3.15	1.01	2.14
1939–1954	—	1.46	—
1955	7.29	1.17	6.12
1956–1960	8.64	0.98	7.66
1961–1965	10.05	0.99	0.06
1966–1970	9.97	1.25	8.72
1971–1975	5.66	1.33	4.33
1976–1980	4.50	0.93	3.57
(1955–1980)	7.74	1.11	6.63

NOTE: The figures are the simple averages of the annual growth rates.
SOURCE: Ryōshin Minami, *The Economic Development of Japan: A Quantitative Study* (London: Macmillan Press, 1986), p. 43.

These war-related factors, however, offer only a partial explanation of Japan's ability to minimize fluctuations in its growth rate. I argue that the many policies adopted to achieve dynamic technological efficiency, along with Japan's institutions, were important. The most significant policies preferentially allocated capital to the most rapidly growing industries, maintained a low yen value to maximize the rate of export growth, and promoted cartels. The principal institutions muting recessions were multidimensional, interfirm relations that adjusted to large or sudden changes or both in relative prices, cooperative relationships between government and industries, the suppression of labor unions in the prewar period, and the docility of enterprise unionism in the postwar period.

For these reasons, in both the prewar and the postwar periods, Japan could facilitate high savings while supporting institutions conducive to capital

Table 4.3   Per Capita GNP in the Developed Countries at Their Modern
               Economic Growth (MEG) Starting Points and in 1965, 1981

	MEG Starting Point (1965 dollars)		1965 (1965 dollars)	1981 (1981 dollars)
Australia	$760	(1861–1869)	$2,023	$11,135
Switzerland	529	(1865)	2,354	17,442
Canada	508	(1870–1874)	2,507	11,409
United States	474	(1834–1843)	3,580	12,819
Denmark	370	(1865–1869)	2,238	13,123
Netherlands	347	(1831–1840)	1,609	11,796
Belgium	326	(1831–1840)	1,835	11,918
Germany [a]	302	(1850–1859)	1,939	13,452
Norway	287	(1865–1869)	1,912	14,059
Italy	261	(1861–1869)	1,100	6,843
France	242	(1831–1840)	2,047	12,186
Great Britain [b]	227	(1765–1785)	1,870	9,140
Sweden	215	(1861–1869)	2,713	14,877
Japan	136	(1886)	876	10,084

[a] The postwar figures are for West Germany, as opposed to Germany.
[b] The postwar figures are for the United Kingdom, as opposed to Great Britain.
SOURCE: Ryōshin Minami, *The Economic Development of Japan: A Quantitative Study* (London: Macmillan Press, 1986), p. 13.

formation because everyone shared the ideologies of catching up with the West and pursuing a strategy of dynamic technological efficiency. This is why the prosavings policies and institutions long remained unchallenged and the leadership, unsubjected to strong political demands to change its policies and institutions—despite the burdens of unequal income distribution and living standards that rose more slowly than the increase in labor productivity.

Had the Japanese people not believed that prewar Japan could become a "first-rate nation," the Meiji government could not have increased capital formation at the expense of farmers and wage earners. That same belief meant that the government in the interwar period could pursue policies favoring the accumulation of capital and the inflationary policies of the largest manufacturing firms, even though these deprived customers of their purchasing power. In the postwar period as well, had it not been for the national consensus to wage a "total economic war," the low interest-rate disequilibrium policy of the rapid growth period could not have long remained in effect because it penalized wage earners who had deposited their savings into banks paying out a low, fixed interest rate. Many other prosavings policies and the close government-business relationship could also never have been maintained. In short, the high savings rate, from the

Meiji period to the early 1980s, which was essential for Japan's acquisition of dynamic technological efficiency, could not have been attained without the shared strong ideology of the need to catch up with the West. The political costs of rapid capital formation were also significantly reduced by the shared perception that Japan had to save to become a "rich nation."

Because of its success in pursuing dynamic technological efficiency, Japan's living standard and quality of life have greatly improved in many other ways over the past century. Real inflation-adjusted personal consumption expenditure rose at an annual average rate of 2.53 percent for the 1889–1938 period and 6.99 percent for the 1956–80 period. This rate was nearly 8 percent during the rapid growth period of 1950–73. These rates were high compared with those achieved by other industrial nations in comparable periods.[31] Consumption patterns also changed as the Engel coefficient fell from 35 to 37 percent in the 1920s and 1930s to 27.8 percent by 1980. In contrast, the expenditure category classified as miscellaneous, or total expenditures minus those incurred for food, housing, heat and light, and clothing and thus available for education, entertainment, medical care, and the like, rose from the 29–30 percent level in the interwar years to 49.2 percent by 1980.[32] There was also a steady rise in the quality and kinds of foods (including many Western foods) consumed; for example, per capita consumption of animal protein (meat and fish) rose from 2.0 kg of meat and 13.9 kg of fish in the 1930s to 23.8 kg and 34.2 kg, respectively, in the mid-1980s.[33]

Better diet, improved medical care, and other lifestyle changes improved the quality and quantity of life. For example, life expectancy for males rose from 42.8 years during the 1891–98 period to 73.4 by 1980 and for females, from 44.2 to 78.8 during the same period. The infant death rate, for which reliable data became available in 1920, declined from 166.2 per thousand live births in 1920 to a mere 7.5 in 1980. These accomplishments have not been surpassed by any large industrialized Western nation.[34] In the past one hundred years, Japan also became better educated. The percentage of students enrolled in compulsory education rose from 28.1 percent in 1873 to virtually 100 percent in the postwar years, whereas the number of years of compulsory education rose from four in the early Meiji period to nine in the postwar period. Those completing at least two years of education beyond the high school level steadily rose from a few percent of their cohort group in the Meiji years to 38.5 percent by 1980 (a figure exceeded only by the United States).[35] Indeed the quality of life in Japan in 1980 bore little resemblance to that of 1867, when the nation began to produce more wealth at an accelerating rate.

Why Success and at What Costs?

Why did Japan's "bridled capitalism" enable it to successfully pursue dynamic technological efficiency and sustain a wealth-creating process for the past one hundred years? Put differently, why did not many of Japan's policies and institutions, as described in the preceding sections, cause inefficiency and stagnation in economic performance as many other nations did when adopting similar policies and maintaining analogous institutions?

The answer, supported by the facts and observations presented in this study, is that, because of its widely shared ideologies of "catching up with the West" and "waging a total war for economic growth" as well as the character of its policies and institutions, Japan was able to provide means and incentives that aided its firms in their pursuit of dynamic technological efficiency while enabling them to compete to increase their productive capacity and productivity over time. Those policies and institutions combined in such salient growth-inducing mechanisms as cartels, subsidies, firm management and control, and dual structure. The "bridled capitalism" of Japan succeeded, then, because its policies and institutions reflected shared ideologies, providing firms with the means, incentive, and opportunities to pursue dynamic technological efficiency and become procompetitive rather than anticompetitive. Of course, the transformation also succeeded because Japan was a follower who had technology to borrow and had a culture that aided the crucial roles played by policies and institutions in the transformation process.

I conclude this essay by stressing that the past one hundred years of Japan's march to become an economic superpower were not cost-free but were paid for by what I characterize as "exploitation of ideology." That is, the temptation to "exploit" ideology was often succumbed to by Japan's political and business leaders. To deny that they did so is to argue that dynamic technological efficiency created a necessary number of "losers" who were "victimized" only to the extent necessary. Such an argument is impossible to sustain. It would argue the necessity of deplorable working conditions, long hours, and low wages for hundreds of thousands of young female workers in the cotton textile industry; the ruthless suppression of the labor movement; the extremely paltry social welfare programs; the harsh lot of tenant farmers and employees of small firms; and many other inequalities and deprivations of the prewar period. Such an argument would also claim as necessary the woefully inadequate housing, overcrowded public transportation and scarcity of parks, prices of manufactured products distinctively higher than similar products in other industrial nations, legal and administratively guided barriers to trade entries, and numerous other strongly criticized facts of Japanese life in the postwar period.

All nations and their respective paths of industrialization created losers, and it is hard to determine which one had more losers than others. No nation, capitalist or otherwise, has achieved an "optimum" trade-off between efficiency and quality, that is, between the number of losers that must be tolerated and the efficiency with which a nation achieves economic growth. Thus, pursuing the strategy of dynamic technological efficiency, Japan created more losers than could be justified because those who had political and economic power and thus were in a position to exploit ideology could adopt policies and create institutions, the effect of which was to bridle capitalism more tightly than necessary. In noting the exploitation that occurred, however, we should not lose sight of the fact that the strategy's success lay in the power holders' ability to exploit ideology, adopt polices, and create institutions.

Notes

1. The institution-based increasing and decreasing returns discussed here are a subset of those discussed in North's essay in this volume. As my examples show, the cumulative effects I have in mind are limited to those that result from interfirm relationships, the nature of modern technology, and readily identifiable social norms within a nation.

2. Eisuke Sakakibara and Yukio Noguchi, "Ōkurashō-Nichigan ōcho no bunseki," *Chūō kōron*, August 1977, p. 110.

3. The most effective and technical critique of those economists who question the "export-led" growth thesis is found in Miyohei Shinohara, "Yushitsu shudo-gata seicho to kawase reto" (Export-led type growth and exchange rates), *Keizai Kenkyū* 40, no. 3 (July 1989): 193–203. His criticisms, in addition to mine, include the fact that most of the arguments are based on nominal values and not real values, use the early 1950s (when exports were high as a result of exports relating to the Korean War) as a basis, and neglect the shortcomings that exist in the export data of Japan.

4. Ibid., p. 195.

5. Juro Hashimoto, "Kyodai sangyo no koryu" (The rise of the giant industries), in Takafusa Nakamura and Konosuke Odaka, eds., *Nijū kōzō* (The dual structure), vol. 6 of *Nihon Keizaishi* (Economic history of Japan) (Tokyo: Iwanami shoten, 1989), p. 98.

6. For these descriptions, see ibid.

7. Beginning in the early 1980s, liberalization and internationalization of the capital market liberalized (decontrolled) interest rates, and various restrictions in regard to financial instruments that could be used by banks and security houses both domestically and internationally were removed.

8. Yutaka Kosai, "Kōdo seichōki no keizai seisaku" (Economic policy of the rapid growth period), in Yasukichi Yasuba and Takenori Inoki, eds., *Kōdo seichō*, vol. 8 of *Nihon Keizaishi*, p. 239.

9. Ibid.

10. Kozo Yamamura, "Structure Is Behavior: An Appraisal of Japanese Economic Pol-

icy, 1960 to 1972," in Isaiah Frank, ed., *The Japanese Economy in International Perspective* (Baltimore, Md.: Johns Hopkins University Press, 1975), pp. 67–100.

11. As made evident in frequent trade disputes that occur between Japan and its trading partners, however, these facts did not mean that, even by the end of the decade, Japanese markets had become as accessible to foreign firms as those of other industrial nations. Although further discussion is outside the scope of this study, this was because various institutions that had evolved to promote exports and restrict imports were changing only slowly and continued to impede exports.

12. Hashimoto, "Kyodai sangyo no Koryu," p. 124.

13. U.S. International Trade Commission (U.S. ITC), *U.S. Global Competitiveness: The U.S. Automotive Parts Industry* U.S. ITC Publication 2037 (Washington, D.C.: U.S. ITC, December 1987), sects 4–13.

14. Tuvia Blumenthal, "Factor Proportions and Choice Technology: The Japanese Experience," *Economic Development and Cultural Change* 39 (1980): 558.

15. John C. Fei and Gustav Ranis, "Less Developed Country Innovation and the Technology Gap," in Gustav Ranis, ed., *The Gap between the Rich and Poor Countries* (New York: Macmillan, 1972), p. 315; as quoted in Blumenthal, "Factor Proportions and Choice Technology," p. 555.

16. Blumenthal, "Factor Proportions and Choice Technology," p. 556.

17. Chalmers Johnson, *MITI and the Japanese Miracle: The Growth of Industrial Policy, 1925–1975* (Stanford: Stanford University Press, 1982), p. 19.

18. Takie Sugiyama Lebra, *Japanese Patterns of Behavior* (Honolulu: University of Hawaii Press, 1976), p. 25.

19. Edwin O. Reischauer, *The Japanese Today: Change and Continuity* (Cambridge, Mass.: The Belknap Press of Harvard University Press, 1988), p. 147.

20. Takeshi Abe, "Men kōgyō" (The cotton textile industry), in Takeshi Abe and Shunsaku Nishikawa, eds., *Sangyō ka no jidai (1)* (The period of industrialization [1]), vol. 4 of *Nihon Keizaishi*, p. 166.

21. Kazuyoshini Oku and Yuzo Yamamoto, "Bōeki" (International trade), in Shunsaku Nishikawa and Kazuyoshi Oku, eds., *Sangyō ka no jidai (2)* (The period of industrialization [2]), vol. 5 of *Nihon Keizaishi*, pp. 97–109.

22. Johannes Hirschmier and Tsunehiko Yui, *The Development of Japanese Business* (London: George Allen and Unwin, 1975), pp. 186–88.

23. Shunsaku Nishikawa and Takeshi Abe, "Gaisetsu" (Overview), in Abe and Nishikawa, eds., *Sangyō ka no jidai (1)*, pp. 13–30.

24. Hashimoto, "Kyodai sangyō no kōryu" pp. 94, 107–12.

25. Ibid., p. 101.

26. Hugh Patrick and Hideo Sato, "The Political Economy of U.S.-Japan Trade in Steel," in Yamamura, ed., *Policy and Trade Issues of the Japanese Economy*, p. 205.

27. Hashimoto, "Kyodai sangyō no kōryu," pp. 105–7.

28. Yutaka Kosai, "Kodo seicho e no shuppatsu" (The beginning of rapid growth), in

Takafusa Nakamura, ed., *Keikakuka to minshuka* (Planning and democratization), vol. 7 of *Nihon Keizaishi*, pp. 302–5.

29. Odaka, "Seicho no kiseki (2)," in Yasuba and Inoki, eds., *Kōdo seichō*, pp. 170–72.

30. Takafusa Nakamura, *Economic Growth in Prewar Japan* (New Haven, Conn.: Yale University Press, 1983), p. 8.

31. Ryoshin Minami, *The Economic Development of Japan: A Ouantitative Study* (London: Macmillan, 1986), pp. 37–38; and Yutaka Kosai and Yoshitaro Ogino, *The Contemporary Japanese Economy* (New York: M.E. Sharpe, 1984), p. 9.

32. Calculated from the Bureau of Statistics, Office of the Prime Minister, *Kakei chosa nenpo* (Annual statistics of family expenditures) (Tokyo: Office of the Prime Minister).

33. Statistics are per year, per person; *Asahi shimbun*, January 1, 1985.

34. Life expectancy data are from *Hundred Year Statistics of the Japanese Economy* (Tokyo: Statistics Department, Bank of Japan, 1966), p. 17; and Statistics Bureau, Management and Coordination Agency, *Nihon keizai tokei nenkan* (Annual statistics of the Japanese economy) (Tokyo: Ministry of Finance Printing Office, 1989). The infant death rate is from Irene B. Tauber, *The Population of Japan* (Princeton, N.J.: Princeton University Press, 1966), and Yano, ed., *Suji de miru Nihon no 100-nen* (One hundred years of Japan seen in numbers) (Tokyo: Kokuseisha, 1981), p. 273.

35. Minami, *Economic Development of Japan*, p. 19, and Yano, ed., *Suji de miru Nihon no 100-nen*, p. 361.

5

Decelerating Growth under Socialism
The Soviet Case

GUR OFER

Introduction

During the last three decades of its existence, the Soviet Union went through a process of declining growth, reaching virtual stagnation.[1] It is therefore understandable why one of the first moves of perestroika in the Soviet Union, back in 1985, was acceleration (*uskarenniya*), an effort to reverse this long-term declining trend. As it turned out, acceleration was sustained at best for one year (1986), and since then growth rates continued to decline, even turning negative at the end, down to the disintegration of the union at the end of 1991 (Bruno 1993, 202, table 7.1). Paradoxically, what perestroika needed at the time was a period of relaxation of pressures on quantitative targets in preparation for the complete abandonment of the old system and the transition to a new one. Since 1991, Russia and all the other former Soviet republics and former socialist countries had suffered from sharp declines in output, resulting from the collapse of the old system and the efforts of economic transition. This collapse, although closely related to the nature and heritage of the old system, had also been an integral part of the new epoch of transition to a new political and economic regime.

Perestroika arrived when the Soviet leadership became convinced that there was no way to reverse the trend of declining growth rates, indeed of near stagnation and possibly even a collapse, except through a major systemic transformation. This assessment, shared by some economists of the old system, was fully consistent with and reinforced the long-standing Western literature on the reasons for the long-term deceleration of Soviet growth rates during the post–World War II period (see, for example, Bergson 1973). Although decelerating rates of growth are normal in most growth processes, and are common to most of the regions covered by this volume, Soviet deceleration and stagnation occurred long before substantial convergence toward output levels of the developed West was achieved.

The factor that was most responsible for Soviet decelerating growth was the failure of the system to generate an adequate amount of growth of productivity, driven by technological change and improvements in the patterns of production. Initially, technological innovations, imported from the West, contributed to Soviet growth, but the natural decline of this factor and the failure to generate indigenous technological capability contributed to the built-in deceleration. This failure, caused by the many systemic, institutional, and strategic economic policy elements discussed below, left the responsibility for growth on the shoulders of the so-called extensive growth model or strategy, where growth depends increasingly, and eventually exclusively, on the rise in labor and capital inputs and finally only on capital, a rise whose rate is bound to decline and eventually be exhausted, leading to stagnation. Although input-led growth is normal and common in the early stages of economic development of many countries, it is the failure to use this stage as a base on which to develop indigenous and sustainable capability of technological and efficiency growth that characterizes the Soviet experience.

The Soviet growth record fits the neoclassical growth model developed by Robert Solow and others during the 1950s, where input-determined growth was directly estimated and the growth of efficiency and technological change were left as "residual" growth unexplained by input growth (Solow 1957). The Soviet case, especially during the last decades, qualifies as a classical example of the Solow model with a rapidly diminishing residual. This is so despite the fact that, in the neoclassical growth model, the calculation of growth is based on the assumption of perfect markets.

In the Solow growth model, technological change is formally treated as "exogenous" to the system of perfect markets, whereas for a long time, before and following its formulation, scholars studying the theory and reality of technological changes in the West emphasized the underlying disequilibrium nature, the various forms of market imperfections of the technologically supportive institutional arrangements. These economic and institutional theories of technological change were developed over the years by economists like Schumpeter, Kuznets, Abramovits, and many others. Recently, however, the apparent contradiction between the neoclassical model of perfect markets and nonperfect market structures and the institutional requirements for technological change was somewhat smoothed in an integrated endogenous growth model developed by Romer (1986, 1989), Lucas (1988), Ethier (1982), Grossman and Helpman (1989), and others and by corresponding empirical work by the above, as well as Barro (1989a, 1989b). The main feature of that work is that the process of technological change is endogenized into market economies that allow increasing returns to scale, externalities, and nonperfect competition. Quasi-rents that are created behind the shelters of an increasing number of new, specialized products and grades of (improved) qualities provide the incentives and the financing for such developments. This new-old approach helps bridge a gap between an apparent theoretical advantage of central planning over a market economy in the generation of technological changes and its obvious revealed failure in this area. The new theories, or the new formulation of old ones, also underlie a number of important elements of the process of technological change that were deficient or altogether missing in the Soviet economy. Hence a more integrated theoretical case can now be made to support the observed advantages of a mixed-market system over a centrally planned one. The Soviet growth and technological failure was clearly a combined outcome of many institutional and policy-driven factors that were an integral part of its economic system.

A second major explanation for growth deceleration in the Soviet Union was the strategy of "haste": the effort to "catch up" with the advanced countries, the readiness to sacrifice future growth in order to secure maximum growth rates as soon as possible, the readiness to borrow resources for present production purposes from future capabilities and to borrow them at high real interest rates reflecting high time (present) preference. Future payments of the principal and interest reduce future growth potential. Haste may have raised initial Soviet growth rates but at the expense of much lower future ones. It caused a much faster exhaustion of potential capital, labor, and natural resources and stifled even further the ability of technological advances, through heavy pressure for immediate quantitative targets.[2]

The failure of the Soviet Union to achieve sustained growth is a comprehensive, systemic one and a failure of its growth strategy. The absence of market forces, market incentives, and market flexibilities, and free enterprise and their replacement with central planning proved to be fatal. One option for this chapter was to go through a laundry list of all the failures of central planning. The alternative that was chosen was to organize the discussion around the two main clusters of factors listed above—the technological and efficiency failure and haste—and on the related policies and institutions as the main explanations for the Soviet growth deceleration since the 1960s (see below). Before that, there is a summary description and analysis of the Soviet growth record as well as changes in the main structural features of the economy.

The Growth and Welfare Record

The wealth of a nation, as a measure of its welfare or productive capabilities, may be summarily defined as the long-term ("permanent") sustainable level of consumption, material and otherwise, per capita, "reasonably" distributed. This is a much broader and different concept than either the level of GNP per capita at a certain period of time or its rate of growth. Some of these issues are dealt with at length in the introductory and concluding chapters of this volume. Let's list here some of the differences that are relevant to the Soviet case.

First, excluded from GNP per capita is the time left to be spent on non-GNP uses like leisure. Thus, wealth is lower the higher the proportion of time spent in the production of GNP per capita. Second, per capita GNP includes the share spent on investment, also an input. If this share is consistently higher in the long run (because of its lower productivity), less is left for consumption, the ultimate producer of welfare and therefore of wealth. Indexes of long-term consumption per hour worked, or per person employed, are therefore better measures of welfare inside the regular framework of national accounting.

In the production of GNP, in addition to labor and produced capital, there is also the use of natural resources. The rate of depletion of these resources, including environmental damage, is sometimes extreme and in some cases not properly measured. In either case estimated GDP growth is overstated.

The GNP is estimated with a set of weights that usually reflect relative prices in the economy. For a number of reasons, relative weights assigned to the various end uses of GNP through established relative prices may not always reflect the true (welfare or productivity) social weights. These weights, and therefore the aggregate measure, do not represent true welfare if consumer sovereignty is absent or when relative prices do not represent consumer utilities and costs of production or both. Per contra, even when a reasonably free combination of consumer sovereignty and social collective decision-making processes prevails, some GNP uses or their direct accumulated consequences are given higher welfare weights than their measured "market" value. An example is the recently developed United Nations human development index (HDI), which gives much higher weights to the level of education and the status of health of the population than their respective shares in GNP and a much lower weight to GNP per capita itself (United Nations 1990). This measure tries to correct biases in the estimation of the productivity of health and education services over time and to account for the size of the stock of human capital. It corrects for longer-term effects missing in short-term GNP estimates. In addition it is motivated by wanting to assign higher welfare and distributional values to health and education than does regular national accounting. There is presently an effort to add a distributional dimension to the HDI to take account of both its productivity and its welfare aspects.

Finally, a major source of human welfare excluded from GNP measures is human freedom in all its dimensions: personal and economic security, political freedom, respect for human rights and personal freedoms, and a number of other human aspirations that are both innate and indirect sources of welfare and productivity. All the above were mainly tailored to underline major systemic differences in the estimation of wealth or welfare between the Soviet Union and market economies in the West at different levels of economic development.

Comparative data on the growth record of the Soviet economy and a number of groups of market economies and of new industrializing countries (NICs) are presented in table 5.1. It starts from the growth records of GDP and GDP per capita, goes through various productivity measures of output per different units of inputs, and ends with comparisons of a number of consumption levels. In terms of the above measures of welfare, the Soviet record appears best when just GDP per capita is compared, but it becomes less and less impressive as more meaningful welfare and productivity measures are introduced. Up to a point, table 5.1 uses the data provided by Maddison in his chapter in this volume and the same country groups as comparisons: the United States, the core group of developed European countries, a group of peripheral, less-developed European countries, and two groups of NICs, an East Asian and a Latin American group. For lack of data, not all the statistics are based on the entire group in each case. Also the periodization follows Maddison as far as possible. The data for the Soviet Union go up to 1985, as in the original (1990) paper, but updating will make little difference. The rates of growth during 1986–1990 continued to decline, and 1990 witnessed the only absolute decline in GDP in the Soviet Union since the Second World War. It has to be said, however, that these declines are partly an outcome of the initial failed reform efforts during Gorbachev's period and partly (especially during 1991 when GDP declined by at least 5 percent) the beginnings of the disintegration of the union.[3] The main findings are as follows:[4]

1. The Soviet postwar growth of GDP per capita was superior to that of the United States and to that of the Latin American group only during the first subperiod. Even the rates of growth of other East European socialist countries was somewhat higher (not shown; see Maddison, this volume). Although catching up, or convergence, can explain the growth advantage over the United States, as it did in two of the three less-developed groups, it fails to show up with respect to the core European group, which is also much more developed. Although rates of growth of all groups deteriorated during the second period, at least part of this decline is credited to the energy crisis. Per contra, the Soviet Union was during this period a large exporter of energy, and the decline in the rate of growth occurred despite the crisis rather than because of it. Furthermore, although some decline in growth rates in the European core group can also be credited

Table 5.1   Growth and Productivity, 1950–1985: The Soviet Union and Country Groups (annual rates of growth in percent)

	Population	GDP	GDP per capita	Land[e]	Capital	Man-hours	Labor quality	Man-hours plus quality (M·Q)	GDP/ (capital)	GDP/ (man hours)	GDP/ (M·Q)	Total factor productivity	Private consumption[f]	Consumption[f] per capita	Consumption[f] per man hour
1950–73															
USSR	1.40	5.00	3.55	1.69	8.64	1.42	1.56	3.00	−3.35	3.53	1.94	0.50	4.00	2.56	2.54
United States	1.40	3.60	2.17	0.11	3.38	1.92	0.48	2.41	0.21	1.65	1.16	2.98	4.18	2.74	2.22
European core[a]	0.80	4.60	3.77	−0.38	4.48	0.57	0.35	0.92	0.11	4.01	3.64	3.35	4.53	3.70	3.94
Periphery[b]	1.00	5.50	4.46	0.00	5.91	0.06	1.15	1.21	−0.39	5.44	4.24	3.32	6.79	5.73	6.72
Latin America[c]	2.48	5.08	2.53	1.68	5.33	1.74	1.08	2.84	−0.24	3.28	2.17	1.62	6.16	3.59	4.34
East Asia	0.74	8.69	7.89	0.01	6.45	3.01	1.25	4.29	2.10	5.52	4.22	4.13	8.25	7.45	5.09
1973–86															
USSR	0.90	2.10	1.19	—	6.46	1.00	1.50	2.52	−4.10	1.09	−0.40	0.00	1.80	0.89	0.79
United States	1.00	2.50	1.49	0.09	2.86	1.27	0.65	1.93	−0.35	1.21	0.56	0.28	2.85	1.83	1.56
European core[a]	0.20	2.10	1.90	1.82	3.44	0.85	0.39	1.24	−1.30	1.24	0.85	1.04	2.18	1.98	1.32
Periphery[b]	0.80	2.60	1.79	0.00	5.20	−0.66	1.52	0.85	−2.47	3.28	1.74	0.08	2.79	1.97	3.47
Latin America[c]	2.10	2.87	0.75	1.03	4.84	2.19	1.36	3.58	−1.88	0.66	−0.69	−0.82	2.96	0.84	0.75
East Asia	0.46	6.30	5.82	−1.49	10.65	1.94	1.81	3.78	−3.93	4.28	2.43	0.97	5.08	4.60	3.09

[a] Austria, Belgium, Denmark, Finland, France, Germany, Italy, Netherlands, Norway, Sweden, Switzerland, United Kingdom
[b] Greece, Portugal, Spain
[c] Brazil, Chile, Mexico   [d] Japan, Korea, Taiwan   [e] European core (France, Germany, Netherlands, United Kingdom), Latin America, Portugal, Spain
[f] 1960–73, 1973–1985 (1973–87 in East Asia, Latin America)

NOTE: Not all the variables were available for all countries in each group.

SOURCES: Population, GDP, inputs: Madison, 1990 (this volume), various tables; consumption: OECD, *Historical Tables, 1960–1985*; *World Development Report,* various years. USSR: Schroeder 1990a.

to converging on the U.S. level, this cannot be said of the Soviet Union, which reached a level of at most 40 percent of that of the United States. In these perspectives, the Soviet record of declining and inferior growth rates seems especially alarming.[5]

2. Despite a Soviet move to reduce weekly hours during the 1950s, and despite the fact that most working-age people had been already drawn into the labor force by 1950, working hours continued to grow faster than the population (column 6); the number of people employed grew even faster (Ofer 1987, table 2; 1992, table 1). Therefore, rates of growth of GDP *per hour* grew at a somewhat slower pace than GDP per capita in the Soviet Union (column 10, GDP per employed, at a much faster pace; Ofer 1992, table 1) and comparatively even slower than those for the other European groups of countries. Only among East Asian countries did the number of hours grow quickly, which is typical for early stages of industrialization.

3. With one exception (East Asia during the second period), the Soviet Union invested more in the level of education of its labor force during the period reviewed (column 7). As a result, GDP per unit of labor adjusted for quality increased less than labor productivity, the relative decline over time was much steeper than in the other groups of countries, and the comparative Soviet record, still poorer (column 11).

4. With one exception (East Asia during the recent period), the Soviet economy enjoyed one of the highest rates of capital growth during this period. Correspondingly, however, it also demonstrated the highest rates of decline of capital productivity (column 5). Capital growth, therefore, did not contribute significantly to rates of growth of labor productivity, as shown above.

5. Finally, high commitment to investments in both human and physical capital did not produce high rates of total factor productivity (TFP) growth for the Soviet economy, either absolutely or by comparison: Soviet TFP, according to Maddison, advanced by 0.5 percent a year during the first period and did not advance at all later (indeed it may have been negative), as compared with positive and higher rates in almost all other country groups (column 12; see also Bergson 1987).

The failure to produce superior rates of labor productivity despite heavy investments in both human and physical capital, and despite the remaining potential for technological convergence, is one of the major symptoms and sources of the failure of both the Soviet economic system and its growth strategy. Because of the complementarity between capital and technology, and the technological embodiment in capital goods, high rates of investment of all kinds should induce, and do induce elsewhere, high rates of productivity growth. This did not happen in the Soviet case, where such high investments assumed mostly a quantitative rather than a qualitative productive role.

As can be seen from the data, there was a much faster growth of capital than of labor. During the later part of the period, labor growth was slow. Such unbalanced growth creates a strong need for technological changes that facilitate intensive substitution of capital for labor in production. The sharp decline in capital productivity also reflects the failure to accomplish such a substitution.

The other side of the coin of high investment rates is the alternative price in terms of foregone consumption, the ultimate goal of economic activity and the welfare of the population. The problem is compounded when large investments do not generate enough technological change and improved productivity. In such cases, to sustain a given rate of growth of GNP, not only the *share of consumption* in GNP has to go down but in certain cases even the *absolute level of consumption* (see Bergson 1973). As can be seen in table 5.1, this did not happen in the Soviet case, partly because rates of growth of the capital stock were somewhat reduced. Nevertheless, rates of growth of consumption both per capita and per hour worked in the Soviet Union declined sharply over time and lagged in each period and over time after those in all country groups (except one period for Latin America), including the United States during the second period. Most rates of growth of consumption per capita and per hour worked in the other country groups are double the corresponding Soviet rates (columns 13 and 14).

In addition to a high and growing share of investment, Soviet consumption growth also suffered from the growing share of defense expenditures (see below). Some claim that the unimpressive Soviet record is even less so, in that the basic Soviet data presented here are biased upward.[6] Some of the criticism is based on elements discussed below, but others criticize even the fundamental calculations presented above. We cannot go into the debate here, except to point out that, under the present state of the art, the above presented data are ceiling levels and the true rate of growth may be even lower.

Let us turn now to elements of productivity and welfare that are not included in "consumption per unit of labor" as estimated more or less routinely in a framework of national accounting. We follow the list of additional criteria presented above but not necessarily in that order.

Let the benchmark for these qualifications be the *level* of consumption per capita or per unit of labor. Central Intelligence Agency (CIA) estimates of the Soviet level of consumption per capita for 1985, made in 1990, was 32 percent of that of the United States (compared with 34 percent back in 1976), which is consistent with data in table 5.1 (Schroeder 1990a, 20). These figures include the social services of education and health; the corresponding relative levels of household consumption alone are estimated at 29 percent for 1976 and 28 percent of the U. S. level for 1985 (ibid.).[7] A reevaluation of these figures put the relative level of Soviet consumption per capita in 1985 at 28.6 percent of those in the United States, but there are also lower estimates (Bergson 1991, 31–33).

The following is a list of qualifications for this level of material welfare:

1. In addition to the higher rate of labor force participation in the Soviet Union, there was also a much higher service burden on the nonwork free time of the population. This was a result of the state of permanent shortage in the consumer markets, the small volume by comparisons of economic activity in trade and other personal services, and the relatively meager supply of appliances and other capital substitutes to household services, including the poor state of housing (Ofer 1987, 1990; Schroeder 1987, 1990a, 1990b).

2. The composition of the consumption bill had always been determined by planners, with little attention paid to consumer choice and in many cases as a residual, after the needs of the other uses had been set aside. People were forced by nonavailability or distorted relative prices to purchase a different basket of goods than they would choose under a state of full consumer sovereignty. This was in addition to the fact that the population had little influence on the share of consumption in GNP, including the narrow assortment and variety of goods within each category. It can hardly be assumed that they would have voted for such a large defense budget or chosen to remain a virtually carless society and with few resources devoted to the service sector or to housing (see also Ehrlich 1989, table 7). It is clear that the welfare value of any such bill of goods was significantly lower than a freely chosen one.

3. The effects of the abnormally large environmental damages on quality of life are not included in the above measure (Feshbach and Friendly 1992; see more below).

4. Within the context of the absence of free consumer choice, the system's directors had a higher priority for public services, especially education and health. These priorities were motivated by both ideological and growth considerations. As can be seen from table 5.2, the relative standing of the Soviet Union in these two categories was higher than consumption per capita in general.[8] The CIA comparisons of consumption of education and health services per capita between the United States and the Soviet Union were estimated in 1976 at 79.7 and 32.5 (!) percent, respectively, compared with the relative total consumption level of 34.4 percent (Joint Economic Committee 1981, 20, table 8).

Yet even before 1985, and more so later, revelations about low-quality provision of health services and a number of major failures, as in the sphere of infant

Table 5.2   Social Indicators, 1955–1985

	Infant mortal-ity per 1,000 births	Life expec-tancy	Physi-cians per 10,000 people	Calorie supply per person per day	SCHOOL ENROLLMENT (AS % OF POPULATION IN RELEVANT AGE GROUP) Pri-mary	Sec-ondary	Ter-tiary	Labor force partici-pation (% of popu-lation aged 15+)
Circa 1955								
USSR	27.60	69.20	480.00	3,231	103.00	72.00	21.00	49.50
United States	24.70	70.20	670.00	2,888	100.00	–	40.00	40.90
European core [a]	18.96	71.49	910.00	2,911	93.83	60.08	12.33	43.34
Periphery [b]	27.50	68.93	916.67	2,796	103.00	43.00	7.00	38.67
Communist countries [c]	39.64	68.66	771.43	3,247	103.29	45.20	7.71	50.60
Latin America [d]	84.75	59.70	1,919.50	2,607	96.25	19.50	5.75	32.50
East Asia [e]	26.87	42.33	1,218.00	1,647	67.00	39.00	6.33	27.87
Circa 1985								
USSR	25.40	68.90	270.00	3,440	106.00	99.00	–	50.70
United States	10.40	75.40	473.00	3,064	102.00	100.00	59.00	49.10
European core [a]	8.29	75.93	423.92	3,379	93.42	82.83	29.25	47.64
Periphery [b]	11.00	75.43	360.00	3,399	108.00	79.33	23.00	39.73
Communist countries [c]	17.36	71.37	414.71	3,537	99.14	75.14	7.29	50.61
Latin America [d]	47.00	67.45	970.50	2,885	110.50	55.98	17.00	34.53
East Asia [e]	10.17	49.17	450.00	1,923	65.33	63.67	20.67	30.40

[a] Austria, Belgium, Denmark, Finland, France, Germany, Italy, Netherlands, Norway, Sweden
[b] Greece, Portugal, Spain
[c] Bulgaria, Czechoslovakia, East Germany, Hungary, Poland, Romania, Yugoslavia
[d] Brazil, Chile, Mexico
[e] Japan, Korea, Taiwan
SOURCES: United Nations, *Social Indicators*, 1990; *World Development Report*, various years.

mortality, where rates increased during the 1970s; birth control, where abortion had been throughout the major tool; high rates of morbidity; high levels of corruption; and extended privileges for the elite reduced the previous higher appreciation for the provision of health services in the Soviet Union (Davis 1987; Feshbach and Friendly 1993). As for education, in addition to similar criticisms over quality, Soviet education had been known for its indoctrinarian and narrow utilitarian and technical biases, including ones bias against humanities and social sciences. The general approach was, as in so many other areas, to target education to narrowly defined occupations, with relatively little attention (and resources) paid to prospects of cross-occupational mobility or changes over time in the assortment of needed occupations. All these reduced the consumption content of education and enhanced its significance as an investment and a tool of political control.

There is not yet an agreed-on methodology or system of weights by which to combine material well-being, as measured by consumption per capita, with other welfare-generating attributes such as health status or educational attainment. If, however, the present provisional U.N. index, which gives equal weights to per capita GDP, the level of literacy, and life expectancy, is accepted, then the pretransition Soviet welfare ranking was much higher than on the basis of GDP or consumption per capita alone (United Nations 1990). I doubt, however, whether the Soviet people, privately and collectively, would have accepted such an index as a true representation of their relative level of material welfare at that time.

Four additional elements that contribute to the general level of welfare and productivity and to the wealth of the nation must be considered: freedom, economic security, equality, and considerations of long-term levels of wealth. The denial of all basic freedoms for a long period of time under the Soviet system had been justified in order to achieve a more affluent and more just society *at the same time.* But the denial of freedom joined forces with the unimpressive material achievements to serve as trade-offs for a high level of economic justice expressed in the forms of economic security and a high level of economic equality. There seems to be a general agreement among scholars that, under the old regime, the Soviet system provided higher levels of job security and lower levels of open inflation and at least somewhat higher levels of economic equality than did most market economies and possibly, but not surely, a lower level of poverty (Bergson 1984; Matthews 1987; Hewett 1988, chap. 2; Ofer and Vinokur 1992, chaps. 4 and 6; Ofer 1992; Houseloner 1989). There is, however a need to question some of these achievements or at least to qualify them: first, shortages on the one side and the inability to own real assets on the other reduced economic security; second, economic and other privileges to the elite seriously damaged the claim for equality. It should be pointed out, however, that the Soviet leaders never accepted any trade-offs between material well-being, economic security, and equality and freedom. The Soviet political and economic system was supposed to provide high levels of these categories. Only recently was the existence of trade-offs fully recognized, and then excessive economic security and equality were criticized, as well as the denial of basic freedoms, as representing part of a distorted concept of socialism. Even the reform-minded leaders of the Soviet Union during the late 1980s did not accept the old mix as anything close to optimal. So why should we? My conclusion, and theirs, is that, although some positive social values were attained at higher levels than in other countries, the cost paid in terms of other goals has been too high. Therefore, the mix was far from optimal and inferior to that of free market economies. But the above-listed trade-offs are only part of the problem.

The most critical observation regarding the pretransition Soviet welfare and productivity posture is that even the low levels of growth reached at the end of the period were not sustainable; indeed, they were supported by heavy borrowing from the future, as shown below. Under any reasonable set of assumptions, a continuation of the old system was bound to increase the economic lag of the Soviet Union behind most market economies. In the following two sections I address the main institutional and strategic factors that contributed to bringing the Soviet economy to virtual stagnation, to a dead end.

Growth Deceleration through Haste

By *haste* we mean a policy that is designed to achieve initially high rates of economic growth even at the risk of low growth in the future.[9] Whether such a move results in a net gain or loss depends on the amounts of present and future gains and losses and on the rate of time of the loss discounted against the present gain. Haste may have a net positive economic result if the early benefit is larger than the *present value* of the later loss. Even so, haste will raise initial rates of growth at the expense of future ones. The economic merit of such a policy depends on the relevant rate of discount or on the rate of time preference of the policy makers. The higher the rate of time preference of the decision maker, the larger the accepted future loss in order to break even. The proposition about haste in Soviet economic growth is that the rate of time preference revealed by the leadership was significantly higher than the average rate of return on the resources whose use had been advanced. In this way, when the present value of haste is calculated on the basis of real, objective rates of return, the net result is a big loss. To a large extent, the high rate of time preference reflected a deliberate choice formulated as a clear goal of the Soviet Union rapidly catching up with the advanced economies of the West. To a degree, however, the gap between the rate of return on investments and the rate of time preference (my measure of haste) may have been wider than intended, mostly due to a lower rate of return than expected in the early use of resources and to higher than expected costs during later years, resulting in shortages and deficiencies associated with the consequences of excessive early use. Put differently, haste can be thought of as a high-interest loan taken from reserves of future resources (instead of from other countries) invested at lower rates of return, a loan that must be paid back at some future date, together with heavy interest payments. The repayment of the loan is manifested in future overdepleted resources. The interest charges are expressed in inefficiencies in the way resources are used as a result of haste.

The proposition about haste, based on the assumption of a high rate of time preference in Soviet growth strategy, is diametrically opposed to the common presumption that the high GNP share devoted to investment, and the low share of consumption in socialist economies, indicated a relatively low rate of time preference, a willingness to postpone consumption, with the ultimate goal of growth in the more distant future. This, however, is not true for several reasons: first, when the increasing share of defense spending is added to consumption, with the total share of consumption is not exceptionally low. Second, given the almost endless postponement of a significant rise in private consumption, one must conclude that the growth of investment, of the capital goods sector, and of heavy industry were the true system's goals and a base for increased power and military capability, rather than a means for eventual growth of consumption. Let's illustrate the strategy of haste with some of its major specific manifestations:

EARLY OVERUTILIZATION OF LABOR

As part of the extensive growth strategy there was a rapid increase in labor force participation rates and in the utilization of human time for social production. At first, after 1928, labor force participation rates grew through the utilization of the labor reserves in the countryside for the construction and industrialization drive, then through the gradual enlistment of most women of working age to the labor force. By the mid-1960s the Soviet Union had the highest rate of participation of women in the world. The means used to achieve the goal were the doctrines of equality of the genders and of independence of women, wage policies (families needed two salaries to make ends meet), and social and other pressures. Although the policy also included opening up all educational institutions and most professions for women, a high proportion of women were blue-collar workers in low-paying and physically difficult jobs. Furthermore, ideology did not carry over into the sphere of supporting household and day care services; given the lagging norms of gender equality inside families, women found themselves under a heavy double burden. The policy of minimizing consumption, with a special bias against services, imposed an additional burden—the self-supplying of many services during off-work hours—on the free time of the entire population. All these must have reduced both short- and long-term labor productivity, especially but not exclusively of women (manifested in lower wages and lower-status jobs), and, given the acute housing shortage, accelerated the decline in the rate of population growth beyond the natural decline associated with modernization. By the late 1970s and 1980s, labor force increments in the European parts of the Soviet Union declined to almost zero, drying up this resource as an input to the extensive growth model.[10]

A major exception with respect to labor force policy was the strong emphasis, from the start, on education. The investment in human capital is no doubt an important contribution to Soviet growth, along with initial efforts to provide adequate medical care, at least to workers. As we saw above, over the years the quality of medical care deteriorated substantially.

OVERUTILIZATION OF NATURAL RESOURCES

There is much evidence of overutilization of natural resources, resulting in long-term damage, and of extreme neglect of the environment, with similar consequences. Examples of the first are the overpumping of oil, which brought water into the wells and damaged future reserves, the overcutting of forests, and the overutilization of arable land through excess irrigation, overfertilizing, and constant planting (Johnson 1983). The environmental damages in water, air, and land pollution, including radioactive pollution, created in the Soviet Union and other socialist countries were almost unprecedented (see, for example, Feshbach and Friendly 1992). All these reduce productivity over time at an accelerating rate (interest payments) and impose large necessary investments (or loss of product) as correction (paying up the principal).

HASTY INVESTMENT

Investment, the main vehicle of the extensive growth model, suffered from a number of haste-related factors. First, the permanent pressure for a high volume and high speed of investment negatively affected the selection and the quality of construction of new projects, lengthened (paradoxically!) the construction time, and kept inactive a growing stock of uncompleted projects. The high targets and taut planning also contributed to the diluted technological content of many investments. High production targets encouraged long service periods of existing capital stock and low replacement rates, further reducing the innovative content and increasing maintenance and repair costs, one manifestation of the rising debt service mentioned above.

Second, with capital stock growing faster than GNP, due at least partly to haste, the ceiling for the share of investment in GNP was rapidly approaching, forcing a decline over time in the feasible rate of growth of the capital stock and thereby of the growth potential of the extensive model. During the last twenty years of the Soviet regime, capital expansion alone was driving growth as labor growth almost stopped, thereby imposing an even higher burden on the R&D sector to substitute capital for labor and further reducing capital productivity.

Third, in order to maximize the effectiveness of capital in the short run, and to maximize the output to capital ratio, less capital was devoted to investments in infrastructure, urban infrastructure, transportation and communication (Ehrlich

1989), storage, and distribution, even to secondary and auxiliary production activities, and more capital was devoted to the core production process and the main technology. Some aspects of such a policy may be beneficial in the short run, but with time, the extra costs and losses, some in the form of major accidents, others in the form of supply bottlenecks and delays, were growing. They also became part of the interest paid on the loan. With time, resources for investment became more scarce and the backlog of needed infrastructure grew. This is when repayment of the principal on the "loans" was due.

HIGH COST PER UNIT OF CHANGE

The entire economic mechanism of the Soviet system was geared and directed toward ambitious *quantitative* targets of *routine* production at the expense of improvements in quality, an expanded assortment of products, flexibility, and innovation. Planning, incentives, and control had been mostly defined in short-term quantitative terms, partly because such an approach was deemed administratively effective. It is much more complicated to plan, direct, or reward administratively for changes of any kind. Thus, the pressure was mostly toward "more of the same" rather than for any kind of change. The pressure also left little slack for experimentation or preparation for change. This may had some short-term benefits but at the cost of high long-term losses. Another aspect of *routine* is the clear Soviet preference for single, well-defined missions and well-targeted products over multioption, flexible, and open-minded products and general-purpose technologies. The first may be cheaper and more effective so long as the predefined mission persists but is much less efficient in the face of constantly changing needs and environments. Again, short-term benefits are paid for by long-term costs. The rigidity of the old system and the high cost of change contributed significantly to the decline in productivity over time, as the economy became more complex and less predictable. They also contributed to the severity of the collapse of output and the instability during the 1990s.

LACK OF FREEDOM AND DEMOCRATIC PROCESSES

Finally, one can make the point that, during the initial stages of the modernization process, some gains were made by a strong, totalitarian regime, with power to impose and pursue its own objective function, impose a simple and "efficient" decision-making process, and make people comply through assertive measures (this does not in any way justify Stalin's regime of terror, which was also counterproductive even in the short run). As time goes on, however, the price for the lack of freedoms and democratic processes increases in terms of reduced motivation and participation and in the form of an accumulated stock of mistakes, bureaucratic deadwood, corruption, and rent seeking. This process of mutual alienation reduced the system's efficiency over time (these were the interest payments). When the time for change came, huge investments were needed to establish the institutional, legal, and mental infrastructure for democracy, as well as the costs demanded for the learning and the transition processes (this was the repayment of the principal).

Declining growth rates are embodied in the basic concept of the extensive growth strategy. In some sense even haste can be thought of as part and parcel of that model. As untapped reserves of resources were being progressively exhausted, efforts to keep growth rates high forced the system to take successively more expensive measures and shortcuts, including higher interest loans, thereby causing a steep and fast decline in growth and a high backlog of accumulated debt.

The relationship between a hypothetical "normal" long-term trend of declining growth rates under Soviet conditions and the "actual" trend, including haste, is presented in figure 5.1. In panel a of the diagram, the relationship between the two trends is presented in terms of annual growth rates, and in panel b, in terms of total output. Because the axes are not calibrated, it is impossible to determine from panel a the economic merit of the policy of haste: there is only a trade-off between higher growth rates during the earlier period and lower ones later. In panel b, however, we do show a negative economic outcome of haste: output could have been higher during the second part of the period by more than the gain (time discount considered) during the early period. The total value of output (the area under the curve) could have been higher without haste.

Why did the Soviet leaders embark on a strategy of haste? They may have believed in the economic merits of initial high rates of investment, or they may have underestimated the downside consequences of haste. They were probably eager to prove the economic superiority of the socialist system, which they most likely believed in. And there may have been noneconomic reasons: the need of the regime to quickly establish its authority and legitimacy or, as some claim, to prepare for World War II and then be ready for the cold war. Whether or not any of the above are true, haste still implies lower rates of growth at the end of the process.

Finally, with some economic merit but facing big losses, the Soviet Union at the end of the 1980s was in a situation of near exhaustion of all its reserves and the need, at the same time, to change the system and assume the heavy debt service burden in the form of accumulating inefficiencies and paying the principal on the debt in the form of needed investments (including a new political system) to compensate for past neglect in infrastructure, environment, and so on. Such needed investments impose a heavy burden on the process of economic transition and may prevent a more drastic reallocation of resources toward consumption. The single-mission strategy, which may have contributed to faster growth in the past, made the shift to a new system much more difficult. Unfortunately, unlike a regular debt, there are limited options for rescheduling or

Figure 5.1   Growth Patterns over Time: With and without Haste

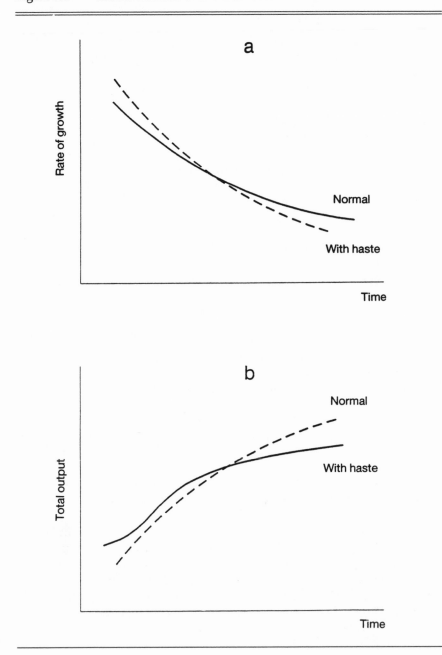

writing off part of the debt, except through shifting part of it to external lenders and investors.

As shown above, haste contributed to the poor record of technological change of the Soviet system. In a way these two concepts contradict each other. When discussing the reasons for the technological failures of the Soviet system in the following section, it becomes obvious that there were elements of haste behind many of them.

The Role of Technological Change

Any growth model without sustainable processes of technological change is bound to reach stagnation. This is the manifestation of the extensive, input-intensive growth described earlier. On the one side there is the diminishing marginal product of all natural and reproducible inputs to the exogenously given low rate of population (and eventually labor force) growth. On the other side there is the gradual exhaustion of technological or other growth reserves available to latecomers into the global process of economic modernization. Among these reserves is the available stock of technological knowledge developed by the leading economies. Although it is reasonable to assume that borrowing out of such a stock also suffers from diminishing returns, it is surprising that it happened in the Soviet case so early, when the technological gap in many areas was still wide. This failure of continuous diffusion, and of generating indigenous technological development, is the subject of this section.

The secular decline in efficiency growth in labor and capital productivity and in total factor productivity, as shown above, is also a result of factors other than technological change affecting efficiency. Let us therefore first list a number of such factors usually associated with declining rates of growth in the Soviet Union over time (see, for example, Bergson 1983). First is the process of the increasing complexity of the economy over time, the rising number and variety of products, and the increasing interdependency among sectors. Even with improved computers, the capabilities to centrally plan must have declined over time. Declining planning and bureaucratic efficiency also resulted from the rising degree of corruption and of rent seeking. Although such tendencies may be general to a variety of organizations and government bureaucracies, dictatorial regimes especially excel in them.[11]

Second is the long-term and increasing burden of defense expenditures. This burden, as estimated by the CIA, had been high all along as compared with most other countries, and it increased over time, at least until 1986. Defense, in addition to being a nonproductive category, also directly competed for resources with investment and R&D, the two main vehicles of economic growth. This competition was especially damaging to Soviet growth because of its comparative disadvantage in R&D, the need to provide first-line technologies to the military, and an almost complete absence of spillover to a civilian sector designed to secure scarce materials and processes for exclusive military use.[12]

Third, there also were diminishing returns to governance through dictatorial powers and oppressive measures based on fear. When the regime was forced to retreat from the most extreme means of coercion, fear declined and aspirations for higher levels of freedom, liberties and democracy rose. This effect may also be included under haste. Finally there was an increasing cost, or loss, of the policies of the "functional" autarky (following Hrncir 1989) of the Soviet Union, to which we come back later.

Much has been written and discussed about the systemic weaknesses of R&D activity and technological change under central planning in general and the Soviet economy in particular. Innovation under central planning suffered from overbureaucratization; rigidity in decision making, in the transfer of information and diffusion, in supplies, in organizational forms; lack of initiative from below, of flexibility and quick response, driven by the right type of reward system (private property rights); and the lack of the push and pull of profit motives and markets — a severe functional autarky as discussed above. There is no need to go through all these in detail (a survey of these problems and an extensive list of references can be found in Ofer 1987).

The negative verdict on the technological ability of central planning comes as at least a partial surprise, given the number and extent of public good and collective good characteristics of R&D and technological advance. Investment in human capital is considered by most countries as a collective service to be provided or encouraged by the public sector. New scientific and technological knowledge, developed by R&D activities, is in large measure a public good and therefore can be best internalized and captured by the entire public, who can develop it without the creation of artificial barriers (such as patents) and diffuse it quickly over the entire system in the shortest time. The public is also the owner of the information system, another public service, and therefore can prevent information barriers from delaying development application and diffusion. Finally, the large size of the Soviet Union (and, for that matter, the entire Eastern bloc) also provided the needed environment to capture the externalities and scale benefits of the scientific and technological efforts. The same should be true about the potential benefits in the import of technology, except for the above-mentioned limitations, mostly self-imposed, of a centrally planned system to interact freely in the world market. All these can be easily internalized by a central planner.

Among those listed above, the main advantage that was exploited by the Soviet system was developing and maintening a large R&D sector, in terms of both manpower and resources, and a constant supply through the educational system of a stream of scientists, engineers, and technicians. The authorities could also master the resources to direct and execute large new technological projects as national missions. Some of these specific advantages of central planning, however, were also adopted through activities of the public sectors in market economies, thereby narrowing the Soviet advantage.

The Soviet R&D establishment was one of the largest in the world, if not *the* largest. By 1985 the Soviet Union was investing some 5 percent of the national income in R&D, and since 1970 the annual rate of growth of this expenditure had been more than 6 percent a year in current prices, probably around 4 percent a year in constant prices. The number of people employed in R&D (a Soviet branch definition) in 1985 was more than 4.5 million, about 3.5 percent of the entire labor force. The annual rate of growth of those employed in R&D since 1950 was 5.4 percent, when they consisted of only 1 percent of the labor force. Similar rates of growth are observed for "scientific workers," people with degrees working in R&D activities in all branches, and for the number of engineers and technicians.[13] A previous comparison of R&D employment between the Soviet Union and the United States (for 1970) showed a Soviet advantage of almost three to one (Bronson 1973). The poor showing of this huge R&D establishment is thus despite the effort rather than because of neglect.

The above quantitative show of strength was first weakened by the large proportion that was devoted to military R&D. The exact proportion of expenditures devoted to military R&D is not known, but Western students estimated it at as high as between 60 and 80 percent of the total for the 1960s, a high proportion indeed.[14] Also there was a heavy burden on civilian R&D institutions to work directly or indirectly for the military, and, more important, military R&D enjoyed a substantial qualitative advantage expressed in better inputs and manpower, better supplies, more flexible work arrangements, a more demanding client, and a general priority environment and direct contact with the leadership. Military R&D enjoyed almost complete immunity from the bureaucratic burdens of central planning, whereas civilian R&D had to operate under conditions of particular disadvantages under that system. Finally, the heavy military involvement in R&D increased the dense secrecy cover that further restricted the free flow of information, both internally and externally.

The need to favor the military R&D sector to such a large degree is explained by efforts to bring Soviet military technology to a level equal to that of the West in order to compete successfully in the arms race. In this way the civilian R&D sector suffered much more than the economy at large from the heavy military burden.[15]

The recent development of theories of *endogenous technological change* provides an interesting organizing framework within which one can focus on some of the main systemic and institutional impediments to technological and efficiency growth under socialism. Although scale advantages and externalities always played a decisive role in theories of technological change, there is now a somewhat more coherent and consistent introduction of the forces that are responsible for technological change (most of which were discovered long ago by people like Schumpeter and Kuznets) into the new neoclassical growth model as endogenous responses to market forces and the profit motive. A somewhat better theoretical case can now be made to support the observed advantages of a mixed-market system. The discussion below fleshes out the main points listed in the opening paragraph of this section in the context of endogenous growth:

STOCK OF HUMAN CAPITAL AND R&D

Endogenous growth is strongly correlated with the stock of human capital and the accumulated stock of investment in R&D in a country over the years.[16] These stocks provide positive external effects on future R&D activities and thus on technological growth. The observed contrast in the Soviet Union between the high rate of accumulation of investment in both physical and human capital and in R&D and the low contribution of these investments to productivity growth is explained by the factors listed in this section on the low level of productivity of R&D activities, including military dominance. It can therefore be assumed that estimates of Soviet growth that include human capital and R&D expenditures as inputs (as done partly by Barro 1989b) should further reduce the evaluation of the Soviet growth record and any kind of productivity growth or residual. Human capital and R&D activities suffered in the Soviet Union from the same problems observed in the case of physical investment: despite (or perhaps because of) high rates of growth, the innovative content of these activities was low.

INFORMATION FLOW

External effects and public good benefits play a key role in the process of technological change. Yet Soviet R&D activities were extremely restricted and segmented by the heavy departmentalism of the economy, the rigidity of the supply system, the perennial shortages of new inputs and materials, the narrow-minded educational system, rigid and predetermined plans, and severe limitations on the flow of information (internally and externally) and of open discussion and free expression, dictated by the nature of the political system. In this way there developed critical limitations on interaction, dissemination, diffusion, and learning across industries and hence a restricted internal utilization of the potential scale effects of the development of knowledge. These eliminated the advantages that could have been gained through the large size of the economy and the ability to centrally internalize the scale and externality benefits of new technologies. At the same time, the limitations on the free flow of information were not used to stimulate technological competition.

DIVERSIFICATION OF PRODUCTS

The Soviet system severely restricted the level of horizontal and vertical diversification of products into different kinds and quality grades. This was true for consumer, producer, and intermediate goods alike. Along similar lines, efforts to improve the quality of existing products were also restricted and limited. These two features of the Soviet system were to a large degree deliberate, as another means to increase quantities and save on R&D costs. Mass production and saving on costs of diversification were more consistent with the nature of the system. Variety was costly because of difficulties in detailed planning and control over plans and the absence of active and selective buyers. Enterprise managers further restricted variety as a means to ease the pressure of taut plan targets. The same factors also limited quality improvements, which were difficult to reward or impose. Furthermore, the reluctance of enterprises to engage in R&D (as a result of pressure to fulfill short-term quantitative targets), the resulting institutional separation between R&D and production activities, and the tendency to invest in new projects rather than restructure existing enterprises depressed and limited the extent of effort toward quality improvements.

It well may have been that, in recognition of its strong relative disadvantage in R&D, the Soviet production system tried to economize on the amount of R&D inputs in the production process and in the proportion of technologically intensive products in general. One way of achieving this was through the method of incremental innovation, standardization, and commonality of production components and the use of off-the-shelf parts in new products (see Alexander 1978; Nimitz 1971, 1974). The savings in R&D achieved in this way were, however, short term and at the expense of long-term technological growth.

Increasing both the variety and diversity of production and the innovative efforts in quality improvements are major sources of technological advances and efficiency growth (see Ethier 1982; Grossman and Helpman 1989a, 1989d, 1989e; Romer 1986, 1988). Quality improvements may amount to half or even more of the value of the final innovation, while diversification is a (the) major source of innovation. The Soviet performance with respect to both aspects, whether deliberate or *ex post*, was another manifestation of the preference of quantity over quality, of short-term over longer-term outcomes, of haste.

FUNCTIONAL AUTARKY

The policy of functional autarky pursued by the Soviet Union prevented it from actively participating in the global process of product cycle innovations in both directions, especially in exploiting the relatively free use of accumulated stock of technological knowledge and the available supply of commercial innovations. The administrative obstacles to trade (through a state monopoly), and the restrictions on technological exchanges, limited the ability of the Soviet Union to borrow technologies from abroad; whenever borrowing or imitation took place, it was delayed by both the external and the internal rigidities described above. Over most of the period the main form of technological imports was through reverse engineering by Soviet technicians with little Western training, an expensive, time-consuming, and inefficient process. Even when more liberal policies of technological transfers were allowed in the early 1960s, they did not include direct foreign investments or even joint ventures; thus the level of scientific exchanges was kept at a low level. The absence of profit-seeking agents, in the form of private entrepreneurs, and their replacement by "planners" were major deficiencies here. The Soviet Union also failed to export technologically advanced goods and thereby to benefit from the technological cycle embodied in trade (see Poznanski 1987; Bornstein 1985; Hanson 1982; Ofer 1992). The trade and technological relationships with the other socialist countries of Eastern Europe suffered from many of the same internal and external problems and policies and therefore also produced only limited benefits. Even with some technological transfer, the Soviet economy ended up with a technology that was incompatible in many respects with that of the West, which severely limited the potential benefits of opening up in the short run and imposed heavy costs on the way to becoming compatible.

Recent developments in the theory of international trade, and the incorporation of these developments into the new theory of endogenous growth, raised the potential contribution of trade to internal and external technological developments. The benefits of diversity and the specific division of labor create scale effects that go beyond the economic size of even large countries (Ethier 1982; Krugman 1979; Helpman and Krugman 1985; Barro 1989a, 1989b). The ability to draw on the accumulated global stock of knowledge, and to participate, as a profit-seeking entrepreneur, in a worldwide product innovation cycle, depends to a large extent on the openness of the economy and trade-conducive policies, as well as on the similarities between the economic systems, on a well-functioning financial and trade infrastructure, and on close technological relationships. Quick response is crucial here because the monopolistic or quasi-monopolistic profits of new inventions and product improvements decline fast as imitators and innovators move in.[17] The potential gains from international trade and openness are thus found to be much larger than those acquired through traditional static comparative advantage and are only partly mitigated by size. Countries that restrict such exchanges, whose institutions are ill-suited for such participation or are too rigid to respond quickly, cannot reap the full benefit. The Soviet Union and other socialist countries have been extreme cases on all counts of international economic nonparticipation, causing and resulting in a comparative disadvantage in technological development.

RENT SEEKING

One major deficiency of any bureaucratically run system is the tendency to replace productive efforts by rent seeking directed at the government. In R&D, given the clumsy reward system for innovation implemented almost exclusively by the government, tendencies developed to invest much effort in the simulation of innovation and in other kinds of related rent-seeking activities (see Grossman and Helpman 1989c; Baumol 1988; Krueger 1974).

Concluding Comments

The decline and stagnation of Soviet growth, although coincident with a decline in rates of growth in many other regions and countries, were only marginally, if at all, related to the general decline. The sources of Soviet slowdown were specific and inherited in the socialist system and its development strategy, which prevented the main factors responsible for modern economic growth anywhere—technological changes and efficiency growth—to contribute their share. Haste accelerated the rate of decline and advanced the point of stagnation. It contributed to initial growth, some only statistical, at the high cost of future decline and eroded the wealth of the nation.

The Soviet economy achieved its postwar economic growth by the unconventional method of extending to the long run the extensive, input-intensive strategy, reinforced by a heavy dose of haste and a declining contribution of technological and productivity growth, which were partly the responsibility of haste. Although extensive growth based on proper increases in the capital stock, both material and human, is a common and healthy start, future growth depends increasingly on the ability to use the accumulated capital stock as a springboard for efficiency and for technology-driven continuous and sustained growth. Failing that, as happened in the Soviet Union, the unavoidable outcome was a trend of declining growth rates toward stagnation. The growth potential of the extensive-plus-haste strategy was exhausted by the 1980s, indeed much earlier. It should have been changed long before, and its preservation created a large internal debt in the form of neglected economic, social, and political infrastructures. The repayment of the loan of haste was imposed on the system on top of the high expected costs of the transition. Pushing the extensive-plus-haste model also left the Soviet economy at the transition with few reserves. So when the change finally came, it required (and still requires) enormous investments over a short time and a deep thawing of a multifaceted rigid system. The difficulties in both, and the need to make a sharp systemic turn over a short period of time, are responsible for the extreme collapse of output and the ensuing high inflation that has developed following the change.

Using the terminology of Douglass North, the system of central planning and of a command economy had a clear *absolute* disadvantage in both allocative and adaptive (dynamic) efficiency but a *comparative* advantage in allocative efficiency. The system was forced to sacrifice much adaptive efficiency to secure a minimum level of allocative efficiency. The extensive model of growth is one manifestation of such a sacrifice. The story of the present transition is one of breaking up the old rigid structure and creating new institutions with much higher levels of built-in adaptive efficiency.

The other side of the story is the great economic growth potential of the posttransition system, when many of the distortions and rigidities of the old one will be eliminated. Included among them is opening up the economy to the global market, with its increasing opportunities. This is the good news beyond the long, risky, and difficult transitional period.

The socialist Soviet epoch was one of the most heroic and costly (in all aspects) social experiments of the modern era. Although not devoid of positive contributions, let alone impact on the rest of the world, it turned out to be a nonviable mode of social organization for long-term human and economic development. In a world of second-bests the dominant model is now that of democratic and free societies with mixed-market economies and strong doses of the welfare state.

Notes

1. This chapter was written in 1990 when perestroika was five years old, still under the leadership of Mikhail Gorbachev, but when most of the former socialist countries in Central and Eastern Europe had already turned away from their past to embrace democracy and the market system. A year later the Soviet Union disintegrated, and shortly thereafter most former socialist countries started on a new road, called *transition*, involving initial sharp declines in production, and outbreaks of inflation, along with improving markets and the beginnings of democracy and freedom. The paper's main task was to study past economic developments and, in this specific case, to understand the factors that contributed to the secular decline and virtual stagnation of economic growth and therefore the crisis. Reading it again five years later, it seems to have performed this task within the realm of economic analysis. It reached the conclusion that the stagnation was not cyclic or temporary but rather deeply systemic, the end of the road for the system and its growth strategy. I therefore decided to keep the analysis pretty much as it was, confined to its defined framework of economic analysis of economic growth. I leave the much broader

postmortem evaluation of the Soviet-type socialist economic experiment for another opportunity.

2. The basic concept of *haste* and the term *rush* were first used by Janos Kornai (1972). The term *haste* was used by Gregory Grossman (1962) and then by Joseph Berliner (1966). It was first developed by the author in 1987.

3. The annual rates of growth of GDP during the second half of the 1980s are as follows: 1986–89: 1.9 percent, 1990: −2 percent, and 1991: −5 percent (data for 1986–1990 are from Bruno 1993, 202, table 7.1). The figure for 1991 is a recent revised estimate by the World Bank (*The Economist* 30).

4. These findings are similar to those presented in a more recent paper by Easterly and Fischer (1995) that also carries the Soviet data up to 1987.

5. Similar comparative results were obtained by the author in earlier papers (1987, table 2; 1992, table 1). The results here are even stronger for the second period because the comparison is carried until 1985 instead of 1980, as in the earlier papers. Although the Soviet growth rates continued to decline, those of the other Western countries seemed to recover somewhat from the crisis of the late 1970s and early 1980s.

6. For recent surveys of the debate over the true Soviet growth record and GNP levels, see Aslund 1990 and Schroeder 1990a, 1990b.

7. The much lower relative level in terms of consumption, as compared with GNP per capita, is a result of the much higher shares in GNP of gross investment and defense (Ofer 1987, table 3).

8. Similar findings were presented by Eva Ehrlich in a study that compared the relative levels of various service infrastructures across countries using the method of physical indicators and economic systems. Although in terms of GDP per capita the Soviet Union occupied in 1980 the twentieth place among the twenty-eight countries included in the study, its rank with respect to a composite index of educational and cultural levels was fifteenth and with respect to health services, sixth, ahead of the United States (Ehrlich 1989, tables 6–9). The USSR's ranking with respect to housing was twenty-sixth.

9. Developed on the basis of Ofer 1987, section V. See also Berliner 1966 and Grossman 1962.

10. The remaining growth in population and labor force occurred almost completely in the Asian republics, where rates of natural increase remained high. These additions to the labor force, however, are less qualified and resistant to moving to the industrial centers in the European USSR.

11. See Olson 1982; Grossman and Helpman 1989; Baumol 1988; Krueger 1974. On Soviet corruption, see G. Grossman (JEC 1987, including many references therein).

12. See Kennedy (1987) and other studies on the relationship between high defense spending and growth. See also Easterly and Fischer 1995 and Ofer 1987.

13. Sources are *Narodnoe Khoziyaistvo* 1987, 25, 364, and corresponding tables in volumes of previous years and Bronson 1973.

14. See discussion in Ofer 1975, 1. Nimitz (1971, 1974), has lower estimates, down to maybe 40 percent. In the Soviet state budget for 1989, civilian R&D is given at 7.5 billion rubles out of a total R&D budget of 29.7 billion rubles but which also includes 3.0 billion

rubles as civilian space activities. The civilian share is thus between a quarter and a third, but there are other military and civilian R&D expenditures outside of the budget (Ofer 1990, table 1).

15. A detailed exposition of the issue is included in Ofer (1975, 1980), which is based on many other studies referred to there.

16. See Lucas 1988; Barro 1989a, 1989b; Romer 1986, 1988; Grossman and Helpman 1989a. This is an addition to the learning-by-doing model for physical capital developed by Arrow (1962) and others.

17. See the above citations as well as Romer 1988; Rivera-Batiz and Romer 1989; Grossman and Helpman 1989a, 1989b, 1989c, 1989d.

References

Alexander, Arthur. *Decision Making in Soviet Weapons Procurement.* London: International Institute for Strategic Studies, 1978.

Arrow, Kenneth. "The Economic Implications of Learning by Doing." *Review of Economic Studies* 29 (June 1962): 155–73.

Aslund, Anders. "How Small Is the Soviet National Income?" In Henry Rowen and Charles Wolf Jr., eds., *The Impoverished Superpower: Perestroika and the Soviet Military Burden.* San Francisco: ICS Press, 1990.

Barro, Robert. "A Cross-Country Study of Growth, Saving, and Government." Working paper No. 2855, National Bureau of Economic Research, Cambridge, Mass., February 1989a.

———. "Economic Growth in a Cross Section of Countries." Working paper No. 3120. National Bureau of Economic Research, Cambridge, Mass., September 1989b.

Baumol, William. "Entrepreneurship: Productive, Unproductive and Imitative; or the Rule of the Rules of the Game." Mimeo, 1988.

Bergson, Abram. "Toward a New Growth Model." *Problems of Communism* 22, no. 2 (March–April 1973): 1–9.

———. "Income Inequality under Soviet Socialism." *Journal of Economic Literature* 22, no. 3 (September 1984): 1052–99.

———. "Technological Change." In Abram Bergson and Herbert S. Levine, eds., *The Soviet Economy: Toward the Year 2000.* London: Allen and Unwin, 1983.

———. "Comparative Productivity: The USSR, Eastern Europe, and the West." *American Economic Review* 77, no. 3 (1987): 342–57.

———. "The USSR before the Fall: How Poor and Why?" *Journal of Economic Perspectives* 5, no. 4 (fall): 29–44.

Bergson, Abram, and Herbert Levine, eds. *The Soviet Economy: Toward the Year 2000.* London: Allen and Unwin, 1983.

Berliner, Joseph. "The Economics of Overtaking and Surpassing." In Henry Rosovsky, ed., *Industrialization in Two Systems: Essays in Honor of Alexander Gerschenkron.* New York: Wiley, 1966, pp. 159–85.

Bornstein, Morris. *The Transfer of Western Technology to the USSR.* Paris: OECD, 1985.

Bronson, David. "Scientific and Engineering Manpower in the USSR and Employment in R&D." In Joint Economic Committee, ed., *Soviet Economic Prospects for the Seventies*. Washington, D.C.: U.S. Government Printing Office, June 27, 1973.

Bruno, Michael. *Crisis, Stabilization and Economic Reform: Therapy by Consensus*. Oxford, Eng.: Clarendon Press, 1993.

CIA Directorate of Intelligence. *Handbook of Economic Statistics, 1989*. Washington, D.C.: CIA, 1989.

Davies, Mark. "Developments in the Health Sector of the Soviet Economy, 1970–90." In Joint Economic Committee, ed., *Gorbachev's Economic Plans: Study Papers*. Vol. 2. Washington, D.C.: U.S. Congress, 1987.

Easterly, William, and Stanley Fischer. "The Soviet Economic Decline." *World Bank Economic Review* 9, no. 3 (September 1995): 341–71.

Ehrlich, Eva. "Economic Development Levels, Proportions and Rates of Growth Based on the Physical Indicators Method, 1937–1980." Paper prepared for the World Bank Planning Conference on the Measurement and Evaluation of the Macroeconomic Performance of Selected Centrally Planned Economies and Yugoslavia, World Bank Headquarters, Washington D.C., May 16–17, 1989a.

———. "Services: An International Comparison, 1960–1983." Paper written for the Fifth Annual Seminar on the Service Economy, Geneva, Switzerland, May 29–31, 1989b.

Ethier, Wilfred. "National and International Returns to Scale in the Modern Theory of International Trade." *American Economic Review* 72 (1982): 389–405.

Feshbach, Murray, and Alfred Friendly Jr. *Ecocide in the USSR: Health and Nature under Siege*. New York: Basic Books, 1992.

Grossman, Gene, and Helpman, Elhanan. "Comparative Advantage and Long-Run Growth." Working paper No. 2809. National Bureau of Economic Research, Cambridge, Mass., January 1989a.

———. "Endogenous Product Cycles." Working paper No. 2913. National Bureau of Economic Research, Cambridge, Mass., March 1989b.

———. "Growth and Welfare in a Small Economy." Working paper No. 2970. National Bureau of Economic Research, Cambridge, Mass., July 1989c.

———. "Quality Ladders in the Theory of Growth." Working paper No. 3099. National Bureau of Economic Research, Cambridge, Mass., September 1989d.

———. "Quality Ladders and Product Cycles." Mimeo, November 1989e.

Grossman, Gregory. "Communism in a Hurry: The Time Factor." In Abraham Brumberg, ed., *Russia under Krushchev*. New York: Praeger, 1962, pp. 205–18.

Hanson, Philip. "The Soviet System as a Recipient of Western Technology." In Hanson, *Industrial Innovation in the Soviet Union*. London: Yale University Press, 1982.

Hauslohner, Peter. "Gorbachev's Social Contract." *Soviet Economy* 3, no. 1 (January–March 1987): 54–89.

Helpman, Elhanan. "Growth, Technical Progress and Trade." NBER working paper No. 2592, Cambridge, Mass., 1988.

Helpman, Elhanan, and Paul Krugman. *Market Structure and Foreign Trade*. Cambridge, Mass.: MIT Press, 1988.

Hewett, Ed A. *Reforming the Soviet Economy: Equality versus Efficiency*. Washington, D.C.: Brookings Institution, 1988.

Hrncir, Miroslav. "Alternative Approaches to the Reform of Socialist Economy: The Case of Czechoslovakia." Paper prepared for the Ninth World Congress of the International Economic Association, Athens, Greece, August 28–September 1, 1989.

Joint Economic Committee. *Consumption in the USSR: An International Comparison.* Washington D.C.: U.S. Congress, 1981.

Johnson, D. Gale. "Agricultural Organization and Management." In Bergson and Levine, eds., *The Soviet Economy.*

Jorgenson, Dale W. "Investment in Education and U.S. Economic Growth." Mimeo, 1989.

Kennedy, Paul. *The Rise and Fall of the Great Powers: Economic Change and Military Conflict from 1500–2000.* New York: Random House, 1987.

Kornai, Janos. *Rush versus Harmonic Growth.* Amsterdam: North Holland, 1972.

Krueger, Anne. "The Political Economy of the Rent-Seeking Society." *American Economic Review* 64 (1974): 291–303.

Krugman, Paul. "A Model of Innovation, Technology Transfer and the World Distribution of Income." *Journal of Political Economy* 87 (1979): 253–66.

Lucas, Robert E., Jr. "On the Mechanics of Economic Development." *Journal of Monetary Economics* 22 (1988): 3–42.

Maddison, Angus. "Growth and Slowdown of Advanced Capitalist Economies: Techniques of Quantitative Assessment." *Journal of Economic Literature* 25 (1987): 649–98.

Matthews, Mervyn. *Poverty in the Soviet Union: The Life-Styles of the Underprivileged in Recent Years.* Cambridge, Eng.: Cambridge University Press, 1986.

Mincer, Jacob. "Comments on Dale Jorgenson's 'Investment in Education and U.S. Economic Growth.'" Mimeo, October 1989.

Narodnoe Khoziyaistvo. Moscow, 1987.

Nimitz, Nancy. *The Structure of Soviet Outlays on R&D in 1960 and 1968.* R-1207-DDRE. Santa Monica, Calif.: Rand Corporation, 1974.

———. *The Structure of Soviet Outlays on R&D in 1960 and 1968.* R-1207-DDRE. Santa Monica, Calif.: Rand Corporation, 1974.

OECD Economic Outlook. *Historical Statistics 1960–1985.* Paris: OECD, 1987.

Ofer, Gur. "The Opportunity Cost of the Nonmonetary Advantages of the Soviet Military R&D Effort." R-1741-DDRE. Report prepared for director of Defense Research and Engineering, Rand Corporation, Santa Monica, Calif., August 1975.

———. "The Relative Efficiency of Military Research and Development in the Soviet Union: A Systems Approach." R-2522-AF. Project Air Force report prepared for the U.S. Air Force, Rand Corporation, Santa Monica, Calif., November 1980.

———. "Soviet Economic Growth: 1928–1985." *Journal of Economic Literature* 25 (December 1987): 1767–1833.

———. "The Welfare State in Soviet Economic Reform: Also Converging?" Paper presented at the Allied Social Science Associations Annual Meeting, Atlanta, Georgia, December 28–30, 1989.

———. "Fiscal and Monetary Aspects of Soviet Economic Reform." Mimeo, January 1990.

———. "Productivity, Competitiveness and the Socialist System." In Bert G. Hickman, ed., *International Productivity and Competitiveness*. New York and Oxford, Eng.: Oxford University Press, 1992.

Ofer, Gur, and Aaron Vinokur. *The Soviet Household under the Old Regime: Economic Conditions and Behavior in the 1970s*. Cambridge, Eng.: Cambridge University Press, 1992.

Olson, Mancur. *The Rise and Decline of Nations*. Westford, Mass.: Yale University Press, 1982.

Poznanski, Kazimiriez. *Technology, Competition and the Soviet Bloc in the World Market*. Berkeley: Institute of International Studies, University of California Press, 1987.

Rivera-Batiz, Luis, and Paul Romer. "International Trade and Endogenous Technological Change." Mimeo, University of Chicago, October 1989.

Romer, Paul. "Increasing Returns and Long-Run Growth." *Journal of Political Economy* 94 (1986): 1002–37.

———. "Endogenous Technological Change." Paper presented at the SUNY Buffalo conference "The Problem of Development," May 1988; revised November 1989.

Schroeder, Gertrude. "USSR: Toward the Service Economy at a Snail's Pace." In *Gorbachev's Economic Plans*. Vol. 2, Study Papers, U.S. Congress, Joint Economic Committee, November 23, 1987, pp. 240–60.

———. "Consumption in the USSR and the US: A Western Perspective." Mimeo, 1990a, pp. 1–41.

———. "Soviet Consumption in the 1980s: A Tale of Woe." Mimeo, University of Virginia, June 1990b, pp. 1–32.

Solow, Robert M. "A Contribution to the Theory of Economic Growth," *Quarterly Journal of Economics* 70, no. 1 (February 1956): 65–94.

Summers, Robert, and Heston, Paul. "A New Set of International Comparisons of Real Product and Price Levels Estimates for 130 Countries, 1950–1985." *Review of Income and Wealth* 34 (March 1988): 1–25.

World Bank. *Social Indicators of Development 1989*. Baltimore: Johns Hopkins Press, 1989.

World Development Report, various years. Washington D.C.: Oxford University for the World Bank, 1989.

PART THREE

WEALTH CREATION AND FAILURE IN THE TWENTIETH CENTURY: SEVEN CASE STUDIES

6

Diverging and Converging Patterns of Wealth Creation

The People's Republic of China and the Republic of China

RAMON H. MYERS

In 1949 China divided into two territories ruled by different regimes. The People's Republic of China (PRC) on the mainland established a socialist system based on central planning, state-owned enterprises, collective forms of life, and public ownership of property; the Republic of China (ROC) created a mixed economy in which state policies, institutions, and state enterprises modulated a private sector based on private enterprise, households, and markets.

These two different economic systems produced divergent economic performances until 1978, when the PRC's leaders decided to reform their economy, first in the countryside and then in the cities, adopting many of the policies and institutional changes long prevalent in the ROC. As a consequence of these reforms, the PRC is becoming a market economy, similar to ROC's, with macro regulatory controls.

The 14,000-square-mile island of Taiwan, about the size of Maryland, Delaware, and Rhode Island combined, in 1993 had a population of almost twenty-one million people and a gross domestic product (GDP) roughly 39 percent of that of the PRC. There is no area of comparable wealth inside the PRC. (One great irony of twentieth-century Chinese history is that, had the PRC experienced a Taiwan-type of economic development, their combined wealth by the 1990s would have made this greater China one of the world's economic powerhouses.)

From the outset, although they were poor and technologically backward, both economies had the potential to create wealth. Both territories had experienced a commercial-industrial revolution after 1900 that lasted until around

1937, when the mainland became engulfed in war and Taiwan's industrialization accelerated under Japanese wartime mobilization.

With a divided China at peace in 1950 (despite the PRC's participation in the Korean War from November 1950 until summer 1953), both Chinese governments tried to modernize. Taiwan's economy took off, with high economic growth, expanding factor productivity, and rapid integration into the world market. Although the Chinese GDP also expanded in the early 1950s, over the next two decades China remained isolated from the world economy, and factor productivity and living standards scarcely improved. After assessing China's economic deficiencies in 1978, the PRC's leaders initiated far-reaching economic reforms, abandoning the planned economy based on public ownership of property, orienting the economy toward the world market, and reconstituting a market economy with private and mixed property rights.

These diverging and converging economic trends are evaluated below, followed by a description of the economic conditions for both regimes in the early 1950s when their leaders, having different ideologies, adopted different economic policies and institutional changes. A comparison of Taiwan and mainland China's policies and institutional changes illuminates the economic performances of these two Chinese societies and how they first diverged and then converged.

Evaluating Economic Performance

Mobilizing resources can produce a rapid increase of output, but without markets neither society's living standards nor the economy will improve on a sustained basis.

Central planning and publicly owned enterprises can produce many capital goods and intermediate products, but these conditions do not infer that organizational efficiency and higher output will be forthcoming. But an economy without markets is not compatible with competition and freedom of choice for producers and consumers. Moreover, transaction costs, such as acquiring current information, are high. Therefore, mobilizing resources without markets has not, historically, led to an efficient allocation of resources and thus higher- or better-quality output.

But consider the opposite pattern: government interventionist policies. Suppose the state tries to integrate markets, expand incentives, define property rights, lower financial burdens, reduce transaction costs, and promote education and skills. These kinds of policies and institutional changes (or rule changes) are likely to enhance opportunities in the marketplace efficiently and creatively.

These two patterns of government interventionist activity, shaped by leadership ideology and policies, explain why wealth creation differed in the first three decades for the two Chinese regimes. Markets are indispensable for economic modernization. Eliminate markets, and society pays a high economic cost: low productivity, technological backwardness, enormous waste, and low standards of living sustained only by rationing.

Both Chinese territories had limited land, abundant labor, and little capital. The PRC's socialist planners emphasized producing capital and intermediate products and limited the output of consumer goods and services, rationing them as early as 1954. At first, central planning and mobilizing resources through state and collective enterprises achieved a high GDP growth rate, but rapidly increasing transaction costs meant that labor and capital productivity did not increase. The wasteful, inefficient, and intensive use of inputs caused the economy's growth rate to decline (see table 6.1, panel A, for the growth slowdown between 1957 and 1978).

Foreign trade, based on bartering to obtain strategic goods, increased only moderately; domestic trade only rose slowly because the regime discouraged specialization and exchange and stressed local self-reliance. The share of capital and intermediate goods of total output, minuscule at first, quickly exceeded consumer goods, and by the 1960s and 1970s living standards were stagnating. The supply of public goods for medical services, education, and welfare for the aged and young increased, but their quality was poor.

Between 1949 and 1976, factor productivity declined; capital productivity, as measured by the ratio of national income generated from every one hundred yuan of capital stock, fell in 1954–55, 1957, and 1959, was negative in 1960, 1967–68, and 1976, and remained low during the 1970s.[1] Total factor productivity in agriculture also stagnated between 1957 and 1978.[2] After 1978, however, factor productivity rose, with the biggest gains in agriculture occurring between 1978 and 1984, perhaps as much as 32 percent, partly because of property rights being redistributed from the production team to the family farm, greater competition, and marketization of the economy.[3]

Meanwhile, population growth increased over the period. People also lived longer, but their living standards barely increased. Living standards improved after 1978 mainly in the coastal provinces and the late 1980s for the hinterland provinces. The regime had allocated too many resources for capital and intermediate products, produced them inefficiently and wastefully, and could not supply enough consumer goods and services to raise living standards. Communes and state enterprises encouraged their wage earners to save a high percentage of their income and used rationing to distribute the necessities. Public goods and services were supplied through the individual's work unit. As a result, urban household spending for food and drink was more than 50 percent of annual household expenditures; not until 1993 did household income increase annual expenditures for food and drink enough to drop to 50 percent (see table 6.2).

Table 6.1   Annual Rate of Growth of the PRC and ROC, 1952–1993
               (in percent)

PANEL A: THE PRC ECONOMY

Period	Gross Value of Output [a]	National Income	National Income per Capita
1952–1956	11.3	8.9	6.7
1957–1978	6.0	4.2	2.3
1979–1989	10.7	8.7	7.3
1990–1993	8.8	9.2	7.6

[a] This column denotes the gross value of output from agriculture, industry, construction, transport, and commerce, excluding military and other services normally subsumed under the Western measure of GDP.

SOURCES: Kuo-chia t'ung-chi-chü (comp.), *Chung-kuo t'ung-chi nien-chien 1990* (China statistical yearbook, 1990) (Beijing: Chung-kuo t'ung-chi ch'u-pan-she ch'u-pan, 1990), p. 36, for measures of national income, p. 51, for gross value of output, and p. 89, for population growth data to estimate the third column. For 1990–1993, *China Statistical Yearbook* (hereafter CTN), 1994, pp. 32–33.

PANEL B: THE ROC ECONOMY

Period	GDP	National Income	Real Income per Capita
1951–1959	8.0	7.9	4.5
1960–1979	9.7	9.3	6.8
1980–1989	7.7	8.4	6.5
1990–1993	6.4	6.4	5.3

SOURCE: Council for Economic Planning and Development, *Taiwan Statistical Data Book, 1994* (Taipei: Council for Economic Planning and Development), p. 27, for the first column, pp. 33–34, for the second, and pp. 36–37, for the third. ROC uses the same accounting standards as do the United States and other Western nations.

When real income per capita rose slightly, the regime managed to limit household consumption, increase household savings, and channel savings into planned investment. In this way the state maintained a high rate of capital accumulation but at the cost of tremendous waste, inefficiency, and low living standards. Not until 1993 did PRC per capita income reach almost US$500 (that of the ROC's per capita income in the early 1970s, when ROC households also spent about 50 percent of household expenditures for food and drink).

Mainland China's rural income distribution before 1937 was similar to that of most poor countries: the poorest one-fifth of rural households received only 5 percent of income compared with 50.4 percent for the richest one-fifth.[4] Land

Table 6.2   Annual Urban Household Living Expenditures per Capita in the PRC, 1957–1993 (in percent)

Category	1957	1964	1981	1985	1989	1993
Food	58.43	59.21	56.65	52.24	54.50	50.14
Clothing	12.00	10.98	14.78	14.56	12.32	14.24
Rent, fuel, power	7.67	8.58	4.31	3.69	3.57	6.63
Household furnishings	7.62	7.06	15.37	18.40	11.06	8.76
Medical care, health expenses	3.14	3.42	1.21	1.43	1.32	2.69
Transport, communications	2.38	1.74	1.44	1.09	0.94	3.81
Education, recreation	1.24	2.39	1.52	2.05	2.49	9.91
Other	7.52	6.61	4.72	6.54	13.80	3.52
TOTAL	100.00	100.00	100.00	100.00	100.00	100.00

SOURCES: *CTN*, 1984, p. 463, for 1957–1981; *CTN*, 1987, p. 807, for 1985–1987; *CTN*, 1990, p. 3, for 1989; *CTN*, 1994, for 1993, p. 260.

reform radically changed income distribution between 1946 and 1951; Charles R. Roll estimates that, by 1952, the poorest one-fifth were receiving 20.4 percent.[5] By 1956 the collectivization of farming made income distribution even more egalitarian. The Gini coefficient for urban-worker income distribution was as low as 0.185 in 1977; in 1978 it was 0.237 for rural workers. During the 1980s, however, these coefficients increased to 0.233 for urban inequality and 0.338 for rural income inequality.[6] (These estimates exclude the income of the privileged communist elite.) Income inequality between cities and the countryside and between rich and poor provinces worsened in the 1990s, but these inequalities are still far below pre–World War II inequality levels.

This socialist economy also improved public hygiene and health: the population's life expectancy, which had been thirty-six years in 1950, rose to sixty-four in 1979[7] and seventy as of 1995.[8] But, after 1978, female life expectancy fell, remaining constant for males. Meanwhile, infant mortality increased for females but slowly declined for males, reflecting the gender discrimination that took place when the government pushed the one child per family program in the 1980s and 1990s. Adult literacy rose from 20 percent in 1949 to 66 percent in 1979 and topped 80 percent in 1995, with primary school enrollment rising from 25 percent to 93 percent of school-age children but then declining after 1979 as rural children left school to work for their families. Living standard improvement has been mixed: as a consequence of society receiving more public goods, people lived longer and enjoyed more education. Yet households were unable to improve their material living standards and often had to toil longer.

As for Taiwan, its mixed economy experienced a high GDP growth rate that continued into the 1960s, when foreign and domestic trade greatly expanded as a proportion of GDP. Not until the 1980s and 1990s did Taiwan's economic growth rate slow down as more resources moved overseas and into the services sector and as the manufacturing and agricultural sectors' contribution to national GDP declined (table 6.1, panel B). Households and business firms still saved more than 20 percent of their income, and investment remained high over the period. Enterprises that did not increase their productivity could not compete and went out of business. Rising total factor productivity accounted for about half Taiwan's GDP growth in the early decades.

Until 1960, Taiwan's households also consumed a high proportion of their income (around 95 percent), but by 1965 they were saving more than 10 percent and by the 1970s, more than 20 percent. Frugality and hard work had always characterized this Confucian society but had never before taken the form of high savings and investment. As early as 1964, 60 percent of household expenditures, just as on the mainland, went for food and drink. But after 1970, the proportion spent for food and drink declined because of the rise in household income. Meanwhile, household savings remained high (see table 6.3). By the 1990s Taiwan household expenditures resembled the household spending of high-income countries.

Taiwan's economy is now highly urban (nearly 90 percent), and the services sector contributes more to GDP (59.1 percent) than both manufacturing (37.3 percent) and agriculture (3.6 percent). Rapid structural change and gains in factor productivity have occurred without severe economic fluctuations. When annual fluctuations in GDP growth rates are compared for the PRC and the ROC (see figure 6.1), we see that the PRC's GDP greatly fluctuated in 1959–61 because of famine and in 1966–67 because of urban turmoil.

Because land reform redistributed income more equally, the Gini coefficient measuring income distribution fell from 0.5762 in 1953 to 0.329 in 1965 and 0.2735 in 1972. That decline continued until 1980. After that, urbanization and rising real estate prices increased the share of nonwage income, and income distribution shifted toward more inequality until 1993, when the trend stabilized, only to become unequal again.

The ROC's economy also increased the supply of public goods. By 1993 average life expectancy had risen to 73.3 years.[9] Primary school enrollments reached 99.8 percent of school-age children, with 100 percent of all primary graduates going on to junior high school; 77.3 percent of the latter enrolled in senior high school; and 85.5 percent of senior high students who graduated in 1987–88 enrolled in higher education.[10] Ninety-two percent of adults are literate. Education is now a permanent way of life in Taiwan, but for many mainland village youth it is still out of reach.

Table 6.3   Annual Household Living Expenditures per Capita in the ROC, 1964–1992 (in percent)

Category	1964	1970	1976	1980	1986	1992
Food, beverages, tobacco	59.70	52.46	46.88	40.35	37.42	29.79
Clothing, footwear	6.30	5.79	6.83	7.03	5.84	6.10
Rent, fuel, power	17.20	18.19	21.45	23.65	23.26	26.38
Household furnishings	3.40	3.96	3.87	4.57	4.30	4.20
Medical care, health expenses	5.30	5.95	4.61	4.20	5.42	5.08
Transport, communications	2.00	3.00	4.99	6.68	8.23	8.97
Education, recreation	1.20	2.66	6.38	8.18	16.03	13.36
Other	4.90	7.99	5.49	5.34	5.50	6.12
TOTAL	100.00	100.00	100.00	100.00	100.00	100.00

SOURCES: *Taiwan Statistical Data Book, 1982*, p. 54, for 1964; *Taiwan Statistical Data Book, 1990*, pp. 61–62, for 1968–1989; *Taiwan Statistical Data Book, 1994*, p. 63, for 1992.

The Historical Benchmark

The market economy of China's coastal provinces rapidly became integrated with the world economy after 1900 through major rivers like the Yangtse, railroads connecting the hinterland with the coastal cities, and treaty ports (a term derived from imperial government treaties during the Ch'ing empire giving foreigners special rights). These coastal markets imported rice from Southeast Asia and textile products from Japan and the West. By the 1930s tens of thousands of privately owned factories and companies in China's port cities produced goods for domestic and foreign markets. Even during the war years (1937–1945), some thirteen thousand modern factories employed more than six hundred thousand workers in twelve major cities.[11] The railway system extended nearly twenty-four thousand miles and connected with fifty large cities.[12] After the war, China recovered Japanese mines, factories, rolling stock, and harbors in the northeast.[13] A private banking and commercial network also existed in every province.

More important, China was on the brink of an agricultural revolution. In 1946 an agroscientific research network linked seventeen agricultural colleges and universities, twenty-five provincial and missionary schools, and nine agricultural technical schools. That network graduated more than six thousand students a year and introduced new cotton and wheat seeds into the villages to raise yields.[14] Mainland China's small modern economy could have been expanded if prudent state policies and institutional reforms had rejuvenated the private sector and the market economy.

Figure 6.1   Annual Growth of GNP

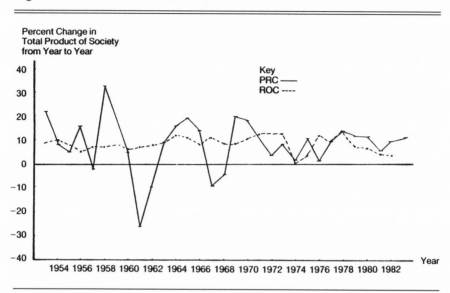

When Taiwan became a colony of Japan in 1895, Japanese officials unified the currency; built an infrastructure of modern transportation, communications, and public health and education; and launched an agricultural revolution by establishing new agro-experimental stations in rural communities and building water control and irrigation projects.[15] By 1937 nearly 15 percent of the island's population lived in five main cities, and an industrial revolution was sweeping the island. The island's per capita product grew twice as fast as that of the mainland.[16] Whereas, by 1937, the small modern base established on the mainland had little influence on the huge traditional sector, by the eve of World War II, Taiwan's modern economy had penetrated every rural district.

In both Chinese societies, people had long privately contracted with one another to exchange and share family resources through customary law agreements. Markets were highly competitive, although not always integrated.[17] The Chinese worked long and hard, saved, calculated costs and benefits, and valued literacy and education.[18] During the first half of the twentieth century, these two economies began their transition to a modern market economy. They possessed similar factor endowments and were at comparable stages of economic development by midcentury.

But the war and early postwar years engulfed both territories in political and social changes that transformed the course of Chinese history. The civil war, which was quickly won by the Communist Party in 1949, left a legacy of hate between the Communists and the elite who had accumulated wealth and technical capabilities in the prewar decades. On Taiwan a rebellion erupted in February 1947 that left a legacy of bitterness between the Taiwanese and those mainlanders who had fled the civil war on the mainland.[19]

By 1952, both Chinese economies had rebounded to achieve their highest output since 1937. Between 1950 and 1961, the Soviet Union supplied the PRC with about $2.08 billion worth of credits to finance new plants, military equipment, and four Soviet joint-stock companies established in 1954.[20] Similarly, the ROC received economic and military aid from the United States of around US$1.5 billion between 1950 and 1965.[21]

Each territory had special difficulties to overcome. Taiwan had absorbed some two million mainlander refugees, most of whom worked in government and the military but had trouble interacting with the local people, who spoke a different dialect and had lived under fifty years of Japanese colonial rule. On the mainland the new socialist government ruled a vast territory that had not been unified since 1911 and worried about counterrevolutionary elements that might undermine its rule. Despite similar backgrounds of modernity, resource endowment, and difficulties, their economic development paths soon diverged, and two very different economies and societies emerged.

Political Centers

THE PRC'S "UNINHIBITED" POLITICAL CENTER

The concept of political center helps clarify the salient differences between these two regimes and why they managed their economies so differently.[22] The Communist Party created an "uninhibited" political center by concentrating enormous power to itself and the state, which then abolished private property, outlawed private businesses, and eliminated markets that had once connected the domestic economy with the world economy. From 1949 until 1978, the party-state-dominated political center adhered to Marxism-Leninism and Mao Tse-tung's ideas. China had no civil society, no free economic marketplace, no private enterprise, and no ideological or political market processes. The leaders of the uninhibited political center, such as Mao Tse-tung, dreamed of building a socialist utopia without classes. In this futuristic society, everyone would share the ethics of self-sacrifice for the people and eschew personal gain. Party members were to adopt "revolutionary enthusiasm and a death-defying spirit" and "work hard and serve the people with their whole heart, not with half or two-thirds."[23] The uninhibited political center used massive national campaigns to transform community organizations and lifestyles and to shame and force opponents to conform to collective forms of life. First there were collectives, followed by rural communes and state enterprises with their schools, hospitals, and homes for the aged, workers, and managers. By the end of the 1950s, Chinese society had been transformed into a collective-communal life in which people lived and worked in their assigned units.

During the 1960s and 1970s, Mao and the party experimented with new communal forms in agriculture and industry to govern how individuals worked and received goods and services from their work units. Every commune and state enterprise strived for self-sufficiency in production and exchange and to produce a surplus to be distributed by central planning. This socialist society demanded universal conformity: to dress in blue cotton pants, shirts, and blouses; to live simple and frugal lives; to receive public goods from their work units; and to adhere to Mao's way of thinking and Communist Party doctrine.

The state expanded the older industrial enterprises while building new ones to produce iron, steel, machine tools, and cement and to develop mining, energy, and transportation. For example, in 1957, the Ministry of Metallurgy expanded the former Japanese-run Anshan Iron and Steel Company in Liaoning province of the northeast, built the Wuhan Iron and Steel Company, and then constructed the Pao-t'ou Iron and Steel Company, the P'an-chih-hui Iron and Steel Works, and the Capital Iron and Steel Company at Shih-ching-shan near Beijing. The Central Planning Commission then connected these metallurgical centers to networks of metal mines and the machine-building industry being built by the Ministries of Mining and Machine Tools. These state enterprises made up the first developmental block built during the first two five-year plans (1952–1962) with Soviet aid.

In the mid-1960s and 1970s, various state ministries began building another developmental block of metallurgical, chemical, and machine tools in Kwei-chow and Szechuan provinces.[24] These two developmental blocks were designed to serve different regions. Without national and international markets, the industries of these two developmental blocks soon accumulated unplanned inventories and lacked spare parts and machines. They could find neither buyers for their excess products nor suppliers for the materials and intermediate products they lacked. By the 1970s both developmental blocks of industries were technologically backward. As these same problems began affecting other industries and the energy sector, China's industrial sector began falling behind that of the advanced countries. By 1978 the socialist core of 150,000 state-owned enterprises was not only backward but costing the government billions of yuan in subsidies.

China's living standards had stagnated for several decades, and rural poverty in many inner provinces was widespread. By controlling information about developments abroad and relying on rationing, the regime limited consumption and allocated resources to expanding capital goods production. Housing had deteriorated; overcrowding was severe in every city, town, and village; transportation and utilities did not keep pace with demand. Although the regime had managed to suppress inflation while producing more capital goods relative to consumer goods and services, by 1978 the strains in the economy had become deep and pervasive. The new leaders who replaced Mao and his few close supporters decided that China's only course was economic reform: gradually opening up the economy to the world market and foreign investment and rebuilding a market economy with state, private, and mixed property rights.

THE ROC'S "INHIBITED" POLITICAL CENTER

In Taiwan, the ROC's Kuomintang (KMT) established an "inhibited" political center that allowed households and other organizations to operate in an economic market process. The ROC's inhibited political center granted households and organizations the freedom to choose their businesses and professions, acquire property, and operate as they pleased but regulated the economy through monetary and fiscal policies and institutional rules.

Adhering to the ideas of Sun Yat-sen, the KMT envisioned making the Chinese people on Taiwan prosperous, encouraging traditional ethics, and nurturing democratization by gradually allowing the people to elect their local leaders and representatives. Sunist doctrine approved of capitalism on the condition that the state alleviate economic fluctuations, unequal income distribution, and unemployment and poverty. That doctrine also stressed building social harmony, promoting national prosperity through "guided capitalism," and opposing any form of class warfare. The KMT leadership adopted Max Weber's "ethic of responsibility," prudently taking responsibility for its policies and emphasizing study and review to avoid mistakes or any unexpected consequences that might produce a backlash of social discontent. Whereas the Communist Party preferred autarky, the KMT affirmed foreign trade and foreign investment to link the domestic economy with the world market. The PRC abolished the marketplace, but the ROC developed an efficient economic market process. Their different policy approaches are best illustrated in land reform.

At the outset, the Communist Party abolished private property rights in the countryside by launching a vendetta against property holders, forcibly dispossessing them, and redistributing their wealth to the community. On Taiwan the government first redistributed public land and then confiscated private land but paid the owners an equivalent market value in bonds or stock shares in state enterprises. The government then sold that land to tenants and landless households, who obtained low-interest loans from banks to purchase their new property. The KMT followed Sun's dictum of "taking precautions against calamity" to enact land reform in a "peaceful and progressive way."[25] In late 1965 only 17 percent of Taiwan's rural people were tenant farmers; four out of every five persons owned their land compared with only two out of five in 1952.[26]

By 1955 the Communist Party had dispossessed all businessmen (except for a favored few) of their private assets. Meanwhile, the KMT had promoted the private sector's growth by selling public enterprise assets to businessmen, discouraging labor unions, and reducing the tax burden. In 1958 the ROC state replaced the dual exchange-rate system with a single fixed rate and lowered taxes to promote exports. In the late 1960s the government established export zones wherein business firms could locate for low rents if they manufactured for export.

By the mid-1960s Taiwan's economy was booming, exports were increasing, and small to medium enterprises (SMEs) were sprouting up everywhere. Taiwan's unimodal system of family farms increased consumer spending, which increased the demand for SME products and services and encouraged those businesses to employ more workers and expand output.[27] Rural migration to the cities reached an all-time high; more villagers sold their land and established new services and manufacturing enterprises in the cities. Specialization and exchange flourished. The domestic market expanded, and household consumption increased. The export-led boom encouraged greater imports, which helped suppress inflation. With investment and savings at an all-time high, people began enjoying higher living standards.

Instead of expanding its power in the economy, the state's economic influence receded and the private sector's influence grew. In the 1970s the state expanded infrastructure projects such as trans-island roads, railroads, harbors, and an international airport but at a huge cost. The government encouraged capital investment in industries with export potential through preferential tax reductions and subsidies. In 1957, for example, the state helped Y. C. Wang establish a new polyethylene plant; Wang went on to become the island's first billionaire.[28] Other businessmen followed Wang's example, and in the 1960s a booming plastics industry supplied both local and foreign market demand. The state also created the Joint Commission for Rural Reconstruction, which helped farmers grow specialty crops, convert their paddy land to aquaculture, and install irrigation works.[29] During 1965–67 the state set up export zones on low-cost land to encourage private enterprises to export.

As a result, a bimodal enterprise structure, consisting of tens of thousands of SMEs, operated alongside large-scale corporations owned by five hundred families, producing nearly 40 percent of GDP in the late 1980s.[30] This bimodal enterprise structure, which was innovative and responsive to changes in domestic and foreign market demands, was the core of Taiwan's economy. By 1993 the island of Taiwan, with a population of less than 2 percent of the mainland's, generated a GDP that was almost 40 percent of the mainland's.

The Two Political Centers
Adjust to New Realities

REFORMING THE PRC ECONOMY

When Mao Tse-tung died in September 1976, the Chinese economy was "cellular," in that communes and state enterprises tried to be self-sufficient and supply only those buyers designated by central planning.[31] The state's rigid control and allocation of labor diverted workers to agriculture, which absorbed "97.3 million workers between 1957 and 1975, or about two-thirds of the overall labor force increase of those years."[32] The state had tried to enlarge the railroad system, but road building lagged because districts striving for self-sufficiency had little incentive to build roads and because labor markets did not exist. The service sector drastically declined after 1957, and public demand for services like telecommunications far outstripped their supply. In 1980 the phone system of Kiangsu province could handle only fifty thousand lines.

In 1978 the regime's leaders began to address the worsening problems: declining factor productivity, high transaction costs, technological backwardness, poverty, and waste. Reform, which began in Anhwei province, spread to other counties as the party abolished the commune system and allowed households to supply a fixed amount of output to the state and market the remainder. Because households could allocate their resources, they worked more efficiently and intensified their production efforts. The output of grain *and* industrial crops rose; for the first time since the Communist Party came to power, there was a marketable farm surplus. Households had income to rebuild their houses, establish new services, invest in manufacturing enterprises, and produce for export. In 1983–84 an economic boom swept the country, bringing prosperity to villages and even the cities. The service sector began to revive. In Szechwan province, for example, the number of registered service businesses went from 36,700 to 811,120 between 1980 and 1986.[33]

In 1985 the Communist Party initiated urban economic reform by allowing state enterprises to find buyers for output that remained after a fixed quota had been supplied to the state. Such contracting was supposed to encourage the inefficient, debt-ridden state enterprises to earn profits, upgrade their technology, and increase labor and capital productivity. It failed because too many state enterprises depended on state subsidy, had costs that were too high, and lacked markets for their products or for labor and capital. Without state subsidies, they could not meet their annual costs. A majority of them were going bankrupt, abandoning their workers to unemployment and leaving pensioners without any means of support.

As the plight of state enterprises worsened, private enterprise and new town-village enterprises having a mixture of property rights were rapidly expanding their production and trade. Although the economy grew more slowly between 1985 and 1990 than it had from 1978 to 1984, exports were still on the rise. After 1978 the coastal provinces also began receiving businesspeople and investments from Hong Kong and Taiwan. The provincial banks defied the Central Bank and expanded their loans. Inflation worsened, forcing the state to intervene and tighten credit. As the money supply expanded and then contracted, the financial condition of the some 150,000 state enterprises became precarious. Finally, at the Communist Party's fourteenth congress in October 1992, China's leaders decided to restructure the property rights of state-owned enterprises by creating new corporate forms that could operate in the marketplace. Some state enterprises would be retained but improved. The party referred to this reform as *building a socialist market economy*, the goal being to put a mixed market economy in place by the year 2000.

Between 1992 and 1995 the State Council eliminated the Planning Commission and began experimenting with large clusters of urban state-owned enterprises to reduce their indebtedness and cut their costs so they could operate independently in the marketplace. Having selected eighteen cities whose state enterprises would be restructured, in 1995 the State Council began surveying their property assets to see how they could become profitable. At the same time, the State Council drafted laws to guarantee unemployment compensation and social security for workers and to regulate the stock markets that were operating in Shanghai and Shenzhen cities. The state was now commited to creating labor and capital markets in which restructured state enterprises could use their resources efficiently and earn a profit.

In 1994, the State Council began reforming the foreign exchange system, the taxation of Chinese and foreign firms, and the banking system in an effort to control inflation in the evolving market economy. The party, recognizing that socialism could not progress without markets and different property rights, seemed to be adopting the economic ideology and policies long practiced in Taiwan.

THE ROC ECONOMY

Taiwan's economy began to slow down in the early 1980s because of rising labor costs and declining profits in the textiles, plastics, and food-processing industries, which made up the developmental blocks of the 1950s and 1960s, and by the early 1990s, manufacturing had begun to experience a gradual downsizing. Many factories and their managers began moving to mainland China and Southeast Asia.

The island's burgeoning trade surplus in the 1980s with the United States brought fierce pressures to open Taiwan's markets. Negotiations between the two nations led to the removal of many quotas and a lowering of Taiwan's tariffs. American pressure also depreciated the U.S. dollar relative to the Taiwan dollar, so that Taiwan's dollar was revalued upward, to around US$1 to NT$27–28 instead of NT$40 as in the past. As Taiwan's currency appreciated, its imports expanded. Even so, the economy's dependency on foreign trade increased. Taiwan firms adjusted their costs and remained competitive in world markets but directed more of their trade and investment to Southeast Asia and the China mainland.

Structural economic change continued, and by the 1990s only about 10 percent of the labor force worked in agriculture, with roughly 40 percent employed in manufacturing and 50 percent in services. As the twenty-first century approaches, Taiwan's economy has become increasingly dependent on services. With a per capita income of more than US$12,000 in 1995, Taiwan now has a high-income economy, with its attendant needs: to upgrade the nation's infrastructure, to educate and train the labor force to maintain competitiveness in world markets, to provide health and social security benefits for an aging population, and to avoid a rising national debt as the social welfare demand increases.

Meanwhile, the government monitors the economy and encourages resources to move into those economic activities in which the island has a comparative advantage. In the 1970s the state encouraged the development of an electronics industry that came to maturity in the late 1980s and now competes in a worldwide market. Similar efforts are under way in the 1990s to transform Taiwan into a financial services center. The island's people still save around a quarter of their GDP, and the Central Bank holds nearly US$100 billion of foreign exchange reserves.

Taiwan's economic power and dependency on foreign markets have encouraged its entrepreneurs to look toward the mainland for new opportunities. Nearly 25 percent of Taiwan's exports now flow to the mainland; if that share increases over the next decade, the mainland could replace the United States as its premier trading partner. As Taiwan and mainland China's economies become more closely integrated, their economic cooperation should promote social and political cooperation. The divergence that characterized these two economies in the three decades after World War II has ended. They are now moving on new trajectories that converge to promote greater economic interdependence.

Notes

1. *CTN* (1990), p. 69.
2. Anthony M. Tang, *An Analytical and Empirical Investigation of Agriculture in*

Mainland China, 1952–1980 (Taipei: Chung-hua Institution for Economic Research, 1984).

3. John McMillan, John Whalley, and Lijing Zhu, "The Impact of China's Economic Reforms on Agricultural Productivity Growth," *Journal of Political Economy* 97, no. 4 (August 1989): 781–807.

4. Charles Robert Roll Jr., *The Distribution of Rural Incomes in China: A Comparison of the 1930s and the 1950s* (New York and London: Garland Publishing, 1980), p. 46.

5. Ibid., p. 98.

6. Li Chengrui, "Economic Reform Brings Better Life," *Beijing Review* 28, no. 29 (July 22, 1985): 22.

7. Judith Banister, *China's Changing Population* (Stanford: Stanford University Press), table 4.12.

8. "Blue Paper Views Economy since 1995," Foreign Broadcast Information Service, *Daily Report: China,* FBIS-CHI-95-101, May 31, 1995, p. 35.

9. *Taiwan Statistical Data Book,* 1994, p. 282.

10. Ibid., p. 264.

11. Yen Chung-p'ing, comp., *Chung-kuo chin-tai ching-chi-shih t'ung-chi tzu-liao süan-chi* (Selected statistical materials on Chinese modern economic history) (Peking: K'o-hsüeh ch'u-pan-she, 1955), p. 106.

12. Ibid., pp. 177–79.

13. Donald G. Gillin and Ramon H. Myers, eds., *Last Chance in Manchuria: The Diary of Chang Kia-ngau* (Stanford: Hoover Institution Press, 1989), p. 32. See also Peter Duus, Ramon H. Myers, and Mark R. Peattie, eds., *The Japanese Informal Empire in China, 1895–1937* (Princeton, N.J.: Princeton University Press, 1989), chaps. 4 and 5. Thomas G. Rawski's new measure of capital stock between 1912 and 1937 shows that the composition of labor and capital did change. See Thomas G. Rawski, *Economic Growth in Prewar China* (Berkeley: University of California Press, 1989), pp. 260–61. Rawski's pathbreaking work strongly argues that output per head increased on a sustained basis; see chap. 7.

14. For a good summary of the remarkable development of the educational system on the mainland before 1949, see E-tu Zen Sun, "The Growth of the Academic Community, 1912–1949," in John K. Fairbank and Albert Feuerwerker, eds., *The Cambridge History of China.* Volume 13: *Republican China, Part 2 (1912–1949)* (Cambridge, Eng.: Cambridge University Press, 1986), pp. 361–420. For a brief discussion on the well-developed agricultural colleges and research institutions, see Ramon H. Myers, "Wheat in China— Past, Present and Future," *China Quarterly,* no. 74 (June 1978): 315. Paul K. T. Sih, ed., *The Strenuous Decade: China's Nation-Building Efforts, 1927–1937* (New York: St. John's University Press, 1970), chaps. 6–8.

15. Ramon H. Myers and Yamada Saburō, "Agricultural Development in the Empire," in Ramon H. Myers and Mark R. Peattie, eds., *The Japanese Colonial Empire, 1895–1945* (Princeton, N.J.: Princeton University Press, 1984), pp. 428–46.

16. Samuel P. S. Ho, *The Economic Development of Taiwan, 1860–1970* (New Haven, Conn., and London: Yale University Press, 1978), pp. 284–85, 319. Taiwan's national

income grew at the annual rate of 2.3 percent between 1911 and 1937, according to Lee Teng-hui's estimates. Mainland China's gross domestic product grew at 1.8–2.0 percent a year according to Rawski's preferred estimates (*Economic Growth in Prewar China*, p. 330).

17. Fu-mei Chang Chen and Ramon H. Myers, "Customary Law and the Economic Growth of China during the Ch'ing Period," *Ch'ing-shih wen-t'i* 3, no. 5 (November 1976): 1–32. See also Fu-mei Chang Chen and Ramon H. Myers, "Some Distinctive Features of Commodity Markets in Late Imperial China: Three Case Studies," in *The Second Conference on Modern Chinese Economic History*, vol. 2. (Taipei: Institute of Economics, Academia Sinica, 1989) pp. 633–81.

18. Evelyn Sakakida Rawski, *Education and Popular Literacy in Ch'ing China* (Ann Arbor: University of Michigan Press, 1979).

19. See Lai Tse-han, Ramon H. Myers, and Wei Wou, *A Tragic Beginning: The February 28, 1947 Rebellion* (Stanford: Stanford University Press, 1991).

20. Carl Riskin, *China's Political Economy: The Quest for Development since 1949* (Oxford, Eng.: Oxford University Press, 1987), p. 74.

21. Ramon H. Myers, "The Economic Development of the Republic of China on Taiwan, 1965–1981," in Lawrence J. Lau, ed., *Models of Development: A Comparative Study of Economic Growth in South Korea and Taiwan* (San Francisco, Calif.: Institute for Contemporary Studies, 1986), p. 47.

22. Edward Shils advanced this concept, developing it to include the central beliefs and norms of the elite, intellectuals, and opinion makers to differentiate from those held by the society or "periphery." See his essays on this concept in Edward Shils, *Center and Periphery: Essays in Macrosociology* (Chicago and London: University of Chicago Press, 1975). S. Eisenstadt further applied this concept of political center to analyze the historical evolution of different societies to modern times. In a series of unpublished essays, Thomas A. Metzger further developed a typology of "inhibited and uninhibited political centers" to understand Chinese modernization.

23. Mao Tse-tung, "Persevere in Plain Living and Hard Struggle; Maintain Close Ties with the Masses," in *Selected Works of Mao Tse-tung*, vol. 5 (Peking: Foreign Languages Press, 1988), pp. 436–39. This essay appeared March 1975.

24. See Barry Naughton, "The Third Front: Defence Industrialisation in the Chinese Interior," *China Quarterly*, no. 115 (September 1988): 351–86.

25. Ch'en Ch'eng, *Juh-ho shih-hsien keng-chu yu ch'i-tien* (How to enable the farmers to till their land) (Taipei: Cheng-chung shu-chu, 1951), p. 4.

26. Council for Economic Planning and Development, *Taiwan Statistical Data Book, 1988* (Taipei: Council for Economic Planning and Development, 1989), p. 65.

27. Albert Park and Bruce Johnston, "Rural Development and Dynamic Externalities in Taiwan's Structural Transformation," *Economic Development and Cultural Change* 44, no. 1 (October 1995): 181–208.

28. Wan-lin Kiang, "Technological Change and Industrial Development: The Plastic Industry in Taiwan," *Industry of Free China* 54, no. 3 (September 25, 1980): 19.

29. T. H. Shen, *The Sino-American Joint Commission for Rural Reconstruction: Twenty*

Years of Cooperation for Agricultural Development (Ithaca, N.Y., and London: Cornell University Press, 1970), part III.

30. Audrey Donnithorne, "China's Cellular Economy: Some Trends since the Cultural Revolution," *China Quarterly*, no. 52 (October–December 1972): 605–19.

31. Thomas G. Rawski, *Economic Growth and Employment in China* (New York: Oxford University Press, 1979), p. 123.

32. These developments are well covered in Chung-kuo lun-t'an, comp., *T'ai-wan ti-ch'u she-hui pien-huan yu wen-hua fa-chan* (Social transformation and cultural development in Taiwan) (Taipei: Chung-kuo lun-t'an tsa-chih, 1985); also Hsin-huang Michael Hsiao, Wei-yuan Cheng, and Hou-sheng Chan, eds., *Taiwan: A Newly Industrializing State* (Taipei: National Taiwan University, Department of Sociology, 1989).

7

Material Progress in Korea since Partition

NICHOLAS EBERSTADT

August 1995 marked the fiftieth anniversary of the partition of the Korean peninsula, which was "temporarily" separated into a Soviet zone (in the north) and an American zone (in the south) in August 1945. Since the summer of 1948—when the Republic of Korea (ROK) was founded in southern Korea and the Democratic People's Republic of Korea (DPRK) was established in the north—the two states of divided Korea have been engaged in fierce and incessant competition with one another. Although they have pursued very different "development strategies" (with communist-style central planning in the north and a much more market-oriented approach in the south), both states have explicitly identified the race for economic development as part of that competition.

By the summer of 1995, any impartial observer would have concluded that this race was no contest at all. On the one hand, the ROK (South Korea), after decades of exceptionally rapid economic growth, was approaching Western levels of affluence—and in fact had formally applied for membership in the Organization for Economic Cooperation and Development (OECD), the institution encompassing the world's affluent industrial societies.[1] On the other hand, the DPRK (North Korea) was struggling with internationally publicized economic difficulties. In North Korea, the 1980s were apparently years of economic stagnation, with the early 1990s marked by absolute economic decline. By 1995 there were even persistent rumors of food shortages in North Korea, rumors seemingly confirmed by the DPRK's discreet requests for emergency food aid from China, Thailand, Japan—even South Korea!

From today's vantage point, one might be tempted to presume that the tremendous economic disparity now evident between the two states meant that South Korea had consistently outpaced North Korea in their contest for material advance. But such a presumption would be badly off the mark. For many years after the partition, it was *North* Korea that managed the more productive, and more rapidly developing, economy of the two. The story of divided Korea's material development is thus more complex, and interesting, than might initially have been supposed.

In the following pages, we will recount that story, first by examining some of the quantitative evidence concerning the economic race in divided Korea, then by reviewing "development" policies embraced by the two regimes, and finally by considering some of the more general lessons this story may offer.

I

To quantify North Korea's economic performance in order to compare it with the records of market-oriented economies, we must cope not only with the theoretical issues that have dogged such estimates for the USSR and communist Europe[2] but also with the fact that the USSR and communist Europe released vastly more information about their economies than has the DPRK to date. Since its founding, for example, North Korea has never published a figure for the country's "net material product," the standard measure of national output in the Soviet-style framework for national accounts.

How, then, to begin an assessment? One starting point for comparing North and South Korean economic performance would be measures of physical production.[3] (Indexes of physical output, though, beg the question of valuation.)[4] Between 1960 and 1989, to judge by the indicators in table 7.1, the balance of basic production on the Korean peninsula shifted dramatically. By these measures, the volume of commodity output would seem to have risen for both Koreas, but especially South Korea. Of the commodities represented, North Korea's estimated output ratio improved only for rice (perhaps for reasons that have little to do with underlying changes in productivity).[5] For some of these products, South Korean output was negligible in 1960 and yet was estimated to be much greater than North Korea's by 1985. When one remembers that South Korea's current population is roughly twice that of North Korea's, one may note that per capita production of such items as cement, steel, trucks, and buses is estimated to be higher today in the south than in the north—exactly the reverse of the situation estimated for 1960.

If these figures can be presumed to be reliable in and of themselves, and to be broadly representative of trends for allied goods, they would suggest that South

Table 7.1 Official U.S. and ROK Estimates of Selected Commodity Output: North Korea vs. South Korea, 1960–ca. 1989

Commodity	1960	1965	1970	1975	1980	1985	1989
Rice (in thousands of metric tons)							
DPRK	1,100	1,300	1,400	2,500	2,300	3,600	3,400 [a]
ROK	4,151	4,470	5,471	6,485	5,311	7,855	5,601 [a]
Cement (in millions of metric tons)							
DPRK	2.3	2.4	2.8	5.0	6.6	8.5	9.3 [b]
ROK	0.4	1.6	5.8	10.1	15.6	20.4	29.9 [b]
Crude steel (in millions of metric tons)							
DPRK	0.6	1.2	2.2	2.6	3.6	4.5	8.0
ROK	–	0.2	0.5	2.0	8.6	13.5	21.8
Electricity (in billions of kWh)							
DPRK	9.0	13.4	16.5	22.0	24.0	30.0	30.0
ROK	1.7 [c]	3.3	9.2	19.8	37.2	58.0	74.0
Trucks and buses (in thousands)							
DPRK	3	4	8	10	12	16	16 [b]
ROK	–	1	9	19	54	71	167 [b]

Ratio: ROK to DPRK DPRK = 100							
Rice	377	344	391	259	231	218	165 [a]
Cement	17	67	207	202	236	240	322 [b]
Crude steel	( ) [d]	17	22	77	239	208	273
Electricity	19	25	56	90	155	193	247
Trucks and buses [e]	( ) [d]	25	118	185	448	444	1,044 [b]

NOTES: – = negligible

[a] 1986

[b] 1987

[c] excluding privately generated electricity

[d] ratio meaningless, North Korean preponderance

[e] ratios may not match production figures due to rounding.

SOURCES: For estimates of South Korean current electricity and truck and bus production: Republic of Korea, National Bureau of Statistics, *Korea Statistics Yearbook* (Seoul: Economic Planning Board), various issues. All other estimates: U.S. Central Intelligence Agency, *Handbook of Economic Statistics* (Washington, D.C.: NTIS, 1981 and 1989).

Korea has caught up with, and then significantly exceeded, North Korean per capita output in many areas of heavy industry over the course of that generation. Insofar as heavy industry enjoys special priority in all Soviet-style economies, broader significance might be ascribed to such a crossover.

Parallel indications come from data on the North Korean labor force, provided to the United Nations Fund for Population (UNFPA) in 1989 to meet the funds' requirements for extending technical assistance to Pyongyang for a planned 1992 census (apparently not yet undertaken). Those data do not reveal any obvious or peculiar inconsistencies, although their reliability may be affected by the ability of the DPRK's statistical authorities to gather and process accurate information on the society under their aegis.[6]

Table 7.2 presents data on the changing employment structure of the civilian labor force in North and South Korea between 1960 and 1985.[7] Both Koreas appear to have made the transition to a predominantly nonagricultural workforce by the late 1980s. In the early 1960s, however, the sector defined as "agriculture" accounted for a much greater share of overall employment in South Korea. By the late 1980s, the share of workers in agriculture was apparently no longer higher in South Korea than in North Korea and was possibly somewhat lower. The correspondence between the sectoral distribution of a country's labor force and its level of per capita output is approximate at best in market-oriented economies[8] and more tenuous still for command economies, where broad sectoral changes can be mandated politically. Even so, the patterns in these figures are suggestive when one recalls that South Korea's population is roughly twice as great as North Korea's, whereas North Korea's reported proportion of "worker" households in its civilian population is roughly twice as high as South Korea's proportion of working population in mining and manufacturing. Given these offsetting differences, it may be that the number of civilian "industrial" workers in the two Koreas in the late 1980s was roughly similar. Yet as we have seen, aggregate production of some basic industrial commodities is believed to have been considerably higher in South Korea than in North Korea. Taken together, the indications are that output per worker was considerably higher by the late 1980s in South Korean industry than in North Korean "industry." Even if per capita output in the residual sectors were equal in the two countries—or somewhat higher in the north— overall output per capita could still be significantly higher today in the south.

Comparative trends of urbanization are presented in table 7.3.[9] Before partition, both North and South Korea were overwhelmingly rural by any reasonable definition, although urbanization rates were reported to be somewhat higher in what is now South Korea. By 1960, to judge from these figures, the DPRK looks to have been more urbanized than the ROK, although some of this differential may simply reflect differences in basic definitions of the term. By 1985, however, South Korea decidedly looked to be the more urbanized society. If current definitions for urban areas are stricter for South Korea than for North Korea, the

Table 7.2   Civilian Labor Force Distribution in North and South Korea, ca.
               1960–1987 (in percent)

	South Korea		
Year	Agriculture, Forestry, and Fisheries	Mining and Manufacturing	Social Overhead and Other
1965	58.5	10.4	31.2
1975	45.7	19.1	35.2
1987	21.9	28.1	50.0

	North Korea		
Year	Farmers	Workers	Officials	Industrial Cooperative Workers
1960	44.4	38.3	13.7	3.3
1963	42.8	40.1	15.1	1.9
1987	25.3	57.0	16.8	0.9

NOTES: South Korean data refer to the proportion of the economically active labor force. North Korean figures for 1987 appear to refer to total population ages sixteen and older. Sectoral classification differs for North and South Korea; thus, figures are not fully comparable. For more information, see sources.

SOURCES: Nicholas Eberstadt and Judith Banister, *North Korea: Population Trends and Prospects* (Washington, D.C.: U.S. Bureau of the Census, Center for International Research, forthcoming).

differential would be even greater than suggested by table 7.3. According to these figures, the pace of urbanization slowed markedly after 1970 in North Korea but continued briskly in South Korea through the 1970s and 1980s.

A final datum relating to the comparative performance of the North and South Korean economies was released but not published by North Korean authorities in May 1990.[10] According to this datum, North Korea's per capita "GNP" in 1989 amounted to $2,580. The derivation of the figure was not explained, and its denomination of North Korean output in American dollars seems surprising and significant. In the past, North Korea has episodically released dollar-denominated figures for the country's per capita output ("national income"). Although their accuracy was questionable (the figure for 1979, for example, was announced on January 1, 1980),[11] they had always been higher than the dollar-denominated, exchange-rate-based estimates of GNP per capita for South Korea. That tradition was broken in 1989, when South Korea's exchange-rate-based GNP per capita was put at $4,968.[12] In releasing the figure of $2,580 in May 1990—after preliminary South Korean estimates for 1989 had already been reported—North Korean authorities not only seemed to be placing per capita output in their country at about half (52 percent) of the contemporary

Table 7.3   Urban Population in North and South Korea: 1960–1987
               (in percent)

Year	North Korea	South Korea
1960	40.6	28.0
1965	47.5	33.6 [a]
1970	54.2	41.2
1975	56.7	48.4
1980	56.9	57.3
1985	59.0	65.4
1990	56.6 [b]	74.4

NOTES:

[a] 1966

[b] 1987

Definition of urban area for North Korea is unknown. In South Korea, urban areas are defined as cities and towns with populations of 50,000 and above. Urbanization rates for North Korea since 1975 refer only to civilian population. Figures may not be fully comparable. For more information, see sources.

SOURCES: Nicholas Eberstadt and Judith Banister, *The Population of North Korea* (Berkeley: Institute of East Asian Studies, University of California, 1992), pp. 21–28; ROK National Statistical Office, *Korea Statistical Yearbook, 1992* (Seoul: Korea Statistical Association, 1992), p. 36.

South Korean level but to be indicating that they knew what they were doing and what they were implying.

Taken together, these data—drawn from a variety of sources and relating to some diverse aspects of economic structure and performance—seem to point toward a single, consistent reading of economic events in postpartition Korea. By the late 1980s, they suggest, per capita output in South Korea was higher than in North Korea—although exactly how much higher is difficult to gauge. Over the generation between the early 1960s and the late 1980s, they suggest, per capita growth was more rapid in South Korea than in North Korea—although, again, precisely how much more rapid is not clear. In contrast, in the early 1960s, by various indications, per capita output may have been higher in North Korea than in South Korea.

The conclusion that per capita output is higher today in South Korea than in North Korea is unlikely to shock many contemporary students of international development. Witnessing as we so recently have the collapse of communism in Eastern Europe and the Soviet Union, we may have become accustomed to presuming that centrally planned economies necessarily and generally perform less effectively than more liberal arrangements. The modern Korean experience may be a discipline against such comfortable and mechanistic presumptions. As best as can be told, South Korea did not catch up with, much less surpass, North Korea's per capita output during their first quarter century of independent government. Even if its rate of material advance has been slower than South Korea's over the past generation, North Korea's pace of progress may still have been quite rapid by international standards.

II

One might be excused for presuming that North Korea—a state commonly judged to be closed, rigidly controlled, and unpredictable—would stand little chance in a long-term economic race with the sort of dynamic, competitive, and open order that South Korea is today widely believed to exemplify. But North Korea's levels of output per capita were likely superior to South Korea's for much, if not most, of the period since partition. Even leading political figures in the Republic of Korea perceived that North Korea's general level of development was higher than South Korea's in the early 1960s.[13]

If all this seems out of keeping with the outside world's image of North Korea, it may be that important elements of the DPRK's policy have not been widely understood or appreciated. If the DPRK is a fanatical government, that fanaticism has evidently not inured its leadership to very practical considerations.

A capacity for sophisticated calculation and adept management, in fact, would seem to be suggested by what has *not* occurred in North Korea. Throughout Asia, for example, the transition to collectivized agriculture was followed by economic crisis and by famine: witness the People's Republic of Mongolia, the PRC, the Democratic Republic of Vietnam, and more recently Democratic Kampuchea. North Korea stands out as the single exception. Not only were famine and disruption apparently averted, but per capita production in agriculture seems to have reached relatively high levels in the early 1960s[14]—just a few years after collectivization was completed.

The practical grounding of North Korean economic policy—external indications to the contrary—may perhaps also be adduced from what did *not* happen after its mass mobilization campaign. In 1958, as China's Great Leap Forward was in motion, North Korea was in the midst of its own Chollima (Flying Horse) movement. As in China, North Korea's mass mobilization was characterized by intensive propaganda, utopian rhetoric, and exhortations that the population push itself to the limits of endurance.[15] Whereas China's campaign brought its economy to a virtual collapse, the Chollima movement ushered in the 1960s— the period in which North Korea was perceived (by the principals in that struggle) to be leading South Korea economically. The ostensible rigidity and inflexibility of the North Korean polity, finally, did not prevent the national economy's assuming a structure suggestive of relatively high productivity. By the late 1980s, North Korea's reported sectoral distribution of its working population looked much more like that of the Soviet Union than did that of China or Vietnam (see table 7.4). The significance of this comparison is not negligible; all these economies have been similarly subjected to the distorting influence of command planning, if to varying degrees. Per capita output in China is widely thought roughly to have doubled between the late 1970s and the late 1980s;[16] in 1987, however, China's workforce was mainly agricultural, whereas North Korea's was roughly three-quarters nonagricultural. Evidently, North Korea's stolid and continuing rejection of "reform" or "restructuring" has not kept its managers and administrators from evincing productivity increases from the national economy over a period of decades.

Little detail, unfortunately, is available on the specifics of North Korean managerial and administrative procedures.[17] Material incentive appears to figure squarely in North Korean economic policy, although the extent of incentives today and in the past is difficult to determine with any precision. An "internal accounting system," for example, is apparently used to allocate performance bonuses—and penalties—in both industry and agriculture,[18] and farm households are reportedly allowed small private plots for their personal use.[19] The outside world's information about these facets of management, however, derive almost exclusively from the recollections of a handful of defectors, few of whom could claim any general comprehension about the mechanics of the national economy. Perhaps the most that can be safely said is that the regime has shown that it prefers to elicit competitive economic behavior from managers and workers through exhortation and indoctrination but relies on material incentives when necessary.

Important as microeconomic conditions are to productivity and aggregate performance, there is not much in the way of reliable information about them for North Korea. One is left largely with the unsatisfying circularity of divining policies and practices from results.

We may speak with greater confidence about some of the broad trends that have characterized the North Korean economy as a whole since partition—and before it. On the eve of partition, per capita output appears to have been significantly higher in the northern portion of the peninsula than in the southern half. In 1940, by one set of estimates, per capita "commodity product"—that is, value added in agriculture and industry alone—was almost 70 percent higher in the northern provinces than in the southern provinces.[20] Even allowing for the possibility that the service sector accounted for a much higher share of overall output in the south, overall per capita output would, by these numbers, almost certainly have been over 25 percent higher in what was to become North Korea.[21]

Before partition, southern Korea was a bit more urbanized (15 percent) than the northern half (11 percent). The northern provinces, however, were much more industrialized. In 1940, for example, per capita output from mining and manufacturing is estimated to have been almost three times higher in the north.[22]

Table 7.4   Distribution of Labor Force by Sector: DPRK and Selected
              Marxist-Leninist Countries ca. 1987 (in percent)

| | SECTOR | | |
Country	Agriculture	Industry	Other
USSR (1987)	19 [a]	38 [b]	43
DPRK (1987)	25 [c]	57 [d]	18
People's Republic of China (1987)	60	18	22
Socialist Republic of Vietnam (1989)	71	12	17

NOTES: Labor force data refer to total employment in national economy for USSR, population sixteen years of age or older by occupation of household head for DPRK, total employment for PRC, and employment of persons thirteen years of age and older for Vietnam.

[a] agriculture and forestry

[b] industry and construction

[c] "farmers"

[d] "workers"

SOURCES: USSR: *Nar Khoz 1988* (Moscow: Finansy i Statistika, 1988), p. 26; DPRK: Nicholas Eberstadt and Judith Banister, *The Population of North Korea* (Berkeley: Institute of East Asian Studies, University of California, 1992), p. 80; China: *China Statistical Yearbook 1990* (Beijing: State Statistical Bureau, 1990), p. 114; Vietnam: *Vietnam Population Census 1989* (Hanoi: Central Census Steering Committee, 1990), table 3.2

Industrial production in the north, moreover, had been directed—by Japanese colonial design as well as by geography—toward heavy industry: mining, electrical generation, chemicals, and the like.[23] By an accident of history, the territory that the DPRK came to rule had already been developed structurally in directions that would please Leninist planners.

Despite administrative, economic, and even direct military assistance from the socialist camp, the period 1944–56 may have witnessed an absolute economic decline in North Korea. The Japanese withdrawal and the partition of the peninsula had a wrenching effect on the local economy. Between 1944 and 1946, grain production reportedly fell by more than 20 percent and electricity output is reported to have dropped by more than half.[24] The Korean War entailed even greater losses. Although it is impossible to give an exact figure for the economic destruction in North Korea during the course of the fighting, by 1953 the country's registered population was almost 12 percent smaller than it had been in 1949. Not until 1956—at the completion of the postwar Three-Year Plan—were the reported per capita production levels for many basic agricultural and industrial products back to the levels reported before partition.[25]

"Socialist construction," in a sense, commenced with the Five-Year Plan of 1957–61 (whose ambitious targets were reported generally to have been achieved by 1960, a year ahead of schedule).[26] The Five-Year Plan saw the collectivization of agriculture completed and the almost total nationalization of production in industry. It also recorded rapid rates of growth: gross agricultural output was said to have increased at an annual rate of almost 7.5 percent, and gross industrial product was said to have grown by more than 36 percent a year.[27] Even allowing for pricing problems, for the problematic conception of "gross output" in a socialist accounting framework, and for North Korea's rapid rate of population growth (then approaching 3 percent a year),[28] it is likely that the plan period coincided with a sharp increase in per capita product.

Official dissatisfaction with economic performance emerged over the next plan, initially scheduled to last seven years (1961–67). In the event, the Seven-Year Plan was extended three additional years and was finally declared completed in 1970. Disappointment with results was indicated a year or so into the plan, as the DPRK ceased publishing updated data for those few statistical series that had previously been routinely released.

Although the North Korean economy is directed according to precepts extolling national self-reliance, its development nevertheless seems to have been affected by international events. At the time of the Sino-Soviet rift, for example, North Korea had been leaning toward China (the aforementioned Chollima campaign, for example, referred to a horse from Chinese mythology).[29] By the early 1960s, the Soviet Union was not disposed to continue its previous flows of economic and technical assistance to the DPRK, and China, still recovering from its catastrophic leap forward, was scarcely capable of doing so.[30] Unexpected shortfalls of aid may have contributed to the economic adjustments of the 1960s.

During the 1960s, North Korea's response to the changes in the correlation of forces in the peninsula and in the world arena was, apparently, to enhance its military potential.[31] In his report to the fifth party congress in 1970, Kim Il Sung was explicit about this. "During the period under review [1961–70]," he wrote, "we undertook a number of radical steps to boost our nation's defense capabilities."[32] Official budget figures certainly seem to bear out his assertion. Reported defense expenditures doubled between 1966 and 1967 and nearly tripled between 1967 and 1971.[33] For the years 1967 through 1971, defense was reported to account for more than 30 percent of the national budget—up from a reported 2.5 percent in 1961.[34] Implausibly low though that initial figure may have been, there can be little doubt that the extension of North Korea's Seven-Year Plan into a de facto Ten-Year Plan coincided with a concerted new effort to finance the development of the country's military industries through the state budget.

Even under command planning, however, military expenditures have consequences. "This increase in our national defense capability," Kim Il Sung warned in 1970, "has been obtained at a very great price. . . . Had we been able to divert even a part of our nation's defense spendings to economic construction, our national economy would have developed more rapidly and the standard of living of our people [would have] been raised markedly."[35] The commitment posed practical problems. Indeed, there are reasons for thinking that North Korea's planners may have inadvertently engineered a major dislocation in their national economy and inaugurated the slowdown reflected in various official data series by attempting to finesse the trade-off between guns and butter.[36]

Evidence of a dislocation is fragmentary and almost entirely circumstantial. A major dislocation, however, would seem to explain and unite some otherwise disparate and contradictory soundings on the North Korean economy in the early 1970s.

Whatever occurred in North Korea's consumer sector in the early 1970s, subsequent North Korean policy appears to have been intent on limiting the impact of discretionary consumer expenditures on the national economy. For in 1987, North Korea's "national income" was reported to be about 47 billion won. In that same year, official figures reported the number of households in the country at 4.05 million. Under the generous assumption that the average North Korean household earned 300 won per month in 1987, monetary compensation would have amounted to less than a third (31 percent) of net material product—and to an even lower portion, presumably, of the country's gross domestic product. More than in any other country at its income level today, and perhaps more than in any other modern society, discretionary personal demand may have been delimited from the forces propelling economic activity in North Korea.

If the consumer market was jolted by dislocation in the early 1970s, it would not have been the only sector to be so affected. During that same period, North Korea's external sector—its international trade accounts—experienced shocks and adjustments from which it had only partially recovered a decade and a half later. The officially extolled doctrine of *juche* (national self-reliance) and the autarkic proclivities of command planning notwithstanding, international trade in fact played an important role in the DPRK's economy in the 1950s and 1960s.[37] Various attempts to measure North Korean trade in current U.S. dollars seem to suggest that North Korea's per capita export volume was roughly twice as large as South Korea's around 1966.[38] On the basis of some crude and highly tentative calculations, it appears that exports amounted to roughly a tenth of North Korea's "national income" in the mid-1960s.[39] If the ratio of exports to "national income" connotes the degree of "openness," North Korea in the mid-1960s looked more "open" than a number of other contemporary communist economies;[40] moreover, it would have been an economy in the process of becoming more "open" insofar as its pace of export growth exceeded its reported growth of "national income."

In the early 1970s, North Korea's trade strategy shifted. Imports from Western Europe and Japan shaped the trend. Between 1970 and 1974, the estimated current dollar value of Western imports was permitted to grow by a factor of thirteen;[41] in 1974, North Korea may have been importing substantially more from "capitalist" countries than from its communist partners.[42] North Korea's import binge—mainly turnkey factories, capital equipment, and grain—was mostly financed by foreign loans denominated in hard currencies. Repayments did not proceed on schedule. By 1976 North Korea was effectively in default on a large portion of its borrowing from Western countries.[43] North Korea's credit rating collapsed, imports from Western countries sharply contracted, and overall trade turnover fell by perhaps nearly a third between 1974 and 1976.[44] According to several estimates, North Korea's total trade turnover in the mid-1980s was about US$3 billion a year.[45] Even if some of these estimates overlooked certain items in the North Korean trade account (such as its unreported but perhaps sizable weapons sales to Iran and other countries),[46] it could well be that the country's trade turnover, valued in constant U.S. dollars, was lower than it had been a decade earlier.

North Korea's poor record of loan repayments, and the serious disruption that it provoked, hase been adduced to a variety of factors.[47] Among the issues about which analysts have speculated are exogenous shocks in the world economy that may have made repayments unexpectedly difficult, North Korea's lack of managerial capacity to put imported Western equipment to use, and its government's lack of familiarity with the workings of the financial and commercial markets in which it was operating. In all discussions of North Korea's trade problems, however, a basic question seems to have gone unasked: Was the new trade strategy that the government suddenly embraced in the early 1970s actually intended to be self-sustaining?

There is considerable, if indirect, evidence that North Korea was quietly embarking on an entirely new phase of militarization during the years that it was embracing this ultimately untenable trade regimen. Around 1970, when two leading specialists described North Korea as "perhaps the most highly militarized society in the world today,"[48] the country was thought to have about 400,000 men under arms.[49] By 1975, to judge by the number of "missing men" in the count of the civilian male population, North Korea's military may have exceeded 700,000 and by the late 1970s could have been approaching one million. (By this indicator, North Korea's military numbers apparently continued to increase during the 1980s, to 1.25 million or more by year-end 1987; in the late 1980s, then, North Korea's military personnel, by these figures, could have accounted for as much as a tenth of the country's total male population.)[50] By the mid-1970s, North Korea's active-duty military forces, according to these estimates, would have outnumbered South Korea's, which had remained stable at about 600,000 for nearly two decades. North Korean forces, it is widely thought, had last had a numerical advantage over the Republic of Korea's army on the eve of the Korean War.[51]

Even if North Korea's military forces were in some measure self-financing (that is, engaged in producing their own food, matériel, and other necessities), a buildup of this magnitude could only constitute an enormous expense for the state—and, as Kim had acknowledged, a diversion of resources from potentially productive purposes. The motivations and intentions guiding the North Korean leadership are often mysterious or obscure to outside observers. Understanding the reasoning behind this military buildup, however, would seem central to understanding the North Korean economy in the 1970s and 1980s.

In a variety of important ways, the situation in the early 1970s in the Korean peninsula was significantly different from that of the period preceding the Korean War. Even so, a number of strategic and tactical parallels can be drawn between the two time frames. Although such parallels do not establish that North Korea was preparing to unleash a surprise attack against South Korea, they seem consonant with that possibility. At the very least, it appears that North Korea had dramatically enhanced its capability to assure unification on its own terms if the opportunity arose.

Gambling on instability in South Korea in the 1970s, if this was an element of North Korean strategy, would not have been unreasonable (in 1979, the head of security assassinated President Park Chung-hee, fomenting a military coup and an uprising in a southern province). But U.S. security commitments to Seoul endured; South Korea's economy prospered, and the Republic of Korea did not collapse. The economic costs of North Korea's gamble, if that is what it was, became increasingly evident as the 1970s and 1980s progressed. Although the Six-Year Plan for 1971–76 was declared fulfilled one year and four months ahead of schedule, no new plan was announced in 1976 or in 1977 (a year later designated as a "buffer year"). A second Seven-Year Plan for 1978–84 ended on schedule, but results for a number of key targets (electric power, steel, nonferrous metals, and various chemicals among them) were not announced.[52] The second Seven-Year Plan was followed by two years of "adjustment." A third Seven-Year Plan, implemented in the years 1987–93, was concluded with a communiqué that acknowledged, for the first time in the regime's history, a failure to achieve major targeted goals and warned that the national economy was in a "grave situation."[53] Although these poor results were specifically and explicitly blamed on the collapse of the Soviet bloc (whose members had been the DPRK's principal trade partners and aid providers in the late 1980s), the North Korean economy had clearly been in trouble *before* the Eastern European "revolutions of 1989."

By the late 1980s, North Korea's political economy was enmeshed in a trap of its own making. To oversimplify, sources of extensive growth had already been assiduously exploited and avenues for intensive growth were by and large politically unacceptable to the regime. By any international standard, labor force participation rates in North Korea were extraordinarily high in the late 1980s: the officially reported working population was about 73 percent of the population of working age;[54] if military personnel were added to the total, it could have been as high as 83 percent.[55] (In South Korea, the reported labor force participation rate for persons fifteen and older was about 58 percent in 1988.)[56] Although exact figures are unavailable, it also seems that North Korea's ratio of consumption to national output is unusually—even extraordinarily—low. Thus, capital stocks and labor supplies could be augmented substantially only through military demobilization and conversion—an option the North Korean leadership has rejected completely.

Indeed, North Korea's leadership has apparently rejected the notion of experimenting with domestic economic liberalization, perhaps fearing the social and political consequences.[57] In a formal sense, the North Korean government did respond to the mounting pressures on its economy with declared "reforms." In the 1980s and early 1990s, for example, the DPRK promulgated a number of laws (including two joint venture laws) seemingly designed to attract foreign capital, technology, and managerial skills. These half-hearted efforts, however, essentially ignored such things as the concerns of the foreign investor—and consequently were by and large ignored by the international investment community.

In contrast to these tentative measures for economic "opening," in the early 1990s the North Korean government enacted stringent economic policies at home. In 1992, for example, the DPRK implemented a "current reform"—permitting authorities to confiscate household savings not properly accounted for and to identify individuals engaged in black- or gray-market activities. In 1992 Pyongyang also decreed a general increase in workers' wages—exacerbating the already considerable disequilibrium in the domestic consumer economy and increasing the importance of direct state provision of goods to the country's households. In the early 1990s laws on "labor discipline" were also apparently toughened, in keeping with official pronouncements that financial incentives for improved work performance would risk a general drift toward "egotism."

At this writing, it would appear that the primary objective of top policy makers in Pyongyang is, quite simply, the continued survival of their system and their regime (what official terminology describes as "our own style of socialism"). To that end, they have evidently been willing to foreswear potentially major improvements in total factor productivity and to accept economic decline as the necessary cost of the policies and practices that provide security for their polity. Outsiders can only guess how much resilience the current North Korean system maintains. Absent a major shift in policy direction, however, the prospects for a resumption of sustained material advance in the Democratic People's Republic of Korea would seem remote.

III

The Republic of Korea's performance since partition includes rapid and sustained economic growth, dramatic expansion of its foreign sector, and far-reaching structural and technical transformations. But a review of South

Korea's economic record since the 1945 partition needs to include three often-overlooked points. First, South Korea's rapid pace of economic advance was achieved not under a policy resembling laissez-faire but under one of active state interventions into economic life. Second, not only were South Korea's policies unashamedly dirigiste during the period of rapid economic acceleration in the 1960s and 1970s, but many of the government's decisions and practices should have undercut or retarded rapid economic growth. Third, due largely but not entirely to distortions imposed on it by policy decisions since 1960, the structure and performance of the Republic of Korea's economy is in some important ways quite different from those of Japan and Taiwan, with which it has been closely grouped or associated in contemporary economic analyses.

Between 1946 and 1960, South Korea's economy stagnated. In fact, some estimates of real "net commodity product" (i.e., value added in the agricultural and industrial sectors alone) for the territory that was to become South Korea suggest a slight decline in the aggregate between 1940 and 1960.[58] During those years, however, South Korea's population grew from about sixteen million to about twenty-five million; by those numbers, real per capita "net commodity product" might have fallen by as much as two-fifths. Even presuming a significant expansion in the service sector (say, from a hypothetical 25 percent of GDP in the colonial period to the 41 percent reported in national accounts for the years 1960–62),[59] South Korea's real level of aggregate output would have been only one-fourth higher in 1960 than in 1940, and per capita output would have been more than 20 percent lower.[60]

Full recovery and rapid development did not commence in the Republic of Korea until the accession of a series of military leaders. Between 1961 and early 1988 the country's two maximum leaders—Park Chung Hee (1961–79) and Chun Du Hwan (1979–88)—were generals in the ROK army who assumed power through their respective coups d'état.[61] The Park junta, in two of its first and most significant acts, established a broadly empowered Korean Central Intelligence Agency (KCIA) to deal with security questions at home and abroad and set up an Economic Planning Board (EPB) to devise and implement multiyear economic plans for hastening and shaping the country's development. If these and other new institutions did not look like instruments of an open, liberal society, they bore at least a passing resemblance to some of the organs of governance from the era of Japanese colonialism—which had, in fact, been the last period of sustained economic expansion in southern Korea.

Like the reintroduction to South Korean political life of various features from an earlier "hard state," the impact of foreign aid is a delicate but central issue in an evaluation of the country's material transformation. Between 1946 and 1961, exclusive of its Korean War help, the United States provided the Republic of Korea with $5 billion (in current dollars) of direct grants. For a country whose entire GNP for 1953 was reckoned at \$2 billion (current prices), this was a fantastic sum of money. In total, this aid roughly matched South Korea's imports from abroad over this fifteen-year period; it distinctly exceeded the country's total allocation for gross domestic investment.

The impact of aid depends in large measure on the intentions of the recipient government,[62] and the regime of Syngman Rhee (1948–60) used U.S. aid essentially as an ongoing program of external relief. Some analysts have even termed Rhee's policies as "aid maximizing":[63] designed to require large and continuing inflows from its U.S. ally to redress the precarious fiscal and financial conditions they engendered. Needless to say, such a strategy did not promote rapid economic growth in these years.

In the 1960s the advent of rapid economic growth in South Korea may have been directly related to U.S. foreign aid, albeit in a somewhat unexpected manner. By the late 1950s, the Eisenhower administration had become displeased by what it saw as the Korean government's unhealthy dependence on and unseemly interest in U.S. aid. With the military coup in 1961, the incoming Kennedy administration's displeasure with Seoul increased further. In late 1962, the Park regime was reportedly informed by Washington that an irreversible decision had been reached: while security assistance would continue, U.S. economic assistance would be terminated in an orderly but deliberate manner, to be phased out entirely in a few years.[64]

Radical adjustments in fiscal and economic policy were required to compensate for this impending loss of central government revenue.[65] Washington's announcement thus seems to have served as a stimulus for the Park regime's decision to embark on an export-oriented development strategy.

South Korea's export-oriented strategy worked. Between 1960 and 1990, the ROK's ratio of exports to GNP rose from about 4 to more than 40 percent. Over that same period, real gross domestic product is estimated to have multiplied by a factor of nine and real per capita GDP is estimated to have more than quintupled. The net national savings rate, which may have been as low as 1 percent in 1960, had reached 30 percent by the late 1980s. South Korea's gross savings rate was, by the late 1980s, finally higher than its rate of gross domestic investment; between 1986 and 1993, in fact, South Korea was, on net, an *exporter* of capital to the rest of the world.[66]

With this record in mind, it is well to remember what South Korean economic policy did *not* do to foster growth and development. It did not, to begin, establish any regular and impartial rule of law for Korean nationals or any regular and impartial system of commercial law or even any regular and impartial system of property rights for Korean citizens.

During the first two decades of rapid growth, moreover, South Korean policy did not attempt to secure the property rights of foreign commercial concerns in Korea in any regular and lawful fashion. (Only in the late 1980s, for example, did the ROK government begin to apply general protection against infringements of overseas copyrights, patents, and licenses within its domestic market.) Nor did government policy attempt to create an attractive "climate" for foreign direct investment. To the contrary—with the exception of a limited number of approved joint ventures in designated industries—the government's attitude toward direct private investment from abroad was almost unremittingly hostile. Virtually all foreign capital employed in the South Korean domestic economy in the 1960s, 1970s, and early 1980s was introduced through the agency of loans contracted abroad—the overwhelming majority of which, in turn, were either contracted to, or guaranteed by, the state.[67]

Government policy did not initially encourage the development of a private and competitive domestic financial market. In fact, a few months after the Park coup, the state nationalized the country's entire formal banking system. For the next two decades, state control over the allocation of credit extended to the point where government officials made the ultimate decision about virtually every major investment project in the country.[68]

The South Korean government did not attempt to eliminate or even reduce barriers to competition in the industrial and export sectors of the economy. Many government interventions, for example, actually attempted to preserve or increase barriers to entry in these areas, often through extralegal means.[69] Government policy also encouraged the concentration of economic power within the industrial and export sector through the general practice of subsidized credit from state banks and at times through specific interventions to restructure particular industries.[70] Largely as a result of government policies, the share of manufacturing output generated by the one hundred largest concerns in South Korea appears to have risen steadily between 1970 and 1982.[71] By the early 1980s, the share of total manufactured output produced by the nation's one hundred largest manufacturers was more than twice as high in South Korea as in Taiwan and almost twice as great as in Japan.[72]

Finally, far from welcoming the establishment of competitive market prices throughout the economy, the South Korean government continuously and actively intervened in the process of commercial price determination throughout the 1960s, 1970s, and 1980s. Although many of these interventions were "informal," the government also managed price controls over a wide range of goods.[73]

In short, during this phase of rapid economic growth, South Korean government policy was not only illiberal by any number of criteria but also seems to have violated some of the basic neoclassical precepts about allocative efficiency. Perhaps no less perplexing to students of the "science" of public policy, the climate of administration in South Korea during these years was clearly personalistic and ad hoc. How was it possible to have "takeoff" under these circumstances?

Such questions can never be answered with complete certainty or to full satisfaction. The importance of the decision to embrace an export orientation, however, might be hard to exaggerate. By its very nature, export orientation seems to have imposed a comprehensive, and dynamic, discipline over the South Korean economy. For exportable goods to be competitive in world markets, for example, the exchange rate for the won could no longer be perennially overvalued.[74] To maintain a realistic foreign exchange rate, in turn, necessitated budget discipline[75]—a quality notably lacking during the Rhee years. Realistic exchange rates and budget discipline generated pressures of their own. Among them was pressure for a more realistic pricing of the society's scarce capital; thus, despite the government's discriminatory approach to credit, interest rates were raised for all borrowers in 1965 with a "reform" that, for a time, brought real interest rates above zero for most borrowers and lenders.[76] In addition to such macroeconomic adjustments, export orientation had the incalculable, but surely important, consequence of forcing South Korean administrators and entrepreneurs to cope with and learn from the world economy in which Korean exports were now to compete. Theodore W. Schultz has written of the "value of the ability to deal with disequilibria";[77] to a considerable degree, this skill may have been forced on South Korean society as a whole by export orientation.

In the hands of a "hard state," export orientation may thus have proved to be an extremely productive strategy. If South Korea's strategy was not optimal from the standpoint of neoclassical welfare economics, it was evidently a good "second best." Like Isiah Berlin's "hedgehogs," South Korea's military rulers may have known "one big thing"[78] when they embarked upon export promotion—but it was apparently big enough to make up for a multiplicity of smaller economic errors and mistakes.

And errors there were. If South Korean dirigisme seemed to be justified by some of its achievements in the industrial sector, there was no similar justification for its agricultural policies. In the early 1960s, South Korea's population was almost three-fourths rural. Under those circumstances, agricultural and rural development might have been deemed significant, if only for their impact on overall development prospects. (Even if one focused principally on industrial expansion, agricultural development might seem necessary, insofar as enhanced agricultural productivity would release labor for nonfarm employment and stimulate demand for industrial produce through the augmentation of rural purchasing power.) South Korean officials, however, accorded agriculture conspicuously low priority in their first Five-Year Plan (1962–66). Although the government did evidence an interest in agricultural extension and new high-yield strains of rice, it placed no emphasis on agricultural investment and spent little on upgrading roads or other aspects of the country's rural "infrastructure."[79] It also enforced an agricultural pricing policy that kept terms of trade with industry and the cities artificially low. In four out of the five years of the first Five-Year Plan, for example, rice producers were paid below-world-market prices.[80] Although estimates of the effective rate of protection for various domestic goods are not available for those same years, one study for 1968 put the effective rate of protection for the consumer durables in the domestic market at almost 40 percent.[81]

Discontent with the government's approach was widespread in rural areas, and in 1971 President Park narrowly won an election in which his campaign advantages were overwhelming. Thereafter, South Korean agricultural policy shifted toward a different extreme: subsidies and price supports were rapidly established and raised, and domestic agriculture was accorded broad protection from imports.[82] By 1979, producer prices for barley were almost two and a half times world market prices; producer prices for rice were at almost three and a half times the world market level.[83] They rose still further thereafter, until by 1988 wholesale prices for rice were more than five times those offered in world markets.[84]

The new approach to agriculture was, in essence, an incomes policy. Although still a developing country, South Korea had adopted some of the most expensive and economically questionable features of more affluent societies' farm policies.

The economic consequences of these agricultural strategies were both predictable and adverse. During the initial phase of export-led industrialization, South Korean rural policies contributed to a widening of incomes between households in cities and those in the countryside, although these differences were partly disguised in official statistics by a procedure that treated farm assets as income.[85] With dualism induced, migration to urban areas (especially Seoul) was correspondingly more rapid, and underemployment in the "informal sector" characterized a correspondingly greater portion of the country's workforce. In the 1970s, by contrast, the combination of price supports for agriculture and neglect of the rural infrastructure tended to raise production costs by limiting the release of farmworkers into the nonagricultural economy and by artificially increasing the cost of food (still the dominant component in the household budget of urban workers).

With agricultural incomes depressed by government pricing policies in the 1960s, and investments in improvements of rural productivity largely neglected in the 1970s and 1980s, the growth of rural output remained slow. Between 1970 and 1987, according to United Nations' national accounts summaries, the output of South Korea's agriculture, forestry, and fisheries sector increased by about 3.4 percent a year, or about 1.9 percent a person, if current prices were adjusted by the implicit GDP deflator.[86] At 1980 constant prices, however, growth of agricultural output averaged only 2.6 percent a year, or about 1.1 percent a person a year.[87] At a time when per capita growth in GDP for the economy as a whole was averaging more than 7 percent a year, the contrast was notable. Over a comparable seventeen-year period in Japan (1952–69), per capita output rose at an annual rate of about 8 percent but per capita agricultural output rose by about 2 percent a year in constant 1965 prices—nearly twice as fast as in South Korea.[88]

Despite the shift in relative prices during the period in question, farm incomes remained unexpectedly low—limiting not only the size of South Korea's domestic market but also its pool of domestic savings for investment. (Although the story of "Why Koreans saved so little" is complex and extends far beyond agricultural policy, agricultural policy may nevertheless have played its part.) High support prices and subsidies in the 1970s and 1980s also served as a drain on the government budget and a stimulus to higher price levels in urban areas— and thus as an impetus for further countervailing deflationary policies and controls. They distorted the rural land market and contributed to distortions in the urban real estate market. The emphasis on support for cereals, moreover, slowed the shift in output mix toward the higher value-added crops and foods that ordinarily figure prominently in the diet of prosperous populations.[89]

South Korea's development is often likened to Taiwan's, but this is misleading. As Harry Oshima has observed, "Korea ended up [in the 1980s] with much larger foreign debts, price rises, devaluations, smaller international reserves, and higher income disparities than did Taiwan. . . . The neglect of agriculture is a major reason that in the early 1980s [South] Korea was struggling with a heavy debt burden, excess capacity in heavy industries, and continuing social unrest."[90]

Industrial as well as agricultural policies wrought uneconomic distortion in the South Korean economy during this phase of rapid growth. Unlike its farm policies, these industrial initiatives were justified by national security concerns. With the announcement of the "Nixon doctrine" and America's subsequent disengagement from Vietnam, notice had been served that the burden of defense in any future emergency or war could fall largely on Seoul's shoulders. To sustain itself against an attack from the north, or to prevail in a conflict with the DPRK, it seemed that South Korea would now have to build its own defense industry. The ROK's third Five-Year Plan (1972–76) placed a new emphasis on developing the chemical and heavy machinery sectors—the basic military industries.[91] Between 1970 and 1975, the share of heavy industry in South Korea's economy grew by 50 percent (see table 7.5). The emphasis on heavy industry continued through the 1970s and on after President Park's assassination. Between 1970 and 1985, the structural growth of the manufacturing share in South Korea's economy was entirely a result of heavy and chemical industries; the share of light, so-called consumer industries in the South Korean economy actually *declined* slightly during this period. Remarkable though it may be, light manufacturing accounted for the same share of South Korean GDP in 1985 as it had in 1965, despite an increase in per capita output of more than 250 percent in the intervening years. Once again, comparison with Japan is instructive. By 1983, per capita output in Korea was roughly at the same level as that attained in Japan around 1965. Whereas only about 35 percent of Japan's manufacturing output in 1965

Table 7.5   Structure of Production in South Korea, 1955–1985, in GDP,
             at Current Prices (in percent)

		SECTOR		
Year	Agriculture	Industry	Heavy and Chemical Industries	Services and Social Overhead Capital
1955	44.5	12.6	2.5	42.9
1960	36.8	15.9	3.2	47.3
1965	38.0	20.0	5.7	42.0
1970	26.9	22.4	7.9	50.7
1975	24.5	27.6	11.9	47.9
1980	14.6	30.9	14.9	54.5
1985	13.5	29.6	15.3	56.9
1990	9.1	29.2	19.2	61.7

SOURCES: Derived from Republic of Korea, Bank of Korea, *National Accounts 1987* (Seoul: Bank of Korea 1988), table 1; and idem, *National Accounts, 1994* (Seoul: Bank of Korea, 1994), p. 35.

was generated in the heavy and chemical industries, these accounted for more than half of manufacturing output in South Korea in 1983.[92]

Metallurgy, heavy machinery, and chemical industries are intrinsically capital intensive. Despite the government's effort to subject the heavy-chemical industry drive to economic discipline (in large measure, by gearing these new enterprises to export a significant portion of their output and thus to face international competition), the thrust required a rapid and abrupt "capital deepening" for the economy as a whole. Between 1965 and 1970, South Korea's incremental capital-output ratio (ICOR), for example, was about 2.0; in 1975–80, it was about 4.8—almost two and a half times as high.[93] Even if high rates of return on capital could be consistently achieved, the decision to make heavy industry the leading growth sector in a low-income (and thus capital-scarce) society would seem to presage a far-reaching misallocation of resources (by the criterion of economic efficiency, if not national security). As it happened, consistently high rates of return to capital could not be maintained in these industries;[94] in the early 1980s, government-directed "restructuring" essentially wrote off excess capacity in South Korea's shipbuilding and petrochemical sectors, among others.[95]

A final distortion worth mentioning concerns South Korea's financial sector. Through the 1960s, 1970s, and early 1980s, South Korea's domestic savings rate was markedly lower than those of other rapidly growing export-oriented economies in East Asia.[96] Some government credit policies seem to explain the paradox of relatively high rates of investment and relatively low rates of savings.[97] When broken down, South Korea's low rate of domestic savings has been found to be due to low rates of household savings; government and business savings rates

compare with, or exceed, those of other rapidly growing export-oriented economies. Segmentation and discrimination within South Korea's domestic financial
markets exposed private households to a relatively unfavorable environment for
accumulating savings. To encourage and subsidize preferred industries, the government attempted to keep its cost of borrowing in domestic markets low, which
meant that real interest rates on time deposits in the formal banking sector were
negative for twelve out of the twenty years between 1962 and 1982 (see table 7.6).
From 1972 through 1980—during the drive to build heavy and chemical industries—real interest rates on time deposits in these institutions were consistently
below zero. Private households were not obligated to deposit their savings in
government-owned banks; an informal, or "curb," sector also existed in which
nominal interest rates were consistently higher than those offered by the government. The curb market, however, was widely perceived as risky—not least because of the risk of episodic government interventions or even de facto confiscations.[98] The disincentives for household savings have consequences for the rest
of the economy, the most obvious of which is the gap between domestic savings
and planned investment, which the government chose to fill through borrowings
from abroad.

Induced distortions in agriculture, heavy industry, and the domestic capital
markets affected not only the structure of output in the South Korean economy
but its patterns of productivity growth. Generally speaking, these distortions can
be seen as tending to increase the ratio of intermediate consumption to gross
output within the production process. By doing so, they correspondingly reduced
the contribution of total factor productivity to overall growth.

Although South Korea's pace of aggregate growth between 1960 and 1985
was similar to those of Japan and Taiwan during their phases of rapid growth, its
components were different. One exercise in growth accounting, for example, has
estimated that the contribution to growth from improvements in total factor
productivity was twice as great in Taiwan as in South Korea in the period from
the early 1950s to 1980 (4.7 percent a year versus 2.3 percent a year).[99] Another
study concluded that more than half the growth in South Korea's national income between 1963 and 1982 could be explained by the augmentation of factor
inputs;[100] by contrast, almost three-fifths of Japan's growth between 1953 and
1971 (a comparable period) would be attributed to the "residual" associated with
improvements in total factor productivity[101] (see table 7.7). Although South Korea's export-oriented policy was capable of generating rates of growth comparable
to Taiwan's and Japan's, the achievement, at least during its first decades, seems
to have derived in large part from success in mobilizing factor inputs. That
distinction may help explain the South Korean government's continuing interest,
in the 1980s and early 1990s, in the liberalization (or, as it is currently termed in
Seoul, the "globalization") of the country's economy. That transition, however,
is still in progress and by a number of criteria still seems to have far to go.

Table 7.6   Real Time-Deposit Interest Rates and Estimated Household
             Savings Ratios: South Korea, 1955–1985 (in percent)

	Real Interest Rate	Household Savings Ratio
1955	−30.9	3.7
1956	−16.4	1.0
1957	−8.4	1.3
1958	13.5	2.4
1959	12.0	2.3
1960	−1.5	−2.7
1961	−1.8	−1.6
1962	−3.4	1.7
1963	−14.3	−0.2
1964	−15.0	0.5
1965	20.2	0.4
1966	11.9	4.2
1967	10.8	3.4
1968	9.1	5.5
1969	8.0	6.2
1970	7.2	3.6
1971	11.6	2.2
1972	−7.2	3.4
1973	−1.2	11.5
1974	−14.6	8.5
1975	−9.7	3.2
1976	−1.5	7.9
1977	−1.9	11.1
1978	−2.0	14.8
1979	−0.7	12.6
1980	−6.3	9.8
1981	0.0	5.1
1982	0.3	14.5
1983	5.1	14.9
1984	6.2	16.3
1985	5.9	18.4

NOTES: *Real interest rate* is defined as a one-year time deposit rate deflated by an implicit GDP deflator. *Household savings ratio* is defined as the ratio of household savings (minus changes in grain inventories) to disposable income. For 1982 to 1985, owing to changes in national accounts procedures, household savings are adjusted by changes in individual stocks rather than grain inventories.

SOURCES: Derived from Bank of Korea, *National Income in Korea, 1982* (Seoul: Bank of Korea, 1982), pp. 202–5, 234, 237; idem, *Economic Statistics Yearbook, 1988* (Seoul: Bank of Korea, 1988), pp. 259–75; Byung-nok Sang, *The Rise of the Korean Economy* (Hong Kong: Oxford University Press, 1990), p. 163.

Table 7.7   Estimated Sources of Growth of National Income for the
               Republic of Korea, Japan, and United States (in percent a year)

	Republic of Korea 1963–82		Japan 1953–71		United States 1948–72	
National income	7.61		8.77		3.65	
Irregular factors	−0.52		−0.04		−0.14	
Standardized national income	8.13	(100%)	8.81	(100%)	3.79	(100%)
Growth of labor force	2.92	(36%)	1.51	(17%)	1.01	(27%)
Growth of capital	1.58	(19%)	2.10	(24%)	0.71	(19%)
Residual	3.63	(45%)	5.20	(59%)	2.07	(55%)
Economies of scale	1.49		1.94		0.32	
Increased education per worker	0.39		0.34		0.41	
Advances in knowledge and miscellaneous determinants	1.09		1.97		1.00	
Minus labor misallocated to agriculture and nonagricultural self-employment	0.66		0.94		0.29	

NOTE: Figures may not add due to rounding.
SOURCE: Kim Kwang-suk and Park Joon-kyung, *Sources of Economic Growth in Korea, 1963–1982* (Seoul: Korea Development Institute, 1985), p. 169.

IV

The central economic and political fact about the performance of the two Korean regimes seems to be that output per person was higher in the north before partition, and apparently for some decades thereafter, and that it was likely higher in the south by the late 1980s—in other words, even before the general crisis of world communism. It is, however, one thing to recognize this fact and quite another to assign it a meaning.

Does one take it as a general reading on the performance of communist and noncommunist systems? If so, only at peril to the facts of the case. Between the early 1960s and the late 1980s, South Korea's measured pace of economic growth was rapid by almost any standard. North Korea's pace of growth, however, appears to have been rapid as well for much of the period since partition, during which time the country may cumulatively have evinced a considerable increase in per capita output (however that may best be measured for centrally planned socialist economies).

It is sometimes said that the modern Korean experience illustrates the superior potentialities of a liberal political order. But for more than a decade after the Korean War, communist North Korea was outpacing South Korea. Moreover, rapid economic growth in the south did not commence until its political order underwent a distinctly illiberal overhaul, following the 1961 coup. By comparison with North Korea, however, South Korea's political and economic arrangements have been extremely open. But as much could perhaps be said of Poland and North Korea—or of Cuba and North Korea. North Korea is an "outlier" on the contemporary political spectrum, and it is easy to fall into errors of ecological composition in comparisons with outliers.[102]

Both North and South Korea achieved their economic results while straying far from the desiderata of a classically liberal order. Both governments embraced a strongly statist approach to economic development in their periods of rapid growth. Whether this is a predictable, or even necessary, characteristic of "late industrialization," as some have concluded, need not detain us here. South Korea's state interventions into economic life have been far more selective than those in North Korea—and, from today's vantage point, look to have been far more effective. If socialist economic planning betrays "the fatal conceit" (in Hayek's words),[103] that given individuals possessed with political power can successfully improve upon, or replace, the complex workings of the market mechanism, South Korea's approach to planning seems to have been tinged by at least some of that hubris. More recently, however, South Korea's performance would not be seen as having suffered obviously for the transgression.

Regimes opting for dirigisme and its various compulsions can often mobilize resources for economic development but seem to be less adept at utilizing those resources efficiently. In both Koreas, economic growth since partition, to some considerable degree, has been driven by the mobilization of inputs: labor and capital. To date, the role of total factor productivity improvements in South Korea's growth, while hardly negligible, has nonetheless been smaller than in other trade-led developing countries, like Taiwan. When factors of production are fully mobilized, and economic processes become more complex, the costs of Hayek's fatal conceit may become more evident. Since the early 1980s, South Korea has taken important steps toward a more liberal political order and some notable steps toward a more liberal economic order. No indications of any parallel movement have emanated from North Korea as yet.

Notes

1. In fact, according to a recent OECD study, "[by its 1996 admission date South] Korea's per capita income will probably be about twice that of Turkey and about the same as in Greece and Portugal." Organization for Economic Cooperation and Development, *OECD Economic Surveys: Korea* (Paris: OECD, 1994), p. 9.

2. Some of these questions are addressed at greater length in Nick Eberstadt, *The Poverty of Communism* (New Brunswick, N.J.: Transaction Books, 1988), chap. 11, esp. pp. 255–63, and Eberstadt, "The CIA's Assessment of the Soviet Economy: Questions, Problems, Implications," in Nicholas Eberstadt, *The Tyranny of Numbers* (Washington, D.C.: AEI Press, 1995), chap. 6.

3. South Korean statistics have long reported on the volume of physical output for a variety of goods, and there seems little reason to question the reliability of these particular figures. The CIA, for its part, has published its own estimates on the volume of physical output in North Korea for a variety of commodities and goods. These estimates are informed not only by North Korea's episodic release of statistical tidbits on agricultural and industrial performance but by the U.S. government's considerable capacities for gathering information by "technical means." One may note that industrial capacity can be assessed, within limits, by aerial and satellite surveillance and that heavy industry is intrinsically more easy to identify through such methods than production in agriculture and small enterprises and is pertinent to any assessment of a country's military capacities. For these reasons, we may be confident in the CIA's estimates of production in North Korea's heavy industries. We should also remember, however, that by comparing only physical output in agriculture and heavy industry, as we do in table 7.4, we are choosing terms that tend to favor a centrally planned command economy over a more market-oriented economy. Physical indexes, after all, take no account of quality differentials and necessarily ignore activity in the service sector.

4. The literature on this issue is extensive. For some early treatments of the question in the Soviet context, see Alexander Gerschenkron, *Economic Backwardness in Historical Perspective* (Stanford: Stanford University Press, 1951), esp. chap. 6; Gregory Grossman, *Soviet Statistics of Physical Output of Industrial Commodities: Their Compilation and Quality* (Princeton, N.J.: Princeton University Press, 1960); and G. Warren Nutter, *Growth of Industrial Production in the Soviet Union* (Princeton, N.J.: Princeton University Press, 1962). The classic effort to estimate Soviet national income is Abram Bergson, *The Real National Income of Soviet Russia since 1928* (Cambridge, Mass: Harvard University Press, 1961).

5. For more detail, see Nicholas Eberstadt and Judith Banister, *The Population of North Korea* (Berkeley, Calif.: Institute of East Asian Studies, 1992), pp. 8–12.

6. Ibid. On the general question of data reliability under socialist command planning, see Jan Winiecki, "Are Soviet-Type Economies Entering an Era of Long Term Decline?" *Soviet Studies* 38, no. 3 (1986).

7. Needless to say, these figures must be handled with care. South Korean data on the country's economically active population have long been treated with a certain measure

of caution by informed users. The North Korean data, for their part, are unusual in a number of respects. For one thing, North Korea's most recent data give a breakdown of sectoral distribution by household, rather than by worker. For another, the most recent North Korean data explicitly exclude the country's huge military sector.

8. For a now-classic exposition on this topic, see Simon Kuznets, *Modern Economic Growth: Rate, Structure, and Spread* (New Haven, Conn.: Yale University Press, 1966), chap. 3. For a more recent examination, see Hollis B. Chenery, Sherman Robinson, and Moshe Syrquin, *Industrialization and Growth* (New York: Oxford University Press, 1986).

9. Urbanization is apparently measured differently in North and South Korea today. In the era of Japanese colonialism, towns or cities of twenty thousand persons or more were defined as urban areas. In the Republic of Korea, urban areas are defined as towns or cities with a population of fifty thousand or more. North Korea has never volunteered a published explanation of what constitutes an "urban area" in the DPRK. Private conversations with statistical authorities from the DPRK, however, suggest that (1) there is no absolutely fixed definition for urban areas in the DPRK today; (2) the approach to defining urban population may have changed since the founding of the state in 1948 and perhaps more than once; and (3) in general, an area can be counted as urban at a lower population threshold today in the north than in the south. Comparisons of urbanization in North and South Korea, therefore, are less straightforward than might be supposed.

10. This datum was transmitted to the author in a meeting with authorities from the DPRK's Central Statistics Bureau, 25 May 1990.

11. Kim Il Sung, *New Year's Address January 1, 1980* (Pyongyang: Foreign Languages Publishing House, 1980), p. 5.

12. Korea Overseas Information Service, *Korea Update*, I, 8, p. 3.

13. For example, author's interview with former Deputy Prime Minister Nam Duk-woo, 18 September 1984.

14. Not all analysts, however, concur with the U.N.'s estimates for crop production in North Korea during these years. See, for example, Robert A. Scalapino and Chong-sik Lee, *Communism in Korea*, vol. 2 (Berkeley: University of California Press, 1972), pp. 1088–93. Official figures report a drop in grain production in 1959 from 3.7 to 3.4 million tons; ibid., p. 1089.

15. For more detail, see ibid., pp. 539–43, 1114, 1219–22.

16. According to estimates by the World Bank, for example, real gross domestic product in the People's Republic of China rose by an average of 10.3 percent a year between 1980 and 1988, whereas population grew at a rate of 1.3 percent a year; if these figures were accurate, per capita GDP would have more than doubled during those years alone. Data from World Bank, *World Development Report* 1990 (New York: Oxford University Press, 1990), pp. 180, 228.

17. Some attempts have been made to outline North Korean economic management policies. See especially Scalapino and Lee, *Communism in Korea*, chaps. 13 and 14; Joseph Sang-hoon Chung, *The North Korean Economy* (Stanford: Hoover Institution Press, 1974), pp. 32–46, 62–75; and Frederica M. Bunge, ed., *North Korea: A Country Study* (Washington, D.C.: U.S. Government Printing Office, 1981), pp. 129–35, 139–46.

In recent years, owing to a lack of concrete information, there has been little updating of these earlier overviews.

18. Bunge, *North Korea*, p. 131.

19. Ibid., p. 146.

20. Suh Sang-chul, *Growth and Structural Change in the Korean Economy, 1910–1940* (Cambridge, Mass.: Harvard University Press, 1978), pp. 132, 137; estimates of "commodity-product" are for 1939–40 (1936 prices), and population figures are for 1940.

21. If, for example, the service sector had accounted for 40 percent of gross domestic product in the south, but only 20 percent in the north, per capita output in the north would have been about 27 percent higher than in the south. If the portions had been 35 and 25 percent, respectively, per capita output in the north would have been about 48 percent higher than in the south.

22. Derived from Suh, *Growth and Stuctural Change*, pp. 132, 137.

23. Ibid., pp. 136–42, 200. See also Chung, *North Korean Economy*, pp. 57–59.

24. Chung, *North Korean Economy*, pp. 48, 86.

25. Ibid. pp. 48–49, 86–87, 146–47; and Suh, *Growth and Structural Change*, p.132. Even so, per capita production of a number of important commodities was still lower in 1956 than it had been in 1944: among them, electric power, coal, graphite, sulfuric acid, chemical fertilizers, cement, and marine products. The figures for the mid-1950s, moreover, may be affected by a certain overreporting of results. See, for example, Scalapino and Lee, *Communism in Korea*, p. 1090, esp. n. 107.

26. Chung (*North Korean Economy*, p. 96) notes, however, that 1960 was officially described as a "buffer year" and infers that the Chollima campaign had exacerbated or induced serious imbalances in the North Korean economy.

27. Ibid., pp. 41–45, 81.

28. Eberstadt and Banister, *Population of North Korea*, p. 34.

29. The horse figures in the classical Chinese novel *Tales from the Three Kingdoms*. Chung, *North Korean Economy*, p. 96.

30. Ibid. pp. 116–24; Suh Dae-sook, *Kim Il Sung: The North Korean Leader* (New York: Columbia University Press, 1988), pp. 182–85. Economic aid from the socialist camp, by one estimate, accounted for more than a quarter of North Korean state revenues for the Five-Year Plan period and was equal to four-fifths of the state's total budget for basic investment and construction. No less significant may have been the indirect impact of security assistance. From 1953 to 1958, for example, the PRC allowed the forces of a "People's Volunteer Army" to serve in North Korea; as late as 1958, as many as 80,000 personnel may have been involved in the operation.

31. Suh Dae-sook (*Kim Il Sung*, p. 180) dates the military buildup back to 1962 and views it as a reaction to the Cuban missile crisis.

32. Kim Il Sung, "Report to the Fifth Congress of the Workers Party of Korea on the Work of the Central Committee, November 2, 1970," in his *Selected Works*, vol. 5 (Pyongyang: Foreign Languages Publishing House, 1972), p. 431.

33. Bunge, *North Korea*, pp. 240–41.

34. Ibid.

35. Kim Il Sung, "Report to the Fifth Congress," p. 432.

36. This interpretation, and the evidence supporting it, is presented at greater length in Eberstadt, *Korea Approaches Reunification*, pp. 18–20.

37. For an overview, see Chung, *North Korean Economy*, chap. 4.

38. Total exports, in current dollars, amounted to a reported $248 million for South Korea in 1966. Anne O. Krueger, *The Developmental Role of the Foreign Sector and Aid* (Cambridge, Mass.: Harvard University Press, 1979), p. 133. Chung (*North Korean Economy*, p. 105) estimates North Korean exports at $244 billion in 1966. At the time, North Korea's population was probably less than half as large as South Korea's.

39. Chung, *North Korean Economy*, pp. 107, 147, at the official exchange rate of $1 = 2.57 won; "national income" refers to the Soviet conception of "net material product" rather than to its meaning in conventional national accounts. Of course, the comparison must be treated with caution.

40. Some rough calculations can illustrate the comparison. On the basis of Chung's dollar estimate of North Korean exports for 1965 and the CIA's 1980 dollar estimate of 1965 GNP for North Korean GNP, deflated back to 1965 U.S. dollars, one arrives at a ratio of exports to estimated GNP of about 8 percent. Chung, *North Korean Economy*, p. 105; CIA, *Handbook of Economic Statistics, 1980* (Washington, D.C.: NTIS, 1980), pp. 24–25. By similar procedures, one arrives at a ratio for 1965 of less than 3 percent for the USSR, less than 3 percent for China, and about 4 percent for "communist countries" as a group. CIA, *Handbook 1980*, pp. 24–25, 88, 90, 93. Such measures, of course, must be treated with caution because of the differences in domestic and international resource costs for a socialist planned economy. For an exercise attempting to measure Soviet trade exposure in domestic resource costs, see Vladimir G. Treml and Barry L. Kostinsky, *Domestic Value of Soviet Foreign Trade: Exports and Imports in the 1972 Input-Output Table* (Washington, D.C.: U.S. Census Bureau, Center for International Research, 1982).

41. Bunge, *North Korea*, p. 255; Youn-soo Kim, *The Economy of the Korean Democratic People's Republic* (Kiel, Germany: German-Korea Studies Group, 1979), pp. 125, 129; growth is in current dollars.

42. Kim, *Economy of the Korean Democratic People's Republic*, p. 122; the estimate includes noncommunist, less-developed countries.

43. See Bunge, *North Korea*, pp. 154–55; Hiroko Kawai, "North Korean 'Open Policies' and Trade with Japan—the Effects and Functions of Japan-DPRK Trade," in Masao Okonogi, ed., *North Korea at the Crossroads* (Tokyo: JCIIR, 1988); and Kim, *Economy of the Korean Democratic People's Republic*, pp. 130–33.

44. Youn-Soo Kim estimates the decline, in current dollars, to have been about 46 percent; by contrast, the U.S. government places the drop at about 23 percent between 1974 and 1976. The CIA estimates a contraction of more than 22 percent, in current dollars, between 1975 and 1976 alone. CIA, *Economic Race*, p. 10.

45. ROK National Unification Board, *Economies of North and South* (Seoul: NUB, 1988), p. 77; Takashi Uehara, "The North Korean Economy," *JETRO China Newsletter*, no. 65 (1986).

46. Mentioned, for example, in Bunge, *North Korea*, p. 157.

47. For one review of these factors, see Joseph S. Chung, "Foreign Trade of North Korea: Performance, Policy and Prospects," in Robert A. Scalapino and Hongkoo Lee, eds., *North Korea in a Regional and Global Context* (Berkeley: University of California, Institute of East Asian Studies, 1986).

48. Scalapino and Lee, *Communism in Korea*, p. 919.

49. Institute for Strategic Studies (ISS), *The Military Balance, 1970–71* (London: ISS, 1971), p. 64; the precise figure given was 413,000.

50. For more details on these estimates, see Eberstadt, *Korea Approaches Reunification*, chap. 2, appendix D.

51. From the end of the Korean War onward, the Republic of Korea Armed Forces (ROKA) has generally had between 600,000 and 650,000 men under arms. Estimates of force size for given years in the 1960s and 1970s can be found in various editions of ISS, *Military Balance*.

52. For more details, see Teruo Komaki, "Current Status and Prospects of the North Korean Economy," in Okonogi, *North Korea at the Crossroads*.

53. For translation of the complete text, see "Communique Issues on Plenum," Foreign Broadcast Information Service (FBIS), *Daily Report: East Asia*, EAS-93-235, 9 December 1993, pp. 12–19.

54. Derived from Eberstadt and Banister, *Population of North Korea*, p. 84; "working age population" is defined here as all men and women aged sixteen to sixty-four, inclusive. Data are for 1986–87.

55. Ibid., pp. 142, 144, 149.

56. Derived from ROK, *Korea Statistical Yearbook 1989*, pp. 76–77.

57. For an elaboration, see Nicholas Eberstadt, "North Korea: Reform, Muddling Through, or Collapse?" *NBR Analysis Series* 4, no. 3 (1993).

58. Derived from Kwang-suk Kim and Michael Roemer, *Growth and Structural Transformation* (Cambridge, Mass.: Harvard University Press, 1979), p. 35; and Edward S. Mason, *The Economic and Social Modernization of the Republic of Korea* (Cambridge, Mass.: Harvard University Press, 1980), pp. 98, 100; the decline is estimated at 2 percent for the period as a whole.

59. Mason, *Economic and Social Modernization of the Republic of Korea*, p. 100.

60. Japanese colonial policy, of course, attempted to suppress the share of output in the Korean economy allocated to local consumption, whereas consumption is estimated to have accounted for more than 90 percent of South Korean output in the early 1960s. Even so, by these numbers it is hard to see how per capita consumption—at least, on average—could have been much higher in South Korea in 1960 than it had been in 1940. The *distribution* of consumption may well have been more even in the postcolonial period, as Mason, *Economic and Social Modernization of the Republic of Korea*, concludes. If so, the median level of per capita consumption in South Korea might have risen between 1940 and 1960. Within the limits of available data, however, there is little reason to believe that *mean* per capita consumption rose during this period.

61. The subsequent president, Roh Tae Woo (1988–93), was elected through a mass

plebescite in 1987; earlier, however, General Roh had participated in the coup that brought President Chun into command.

62. For further discussion of this issue, see Nicholas Eberstadt, *Foreign Aid and American Purpose* (Washington, D.C.: American Enterprise Institute, 1989), chap. 4.

63. David C. Cole and Princeton N. Lyman, *Korean Development: The Interplay of Politics and Economics* (Cambridge, Mass.: Harvard University Press, 1971), pp. 170–72.

64. See, for example, the *New York Times*, 4 April 1963, p. 1. Remarkably, this incident in U.S.-Korean relations seems not to be discussed directly in any of the published accounts on modern South Korean development.

65. In 1960, government expenditures equaled roughly 18 percent of South Korea's estimated GNP; U.S. economic assistance alone equaled an estimated 8.6 percent for that same year. Mason, *Economic and Social Modernization of the Republic of Korea*, pp. 207, 307.

66. Estimates derived from Republic of Korea, Bank of Korea, *National Income 1988* (Seoul: Bank of Korea, 1989), and idem, *National Accounts, 1994* (Seoul: Bank of Korea, 1994).

67. For more detail, see David C. Cole and Yung Chul Park, *Financial Development in Korea, 1945–1978* (Cambridge, Mass.: Harvard University Press, 1983), pp. 60–61; and Alice H. Amsden, *Asia's Next Giant: South Korea and Late Industrialization* (New York: Oxford University Press, 1989), chap. 4.

68. Amsden, *Asia's Next Giant*, chap. 6; Mason, *Economic and Social Modernization of the Republic of Korea*, chap. 8.

69. Leroy P. Jones and Il Sakong, *Government, Business, and Entrepreneurship in Economic Development: The Korean Case* (Cambridge, Mass.: Harvard University Press, 1980), chap. 4.

70. Amsden, *Asia's Next Giant*, p. 15, provides a number of examples. See also World Bank, *Korea: Managing the Industrial Transition*, vol. 1, p. 50; after describing a number of these major interventions (some as recent as 1983), the report comments that "it is clear from these cases that Government has bypassed competitive solutions in most of its restructuring operations."

71. Ibid., vol. 2, p. 31.

72. Ibid.

73. Amsden, *Asia's Next Giant*, p. 17.

74. For a more detailed treatment, see Bela Balassa, "The Lessons of East Asian Development: An Overview," *Economic Development and Cultural Change* 36 (supplement, 1988).

75. Ibid., and Bela Balassa, "Outward Orientation," in Hollis B. Chenery and T. N. Srinivasan, eds., *Handbook of Developmental Economics*, vol. 2 (Amsterdam: North Holland, 1989).

76. For more details, see Cole and Park, *Financial Development in Korea*, pp. 64–65, 198–211.

77. Theodore W. Schultz, "The Value of the Ability to Deal with Disequilibria," *Journal of Economic Literature* 13, no. 3 (1975).

78. Isiah Berlin, *The Hedgehog and the Fox: An Essay on Tolstoy's View of History* (New York: Simon & Schuster, 1986). One may recall that Sir Isiah's sympathies were with the fox, "who knows many things."

79. One indication of the relative neglect of rural infrastructure may be seen in South Korea's statistics on paved roads. According to Ministry of Construction figures, paved roads as a fraction of total road mileage were 14.9 percent in 1963; by 1969, they had risen to only 17.6 percent. Sung-Hwan Ban, Pal-Yong Moon, and Dwight H. Perkins, *Rural Development* (Cambridge, Mass.: Harvard University Press, 1980), p. 149.

80. Dong-Hi Kim and Yong-Jae Joo, *The Food Situation and Policies in the Republic of Korea* (Paris: Organization for Economic Cooperation and Development, 1982), p. 65.

81. Larry E. Westphal and Kwang Suk Kim, "Industrial Policy and Development in Korea," World Bank Staff Working Paper no. 263 (1977), cited in Krueger, *Foreign Sector and Aid*, p. 184.

82. Kim and Joo, in *The Food Situation*, p. 32, trace the shift back as far as 1968; extremely high nominal rates of protection, however, did not occur until 1971.

83. Ibid., p. 65.

84. Derived from ROK, *Korea Statistical Yearbook 1989*, pp. 277, 437; International Monetary Fund, *International Financial Statistics* 43, no. 12 (1990): 84. Korean prices are for polished rice, average quality; world market prices are for Thailand, white-milled 5 percent, broken, FOB.

85. Ban, Moon, and Perkins, *Rural Development*, appendix C.

86. Derived from United Nations, *National Accounts Statistics 1987*, vol. 1 (New York: United Nations, 1990), p. 840.

87. Ibid., p. 841.

88. Derived from Edward F. Denison and William K. Chung, *How Japan's Economy Grew So Fast* (Washington, D.C.: Brookings Institution, 1976), p. 19.

89. Harry T. Oshima, *Economic Growth in Monsoon Asia: A Comparative Survey* (Tokyo: University of Tokyo Press, 1987), pp. 150–52.

90. Ibid., p. 148.

91. The so-called HCI Drive is conventionally dated from 1973, when it was formally announced in a speech by President Park. See, for example, World Bank, *Korea: Managing the Industrial Transition*, vol. 1, p. 38. In actuality, its origins can be traced back several years earlier.

92. Ibid., vol. 2, p. 20.

93. Ibid., vol. 1, p. 47.

94. Amsden (*Asia's Next Giant*, p. 89) estimates that the rate of return on investment was higher in light industry than in heavy industry for eleven of the thirteen years between 1972 and 1984, inclusive.

95. For more details, see World Bank, *Korea: Managing the Industrial Transition*, vol. 2, chaps. 4, 5, and 6.

96. Jeffrey G. Williamson, "Why Do Koreans Save 'So Little'?" *Journal of Developmental Economics* 6, no. 3 (1979).

97. Ibid.

98. For a description of what the authors describe as the government's 1972 "assault" on the curb market, see Cole and Park, *Financial Development in Korea*, pp. 162–68.

99. Oshima, *Economic Growth in Monsoon Asia*, pp. 140, 142; the estimates are for 1952–80 (Taiwan) and 1953–80 (South Korea).

100. Kim Kwang-suk and Park Joon-kyung, *Sources of Economic Growth in Korea, 1963–1982* (Seoul: Korea Development Institute, 1985), p. 170.

101. Ibid.

102. For a masterful presentation and critique of such methodological errors, see David H. Fischer, *Historical Fallacies* (New York: Harper and Row, 1970).

103. Friedrich A. Hayek, *The Fatal Conceit* (Chicago: University of Chicago Press, 1989).

8

Economic Policies and Performance of India and Pakistan

ALAN HESTON

Introduction

Following the lead of many other low- and middle-income countries, India and Pakistan in the 1990s embarked on major programs of economic liberalization that marked a sharp break from their previous experience with economic planning. These efforts at reform in India and Pakistan will be discussed in this chapter as part of a longer sequence where policies were adopted following independence that by the 1980s were not adequate to cope with the changing world economy.

India and Pakistan make an interesting contrast in development performance because their shared economic history before 1947 permits one to focus primarily on the results of different sets of policies since independence. Terms like *economic miracle* were applied to Pakistan in the 1960s, whereas terms like *stagnation* or *Hindu rate of growth* were often associated with India. Pakistan has been said to have followed more growth-oriented policies, whereas India's planning effort, with its early emphasis on heavy industry, has often been criticized both within and outside of India. Further, Indian economic performance has frequently been judged unfavorably in comparison with China, with the inference that policies in India have been misguided. The relative performance of India and Pakistan in other areas, such as regional balance, poverty alleviation, and provision of public services, was more mixed.

This chapter takes issue with many of the received views about the economies of India and Pakistan, giving more emphasis to similarities rather than differences in experience. In my view, the shared heritage of these countries deserves more emphasis than it has received, not only in terms of the carryover of colonial institutions of administration but also in terms of regional imbalances, federal structure, and provision of public services. Often the similarities in experience are best captured by comparing India and Pakistan with other developing countries or by comparing comparable regions within each country, such as the two Punjabs.

Economic performance in this chapter considers the usual national accounts numerators, as well as denominators related both to productivity and welfare. In addition, personal and regional distribution of income, provision and access to medical and health facilities, and economic influence and mobility of various "deprived" South Asian communities are also considered. Finally, the chapter discusses some less quantifiable aspects of economic performance, such as expansion of opportunities and choice.

The first section examines economic growth before 1947 and compares it with the experience of India and Pakistan from 1947 to 1990 including a discussion of the aggregative saving and investment performance. The second section reviews the almost canonical critiques of government control policies that seem as frequently espoused within South Asia as in Western academic journals, or by institutions like the World Bank. The third section takes up government policies more directly related to the goals of social, regional, and gender equality. The fourth section briefly looks at the achievements in education and health. The last section concludes with a discussion of reforms in the two countries since 1990.

Growth Experience, Pre- and Post-1947

This section begins with an historical discussion of growth in South Asia before the creation of India and Pakistan, followed by an examination of the economic performance during the plans from 1950 to 1990. Compared with the colonial period, economic performance during the first forty years of independence was excellent, but compared with the performance of economies like Korea, the record of India and Pakistan from 1960 to 1990 was lackluster.

ECONOMIC GROWTH BEFORE INDEPENDENCE

If one were to sum up what has been written on the economic relationships between Britain and India in the 1857 to 1947 period, adjectives such as "polemical" come to mind. To be sure, there are an increasing number of solid pieces of scholarship, but even these tend to be classified in the literature as apologist,

Marxist, orientalist, or some other tag. My own view on the subject, which others might, in kinder moments, label apologist, is the following.

All measures suggest that, in the century before 1947, the growth in per capita income in Europe, America, and Japan was unusually high in terms of their past trends. Trend acceleration certainly did not occur in South Asia under the British. Some, like Radakamal Mukherjee or William Digby, would say that real per capita income in the subcontinent declined during the British period. In his contribution to this volume, Maddison suggests that per capita GDP may have risen from $350 (1980 international dollars, discussed below) in 1830 to $399 in 1913 and fallen back to $359 just after independence. I have suggested small growth but somewhat larger than Maddison for this period (Heston 1980; Heston-Summers 1982). This is similar to the conclusion reached by M. Mukherjee (1969), one of the pioneers in Indian national accounts. What I conclude from all this is that the range of estimates for India is small compared with the difference between Indian growth and that in the industrial countries. It is also clear that the pre-1947 estimates for India imply that post-1947 per capita growth in India of 1.9 percent per annum and in present-day Pakistan of 2.1 percent represent an acceleration compared with the previous thirty years, if not the previous century.

This relatively slow growth under the British masks many changes occurring in the subcontinent during the period. These include the rise of a number of large and diversified business houses, different regional growth records on a total and, perhaps, per capita basis, major changes in the agricultural cropping pattern, growth of a professional administrative cadre, development of major educational institutions, and creation of a large railroad network; others might add to this list. Many of these changes were either positive or, as some would say for the railroads, mixed contributions to the colonial Indian economy. Given that there were a number of stimuli to the colonial economy, why was there not an acceleration in growth in the British period? There is also the related question of whether policies or institutions developed by the British prevented more rapid growth and might have carried over as a negative legacy for independent India and Pakistan.

We will return to these questions later in the chapter; for now we will simply note one important legacy of the British period that affected India and Pakistan differentially. The relatively stagnant performance of the Indian economy under the British served as grist for the mill of nationalist economic historians, who in turn had an indirect influence on early economic policies after 1947, especially in India. The interpretations of nationalist economic historians of the pre-1947 period emphasized the apparent drain on the Indian economy due to tax, expenditure, and trade relations, and they emphasized that India was transformed from an exporter of manufactures in the eighteenth century to an exporter of primary products by the late nineteenth century under the international trade regime imposed by the British. It was characteristic of Nehru and some of his advisers, such as P.C. Mahalanobis, in the early planning period to view foreign trade not as a potential vehicle for economic growth but as an international involvement that, to the extent possible, should be minimized.

This was much less true for Pakistan, whose leaders, compared with those in India, had little economic ideology or expertise, bad or good. Few Muslims wrote economic critiques of the British or were actively involved in the discussions of a possible socialist future for the subcontinent. As early as the 1930s, Motilal Nehru, his son Jawarhalal, and many others in the Indian National Congress were involved in setting out an alternative economic and political blueprint for India in reaction to the Simon Commission, which had been given that charge but, in typical British fashion, had no Indian representation. Those who were to become leaders of Pakistan were generally not involved in this exercise and thus did not take with them this heritage in the formulation of their policies. There were also few economists who after 1947 ended up in Pakistan compared with India; thus the legacy of expertise was quite different in the two countries. In the realm of economic ideas and programs, India's leadership entered independence running, though with a number of conflicting visions; Pakistan's leadership, preoccupied with obtaining their nation and the tremendous upheavals of partition, made economic policies far from their first priority. With no port in East Pakistan and only Karachi, then under 200,000 in population, in West Pakistan, with jute and textile mills in India and the raw materials in Pakistan, and with the departure of almost all bankers at partition, economic policy required many fingers in the dike, not great vision.

PERFORMANCE FROM 1947 TO 1990, PER CAPITA GDP GROWTH

The post-1950 record of growth used in this chapter is based on the work of Summers and Heston, which converts all national currency-level measures to common international dollar expenditures based on detailed relative price comparisons.[1] Although useful, conversions by price parities cannot improve the accuracy with which GDP is measured in national currencies. For example, if legitimate economic activity is not fully reported for reasons of tax evasion, GDP in national or international prices will be understated. Further, this poses a problem for comparisons over time, when there is a trend in the share of underreporting, and for comparisons across space, when the extent of underreporting differs across countries. With respect to interspatial comparisons, the underground economy has received more attention in India than in Pakistan but certainly is thought to exist in both countries. Quantitatively, the estimates—based on methods that at a minimum use some assumed relationship between unreported income and observed economic magnitudes—of the understatement of GDP in India run from the 10 percent range upward to almost 50 percent (Kabra and Jagannathan 1985, 41). If 30 percent were an average, it would have a large error associated with it. There has probably been an upward trend in the share in both countries from 1970 through part of the 1980s, with some likely decline following reforms and reductions in high marginal tax rates. These are qualitative guesses, and no further attempt will be made to take undercounting of GDP into account.

The modest growth rate of India (1.9 percent per annum) and Pakistan (2.1 percent) from 1950 to 1990 is well below the rate for Korea, which was 5.9 percent between 1953 and 1990. India and Pakistan did, however, grow substantially faster than during the British period (1870 to 1947), during which growth was less than 0.5 percent per annum. In comparison with Korea, as above, or even a large country such as Brazil (2.9 percent from 1950 to 1990), the India-Pakistan performance is not spectacular, but by African standards it is quite good. As to levels, in 1950 Pakistan would be at $602 and India $590 in 1985 dollars, growing to $1,394 and $1,264 in 1990, whereas Korea moved from $796 in 1953 to $6,673 in 1990. Thus, India and Pakistan can look to their first forty years as a period of some important economic improvement but also as a period of lost opportunities.[2]

Investment and Savings Performance

Both India and Pakistan undertook ambitious planning exercises, including efforts to expand investment as much as possible from domestic resources. India increased its investment share of GDP from about 10 percent in 1950 to more than 25 percent in 1990 in national currencies. Typically, 90 percent of this investment was financed from domestic resources, meaning that the share of savings was also expanding rapidly. For Pakistan, the investment share rose from about 5 percent in 1950 to about 19 percent of GDP in 1990, with often only 60 percent or less being financed from domestic sources. One obvious point is that Pakistan was much more dependent on foreign assistance than was India.[3]

These figures suggest that India invested more than Pakistan, and in fact the ratios in national currencies slightly understate the difference in the additions to plant and equipment in each year in the two countries. When both GDP and investment are measured at international prices, then the investment share is comparable between countries, which is not the case when national prices are used. National prices include duties and scarcity premiums, and in India and Pakistan there have been major distortions in the prices of investment goods.

To illustrate, the real shares of investment in 1990 in India and Pakistan were 17 and 10 percent as opposed to 27 and 19 percent in national prices. This means that investment goods' prices were high, relative to other goods and services, in both countries with the distortions being somewhat more in Pakistan, whose real share is almost cut in half. The curious result of this comparison is that the higher real investment in India has not produced higher growth there.

Can any of this be explained simply by the composition of investment? It seems that there is little difference between the composition of gross domestic investment between India and Pakistan. Both countries in national prices allocate about the same percentage to producer durables and to residential construction, although the construction total for Pakistan appears to be somewhat larger than for India. Producer durables, which are perhaps most closely associated with growth, are in international prices a smaller percentage of investment in India, Pakistan, and Korea than in Japan and the United States. We conclude that the composition of investment tells us little about India-Pakistan differences but perhaps something about differences between these and the industrial countries. The relatively smaller contribution of investment to growth in India compared with Pakistan is more likely a reflection of the larger share of investment in producer versus consumer goods industries in India.

Modes of Government Economic Control

Both India and Pakistan instituted major governmental efforts to guide their economic development by using the framework of their five-year development plans and by specific policies aimed at controlling the direction of industrial expansion. A legacy of the British was that Indian businesses wanted to have access to government to obtain the rents created by government licensing procedures. Indian businessmen resented what they considered to have been the favored role of British business in India (Kidron 1965). British firms often had access to contracts through the social network of the clubs or by policy in matters such as monopolies of mail transport. Indian businesses often felt that obstacles were put in their path if their interests conflicted with those of British business: for example, Jamshed Tata's first attempt at building a steel mill in India.

In Pakistan there were initially close ties between government and business but for different reasons. Because most Muslim businessmen had interests in Bombay and Western India or had migrated to Africa or other places before 1947, few were active in what was to become East and West Pakistan. When virtually all Hindu businessmen left West Pakistan in 1947, there was a major void in banking, insurance, international trade, and, of course, any new industries. The group of Muslim businessmen who filled this void and obtained most of the initial import licenses were migrants from western India or from outside the subcontinent. The contacts of these groups with the new government of Pakistan were close, and in some cases the government actively attracted the migration of business groups to both wings of Pakistan, but particularly the west, for example, the Adamjees from Burma, the Fancys from East Africa, and the Habib, Dawood, and Bohra families from Bombay (Altaf 1984).

INDUSTRIAL POLICY IN INDIA THROUGH THE 1980S

The Industrial Policy Resolution of 1948 and its implementation under the Industries Development and Regulation Act (IDRA) of 1951 set the framework for government control of the direction of investment in India. The act suggested priorities for industrial expansion and indicated scheduled industries where the private sector could expand capacity with a license; the act also was aimed at aiding small industries, preventing concentration of private capital, and spreading industrial expansion across regions.

The 1951 IDRA established the framework for implementing the Industrial Policy Resolution. It called for registering undertakings and licensing all increases in capacity, which called for clearance by a Licensing Committee set up in 1952. Apart from the licensing, imported capital goods had to be cleared through the Capital Goods Licensing Committee; where government finance was required, additional approvals were necessary.

If one were to choose a particular control agency in India for a bad press award, the Directorate General of Technical Development (DGTD) would have serious competitors but might still win by acclamation. The lower-level civil servants in DGTD, as in many organizations, wielded power by saying no and risked review by saying yes. In this the DGTD is no different, except that it was initially assigned more checkpoints in the licensing procedure. These checks included the technical soundness of the project, the environmental impact of effluents, the need for additional capacity given existing production and export possibilities, the relation of the capacity sought to the capital stock of the enterprise, and the degree to which the additional capacity would make use of indigenous inputs. Based on government reports and interviews, Bhagwati and Desai (1970, 249–73) produced a sharply critical appraisal of the whole licensing process, including the practice of treating applications sequentially, without regard to alternative proposals in the pipeline; the DGTD was singled out for failing to establish criteria for their decisions, poor handling of information, and failing to review implementation of approved projects.

There were many proposals for reform in the late 1960s, but, in fact, the early populist years of the Indira Gandhi era added important additional hurdles. In 1973, a reorganization established a Secretariat for Industrial Approvals (SIA) that was to coordinate and expedite applications. Under the Monopolies and Restrictive Trade Practices Act (MRTP) and the Foreign Exchange Regulation Act (FERA), foreign or large firms faced additional committees for approval. Although there were time limits set for turning around applications at each stage, the powers granted to various ministries and committees meant that an application could be reviewed by up to thirty-five persons in up to twelve different departments. Rarely would an application be approved in less than six months, and delays of a year were frequent. The tradition that one department would not overrule the decision of another department also added to the complications of obtaining approval. Of the five or ten committees that reviewed the licensing procedures in the past twenty years, all have called for extensive liberalization and reform.

But strong vested interests, whose lobbying efforts could easily be financed by the rents from the licenses and quotas they had obtained, continued to make reform difficult in India. Other vested interests included the bureaucrats, whose powers bred bribery and corruption. Clearly, the confrontational character of some business-government relations of the 1970s, however, had given way to a situation of accommodation by the 1980s. Under Rajiv Gandhi, several attempts at sidestepping the bureaucratic apparatus were introduced, with some successes. These included broader interpretations of capacity, so that a firm with a license to expand, say, bus production may expand production to include any vehicle (previously, that was not allowed). New small-sized firms or firms seeking small increases in capacity were approved more quickly, and whole areas of production were exempted from a number of the licensing hurdles. Because these reforms often substituted political exemptions for regulatory reform, however, charges of high-level corruption undermined Rajiv's reform efforts and his subsequent election bid.

INDUSTRIAL POLICY IN PAKISTAN UP TO THE PRESENT

In 1948 Pakistan set out an industrial policy statement that left to the private firms all sectors except hydroelectric power, railway cars, communications apparatus, and arms and munitions. Permits were required for ventures of more than 100 million rupees or ventures requiring large imports. One legacy of the British that symbolizes the continuity of bureaucratic rule is the NOC, or *no objection certificate*. In Pakistan an NOC was needed from an industrial committee at the provincial level; if foreign exchange and government loans were involved, additional approvals were required. Industrial development corporations, established in both wings of Pakistan in 1962, were a major lending source and an additional point of control for increases in capacity.

The emphasis in favor of private ownership was substantially modified under Z. A. Bhutto, whose government from 1971 to 1977 nationalized several industries, such as life insurance, cooking oil, and flour milling. The managing agency system was abolished, and the reforms concentrated most heavily on those sectors owned by the infamous "twenty-two families," who had been receiving the rents associated with the early issuance of licenses for foreign exchange discussed above. Many of these policies evoked a negative reaction from business houses, and a number of these houses, especially those that had factories subject to labor actions, simply stopped production and took what capital they could out of Pakistan.

When Muhammed Zia ul-Haq came to power in 1977, he rolled back many of the nationalizations and sought to restore business confidence. Although some of the older business houses responded, much business activity was controlled by new groups, such as the Chiniot Sheiks from Punjab, who had begun to expand their operations in Sind and other provinces. Pakistan had from the beginning a distorted system of tariffs, taxes, and quotas that provided high rates of effective protection. By 1980, effective protection rates in manufacturing averaged 60 percent (Naqvi, Kemal, and Heston 1983, table 2). Because custom duties and excise taxes provided most of the government's revenue, reforms were difficult and institutions such as the IMF opposed cutting tariffs until alternative tax sources were in place. In comparison with India, Pakistan imposed few controls on the expansion of capacity and on the use of imported capital and foreign collaboration. Dismantling existing controls has not been easy, however, and, like India, Pakistan has frequently found it simpler to exempt new capacity creation from bureaucratic review by, for example, raising the investment limit requiring approval.

Income Distribution and Poverty Programs

This section examines income distribution in two parts. The first part looks at personal income distribution, with an emphasis on the poor rather than the rich, in part because there are fewer data on the rich and they are less numerous. The second part takes up the distribution of education and health services, which involve a large, publicly provided component in both countries. The regional distribution of income is taken up later in the essay.

INCOME DISTRIBUTION IN INDIA AND PAKISTAN

By example and by contributions to the profession, India and Pakistan have greatly enriched world discourse on income distribution.[4] India adopted its famous poverty line of 20 rupees per capita a month in rural areas in 1960–61 prices as part of its third Five-Year Plan. This expenditure level, which is about 100 rupees today, would provide a caloric intake of 2,150 calories per day as the threshold above which all poor were to be raised in an effort extending into the 1990s. This poverty line was intended to make income distribution goals, which had previously been qualitative in nature, take on a quantitative dimension, allowing achievements in this arena to be measured and made operational. The World Bank, using purchasing power parities (PPPs) (unfortunately at a very aggregate level), took the 20-rupees figure as an international measure for the 1990 *World Development Report*.

Pakistan's contribution to the income distribution literature came at the upper end of the distribution and included the twenty-two families who purportedly owned most of the industrial capital in Pakistan during the presidency of Ayub Khan. The twenty-two families were referred to in a speech by Mahbub-ul-Haq in 1968 that was intended to refer more generally to distribution problems rather than to attack the business community (Kochanek 1982, 183) Although several parts of the speech were inaccurate about the number and names of the families (White 1974), the speaker nevertheless soon joined the World Bank to help formulate policies for a more just distribution of the fruits of economic planning.

Poverty Line Measures

Much has been made of the middle class of 300 million in India that supposedly make India an attractive investment target for multinationals. That 300 million, who do have the money to buy consumer durables and eat the meals of world restaurant chains, however, are only the top one-third of the Indian population. The middle third has little surplus for discretionary expenditures, and the remainder are perhaps a million superrich and more than 300 million who fall below the poverty line. This large group of poor produces differences between those policy makers who would focus on reducing the numbers in poverty and those who would emphasize rapid overall growth as the best way to reduce the numbers in poverty (Bhagwati 1993). Certainly the direction of recent reforms in both India and Pakistan have reduced social expenditures, including a number of direct interventions aimed at the very poor.

Evidence supports the contention that increased economic opportunities reduce the numbers in poverty. Burki (1988) makes a strong case that the proportion in poverty in Pakistan has declined in the last twenty years. He bases part of this conclusion on the incidence of Middle East remissions and part on the apparent increase in consumption of food per capita. Leaving aside the Afghan refugees, Burki thinks there may be significant numbers in poverty in Pakistan, but he thinks the problem is much less than in Bangladesh or India, with which I would agree.

One early critique of the poverty measures was by A. K. Sen, who argued that the distribution of the poor below any poverty cutoff was also important. In India this distributional aspect of poverty has been partially taken into account by counting the "ultrapoor," those whose income is more than 25 percent below the poverty line. Using the poverty line of 90 rupees in 1988 would take all below that as in poverty and all below 67.5 rupees (.75 × 90) as in ultrapoverty (World Bank 1989). Using these numbers, let us look at the situation between 1970 and 1988 in India.

First, the absolute numbers in poverty have risen from 237 million in 1970 to 252 million in 1988 in rural areas and from 50 million (1970) to 70 million (1988) in urban areas. Second, urban areas often receive migrants in poverty from rural areas, not vice versa. This means that the decrease in the number in ultrapoverty in rural areas from 30 to 20 million and the increase in urban areas from 28 to 33 million may simply reflect the migration of ultrapoor to urban areas. Third, the share of persons in poverty decreased between 1970 and 1988, and the total number in ultrapoverty decreased. These can at best be called modest gains and are probably less than those achieved by Pakistan. As we note in the next section, however, if one compares subregions, areas of India have done as well as comparable areas of Pakistan.

Target Group Programs

Like much of the world, India and Pakistan have attempted to improve the position of the poor by general policies promoting economic growth and employment, while also singling out certain groups for special treatment. In the next section we will touch on evidence on the success of general growth policies trickling down to the poor. In this part I take up the Integrated Rural Development Programme in India, discuss how certain policies may affect the positions of scheduled castes (SC) and scheduled tribes (ST) in India, and discuss policies affecting women in both India and Pakistan. No attempt is made to deal with a variety of other measures, including food and essential commodity distribution programs. Land reform efforts in Pakistan (minimal) and in India (modest) are discussed by Herring (1983). These efforts are not treated here, even though they are important because of the association of rural poverty and landlessness and because a high proportion of the SC are landless.

Integrated Rural Development Programme (IRDP). One target group in rural India are those whose entitlements are basically their labor, usually not enhanced by skills or education. Other assets may include a homestead site but typically little or no land or other capital. Programs aimed at these groups include the National Rural Employment Programme (1978–79) and the Rural Landless Employment Guarantee Programme (1983), which in some states offer fifty or so days employment a year. These programs do not provide long-term skill training, nor do the benefits go only to the rural poor, except to the extent that landlessness and poverty are highly correlated. The combined employment of these programs is about 700 million person-workdays. With 44.4 million poor rural households, the goal of providing 100 workdays a year for one member of the household would entail 4,440 million workdays.

In contrast to these short-term income-generation programs, IRDP was to provide the poor with assets that would allow them to develop long-term increases in their potential income. A model activity would be the provision of animals, which in principle could feed on the common property of a village and which could generate income from milk, transport, and other rural work. The IRDP was supposed to reach 27 million poor rural families between 1980 and 1988, on average providing 3,000 rupees (perhaps $500) in assets in an effort to release the latent entrepreneurial talents of the poor. This has frequently, however, brought the poor in conflict with better-off villagers who have tried to privatize common property, such as grazing land, thwarting the efforts of poor villagers trying to develop animal husbandry as a source of income and employment. The IRDP, which has been administered through the existing bureaucracy, has been criticized for helping the nonpoor and lending to the better-off areas, among other things (N. J. Kurian 1989). Its annual costs have been roughly the same as the employment programs. If the total expenditures made it to the target families, it would average a transfer of somewhat more than 10 percent of the income of those families just at the poverty level in 1984–85.

Those poor who are unable to work or to manage or use productive assets are clearly left out by these programs, a standard criticism. Among those receiving assets under IRDP, a significant number have sold them, often at a "loss" because IRDP shifted out local demand for animals, providing room for setting "excessive" values on animals provided to the poor as capital, a phenomenon aggravated by 35 percent of the budget being spent in March, the last month of the fiscal year. In terms of the bottom line, those families moving out of poverty as a result of these schemes is put at under 10 percent.

Advances among Special Groups, Scheduled Castes, and Tribes.   The scheduled castes and tribes in India have been targeted for affirmative action–type policies since the Indian Constitution was adopted in 1950. Many of those policies, however, have provoked backlash in India because they reserve government employment and admission slots in higher education programs for persons from scheduled castes and tribes. In 1988 in India the scheduled castes and tribes were 9.3 percent of the urban population, representing 13.1 percent of those in poverty and 14.7 percent of those in ultrapoverty; they were 24.2 percent of the rural population, 33.0 percent of those in poverty and 36.8 percent of those in ultrapoverty (Hanson and Lieberman 1989). Although these groups are disproportionately rural, most education and employment policies affect the urban poor. Because the scheduled castes and tribes are one-third of those in poverty in rural areas, all the above rural programs should benefit them, to the extent they are in poverty. It would appear, however, that many of the poorer scheduled castes and tribes have not received their share of IRDP resources. And because of their low literacy levels (60 percent of all rural males and 40 percent of all rural females), the likelihood that they are able to take advantage of IRDP is reduced. More on this when we discuss education.

Female Incomes and Status. Traditionally, in much of North India and Pakistan (as well as in China), women marry outside their village. This puts little premium on investing in females, whose contributions to output and progeny will accrue to another family in another village. The female, once married, will tend to favor sons, as will her in-laws, because a son will support that family for the rest of her life. It has been suggested that, the more women contribute to nonhousehold income, the higher is their status, and some have generalized this to suggest that rice agriculture is kinder to women than wheat. In any event, throughout North India and Pakistan, there is a high masculinity ratio (105 to 110 males per 100 females) not observed in South India (where marriage is typically not outside the village) or most of the rest of the world, except some areas of the Middle East and North China at various recent times.

The two approaches to breaking this cycle are investment in education, discussed below, and creating more money-making opportunities. In almost all regions of India, voluntary organizations have been trying to increase income-making opportunities for poor women. One of the most well known of these in India, SEWA (Self Employed Women's Association), in Ahmedabad, has worked in both urban and rural areas. One characteristic of such groups in India and Pakistan is that middle- and upper-class university-educated women, often with husbands in high positions, are the "temporary" intermediaries between the poor women and authorities that must be dealt with in establishing a co-op or a bank, for example. In Pakistan, there is in the Planning Commission, a special women's division that has sought the expansion of work income opportunities for women outside the home.

EDUCATION AND HEALTH

As the last section suggested, there are major educational shortfalls in both India and Pakistan but with substantial regional variations. Overall literacy in India was reported as 34 percent in the 1970–1975 period, rising to 48 percent in 1990, with the 1990 rate for females at 34 percent; in Pakistan for 1970–1975 it was 21 percent and by 1990 was 35 percent, with female literacy at 21 percent (World Bank Social Indicators 1995). Kerala—the model state, where high educational and health achievements have been attained with modest income—has a literacy rate of nearly 80 percent for males and nearly 70 percent for females, whereas Rajasthan, Bihar, and Uttar Pradesh had literacy rates of under 40 percent for males and under 15 percent for females. No province in Pakistan approaches Kerala, Karachi in 1981 having 60 percent males and 49 percent females literate. The remainder of Sind has literacy rates of 30 percent (male) and 10 percent (female), Baluchistan's rates are 13 percent (male) and 3 percent (female), and Northwest Frontier Province's (NWFP's) rates are 23 percent (male) and 5 percent (female), all below the lowest states in India in 1981.

Clearly mass education has had little priority in either country, but Pakistan has performed much less satisfactorily, especially with respect to female education. Even in 1981, enrollment rates in primary schools in Pakistan outside of Karachi (70 percent) were under 40 percent, whereas in India they were 80 percent or more.

Women are the carriers of culture and change to the next generations, and they monitor health and nutrition practices in the household. It is not surprising that many observers of Pakistan and India regard the limited gains in education as a major negative element in their post-1947 performance. The elite character of both societies, but particularly Pakistan's, is often offered as an explanation. On the higher education level, Indian performance has been impressive, which only in part reflects an elite orientation, the main push being strong demand by a growing and diverse middle class.

As mentioned, one correlate of women's education appears to be the health status of the family and particularly children. It is frequently observed that better feeding, sanitation, and precautionary medical practices are associated with female education. Local demands may also generate government delivery of health services to specific areas or at least explain why most indicators of government health inputs are less correlated with incomes than educational levels, particularly of females.

Because women are the first teachers of children, they have a major impact on the acceptance of new ideas. On most measures of attitudes toward change, education and willingness to innovate are positively associated. These important benefits of education have in India not yet completely overcome long-standing conditions on both the supply side (a colonial and indigenous heritage of elite education) and the demand side. It was suggested above that the unwillingness on the demand side of families in rural areas to invest in the education of female children may be traced to the practice of women marrying outside of their village so that the investment is lost to the family. Whatever the reasons, the evidence is that many of the measured and nonmeasured correlates of poverty are associated with low levels of education of women.

Another strong force operating to reduce school completion rates in rural areas is that large landowners often do not want education for their illiterate laborers' children. The village has an interest in *enrolling* children in school because education grants are based on enrollments, not completions. The village teacher may wish to encourage students of backward castes to remain in school but may not be willing to try to convince their parents if the latter's employers are influential in the local area. Further, school-age children can often contribute to family income in rural and urban areas, providing a strong incentive for their leaving school and continuing a family cycle of illiteracy.

In rural Pakistan there is a similar lack of interest on the part of landlords in encouraging widespread education, a lack of interest that is often shared by the mullahs, the local religious leaders. Both Pakistan and India are painfully aware of their poor performance in the field of primary education, which Pakistan primarily attributes to lack of demand. Under Rajiv Gandhi, India extensively reviewed the weaknesses of its education system but took the easy and elitist way out. Rather than reform the existing system, model schools with higher pay scales for teachers were established in most districts, providing a new track for children of the middle and upper classes. One hopes that the underlying demand factors will change with the expansion of television and other media to remote areas, but, for now, this is an area of poor performance in both countries.

Given the association between health status and education of females, it should come as no surprise that there is substantial regional variation and that health improvements have not been as widespread as in some other countries. Both India and Pakistan have major medical schools and hospital facilities; India also has major medical research facilities. These have been urban based, however, though both countries are seeking to expand primary health facilities in rural areas.

The model India has adopted uses as the key agent a village health worker who is responsible for diagnoses and referral. The tasks heaped on this worker would be daunting to someone well trained and well paid, which these health workers are not. The program is a step in the right direction, however, and has achieved the widest geographic coverage of health care in India to this point.

Regional Income Balance

The colonial legacy left many arbitrary national boundaries that have produced civil wars, as in Nigeria, or continued political agitation, as in many parts of Africa and Asia. These artificial national borders could not be maintained in Pakistan, whose two wings became separate countries in 1971. The Awami League of then East Pakistan listed a number of grievances against the West, most of which related to provincial income differences and discrimination with respect to access to job opportunities, foreign exchange, and investment funds. Although provincial income statistics in Pakistan were and are weak, the usual differential puts the East at perhaps half that of the West and perhaps 40 percent that of Sind, the most affluent province. Because this type of regional difference is not large by international standards of poor or rich countries, clearly, language differences, access to power, and sheer physical distance contributed to the eventual split. The famous "fissiparous tendencies" in the subcontinent, however, have made both India and Pakistan keenly aware of regional interests in their development programs.

THE LEVEL OF REGIONAL DISPARITIES

India.   State domestic product per capita in the richest state, Punjab, was 8,281 rupees in 1990–1991, 3.2 times that of the poorest state, Bihar (Government of India, *Economic Survey 1992–93*). The relative difference has if anything risen in the past ten years, despite programs designed to reduce the disparities. In India the center collects certain revenues that are distributed to the states each year; these allocations are reviewed every five years by a finance commission. Although the finance commissions are supposed to allocate funds so as to reduce disparities, their scope is limited and their effect, minimal.

In recent allocations the low-income states got 208 rupees per capita as opposed to 142 rupees per capita in the high-income states. This difference of 60 rupees is less than 5 percent of the difference in state domestic product between the two groups of states and too small to offset lower state revenues and lower private savings in the poorer states. As a consequence, capital formation is usually more per capita in the more affluent states. Public sector investments by the center are not distributed in favor of the poorer states, so one is left to conclude that public policy has not tended to equalize state incomes. Within the states of India there are attempts to stimulate growth in backward areas, but most of these suffer from the same types of problems as discussed below for Pakistan.

Pakistan.   Estimated data on per capita domestic product in the four principal provinces usually indicate that Punjab is near the average, Sind substantially above the average, and Baluchistan substantially below the average. These estimates are not thought to be reliable, however. By weight of its population (57 percent of the total) and its historically important position in the armed forces, Punjab has dominated national politics. The NWFP, with a strong Pathan group in the military, has often been aligned with Punjab. For Punjab to have a provincial income close to the national average indicates that its alleged discrimination against the other provinces was nonexistent. Sind's high income, which probably results from the high proportion of industrial establishments around Karachi, makes its complaints about Punjab sound groundless. But life is not so simple; Sindhis are not the majority in Karachi, and there are many poor Sindhis within and outside Karachi. Further, many large land grants in Sind have been made to retired military personnel, which, by composition of the military, tend to be Pathan or Punjabi. Further, when Punjabi businessmen purchased factories in Sind, beginning with the first wave of Pakistan businessmen who left under Z. A. Bhutto, they have frequently recruited labor from Punjab. Baluchistan is still more complicated because the majority in its capital, Quetta, are not Baluchis but rather from Punjab or NWFP. Further, there are many poor Baluchis in rural areas and many well-to-do Baluchis in Karachi.

The principal programs for backward regions in Pakistan relate to investment incentives in certain designated areas classified as backward, semideveloped, or containing new industrial estates. The incentives include tax holidays for five years and customs duty reductions on imported machinery. During the 1978–1983 period, these incentives produced substantial shifts in the location of investments. These types of incentives, however, usually favor capital-intensive production in areas where labor is cheap, producing disappointing gains in employment. Backward areas in Pakistan have probably benefited more from the remissions of migrants to the Middle East than from any other source. Burki (1988, 81–82) suggests that most migrants came from a group of poor districts in the northwest of Pakistan and were in general low skilled and low income.

THE TWO PUNJABS

The problems of dividing the former Punjab province among Muslim and Hindu majority areas, while at the same time placating the Sikhs, were among the most difficult associated with the partition of British India in 1947. A line did get drawn, with subsequent mass migrations and loss of life, and some of the consequences are still being played out by Sikhs in and out of India searching for their imagined homeland of Khalistan. Punjab was the favored province of the British, with its famous canal colonies, martial traditions, and yeomanlike peasants. Much interest has attached to comparing the economic performance in the Punjab province of Pakistan with the present Indian states of Punjab and Harayana because of their common past, because the land of the five rivers is homogeneous, and, I suspect, because foreign advisers, like the British before them, have found in the Punabi farmers in both India and Pakistan an attractive counterpart.

What conclusions can be drawn from such a comparison? Sims (1988) examined agricultural performance in both sides and concluded that Indian Punjab has had the better of it. Valuing eleven principal crops at the same prices, Sims found that growth was about 3 percent a year up to 1965 in both Punjabs but that thereafter growth was 8.5 percent a year in India (until 1985) and 4 percent in Pakistan. This was achieved mainly by more rapid increases in yields per acre in India, which Sims attributes to a more equal land distribution in India, better incentives, better rural infrastructure and administration, and a broader base of scientific research. (Pakistan had 260 Ph.Ds in agricultural research in the 1980s and India, 30,000 [Sims 1988, 41].) In transport infrastructure, Pakistani Punjab had 5.5 kilometers of roads per 100 square kilometers in 1978 and Indian Punjab, 47.2. Tube wells were more expensive in Pakistani Punjab and electricity less available.

Agricultural performance and the associated expansion of small-scale industry was world class in both Punjabs, however, comparing favorably with model countries like Taiwan and Thailand. Further, Pakistan was limited in its expansion of output because it could not draw on cheap migrant labor from other parts of Pakistan in the way that Indian Punjab could from Uttar Pradesh. The yields in Indian Punjab are higher than in Pakistan in part because labor is applied more intensively in Indian Punjab because it is cheaper there.

The superlative performance of Indian Punjab tends to be dwarfed by the large populations of eastern India that have experienced slow growth. In Pakistan, Bangladesh is no longer around to overwhelm the good performance of Pakistani Punjab, which partly explains why the overall performance of the Pakistan economy looks better than India's. To the extent the comparison of the two Punjabs holds initial conditions and opportunities constant, one would have to conclude, with Sims, that the comparison favors India.

POVERTY AND OPPORTUNITY BY REGION

A mapping of poverty in India, based on a study of fifty-six agro-climatically homogeneous regions of rural India that examined poverty levels and average per capita consumption, reveals a broad belt running east to west (Jain, Sundaram, and Tendulkar 1988). The high poverty regions include areas of the states of West Bengal, Bihar, and eastern Uttar Pradesh. The belt moves slightly south, taking in parts of Orissa and Madhya Pradesh, and then moves west and north, taking in parts of Maharashtra, Gujarat, and Rajasthan. Other pockets of poverty, albeit less severe, are in parts of Tamil Nadu and Andhra Pradesh. The poverty in the main east-west belt reaches a high of 85 percent in the southern part of Orissa, 67 percent in southern Bihar, 72 percent in eastern Gujarat, and 82 percent in southern Rajasthan. By way of contrast, both regions of Punjab and Harayana states and two of the three regions in Jammu and Kashmir have ratios under 5 percent. Not surprisingly, the latter six regions have higher than average per capita consumption.

The regional differences are fairly easy to summarize. The east, which by its natural resources endowment is the richest area of India, has low levels of state income per capita, low growth, and the least satisfactory performance with respect to poverty reduction. The south, beginning with levels of poverty similar to those in the east, has reduced the absolute numbers in poverty in rural and urban areas. Because the incidence of poverty and poor economic performance are highly correlated, if poor economic performance could be turned around, poverty would be reduced. Recent indications are that the economic situation in Bihar is finally improving, which, if it continues, is likely to do more to improve the position of those in poverty than direct programs.

Let me conclude this section by calling attention to some issues raised in an article by N. S. Jodha (1988). Jodha looked at two nonirrigated villages in Rajasthan in 1963–1966 and again in 1982–1984. There had been a slight rise in per capita income (162 rupees to 175 rupees) in constant prices (1964–1965) over the period, but the percentage of families in poverty had increased from 17 to 23 percent in these villages. Of those families in poverty in 1982–1984, 47 percent reported gains in per capita income of more than 5 percent, 15 percent essentially had no change, and 38 percent experienced declines in per capita income. Jodha asked the thirty-five households whose per capita income had declined how they perceived their fortunes to have changed over the years.

Jodha asked if the families thought they were "better off" as a lead-in to a number of specific questions that referred to different aspects of village life. Jodha found that these families felt significantly less dependent in 1982–1984 on a large farmer or patron for credit, for work as attached laborers, for residential space, for off-season loans, or for marketing produce than in 1964–1965. These same households were less dependent on gathering activities and other low-paying tasks in 1980–1985, nor did they need to take children out of school as much as in 1964–1965 to help earn money. In general their liquidity and fixed-asset position had improved, their diet had become more varied, including greens and sugar, and they had a reduced incidence of guinea worm. Jodha reports that these families *perceived* that their economic situation had improved, in contrast to our standard poverty measures. Jodha's observations were made before the rapid improvements in communications and media availability in rural areas of both India and Pakistan. To the extent the perceptions of the very poor are influenced by a number of factors not captured in standard income measures, which may paint too stagnant a picture of the changes affecting these households.

Economic Reforms since 1990

Worldwide patterns of economic reform have many common elements, such as the convertibility of currency on current (and capital) account, the removal of quantitative and other trade restrictions, the elimination of subsidies, the privatization or restructuring of state-owned enterprises, the encouragement of private foreign investment, and the achievement of macrostability, typically calling for reduced budget deficits. These common elements of reform play themselves out very differently around the world, however, depending on the political structures of the country and the initial conditions and extent to which reforms are a response to crisis. Many of the reforms bear significant political and human costs, which often influence the speed with which countries undertake their reforms. In countries that operate within a democratic framework, such as India and Pakistan, opposition parties can easily capitalize on policies that appear to hurt certain groups, like workers laid off from unprofitable public enterprises or beneficiaries of subsidies that have been eliminated in efforts to balance government budgets. Vested interests can often blunt reform efforts; for example, it is often said that although India has gotten rid of hundreds of regulations, it has not gotten rid of one regulator.

SOME KEY AREAS OF REFORM

In the continuum from gradual to rapid reform, both India and Pakistan are on the gradualist side. Both countries were affected by the Kuwait crisis, Pakistan perhaps more than India in terms of lost earnings of migrant workers in the gulf. The foreign exchange crisis that India faced in spring 1991 clearly required an immediate response. Compared with the earlier reform efforts, what appeared different in the policies of Prime Minister Narasimha Rao and his finance minister, Manmohan Singh, was their sense of commitment to reforms, including key appointments, and their explicit policy changes, many in response to the foreign exchange crisis.

Currency Convertibility

India and Pakistan had both attracted accounts from nonresidents, and both saw those accounts drawn down as confidence in the two economies dwindled. One major goal of both countries in the 1990s was to achieve convertibility on current account. The policies adapted included a major devaluation of one-third by India in 1991 and removal of import restrictions in both countries. These policies, as well as freedom of exporters and importers to retain or obtain foreign exchange, have greatly facilitated export growth, especially in India, and have generally made it attractive to carry out business in the subcontinent. Firms can borrow short term from abroad to finance production and exports or to finance imports.

Capital account convertibility has been another matter, and the gradual approach of both countries has been reinforced by the problems faced by the Mexican peso. India has seen its foreign exchange reserves go from the dangerously low level of $1.1 billion in June 1991 to more than $20 billion in 1994. Although $20 billion is a good cushion against current account fluctuations, it would do little against a speculative attack on the rupee of the type that Mexico experienced against the peso.

State-Owned Enterprises

Pakistan has moved more rapidly than India to privatize publicly owned firms, in part because such firms were a smaller segment of Pakistan's economy. Some 60 of 108 firms offered in Pakistan had been transferred from public to private ownership by 1993 (Government of Pakistan, *Economic Survey, 1992–93* 1993). In several cases, including one bank, the transfer was to an employees' management group, reflecting the concern that workers are often the major losers in privatization. As in India, two sectors that had been reserved for public own-ership—power and communications—have in Pakistan become open to private-sector initiative.

In India, many of the public-sector firms are state owned, and thus linking unemployment and tax loss to the closing of these enterprises is visible, direct, and political. Further, India has moved more gradually in liberalization, proceed-ing sector by sector, meaning that the more viable sectors will face world prices in three to five years. Less viable sectors, which may face major employment losses, have been given a longer time to adjust to world prices.

Private Foreign Investment

The major obstacles to direct foreign investment, such as percent of owner-ship, repatriation of profits, and approvals needed, have been simplified in both India and Pakistan. The result has been a heightened interest by multinationals in both economies and a significant flow of investment funds or technology and management practices or both from abroad. The results have been striking in the communications sector and in the use of the skilled labor forces of both countries by multinational firms.

SOME PROBLEM AREAS

The gradual nature of the reform process is judged by some to be wise policy, for example, the slow movement to convertibility on capital account. Giving in to vested interests, however, can also lead to glacially slow reforms, as in the agricultural sector. The model of China, which has relied on attrition of its large state enterprises rather than reform, may provide support for the gradual approach of India and Pakistan.

Economic reform is usually associated with political decentralization. Both India and Pakistan have highly centralized administrations, and for the reforms to spread widely from Delhi and Islamabad, provincial, state, and local adminis-trations must become involved. However, the incentives often do not work that way. When the center reduces its budget deficit in India, it is often at the expense of the states. If unemployment results from plant closures, the impact falls within local jurisdictions, so central policies that produce closings by, say, lowering import restrictions impose a burden the center does not bear.

Also, many of the central licensing controls that were eliminated had their counterpart in the states of India. Fortunately, the competition of states to attract new domestic and foreign investment is likely to ensure that these controls also are eliminated in the states. The same local initatives can also turn to protectionism, as has occurred in both China and India, where imports from other provinces or states face taxes from which local production is exempted. For state governments to generate the kind of confidence businesses need to locate in their jurisdictions, their political leaders will need the type of political vision that the Rao-Singh policies have reflected at the center, coupled with a minimum of protectionist policies.

Conclusions

By historical standards, both India and Pakistan have experienced major accelerations in their economic growth since 1947. That growth has been spotty; even though both countries experienced fairly substantial growth in the 1980s, by the end of the decade, both felt the need for substantial economic reforms. Two areas of performance in Pakistan have been weak—savings and providing basic education on a mass basis. If Indian investment figures are roughly comparable with those in Pakistan, then India has had less output increase per rupee than Pakistan. However, some of the output increases were easy for Pakistan: setting up its own shoe and textile factories, for example, to process the raw materials that had been previously processed in Ahmadabad or Bombay. And the direction of investment in Pakistan has been to less capital-intensive projects, and some of its major output gains in agriculture were built on water supplies already in existence.

The reforms of the early 1990s reflect a clear break from the quantitative restrictions of the previous forty years and have raised expectations of substantial economic growth in both countries. However, problems remain for both countries associated with national integration. Violence in Punjab and the communal character of recent state elections in India lead one to wonder whether the conflicts in Sri Lanka were a harbinger for other South Asian polities. None of this can make Pakistan complacent because the daily violence in Karachi and the refugee problem with Afghanistan pose major potential problems for Islamabad. Further, the potential for a more open South Asian regional market probably must await some resolution of the Kashmir dispute between the two countries. It would be nice to conclude that rapid economic growth will placate these communal conflicts, but considering that some of the centers of violence are in rapidly growing areas of both countries, that does not seem a good reading of recent history. However, broadly based economic growth, a continued commitment to reforms, and expansion of educational opportunities are certainly priorities for both countries, and one can take considerable encouragement from the developments of the past decade.

Notes

1. The growth and level estimates used in this chapter are taken from Summers and Heston (1991) as modified in Penn World Table 5.6 (1995) as distributed by the National Bureau of Economic Research. That table incorporates a substantial downward revision in the growth and level estimates for China, which is used in some of the comparisons with India and Pakistan.

2. The combined performance of the original Pakistan over the 1950–90 period is rather less impressive than present-day Pakistan because Bangladesh appears to have grown by only 1.3 percent per annum during this period. Thus the combined growth would be somewhat under India's experience. Any overall assessment of Pakistan's economic performance needs to somehow consider the economic relationship of the two wings of Pakistan before the civil war; some further comments on this point will be made below.

3. The heavy dependence of Pakistan on foreign loans and assistance throughout the period may not be as well known because, even though the loans and assistance India has received have not been that large in India's total investment, they are still large absolute sums given India's large population. (In 1991, the population of India was about 7.5 times that of Pakistan.) The indebtedness figures of India and Pakistan only partially reflect this dependence because, as compared to India, Pakistan has received much more assistance in the forms of grants than in loans. In dollars at exchange rates, the debt of Pakistan was $3,069 million in 1970 and rose to $13,205 million in 1987, while for India the figures were $7,938 million and $40,767 million. Relative indebtedness in Pakistan is higher on a per capita basis and as a percent of GNP at exchange rates (38.2 percent of GNP for Pakistan versus 16.5 percent for India in 1987). However, debt service as a percentage of exports was about 25 percent in both countries in 1987. (Data from *World Development Report* 1989, 208.)

4. For a general discussion of Pakistan, see Naseem (1981); for India, see Srinavasan and Bardhan (1988) and Heston (1990).

Selected References

Ahluwalia, I. 1985. *Industrial Growth in India: Stagnation since the Mid-Sixties*. New Delhi: Oxford University Press.

Alagh, Yoginder. 1991. *Indian Development Planning and Policy*. New Delhi: Vikas Publishing House.

Altaf, Zafar. 1984. *Pakistani Entrepreneurs: Their Development, Characteristics and Attitudes*. New Delhi: IBD Publishers.

Bhagwati, J. 1993. *India in Transition: Freeing the Economy*. Oxford, Eng.: Oxford University Press.

Bhagwati, J., and Padma Desai. 1970. *India, Planning for Industrialization: Industrialization and Trade Policies since 1951.* London: Oxford University Press.

Burki, Shahid Javed. 1988. "Poverty in Pakistan: Myth or Reality?" In T. N. Srinivasan and Pranab K. Bardhan, eds., *Rural Poverty in South Asia.* New York: Columbia University Press.

George, K. K. 1989. "Ninth Finance Commission's First Award: An Evaluation." *Economic and Political Weekly,* April 1.

Government of India. 1988. *First Report of the Ninth Finance Commission (for 1989–90).* New Delhi: Ministry of Finance, July.

Government of India. 1993. *Economic Survey, 1992–93.* New Delhi: Ministry of Finance.

Government of Pakistan. 1993. *Economic Survey, 1992–93.* Islamabad: Finance Division, Economic Adviser's Wing.

Hanson, James A., and Samuel S. Lieberman. 1989. *India: Poverty, Employment, and Social Services* (World Bank country study). Washington, D.C.: World Bank.

Heston, Alan. 1982. "National Income 1857–1947." Vol. 2, *Cambridge Economic History of India.* New York: Cambridge University Press, chap. 4.

———. 1990. "Poverty." In Marshall M. Bouton and Phillip Oldenburg, eds., *India Briefing, 1990.* New York: Asia Society.

Heston, Alan, and R. Summers. 1980. "Comparative Indian Economic Growth, 1870–1970." *American Economic Review,* May.

Jaggannathan, N. Vijay, and Animesh Halder. 1989. "A Case Study of Pavement Dwellers in Calcutta: Family Characteristics of the Urban Poor." *Economic and Political Weekly,* February 19.

Jodha, N. S. 1988. "Poverty Debate in India: A Minority View." *Economic and Political Weekly,* special number, November.

Kabra, K. N., and N. S. Jagannnathan. 1985. *Black Money,* Monograph Series No. 8. New Delhi: India International Centre.

Kardar, Shahid. 1987. *The Political Economy of Pakistan.* Lahore, Pakistan: Progressive Publishers.

Kidron, Micheal. 1965. *Foreign Investments in India.* London: Oxford University Press.

Kochanek, Stanley A. 1983. *Interest Groups and Development: Business and Politics in Pakistan.* Delhi: Oxford University Press.

———. 1985. "The Politics of Regulation: Rajiv's New Mantras." *Journal of Commonwealth and Comparative Politics.*

Kohli, Atul. 1987. *The State and Poverty in India; The Politics of Reform.* Cambridge, Eng.: Cambridge University Press.

Kravis, I. B., A. Heston, and R. Summers. 1982. *World Product and Income: International Comparisons of Real GDP.* Baltimore, Md.: Johns Hopkins University Press.

Kurian, N. J. 1989. Anti-Poverty Programme: A Reappraisal." *Economic and Political Weekly,* March 25.

Maddison, Angus. 1983. "A Comparison of Levels of GDP per Capita in Developed and Developing Countries, 1700–1980." *Journal of Economic History,* March.

Marathe, S. S. 1986. *Regulation and Development: India's Policy Experience of Controls over Industry.* New Delhi: Sage Publications.

Mukerjee, M. 1969. *The National Income of India, Trends and Structure.* Calcutta: Statistical Publishers.

Naqvi, S. N. H., A. R. Kemal, and A.Heston. 1983. *The Structure of Protection in Pakistan: 1980–81.* Vol. II. Islamabad: Pakistan Institute of Development Economics.

Naseem, S. M. 1981. *Underdevelopment, Poverty and Inequality in Pakistan.* Lahore, Pakistan: Vanguard Publishers.

Prasad, Pradhan H. 1988. "Roots of Uneven Regional Growth in India." *Economic and Political Weekly*, April 13.

Sivaram, B. 1980. *Report of the National Committee on the Development of Backward Areas.* New Delhi: Government of India.

Srinivasan, T. N., ed. 1994. *Agriculture and Trade in China and India: Policies and Performance since 1950.* Washington, D.C.: International Center for Economic Growth, ICS Press.

Srinivasan, T. N., and Pranab K. Bardhan, eds. 1988. *Rural Poverty in South Asia.* New York: Columbia University Press.

Summers, Robert, and A. Heston. 1991. " Penn World Tables, 1950–88." *Quarterly Journal of Economics*, May.

White, Lawrence. 1974. *Industrial Concentration and Economic Power in Pakistan.* Princeton, N.J.: Princeton University Press,

Zaidi, S. Akbar. 1989. "Regional Imbalances and the National Question in Pakistan: Some Indications." *Economic and Political Weekly*, February 19.

9

Brazilian and Colombian Economic Development in the Twentieth Century

ALBERT FISHLOW

Introduction

Both Brazil and Colombia have had favorable long-term development records. Maddison's estimates of per capita income growth show both countries to be above the regional average, not only for the earlier part of the twentieth century but for the more recent post-1950 period as well.[1] Both began the twentieth century with incomes per capita much below those of Argentina and Chile; both at the end of the 1980s were comparable, at a level of about $3,000 in 1980 international purchasing power. In this aggregate respect and others, the distinction between Brazil and Colombia is much less pronounced than other country pairs in this volume. This similarity in performance does not eliminate the usefulness of a closer comparative look. What emerges is a significant contrast in policy styles that has led to differences both in the implementation of the import substitution model of industrialization after 1950 and in the reaction to the oil shocks of the 1970s and the debt crisis of the 1980s.

In successive sections I briefly characterize in these countries' four periods of twentieth-century economic development: the pre-1950 expansion driven largely by integration into the world economy, positive until 1929 and negative thereafter; deliberate import substitution from 1950 to the mid-1960s; liberalization in the subsequent period until the oil shocks; and adjustment to highly variable international economic conditions, especially access to capital markets, in the 1980s. In conclusion I focus on differences in policy style and its implications not only for growth but alleviation of poverty and reduction of inequality.

Integration into World Markets before 1950

Modern Colombian economic development dates from the country's twentieth-century coffee takeoff. After the disorder of the Thousand Days' War at the turn of the century, rapid and sustained export growth of coffee undergirded continuing economic growth until 1929. Colombian export volume increased from 1905 to 1929 at an annual average rate of 7.4 percent; expanded production of coffee was the driving force in this surge, leading to a rising participation in total foreign exchange earnings (see table 9.1). Import volume, aided by capital inflows in the 1920s that underwrote investment in infrastructure, increased even more rapidly than exports from 1913 to 1929. The results from this outward orientation were positive; when reliable product data first became available in the mid-1920s, they revealed economic growth in excess of 7 percent a year between 1925 and 1929.

The contrast to Brazil in the same period could not be plainer. Brazilian export volume growth was sluggish between 1905 and 1929, amounting only to about 2 percent a year (see table 9.1). Favorable coffee prices and foreign investment underwrote expansion of imports at an only slightly higher rate (3 percent). Brazil, even before the Great Depression, thus had already begun to deviate from a simple export-led model of economic growth. By the beginning of the twentieth century, despite relatively low levels of income, domestic demand and internal productive capacity were important elements determining economic growth. A first burst of industrialization occurred in the 1890s that was preserved through high rates of tariff protection even as a new wave of foreign capital inflows entered before World War I. The war was not uniform in its impact: a reduced import supply created demand for domestic substitutes but also handicapped production; on balance, the artificial shortage had a modestly positive effect on Brazilian industry. In addition, Brazil's balance of payments was somewhat improved by the reduced pressure of debt service that came with the wartime jump in the price level.[2]

At a time when Brazil was already diversifying its productive structure, Colombia was just beginning to enter the world economy. By gaining a progressively larger market share for its higher-quality coffee under the umbrella provided by Brazil's policy of stockpiling, Colombia could and did expand its exports at a favorable rate independent of the slowly expanding international demand for the product. Yet even while pursuing an export-led growth model, Colombian ideology was far from free trade in its inspiration. Tariffs were high. As a percentage

Table 9.1   External Sector of Brazil and Colombia, 1905–1993

	1905	1913	1929	1950	1965	1973	1980	1987	1993
			Export Volume (1970 = 100)						
Brazil	20	25	32	43	64	150	193	324	491
Colombia	7	14	39	54	82	121	154	170	364
			Share of Coffee Exports (%)						
Brazil	48	62	71	64	44	20	12	8[a]	3[b]
Colombia	37[c]	—	67	78	64	51	60	49[a]	18[b]
			Import Capacity (1970 = 100)						
Brazil	31	34	48	64	60	161	179	256	374
Colombia	—	27	64	69	79	135	194	293	320
			Import Volume (1970 = 100)						
Brazil	21	35	42	50	40	174	219	158	271
Colombia	—	17	57	55	58	105	205	197	396
			Exports/GDP (constant 1973 prices)						
Brazil	28[d]	27	20	10	7	8	6	9	12[b]
Colombia	—	—	33	22	16	15	14	16	19[b]

[a] 1983–1987
[b] 1992
[c] 1906–1910
[d] 1900

SOURCES: CEPAL, "América Latina, Relación de Précios del Intercambio, 1928–1976," mimeo 1977. CEPAL, "Balance Preliminar de la Economia Latinoamericana," various years. CEPAL, *Statistical Yearbook*, 1993 IBGE, *Estatísticas Historicas do Brazil*, vol. 3, 1987. José Antonio Ocampo and Santiago Montenegro, *Crisis Mundial, Protecciône Industrialización*, 1984. IDB, *Economic and Social Progress*, 1989, 1993. Maddison, this volume.

of imports, collections were between 40 and 50 percent before the First World War and, after an intermediate decline, rose again to 30 percent in the latter part of the 1920s. Protection was inevitable as a consequence of fiscal requirements; as late as 1929 about two-thirds of national revenues derived from customs duties. But even behind such barriers, internal industrial growth was secondary to expanding the agricultural frontier to increase production for export.

Economic backwardness did not lead to novelty in the style of Colombian economic development. As a late follower, Colombia simply replicated, with considerable success, commodity export specialization. There was no compelling reason to do otherwise. What was missing, and frequently forgotten in the now-fashionable extrapolation of the Gerschenkron backwardness model, was the national security motive for economic performance. Within Europe, and later in Japan, national security drove states to pursue interventionist policies to accelerate industrialization.[3] For Latin America, despite occasional nineteenth-century conflict, there was no parallel dominating the formation of national policy. It was the dramatic change in external conditions ushered in by the Great Depression that provoked definitive and increasingly deliberate abandonment of the export-led growth paradigm.

The fall of coffee prices with the onset of the Great Depression in 1929 added on to a slide that had begun as a result of overproduction in the 1920s. In both countries, coffee in 1929 generated upward of two-thirds of total export receipts (see table 9.1). When prices fell by more than a third in 1930, total Colombian export earnings contracted by 11 percent and Brazilian by almost 30 percent. As the coffee price continued to erode, export receipts continued to fall, bottoming at 40 percent of their 1929 level for Brazil and almost 50 percent for Colombia in 1932–1933. Such reductions occurred despite increases in export volume.

Because import prices also declined in the early 1930s, export purchasing power was not affected as much as the simple dollar totals suggest. But the cessation of capital inflows and initial maintenance of debt service also took their toll in restricting import demand. In those difficult circumstances, both countries increasingly resorted to new quantitative restrictions on imports, including licenses and exchange controls, as well as devaluations in real terms. Both countries also ceased to service fully their external debts. Added to these commercial policies was an eventual anticyclical expansion of domestic demand via looser credit and fiscal deficits.

Yet the conversion to heterodox economic response was neither immediate nor determined by Keynesian logic. The initial reaction to the depression in Colombia was an orthodox fiscal and monetary contraction, lasting about two and a half years. The memory of the monetary disorder of the Thousand Days' War (1899–1902) was an important constraint. President Olaya Herrera in 1931 affirmed his view of "the fundamental need to preserve sound money and to maintain the gold standard. All the sacrifice is little if, with it, we avoid the return to a paper money regime that together with the civil wars, signified for the country misery and discredit."[4] Suspension of convertibility with the pound in September 1931 marked the beginning of a more active policy. It resulted from the magnitude and duration of the global contraction on the one side and increased domestic pressure from coffee producers on the other. The war with Peru in 1933–1934 further provoked expansion. Once such policies took force, more control had to be exercised over imports to avoid disequilibrium in the balance of payments.

In Brazil the conversion to heterodoxy occurred more quickly. There was no equivalent historical memory in the first instance; second, coffee policy had been much more interventionist and was again beginning as early as 1930 in the state of São Paulo; third, civil war led to a large federal deficit in 1932, which was succeeded by continuingly lax fiscal discipline and accommodating monetary policy.[5]

This conjunction of limited imports and sustained internal income in both countries generated demand for manufactures that spilled over into spontaneous import substitution. The 1930s were important for industrialization in both countries but with a fundamental difference. In Colombia the decade provided the first prolonged impulse to industrial development in which domestic textiles played a leading role. In Brazil, industrialization had already proceeded beyond that rudimentary starting point; intermediate goods and even some capital goods began to be produced locally.

In both countries the vitality of the industrial sector helped overcome the initial income decline and sparked a recovery that led aggregate output to much higher levels during the depression decade. In Colombia, 1939 gross domestic product had increased by 45 percent over 1929; in Brazil, by 52 percent. Industrial growth was especially strong in Colombia and the highest among all Latin American countries including Brazil.[6]

The vast scope for Colombian import substitution in basic consumer goods is clear. In 1929 imports supplied 86 percent of the demand for cotton cloth; in 1939, only 50; and by 1945, a mere 6 percent. Cotton textile production expanded at a rate of 21 percent a year between 1932 and 1939 and 17 percent between 1939 and 1947, twice the rates of manufacturing as a whole. The expansion of textiles was responsible for more than half the increment in value added of manufacturing activity in the 1930s and two-thirds during the war. In Brazil, by contrast, domestic production was already supplying more than 85 percent of textile demand when the depression struck. Brazilian textile growth was sustained at high rates by income growth and a greater-than-unity income elasticity. But through import substitution, new sectors such as cement, metallurgy, and paper expanded much more rapidly.[7]

A common characteristic of industrial development in Brazil and Colombia in the 1930s was its limited ability to incorporate the import and production of technologically advanced new machinery and equipment during this phase of accelerated growth. Because of import constraints, a lack of functioning capital markets during the depression, and later limitations on supply during the war years, Latin American import substitution proceeded under a significant handicap. This is not to deny that imports recovered after 1932 in both countries and were reallocated to capital and intermediate good categories. But total real machinery imports in both Brazil and Colombia in 1935–1939 still fell short of their 1925–1929 level, despite much higher levels of production. Rationing occurred.[8]

As a result, the presumed Gerschenkron technological leapfrogging in which latecomers might engage was limited. Instead, domestic industry was directed toward more labor-intensive improvisation. The Gerschenkron model implicitly requires an elastic supply of capital and capital goods for its feasibility. A second consequence was an inadequate capital stock to support an industrialization that could be internationally competitive. As a result, it would be necessary to rationalize industry in the postwar period by relying on large imports of equipment. These helped to contribute to balance-of-payments problems. A capital-scarce, technologically limited industrialization did not provide an efficient basis for exports of manufactures and continued to require high rates of protection at exchange rates determined by comparative advantage in coffee.

Postwar Deliberate Import Substitution

Industrialization after 1945 emerged from such origins. The ratio of exports to product in 1950 had fallen by half in Brazil and a third in Colombia from their 1929 levels (see table 9.1). Correspondingly, the volume of imports in both countries, despite a more than doubling of output, had remained stable. In both countries, rising coffee prices tempted a return to pre-1929 primary export emphasis. But in both the recovery of export earnings instead became the basis for a deliberate strategy of import substitution industrialization.

In Brazil, farther along as a result of an earlier start and with a larger internal market, there was a more conscious emphasis on the industrial sector and, in particular, its extension to intermediate goods and consumer durables. The principal policy instrument was highly differentiated import protection, used primarily not to defend a soon weakened balance of payments but rather to motivate a transfer of resources from agriculture to industry.

As practiced in Brazil in the 1950s, the import substitution strategy had three salient characteristics.[9] One was an overvalued multiple exchange-rate system that permitted cheap but rationed imports. That made needed capital imports, petroleum, and wheat available even while magnifying the degree of effective protection provided to domestic import substitutes. Second were larger government expenditures to support accelerating economic activity. In the absence of adequate counterpart generalized tax revenues, initially bolstered by the revenues obtained from implicit taxes on coffee, such a larger state role was increasingly financed by monetary expansion. Third was a reliance on foreign capital that in the 1950s came primarily in the form of foreign equity investment, providing essential technology as well as a flow of foreign exchange necessary to supplement export earnings.

By its very nature, such an industrialization policy could not be pursued continuously. It provoked disequilibrium in its implementation, as might be expected from any special incentive. Exchange overvaluation took its toll, discouraging all exports except traditional commodities; thus import substitution partially provoked balance-of-payments problems rather than responded to them. The fiscal problem equally contained an element of deterioration. Forced saving induced by the inflation tax confronted an offsetting response by private agents through their reduction of money balances. Only by accelerating inflation could collections be sustained. Reliance on foreign investment was also potentially unstable. Not only was it more sensitive to domestic circumstances, because of the broader range of options enjoyed by foreign capital, but import substitution foreign investment was lumpy and discontinuous. When new sectors such as automobiles were being promoted, it might come in large amounts but then dry up, complicating internal macroeconomic management as well as leading to deterioration in the balance of payments. In the end, these three problems helped decelerate the until then highly successful Brazilian industrialization at the end of the 1950s.

The Colombian experience was somewhat at variance, although retaining generic similarity. For one, the industrialization objective was not as dominant as in Brazil, although the lesson of the depression was not lost on Colombian leaders. Colombia was content to accept the postwar coffee bonanza so as to liberalize imports at a time when Brazil was retreating from an earlier liberalization in 1947–1948. The share of imports in total product in Colombia actually rose, from 17 percent in 1945–1949 to 21 percent in 1950–1954.[10] Note the reliance on devaluation in 1951, not to correct a foreign exchange deficit but to afford an opportunity to reduce import protection. Although domestic industry expanded at a high rate during this early period, it was on the basis of externally induced prosperity rather than vigorous import substitution.

In the last analysis, and different from Brazil, "in the Colombian case, the weight of an agrarian and agroexport economy with ample position in the productive structure and in the circles of power acted itself as a restriction against an excessive bias in favor of industrialists."[11] Import substitution became a generalized modernization strategy that extended to the agricultural sector as well. In Brazil the coffee interests could impede direct subsidies to industry and avoid direct taxation, but they were not strong enough to prevent the benefits of higher coffee prices being indirectly passed on to industry by overvalued exchange rates providing access to cheap imports of capital and intermediate goods. In Colombia the coffee sector was subject to less taxation and less discrimination than in Brazil; more revenues from the unfavorable coffee exchange rate found their way back to the coffee producers.

Thus in Brazil the ratio of the coffee export exchange rate to the import rate was significantly lower than in Colombia over this period. First, in Brazil, the relative value ranged from 0.75 to 0.5 at the end of the period; in Colombia it was 0.9 and larger, falling in the early 1960s to about 0.8. Second, because coffee was expanding, the Colombian import rate was actually comparatively more overvalued relative to an inflation-adjusted 1963 level than was the Brazilian rate. Third, the bias against exports in Brazil was stronger than that in Colombia, as measured by the ratio of import-to-export exchange rates.

These last two characteristics also help differentiate the import substitution processes pursued in the two countries. In Brazil, there was more emphasis in the 1950s on devising sophisticated mechanisms of import control through the auction of foreign exchange and a multiple-rate system. There was thus more frequent adjustment of the rate, leading to less overvaluation. Note that Brazil's import volume actually declined by 20 percent between 1950 and 1965, while it modestly increased in Colombia (see table 9.1). Correspondingly, there was more taxation of the export sector and more incentive provided to domestic industrial production at the expense of the export sector, to which attention was devoted only later.

Brazil pursued accelerated economic growth and avoided the foreign exchange constraint by using foreign investment proceeds and substituting domestic supply. Colombia, both because of its inflation phobia and its more-limited stage of industrial development, pursued a more orthodox response to balance-of-payments pressures: it slowed domestic growth to regulate import demand. There was much more stop and go in Colombia than in Brazil during this period and much less aggressive public sector leadership. Brazil wound up with inflation rates that rose to 90 percent in 1964, while Colombia, with the exception of the postdevaluation surges registered in mid-1957 (20 percent) and early 1963 (30 percent), experienced comparative price stability with inflation rates of about 5 percent.

These results help qualify Jeffrey Sachs's argument for Asian export orientation on the basis of extensive rural sectors exerting their influence in behalf of less overvalued exchange rates.[12] Large rural sectors in both these countries, especially Colombia, did not support more-aggressive exchange-rate policies for two reasons: First, coffee was not a dynamic product experiencing rapidly expanding international demand; for these large producers, a rational policy of exploiting their monopoly position did not involve price competition. Second, within each country, the key question was not the absolute exchange rate but rather the relative divergence of the coffee rate or implicit tax imposed on the sector;[13] that was a matter of debate, in which, predictably, the Colombian coffee interests emerged on top. Sachs's causality presumes a highly competitive international market and an unorganized rural sector. But these characteristics precisely differentiate Latin America from East Asia and thus undermine the validity of the simple rural-urban distinction. Rather, it was the need to tax the important Latin American rural sector indirectly that made exchange-rate overvaluation a specially favored instrument.

Subsequent criticism of the import-substituting model of development should not obscure its positive accomplishments during the period from 1950 to 1965. Maddison's tables in this volume (chapter 2) show that per capita growth in Brazil rose at a rate of 2.6 percent a year, and in Colombia, 1.6 percent. Both continued the expansion achieved post-1929. Equally important, in view of the attacks directed to the inefficiency of industrialization during this period, is the estimated increase in total factor productivity. Although estimates are necessarily imprecise, they suggest clear technological progress, not simply more use of inputs. For Colombia economywide gains, including those ascribable to education, were of the order of 1.2 percent a year in the period from 1956 to 1967. In Brazil, capital-intensive, modern industrial development was accompanied by annual productivity growth of about 1.5 percent. In Brazilian industry alone, the estimated increase is 2.4 per cent annually.[14]

Yet it was clear by the early 1960s that slow-growing exports were becoming a serious impediment to sustained growth as well as to macroeconomic stability, as exchange-rate devaluation reverberated into accelerated inflation. Both Brazil and Colombia undertook trade liberalization policies accompanied by fiscal reform. The changes in Brazil, accompanied by a military coup in 1964, were more far-reaching, but the Colombian reforms in 1967 also were significant. For both countries, they helped initiate a period of improved economic performance.

Toward an Outward Orientation

The late 1960s and early 1970s represented the peak of postwar, historic, economic achievement. Brazil's miracle years between 1968 and 1973 saw average annual per capita growth rates in excess of 7 percent, but Colombia's 3.8 percent over the same period was an equivalent record. In both instances, output growth proceeded from two bases. One was domestic reform, which improved fiscal performance, and in Brazil, by indexing, gave greater scope to relative price signals in resource allocation. Second was external reform, in particular, incentives to exports that helped relieve foreign exchange constraints that had increasingly rendered the import substitution model unproductive. This particular conjuncture was also favored by an expanding international economy; terms of trade were favorable but so was access to private and public capital inflows.

In both countries, government was part of the solution rather than part of the problem. In Brazil, although presided over by a military leadership, the new strategy was directed at curbing the excesses of populism rather than implanting a neoliberal alternative model. Public investment led the way to economic recovery and remained an important component during the miracle period. In Colombia, a new president concerned with economic renewal, Carlos Lleras Restrepo, took energetic action in apparently the opposite direction, that is, imposing import controls and resisting IMF pressures for devaluation to realistic exchange rates. But what emerged was a crawling-peg exchange rate and subsidies to minor exports that were the basis of diversifying and increasing Colombian exchange earnings.

In both countries, internal and external liberalization was secondary to a stable set of rules, an ample—indeed, expanding—but fiscally sound role for the public sector, and a new policy commitment to export growth as an important component of economic strategy. Industrialization and expanded participation in the world economy were no longer a contradiction. Colombia had hopes for the Andean free trade area as a source of increased and more efficient trade in manufactures, but those expectations were never realized. Export-led development of an Asian style was still far from contemplation during this period.

In the event, the Brazilian export response was much greater and more diversified. Export volume more than doubled between 1965 and 1973 (see table 9.1). At the same time, the share of coffee fell to only 20 percent in 1973. Manufactured exports increased rapidly, reflecting the sophistication and extent of Brazilian industrialization. In addition, nontraditional agricultural crops like soybeans also came to the fore. Under the changing incentives of export promotion was a responsive productive structure that could rapidly alter its product mix.

The contribution of improved terms of trade is reflected in import capacity growing more than export volume. But that margin is smaller than the additional foreign exchange provided by Brazilian access to external borrowing. The current account balance changed from a modest surplus in 1965–66 to a deficit of 2.3 percent of GDP in 1971–73. External debt mounted to 17 percent of product at the end of 1973. This was debt led, rather than export led, growth, a style of expansion that underwrote expansion of real imports at a staggering rate of 20 percent a year. These years saw the first reversal of a declining import ratio since the immediate postwar period, when increased access to foreign inputs underwrote a surge in domestic investment.

In Colombia, the changes in external accounts, like output growth itself, were more moderate. Export volume increased by 5.7 percent annually, while imports rose almost identically, to 6.5 percent. Minor exports increased their participation, but the coffee sector still accounted for a majority of exports in 1973. Capital inflows, primarily from official sources, likewise increased. A gradual reduction of import restrictions accompanied the greater availability of foreign exchange. This Colombian approach to import liberalization received high praise from an analyst writing in 1974: "In retrospect, the Colombian experience vindicates the case for gradualism in import liberalization that went pari passu with export expansion. It was not necessary to dismantle the protective system before that export expansion could be generated. The wisdom of avoiding shock treatments while keeping control over macroeconomic management policies remains relevant for anti-inflationary policies."[15]

Yet under the trying international economic conditions set in motion by the first oil shock in late 1973, neither country managed to sustain its stellar performance. Despite very different circumstances, neither managed its integration into the international economy entirely satisfactorily, a deficiency that became apparent in the 1980s.

Brazil was the largest (developing country) importer of petroleum: four-fifths of its oil consumption was satisfied by imports. The quadrupling of oil prices thus had a significant impact, the more so because internal bottlenecks and excess demand were creating adjustment problems and because inflation was in ascendance after its reduction to less than 20 percent annually in 1973. In the face of a sudden balance-of-payments deterioration, Brazil opted not for devaluation or for domestic austerity but rather for larger external flows. The logic was dual. If the price rise were temporary, such finance was the reasonable adjustment path; if it were permanent, foreign savings could help make feasible the massive program of import substitution investment in intermediate activities that had already been projected before the shock. There was also a strong political impulse to the choice of a debt strategy: planned easing of repression was much easier under continuing conditions of consumption expansion.[16]

In a context of continuing high growth, the balance-of-payments problem was not the only one. State activity increased, partially in the context of implementing the planned industrialization, partially to attract continuing inflows of foreign resources. To satisfy the private sector, whose complaints were becoming more vocal, new subsidies and credits were made available. The proliferation of incentives canceled their allocative impact, succeeding only in exposing the fiscal weakness of the state. Macroeconomic management was complicated by the impact of borrowing on reserves and hence monetary policy. By the end of the decade, Brazil was reduced to a stop-go alternation to dampen inflation that was rising to the 50 percent level; the miracle was only a memory.

Although aggregate growth rates remained respectable and export diversification continued, Brazilian performance was increasingly vulnerable to its accumulating external debt. There had been a subtle but important shift from the debt-led growth between 1965 and 1973 to the debt-led debt after 1973, as larger proportions of gross inflows went to pay interest on previous debt and less was left to finance new imports. In fact, between 1974 and 1978 nominal imports did not increase. The progressively larger debt was a barrier to more-rapid product growth, as well as a deterrent to devaluation because of the consequences for increased public payments for debt service. Without the added stimulus of exchange-rate adjustment to the deterioration in external accounts, export volume increased at the inadequate rate of 3.7 percent per year.

Colombia was able to avoid indebtedness. That path was an option in the troubled 1970s in part because it had been a modest oil exporter; its balance of payments were virtually unaffected in 1974, although some limit on imports was established late in the year because of reserve losses. The rise in coffee prices owing to a freeze in Brazil in 1975 was a second factor; Colombia thus benefited from an unanticipated bonanza. Still a third element was the rising receipts from illicit drug traffic. The Colombian problem became an accommodation to an external boom rather than an adjustment to a substantial oil tax.

The government's concerns focused on countercyclical reduction of the domestic spillover effects rather than immediate exploitation of the windfall. Such caution stemmed from previous experience with coffee price booms, on the one hand, and the sensitivity to domestic inflation, on the other. The latter, in an international environment of rising prices, was given a quantum boost. In the event, exchange-rate appreciation became a way of dampening internal inflation; authorities wisely turned down proffered loans from international banks that would have made the situation even more difficult.

The consequences of this policy were to slow domestic growth. Industry experienced its lowest rate of expansion relative to total income since the 1920s. For one, import competition, legal and illegal, became more substantial. For a second, relative prices of food rose significantly, changing the composition of demand. Third, exports of industrial products were considerably set back by the double blow of reduced subsidies and exchange-rate appreciation. This all added up to a reduction in the rate of fixed investment from 1974 to 1980 even as public sector savings increased.[17]

Recorded growth rates from 1973 to 1980 compared favorably with previous periods for both Brazil and Colombia and indeed for developing countries as a whole. Per capita income increased by 4.2 percent in Brazil and 2.9 percent in Colombia. Yet each was poised for severe problems in the next decade. Brazil had integrated asymmetrically into the world economy, favoring capital inflows more than export penetration, and its fate depended on its capacity to escape the Damoclean sword represented by its high debt/export ratio. On the eve of the second oil shock, to complicate matters, Brazil opted for a return to rapid growth.

Colombia, after eschewing opportunities to borrow earlier in the decade, increased its exposure sharply at the end. Between the beginning of 1979 and the end of 1981, its external debt increased by more than 70 percent; having avoided the first round of abundant finance after 1973, it fell victim to the second surge as government expenditures led an expansion of domestic demand designed to improve economic performance.

Thus in both countries the objective of matching earlier special achievement contributed to increased vulnerability. When international economic conditions were favorable, as they had been from the mid-1960s to 1973, each could become more outward oriented in a gradual and controlled manner. When conditions turned more hazardous thereafter, policies proved inadequate to facilitate adjustment. The extent of the problem was concealed by the coffee bonanza and external capital inflows. In the 1980s it became painfully apparent.

A Lost Decade of Development

The 1980s definitively reversed the pattern of earlier twentieth-century economic growth for both countries. Colombian per capita production eked out an advance of 0.9 percent a year between 1980 and 1987, while Brazil managed a stark 0.3 percent. Yet these were the best performances in Latin America. Colombia achieved another distinction: it was the only country in the region that managed to meet its external obligations in a continuing fashion without resorting to organized rescue by the IMF in conjunction with the commercial banks.

A combination of industrialized-country recession, high real interest rates, adverse terms of trade, and the end of elastic supply of external capital proved insuperable to the Latin American countries. Although it is conventional wisdom that the East Asian countries suffered more from the changes in external circumstances, owing to their greater reliance on exports, such a conclusion is deficient in two respects. First, it ignores the consequences of diminished capital flow that had begun in 1981 and on which Latin American countries dependend to meet their prior claims. Second, it relates these effects to total product rather than to export earnings; yet the burden of the external shock had to be met in foreign exchange. Such a revised calculus places Brazil as the most affected country in both regions and Colombia as one of the least.[18]

Under this pressure of deteriorating external accounts from the second shock, the only solution was an immediate reduction of imports. That, however, could not be accomplished without a magnified effect on income; the smaller and more necessary imports were, the larger the consequence. Whereas Colombia had the benefit of greater gradualism, and continued voluntary inflows of private capital, Brazil did not. Between 1981 and 1983 Brazilian imports were compressed by more than 30 percent; Colombia's actually increased.

The explanation of the poor absolute but relatively good Colombian performance in the 1980s is its avoidance of the debt crisis, on the one hand, but continuing susceptibility to specialization in commodity exports, on the other. As late as 1983–87, slow-growing coffee constituted half of total export earnings. Only after 1984 did the real exchange rate depreciate significantly as an incentive to other minor exports. Since that time export volume has increased. But Colombia is far from the model of Japan in Latin America that policy makers dreamed of in the 1970s.

Rather, macroeconomic policy, and hence support for internal demand, continues to be tied to exogenous circumstances. Significant improvement in the coffee price in 1986 was accompanied by a growth rate of 5.8 percent, the highest in the decade, and reduced inflation. A subsequent decline in prices meant slowed expansion. Debt continued to expand after 1984 and in 1988 amounted to 45 percent of product compared with little more than 20 percent in 1980. It was almost a repetition of the debt-led debt experience of Brazil in the latter part of the 1970s.

The dynamic of the Colombian response in the recent period is also affected by the increasing incompatibility of illegal drug activities and economic modernization. No longer merely a disturbing factor in the balance of payments and an important source of smuggled imports, the drug traffic has become an overt challenge to public order and the capacity to govern. Its implications for private investment and the attendant potential expansion of trade in manufactures are clearly negative. That new factor adds to the conventional but continuing difficulty of defining an appropriate style of integration into the international economy.

If Colombian experience and policy conform broadly to the mold of earlier periods, the Brazilian stagnation of the latter 1980s constitutes a distinct and unpleasant novelty. Despite the severe and multiple shocks of the early 1980s, Brazil had returned to a more normal growth rate of 5.1 percent in 1984, with even a better 8.3 percent in 1985. Expansion of exports and control over imports had made possible a large trade balance that satisfied the service requirements of the external debt. With the transition to civilian government in 1985, and the formulation of the Cruzado plan in February 1986 to deal with intolerably high inflation exceeding 200 percent a year, prospects for a full economic recovery seemed bright. Brazil, the finance minister proclaimed, would have the inflation rates of Switzerland and the growth rates of Japan.

Such hopes were dashed by a resurgence of inflation several months later, and its apparent immunity to a succession of subsequent plans, the last in early 1991, after the ambitious policy of March 1990 mandated by the new popularly elected President Collor had failed. Inflation, rather than the external accounts, has moved to center stage. The growth of export volume from 1980 to 1988 was at a rate of more than 6 percent annually and of actual receipts, almost as fast. This compares favorably even with the years of rapid expansion in the late 1960s and early 1970s. Yet it is all for naught. Growth rates since 1986 have been low and even negative in response to the tightened monetary policy associated with periodic efforts to defeat inflation. The earlier technique of indexation, which assured stable real exchange rates and interest rates despite high rates of inflation, could not survive the accelerating prices that have continuously threatened to degenerate into hyperinflation.

Although analysts may differ on the specifics of the deficiencies of the Cruzado plan and its successors, two general conclusions seem valid. One is that the failures of these heterodox efforts are in large measure due to the precarious fiscal position of the government. Fiscal policy is not in a position to regulate aggregate demand to provide support for various price and wage control schemes. In its absence, monetary policy cannot serve because real interest rates are themselves destabilizing by increasing government interest payments.

The second is that Brazilian governments in the 1980s have overestimated the importance of immediate credibility and underestimated the need to alter expectations through cumulative and perhaps lengthy periods of slower, but controlled, growth. While sustaining the impossibility of not growing, efforts to avoid recession have not meant prosperity but rather unproductive recession. The uncertainty attendant on repeated failure has reduced real investment in favor of financial speculation and even capital flight. Even the large trade surpluses that have been achieved are tainted by their dependence on low real wages. Technological change has lagged behind Brazil's East Asian competitors.

Brazil's recent poor performance stands in contrast to Chilean recovery and Mexican structural reforms and even Colombian muddling through. Increasingly, explanations are political rather than economic: the ineffectiveness of economic policy under congressional auspices; the inadequacy of the 1988 constitution; the blocking role of organized labor to economic austerity; and so on. The apparent Argentinization of Brazil in recent years is a challenge not only to policy makers seeking solutions but to analysts seeking to understand its causes.

In mid-1995, both countries stand on the brink of new political and economic opportunities. Both had new presidential elections in 1994. For Brazil, the key question is whether price stabilization can become a new way of life; it has been recovering from the shock of the Collor years and shows new signs of vigor and growth. For Colombia, the issue is twofold: whether new exports can provide a strong basis for a continuing, but more rapid, economic expansion and whether the importance of the drug traffic can be diminished. For both, the issue of closer alignment of trade with the United States poses important opportunities as well as challenges.

Conclusion

In this final section, I derive four conclusions drawn from the comparative analysis of Brazilian and Colombian twentieth-century experiences.

First, the satisfactory long-term development record of both countries owes itself to pragmatism and eclecticism in economic policies. In neither has there been a strong and exclusive ideological position. Even under Brazil's military leadership, the public sector flourished; Colombia's import substitution did not pit the industrial sector against the rural. Both countries converted in the 1930s to more inward-looking policies but again in the 1960s looked to greater exports of new products as a basis for economic expansion. Each found ways to keep the key relative prices, the exchange rate, real interest rates, and real wages within bounds and limited their control to achieve other objectives. Colombia's use of the crawling-peg exchange rate in 1967 and Brazil's indexation are illustrative of policy innovations emanating internally and initially meeting criticism from the international financial institutions.

Of the two countries, Colombia shows the greater restraint and the greater sensitivity to international economic conditions. Its smaller size and larger reliance on commodity exports, as well as a strong consensus against internal inflation, have narrowed the band of the tolerable. But its capacity to use monetary and fiscal policy has also limited the reliance on exchange-rate policy to fight inflation and thus has avoided the extremes of the Argentine price instability and disincentives to exports. In failing better to take advantage of the coffee bonanza in the mid-1970s, Colombia showed the downside of a preoccupation with short-term macroeconomic management rather than a coherent development strategy based on export penetration of its industrial sector.

Brazil's higher growth rate and more intensive industrialization were accompanied by disequilibrium, internal and external. Economic policy change was abrupt and guided by an emphasis on achieving rapid expansion. Economic growth came closer to being a national solution both for poverty as well as for national security.

In the 1980s, Colombia's incrementalism persisted in the midst of a difficult international economy. It averted the soaring inflation found elsewhere in the region, and it allowed more continuity. The price was less rapid economic growth at a time when internal disorder became a major challenge. But the instability of accelerating inflation would have been worse. Politics has been given scope to reconcile rural opposition and find a solution to the independent power of drug traffickers.

Brazil in the 1980s abandoned incrementalism for more dramatic efforts to bring domestic disequilibrium under control at the very time that its export performance was becoming regular and attaining a high rate of increase. Neither the experiment with rational expectations and target exchange rates in 1980 nor the Cruzado plan in 1986 nor the Collor plan in 1990 proved successful. A stop-go alternative cannot work because initial inflation rates are too high. But successive failures, which have eroded confidence and reduced long-term investment, have made executing new strategies of import liberalization more difficult. They have also hardened domestic sectoral interests and contributed to a spreading sense of political failure. But the Real plan and Fernando Henrique Cardoso's inauguration in 1995 may alter that.

A second conclusion is that both countries faced the international economy with the disadvantage of inadequate domestic surpluses. The national savings rate in Colombia is on the order of 20 percent; in Brazil, it has been even lower in recent years owing to large public sector deficits. This has meant excessive reliance on external savings and contributed to the diagnosis of foreign exchange constraint as the rationalization rather than to more aggressive export orientation. National ideology emphasizing autonomy has thus been inconsistent with the reality that such resources have been necessary. Although the divided positions regarding foreign investment are less polarized than before, they persist below the surface. Integration into the international economy, however much economists may agree, is by no means a settled matter in either society. There is a lingering nostalgia for import substitution among many.

In the third instance, private and public sectors seem to have coexisted reasonably in both countries through this period. Even with a rising degree of public participation, there was a recognition of private capabilities and the strength of private sectors. Despite the range of quantitative controls, benefits do not seem to have been diluted into nonproductive rent seeking. Incentives and subsidies elicited private investment and expansion of productive capacity. In neither country was such a productive structure highly inefficient; on the contrary, industry could and did become an increasing source of exports. In Colombia, however, the coffee sector has persisted far longer and far stronger than in Brazil, exerting its influence not in favor of rural exports generally but against taxation of its proceeds. Now, in the 1990s, petroleum is a rising export as the importance of coffee diminishes.

In neither country does one see the close association between private sector and public agencies that is characteristic of the East Asian model. Indeed, in Brazil in the 1980s, the government has come to blame lack of private sector cooperation for the failure of price stabilization; relationships are increasingly seen as antagonistic. State technocrats are not a committee of the national bourgeoisie but have independent objectives. As inconsistencies rise to the fore so does neoliberal sentiment. But in neither country is such an alternative a likely outcome; it is more a rhetorical effort, often on both sides, to improve bargaining outcomes. These interactions, and not simply a set of rules, are likely to be central to better economic performance in the 1990s.

The fourth and final point relates to different styles of accommodating to the high levels of income inequality in the two countries. In the 1960s both countries had roughly comparable levels of inequality, with Gini coefficients of the order of 0.55.[19] That translates into the top decile of the population with almost 50 percent of the income, the bottom half of the population with less than 15 percent. By international standards, such inequality is an extreme.

Whereas in Brazil economic growth became the principal vehicle of alleviating poverty, by raising all incomes even while inequality actually increased, in Colombia, inequality actually declined and thus contributed to increasing the incomes of the poor. Thus World Bank calculations measure an observed reduction of poverty in Brazil of 29 percentage points from 1960 to 1980; if the income distribution had remained constant, there would have been a further 5 percentage point decline. For Colombia an equivalent methodology shows an improvement of some 20 points between 1971 and 1978, a higher annual rate to which diminished inequality contributed about half the gain. In the 1980s, with slow growth, Brazil saw poverty grow by 5 percentage points while Colombia's grew by only 1.[20]

To some degree these results reflect different economic circumstances. The poorer and larger rural sector in Colombia benefited from the coffee boom, bringing with it a rise in urban unskilled wages and thereby ameliorating poverty. The economic miracle and the subsequent emphasis on import substitution industry in Brazil substantially bypassed the northeast, where poverty is concentrated.

Yet these different economic environments themselves accurately reflect the emphasis of policy makers in the two countries. In Brazil the solution to poverty was accelerated economic growth, with less attention to targeting the poor. In Colombia integration of the poor was a conscious political goal, made more salient by the constant threat of rural unrest. Recognizing that growth would be moderate, more attention was placed on social expenditures and education.

Measures of human development, difficult as a meaningful aggregation is, reinforce this distinction. The United Nations human development index shows Colombia with a ranking higher than its income per capita, with Brazil the reverse.[21] The *Report* further characterizes the two countries differently. Colombia is a case of disrupted development, where earlier progress was slowed as a consequence of slow growth and adjustment in the 1980s. Brazil "failed to achieve satisfactory human development despite high incomes, rapid growth and substantial government spending on the social sectors."[22] Inefficient targeting of such expenditures directed benefits to the better off, as reflected in the relatively high social security and housing outlays.

In their more successful direct efforts to alleviate poverty, Colombian policy makers also carved out space for their incrementalism and moderate growth objectives. In Brazil, by contrast, the reliance on rapid growth and mobility to ameliorate the conditions of the poor contributed to a metapopulism: a felt need to sustain expansionary policies when more restraint might have been advisable.

The immediate challenge to policies in these countries is thus correspondingly different. In Brazil it is to achieve macroeconomic stability and to rely less on economic growth and more on equity as a basis for broad-gauged increases in living standards. In Colombia it is to achieve higher average growth through greater export diversification and less susceptibility to cycles in the international economy. In both, past experience, properly interpreted, will be a useful guide.

Notes

1. See Angus Maddison, this volume, table 2.4.

2. See my "Brazilian Development in Long-Term Perspective," *American Economic Review*, May 1980.

3. For a brief discussion of the Gerschenkron model and references, see my entry, "Alexander Gerschenkron," in the *New Palgrave Dictionary*.

4. Quoted in José Antonio Ocampo and Santiago Montenegro, *Crisis Mundial, Protección e Industrialización* (Bogota, 1984), p. 88. My translation.

5. For more detailed discussion, see my "Origins and Consequences of Import Substitution in Brazil," in L. Di Marco, *International Economics and Development* (New York, 1972), pp. 327ff.

6. These data come from Rosemary Thorp, ed., *Latin America in the 1930s* (London, 1984), pp. 334–35.

7. Ocampo and Montenegro, *Crisis Mundial*, pp. 181–200, for a discussion of the textile sector in the 1930s; see Fishlow, "Origins," pp. 330–39, for Brazilian industrial development.

8. These import data come from Instituto Brasileiro de Geografia e Estatística, *Estatísticas Históricas do Brasil*, 1986, vol. 3, p. 345; and Ocampo and Montenegro, *Crisis Mundial*, p. 189. Note that Ocampo argues in favor of much capital expansion occurring in Colombia during the depression itself rather than previously and hence that "the external sector was not, therefore, an import limit for the expansion of productive capacity during the decade of the '30s" (p. 126, my translation). That was obviously true but nonetheless consistent with changes in the capital-labor ratio as well as technology content that I discuss.

9. For a more detailed discussion, see my "Origins and Consequences."

10. José Antonio Ocampo, ed., *Historia Económica de Colombia* (Bogotá, 1987), p. 253.

11. Ocampo, ed., *Historia Económica*, p. 260. My translation.

12. Jeffrey Sachs, "External Debt and Macroeconomic Performance in Latin America and East Asia," *Brookings Papers on Economic Activity*, no. 2 (Washington, D.C., 1985).

13. The same point is made in R. Nelson, T. P. Schultz, and R. Slighton, *Structural Change in a Developing Economy* (Princeton, 1971), pp. 249ff.

14. For Colombia, see Inter-American Development Bank, *Economic and Social Progress in Latin America, 1989* (Washington, D.C., 1990), p. 182. For Brazil, see Henry Bruton, "Productivity Growth in Latin America," *American Economic Review*, December 1967, p. 1103. For the results in manufacturing between 1950 and 1960, see my "Origins and Consequences."

15. Carlos Diaz Alejandro, *Foreign Trade Regimes and Economic Development: Colombia* (New York, 1976), p. 251.

16. See my "Tale of Two Presidents," in A. Stepan, ed., *Democratizing Brazil: Problems of Transition and Consolidation* (Oxford, 1988) for extensive treatment of this period.

17. I am following Ocampo's discussion in *Historia Económica*, pp. 278–79. See also Inter-American Development Bank, *Economic and Social Progress, 1989*, pp. 150ff.

18. For these calculations, see my "Some Reflections on Comparative Latin American Economic Performance and Policy," Department of Economics, University of California, Berkeley, Working Paper no. 8754 (September 1987), table 2. For the conventional calculation, see Bela Balassa's decompositions in his "Adjustment Policies in Developing Countries, 1979–1983," World Bank Staff Working Paper, no. 675 (Washington, D.C., 1984).

19. For the Brazilian household distribution in 1960, see my "Brazilian Size Distribution of Income," *American Economic Review*, May 1972, p. 392. For Colombia, World Bank, *World Development Report, 1990* (New York, 1991), p. 49.

20. World Bank, *World Development Report, 1990*, p. 48.

21. U.N. Development Program, *Human Development Report, 1990* (New York, 1991), p. 129.

22. Ibid., p. 56.

10

Growth and Equity in Nigeria and Indonesia

DAVID BEVAN,
PAUL COLLIER, and
JAN WILLEM GUNNING

Introduction

Nigeria and Indonesia are large, populous, and ethnically diverse; both have a long history of agricultural exports and experienced oil windfalls of comparable magnitude. Yet their patterns of economic development diverged dramatically.

From 1950 to the mid-1980s, Indonesian living standards tripled relative to Nigerian, which fell absolutely. The incidence of poverty declined substantially in Indonesia and increased in Nigeria. The distribution of income became slightly more equal in Indonesia, whereas inequality may have increased in Nigeria. By the end of the period, Indonesia was considerably the more equal society. These outcomes have not evolved as a steady progression; both economies have experienced massive domestic and external shocks. The domestic shocks (war and hyperinflation) were country specific, but the main external shocks (the temporary oil windfalls) were common.

These remarkably divergent outcomes were attributable to the period after 1973 during which external shocks were similar and well after the differing domestic shocks. Hence, the key question is, why did the oil shocks give rise to accelerated growth with equity in Indonesia, whereas in Nigeria they generated negative growth and, possibly, rising inequality?

The divergence after 1973 was largely the result of differences in economic policy, which can be partly traced to conditions before the boom, as described below, in six developmental phases. Within these phases, economic growth and distributional outcomes are compared by relating them to different economic policies and performances in the agricultural and industrial sectors. The chapter concludes by examining why policies diverged so substantially.

Phases in Development

For both economies it is useful to distinguish between six phases. The five events that separate these phases are independence, the collapse into crisis, the oil price increase of 1973, the post-1981 decline in the Organization of Petroleum Exporting Countries (OPEC) share of the oil market, and the oil price crash of 1986.

The colonial legacy in both economies was predominantly that of an infrastructure oriented toward export agriculture. In Indonesia by independence (1949), however, this had been severely damaged by the war against the Japanese followed by that against the Dutch. Nigerian independence (1960) was achieved without such costs. After independence both societies drifted into crises. In Indonesia during the first seven years of independence, there was an attempt at democracy, but no party or coalition was able to sustain a government. Regional rebellions were resolved by military victory for the Javanese, who constituted two-thirds of the national population. In 1957 President Sukarno forged an uneasy alliance between the Communist Party and the army, which lasted until 1965. During this period the economy collapsed into hyperinflation, largely caused by the collapse of state revenues partly triggered by a deterioration in the terms of international trade. However, it was widely misinterpreted as being due to an uncontrolled increase in public expenditure. At the peak of this hyperinflation, the Communist Party launched a coup, which the army crushed in 1965. The new regime, headed by General Suharto (who later became president), still governs.

In Nigeria the first six years of independence were dominated by regional conflicts. The original constitution was a federation of three regions: the North, with about half the population, a majority of the army, but the weakest economy; the West, with the export crop (cocoa) and the main cities (Lagos and Ibadan); and the East, where oil was discovered. A North-East alliance to benefit from the cocoa wealth of the West gave way to a North-West alliance to benefit from the oil wealth of the East. The East then withdrew from the federation, and a civil war ensued, lasting until the federal army achieved victory in 1970.

Indonesia in 1966 and Nigeria in 1970 were thus both governed by military regimes that had emerged from a period of disaster they were determined not to repeat. However, the different form of the disasters was reflected in different solutions. The Indonesian government emphasized confidence in the currency, making the rupiah fully convertible, and (largely in response to the hyperinflation experience) a balanced budget became an explicit political commitment. The Nigerian government, having split the original three regions into thirty states, devised a formula for sharing oil revenue among them, thus enhancing the authority of the federal government. Thus, just before the first oil boom, Indonesia had in place a system that implied some exchange-rate flexibility and budgetary control. Nigeria had, by contrast, just created a series of state governments whose primary function was to spend revenue distributed by the federal government.

The post-1970 period is dominated by the oil booms. These were not the first export booms the economies shared, however, because both had benefited from the Korean War boom. It is therefore of interest to contrast policy responses to the three booms. In neither country did the Korean boom directly confront the government with a policy problem. Although the oil windfalls accrued, to a large extent, directly to the government, in the case of the Korean boom this was true only to the extent that revenue from trade taxes rose. In both countries the policy response was largely passive, resulting in reserve accumulation. In Nigeria this was because the marketing boards, in keeping with their stabilization role, did not adjust producer prices for export crops in line with world prices. The resulting accumulation was unintentional in that the boards did not foresee the boom's magnitude. Similarly, in Indonesia the accumulation of reserves was largely unplanned, resulting from the failure quickly to adjust import licensing to increased foreign exchange availability. Whereas in Nigeria adjustment during the downturn was semiautomatic because an independent monetary policy was impossible, Indonesia was less constrained, and the downturn resulted in both a fiscal and a balance-of-payments deficit.

The oil booms accrued to the governments. The Indonesian government had constrained its own policy choices by its commitment to convertibility and budget balance. In Nigeria the policy response was a massive increase in federal expenditure (which doubled both in 1974 and in 1975), with heavy emphasis on capital formation. Investment absorbed 90 percent of the "windfall,"[1] reflecting the commitment of the civil service to economic growth. There was a rapid increase in the share of industrial investment, particularly in large-scale projects (steel, petrochemicals). Current expenditure rose little and fell as a percentage of GDP.

The Indonesian reaction differed in two respects. First, there was less emphasis on capital formation. Whereas public investment rose in Nigeria from 2.2 percent of GDP before the boom to 15 percent in 1978, the Indonesian share rose in the same period from 5.0 to 10.3 percent. The numbers are not completely comparable, but the difference is large enough that the conclusion that Indonesia invested a much smaller proportion appears robust.

One reason for this difference was the Pertamina crisis of 1975. Pertamina, the national oil company, used its expanded revenue to become a state within a state, borrowing heavily on the world capital market to invest in an array of prestige projects. In 1975 it was no longer able to service its external debt, and the government had to step in. The political shock reinforced fiscal conservatism and put a severe brake on state investment. The result was not a difference in the direction of industrial policy, in that both countries adopted a structuralist emphasis on heavy industry, but a difference in scale. Indonesia severely pruned its investment plans in 1975, while Nigeria accelerated its investment.

Second, and relatedly, whereas in Nigeria the boom induced expenditures well in excess of the extra revenue and thus (in addition to a planned use of reserves) a loss of control, in Indonesia the balanced budget principle, now tested for the first time, was upheld. In fact, there was considerable underspending, and substantial foreign exchange reserves were accumulated. In Nigeria a much smaller proportion of the second oil windfall was invested than of the first. The emphasis on industrial investment remained, but investment was primarily valued as a channel for patronage. The efficiency of investment declined dramatically. In Indonesia the response to the second oil price increase was slow. Initially, through the underspending of amounts transferred to the regions, the government ran a surplus. Subsequently the boom was used for three major subsidies on fuel, rice, and fertilizer.

During the post-1981 slump, trade controls were tightened in both countries. In Indonesia the emerging budget problems led to drastic expenditure cutting; in 1983 speculative capital outflows triggered a devaluation. In both cases the adjustments were inevitable because of the constraints imposed by the budget balance. By contrast Nigeria, through a combination of reserves, borrowing, and trade controls, postponed its adjustment until 1986. It then embarked on a far-reaching economic reform program, including trade liberalization and exchange rate adjustment. In 1993, however, this liberalization was virtually completely reversed.

Economic Development Compared

GROWTH, SAVINGS, AND INVESTMENT

For Nigeria, usable estimates of GDP begin in 1950, for Indonesia, in 1953. (For summary statistics on the rate and composition of GDP growth, see table 10.1.) In Nigeria, GDP increased by 364 percent in real terms over the period 1950–1991, in Indonesia by 578 percent over 1953–1991. In terms of GDP per capita, these figures translate into annual average rates of growth of 2.9 percent for Indonesia, compared with only 0.7 percent for Nigeria. This massive

Table 10.1   GDP Growth of Nigeria and Indonesia Compared

		SHARE IN GDP GROWTH [b] OF	
	GDP Growth [a]	Agriculture	Manufacturing
Nigeria			
1950–60	42	60	12
1960–73	125	11	12
1973–79	23	−18	28
1979–84	−14	16	9
1984–91	36	42	24
Indonesia			
1953–59	21	51	5
1960–73	87	30	12
1973–79	52	17	22
1979–84	36	23	25
1984–91	48	11	42

[a] Percentage increase in GDP at factor cost (constant prices) over the period.
[b] Increase in sectoral GDP over the period, as a percentage of the absolute value of the increase in total GDP.

difference in long-run performance was not uniformly distributed over the period; the Nigerian record compares favorably before 1973 (see table 10.1). Much of the explanation for the subsequent difference lies in how each country handled its oil windfalls. Performance continued to diverge in the 1980s; Indonesia grew much faster in 1984–1991 than Nigeria did. The other notable difference is in the composition of growth in the two countries, with agriculture growing much more in Indonesia than in Nigeria (see table 10.1). By the beginning of the 1990s, the two economies had radically different structures. In Nigeria agriculture and industry each accounted for about one-third of GDP in 1991; in Indonesia agriculture had declined in relative terms (to 20 percent of GDP), and the industrial sector was almost twice as large.

In both countries the period started with extremely low investment rates (see table 10.2). In Indonesia the rate fell during the Sukarno period, reaching only 6.3 percent of GDP in 1965 (compared with 18.3 percent in Nigeria). Price control and rationing imported raw materials made the accumulation of domestic real assets unattractive (the data do not reflect the illegal acquisition of foreign financial assets, which reportedly happened on a large scale; to that extent, low investment rates need not imply low savings rates). At the same time Nigerian economic policies (through tax and tariff incentives) actively encouraged investment, particularly in industry. In the 1960s a substantial part of Nigerian investment was financed from direct foreign investment and external loans. In 1965

Table 10.2   Investment Rates, Nigeria and Indonesia, 1950–1990
               (gross domestic investment as percentage of GDP at market prices;
               in current prices)

	1950	1955	1960	1965	1970	1975	1980	1983	1990
Nigeria	7.2	12.2	13.2	18.3	14.9	25.2	22.2	14.7	14.6
Indonesia	9.4	9.9	7.9	6.3	13.6	19.5	26.6	25.1	36.6

SOURCE: *World Tables* (1976, 1980, 1994).

these amounted to almost 7 percent of GDP, whereas in Indonesia they totaled less than 1 percent.

In the period of the oil cycles, savings and investment rates were similar. There was rapid industrial growth in both countries during the first cycle, but in the case of Nigeria capital costs rose enormously; relative to capital accumulation there was in fact little output growth. There were three reasons for this difference. First, in Nigeria much of what was classified as investment did not represent capital accumulation but bribes. Second, Indonesia could still embark on industrial investment with relatively low capital intensity, which Nigeria had already undertaken in the 1960s. Third, Nigeria attempted quickly to convert the windfall into domestic real assets, which, even without corruption, would have reinforced the Dutch disease spending effect. Spending on goods and factors that were, or effectively became, nontradable resulted in rents rather than output increases. Although to some extent inevitable, this problem was less serious in Indonesia, which adjusted spending less quickly, hoarded part of the oil revenues, invested a smaller proportion out of the remainder, and scrapped the most extravagant investment projects after the Pertamina crisis. In the 1980s performance further diverged. The rate of investment continued to increase in Indonesia, reaching 36.6 percent in 1991 while falling to less than half that in Nigeria.

Living Standards, Poverty, and Equity

We begin by comparing trends in living standards as indicated by mean per capita private consumption. Trends in real private consumption are related to, but distinct from, trends in per capita GDP. Over the period since 1950 Indonesians have increased their living standards threefold relative to Nigerians. Comparisons become even more remarkable, however, when we consider subperiods. Between 1950 and 1955 living standards rose at a rate of 2.7 percent per annum in both countries. From 1955 until the mid-1960s there was stagnation in Nigeria and decline in Indonesia. Between the mid-1960s and 1973 there was a hiatus in Nigeria due to the civil war and a slow recovery in Indonesia.

By 1973, at the start of the oil boom, both countries had recovered from their respective phases of decline and had slightly exceeded the previous peak living standard. Thus, over the whole period 1950–1973, despite different brief phases of decline, living standards in both countries had increased by around 20 percent.

All the divergence in living standards therefore occurred in the period 1973– 1984, during which relative performances diverged by 8 percent per annum. Even within this period, it was during the oil slump rather than the oil boom that most of the differences lay. During the boom (1973–80), living standards rose in Nigeria by 2.3 percent per annum as against 7.0 percent in Indonesia. During the slump (1980–84), Indonesian living standards continued to rise, though at the slower rate of 2.7 percent, whereas Nigerian living standards declined at an annual rate of 15.2 percent.

The rise in living standards in Indonesia and decline in Nigeria suggest that the incidence of absolute poverty declined in Indonesia and rose in Nigeria. For Indonesia there is firm evidence that this occurred; for Nigeria the database is too fragile to support analysis.

Despite the decline in private consumption in Nigeria, public services improved, so overall well-being may also have improved. In both countries, life expectancy increased and infant and child mortality declined. Because Nigeria began with a much lower life expectancy, it is not possible to conclude which country had the more satisfactory improvement.

We now consider distributional outcomes. In both countries the politically dominant distributional dimension was regional. In both the most powerful political region was the largest, and in both it happened to start the period as poorer than average. An interesting comparison is, therefore, the trends in the income differential between the political core region and the periphery. In Indonesia, there was a clear and continuous trend between 1963 and 1984 under which Java gained relative to the periphery. Indeed the differential growth, of 1.8 percent per annum, was sufficient to reverse the initial income ranking; by the end of the period Javanese households had a higher income than those in the periphery. For Nigeria the data are shaky, but there is no basis for a claim that the North gained relative to the other regions.

Another significant spatial dimension of inequality is rural/urban. In Nigeria, urban incomes, particularly those of wage earners, were well above the supply price of labor from rural areas in the first half of the period. During the 1970s, and more especially in the oil slump, this differential was eroded and, by the end of the period, reversed. In Indonesia for most of the period, urban incomes were closely pinned to the rural supply price of labor, and there was no long-term trend in the rural/urban differential.

The obvious distributional question to ask in any comparison is which country was more equitable. This question is almost unanswerable because of the poor state of Nigerian data. To date, no national distribution of income has been published, and the best that can be done is to calculate a range of possible distributions dependent on alternative assumptions. Such an exercise suggests that, by the end of the period, Indonesia had a more equal distribution of income in both urban and rural areas. In almost all cases the Indonesian distribution was more equal than the most equal of the possible Nigerian distributions. For example, in rural areas the poorest 40 percent had a 22.4 percent share in Indonesia and 13.4–22.0 percent in Nigeria. The income differences were most marked between the top quintiles, especially in urban areas.

National trends in the distribution of household income are not measurable for Nigeria and are measurable for Indonesia only since 1963. In Indonesia there was a modest trend toward greater equity for the years 1963–1984. The poorest 40 percent gained relative to the mean at an annual rate of 0.3 percent. Because the mean was itself rising by 3.4 percent, nearly all the gains of the poor were the consequence of growth rather than redistribution.

Policies Compared

THE PUBLIC SECTOR

Table 10.3 suummarizes the major budgetary magnitudes as annual averages for a set of periods covering the years 1951–1990. It highlights two important features of the fiscal history of the two countries. First, although it is true that fiscal management in Indonesia greatly improved in the "New Order" period,[2] the absolute magnitude of the required fiscal correction was not great. Second, the Nigerian budget has shown a long-run secular tendency to deteriorate, with expenditures growing even when revenue is relatively stationary.

The relative size of the average Indonesian budget deficit is remarkably constant, in the range of 2.8–3.6 percent of GDP except during the period of fiscal collapse, when it rose only to 4.8 percent, and in the second half of the 1980s, following the collapse of oil prices in 1986. The period 1951–1957, which was generally regarded at the time as characterized by a severe deficit problem, appears in retrospect to have been characterized by a relatively small deficit. Indeed, the average deficit for the entire "Old Order" period averaged 4.0 percent, whereas that for the New Order was only a little lower, 3.7 percent.

The crisis of the 1960s was essentially a revenue and financing crisis, not an expenditure crisis. Government spending was trendless, averaging around 12.5 percent of GDP for the quarter of a century between independence and the first oil boom. The nature of the fiscal problem in 1958–1966 was twofold. First, there was a considerable erosion of domestic revenue, falling from 9.8 percent in 1951–1957 to 7.4 percent in 1958–1966. What is more, it never recovered, with

Table 10.3   Comparative Budgets, Nigeria and Indonesia, 1951–1990
(annual averages in percent of GDP)

Period	NIGERIA [a]			INDONESIA [b]		
	Revenue (oil revenue)	Expenditure	Deficit	Revenue (oil revenue)	Expenditure	Deficit
1951–1957	10.4	7.7	2.7	9.8	12.8	3.0
1958–1966	11.6	11.7	0.1	7.4	12.2	4.8
1967–1973	14.6 (5.3)	16.6	2.0	9.7 (3.0)	12.5	2.8
1974–1979	25.0 (19.2)	25.4	0.3	17.4 (9.8)	21.0	3.6
1980–1985	23.0 (16.8)	29.2	6.2	20.3 (13.5)	23.9	3.6
1986–1990	26.0 (19.7)	31.9	5.8	16.6 (7.4)	22.0	5.4

[a] Allocation of federally collected revenue to the states is treated as expenditure in the Nigerian case.
[b] Development receipts excluded from revenue in the Indonesian case.

averages of 6.7 percent during 1967–1973, 7.6 percent during 1974–1979, and 6.6 percent during 1980. Second, there was a dearth of noninflationary means with which to finance a deficit. There was in any case no domestic bond market, and the policy of confrontation led to a cessation of the already limited access to international capital. In consequence the expansion of the money stock (M_1) during 1958–1966 coincided with the deficit, averaging 4.8 percent of GDP. Because the money stock was in any case small (around 10 percent of GDP), this rate of expansion was massively inflationary.

What made such a rapid fiscal recovery feasible was the relatively small scale of the underlying problem. The advent of major oil revenues (3 percent of GDP) offset the further decline in domestic revenues, so that the deficit was reduced from 4.8 percent to 2.8 percent. This level of deficit would be comfortably covered by the resumption of development aid.

The Nigerian budgetary story over these three periods could not have been more different. In place of stationary expenditure, there was now a strong upward trend of around one-half of a percent of GDP per annum. The share of government expenditure in GDP in 1967–1973 was more than double that in 1951–1957: it also moved from being substantially smaller than that in Indonesia to being substantially larger.

In consequence, despite the relatively rapid growth of revenue, the budget swung increasingly into deficit, with a total swing of nearly 5 percent of GDP. However, the position in 1967–1973 was not particularly problematic. The average deficit was only 2 percent, and that was entirely attributable to the civil war. The remainder of the change was the elimination of the inappropriate and large budget surplus (2.7 percent) run during 1951–1957 by the colonial authorities.

The next two periods also show a very different pattern. Nigerian government oil revenue was much higher during the first oil cycle, 1974–1979 (19.2 percent of GDP), than was that of the Indonesian government (9.8 percent). In the second cycle, 1980–1985, the gap closed, with the Nigerian government obtaining revenues of 16.8 percent and the Indonesian government, 13.5 percent. Interestingly, the Nigerian government ran a somewhat smaller deficit over the whole decade, 3.3 percent, than did the Indonesians, with 3.6 percent; but the pattern is quite different, with the Indonesian deficit stationary between the two cycles and the Nigerian deficit increasing alarmingly, from near balance to 6.2 percent of GDP in 1980–1985.

Because these were cycles, it is of interest to disaggregate them further. Table 10.4 presents similar information for four subperiods within the cycles, chosen to isolate the upswing phases, 1973–1977 and 1979–1982, from the stationary and downswing phases, 1977–1979 and 1982–1984.

There are two interesting features in this table. First, the pattern of a relatively stationary deficit in Indonesia and a secularly increasing deficit in Nigeria is preserved within the subperiods. Second, revenue instability was much greater in Nigeria than in Indonesia, particularly during the second cycle. Hence the Nigerian government faced a more severe budgetary adjustment problem. Between 1979 and 1984 the state suffered a revenue deterioration of 6 percent of GDP and achieved an expenditure reduction of 3 percent. By contrast, Indonesia's revenue decline was 1.6 percent and the expenditure was reduced by 0.9 percent. In each case, expenditure was reduced by around half the revenue decline, but because the revenue shock was much larger in Nigeria, the deterioration in the deficit was more severe.

As these tables show, the Nigerian deficit during the decade of the oil booms was considerably larger (relative to GDP) than the deficit that produced hyperinflation and destroyed the Old Order in Indonesia. The severe domestic consequences in the Indonesian case were due to a lack of foreign finance. The Nigerian government avoided similar consequences because it was able to cover the deficit by foreign borrowing. It accumulated a large debt, which posed major problems for future macroeconomic policy makers.

Returning to Table 10.3, the last period covered is 1986–1990 following the collapse of oil prices. Paradoxically, the budgetary dependence of the Nigerian government actually rises in this period. This partly reflects the earlier impact of volume fluctuations but is also a consequence of the lack of diversification in the Nigerian economy: the capacity to substitute into other export and revenue generating activities was limited. The story in Indonesia is again very different. There

Table 10.4   Comparative Budgets in Nigeria and Indonesia
during Booms and Busts (annual averages in percent of GDP)

| Period | NIGERIA [a] | | | INDONESIA [b] | | |
	Revenue (oil revenue)	Expenditure	Deficit	Revenue (oil revenue)	Expenditure	Deficit
Boom 1973–1977	24.3 (18.8)	23.3	−1.0	15.7 (8.2)	18.9	3.2
Bust 1977–1979	23.9 (17.0)	27.0	3.1	17.5 (9.6)	21.5	4.0
Boom 1979–1982	26.3 (20.1)	31.1	4.7	20.8 (14.1)	24.2	3.4
Bust 1982–1984	20.4 (14.3)	28.0	7.7	19.2 (12.7)	23.3	4.0

[a] Allocation of federally collected revenue to the states is treated as expenditure in the Nigerian case.
[b] Development receipts excluded from revenue in the Indonesian case.

is a sharp contraction in the level of revenue generated from oil (13.5 percent of GDP down to 7.4 percent); there is a major effort to replace the lost revenue from domestic revenue sources, which is partly successful (6.8 percent of GDP up to 9.2 percent); there is some contraction of government spending, by around 2 percent of GDP; and in consequence the deficit widened to 5.4 percent of GDP. The net outcome, a deficit of 5–6 percent of GDP, is similar in the two countries; but whereas in Indonesia it represents a major but incomplete adjustment to external changes in a diversifying economy, in Nigeria it reflects a failure to adjust in an economy that remained locked into close dependence on oil.

We now consider the composition of public expenditure. Despite problems of budget classification, it seems clear that this composition diverged markedly following the first oil boom. Before this, government spending was dominated by recurrent items in both countries. In the period 1967–1973, for example, current expenditure accounted for 73 percent of federal expenditure in Nigeria and 67 percent in Indonesia. In Nigeria, however, this share fell to 38 percent during the upswing of the first oil boom (1973–77), a figure that was repeated during the downswing. During the next upswing (1979–82), the current share recovered slightly, to 43 percent; the breakdown is not available for later years. In Indonesia the most nearly comparable figures are 50 percent, 49 percent, and 50 percent. These figures almost certainly exaggerate the role of capital expenditure in the

Indonesian budget because they exclude a variety of current expenditures, such as most defense expenditure and the fertilizer subsidy. Even so, the difference between the two countries is striking: capital expenditure jumped in each case with the oil boom, from one-third to one-half of the total in Indonesia but from one-quarter to three-fifths in Nigeria. The shift toward capital expenditure was far more pronounced in the Nigerian case.

Another way of looking at this phenomenon gives a somewhat different interpretation. Current expenditure rose only slightly between 1967 and 1977 in both countries, from 8.9 percent to 10.0 percent of GDP in Nigeria and from 8.3 percent to 10.0 percent in Indonesia. The overwhelming proportion of incremental revenue went into the capital or development budgets in both cases. The marginal propensity to spend incremental revenue in this way was 0.78 in Indonesia and 0.92 in Nigeria. The larger switch in Nigeria, then, only partly reflects a higher marginal propensity to spend revenue on capital; it also reflects the larger relative impact of the first boom on the Nigerian budget.

TRADE AND EXCHANGE-RATE POLICIES

Indonesia inherited from the colonial government a highly restrictive system of trade and exchange control measures, which had largely been set up in the 1930s in response to the Great Depression and the threat of war. Many of these policies were kept in place. The foreign exchange regulations of 1940, for example, survived until 1964. The unified exchange rate was abandoned by the first cabinet, which introduced special rates for exports and imports, a system that implicitly imposed a heavy export tax. Throughout the Sukarno period there were systems of foreign exchange certificates, entitling exporters to acquire domestic currency at a favorable rate. In 1954 quantitative restrictions on imports were introduced. In the 1950s exchange-rate policy was used not as a macroinstrument but as an element of regional policy. In 1957, for example, there was a large devaluation to placate the outer islands, which threatened secession and where export production was concentrated. The Suharto regime abolished foreign exchange control, establishing full convertibility. It also dismantled the bewilderingly complex system of multiple exchange rates and allowed the rupiah to float (which led to a substantial devaluation between 1966 and 1968: from 85 to 326 rupiah per dollar).

Nigeria's trade policy in the 1960s was quite liberal, the system of quantitative restrictions used in the 1950s having virtually disappeared. Domestic industries lobbied successfully for tariff protection, and tariffs were also raised for balance-of-payments reasons. Nigerian trade policy in the 1950s included quantitative restrictions that were removed during the 1960s, and there was increasing pressure from domestic industries for tariff protection. In response both to this pressure and to balance-of-payments problems, tariffs were increased.

The two countries also responded differently to the two oil shocks. During the first oil cycle both countries initially liberalized trade restrictions but reversed that policy during the slump. Nigeria, however, maintained a virtually fixed exchange rate throughout, whereas Indonesia devalued substantially in 1978, partly with the intention of offsetting the adverse Dutch disease effects of the oil boom on local industry.

Policies differed most markedly during the second oil cycle. As before, Nigeria maintained a fixed exchange rate, accumulated reserves during the boom (some $8 billion in 1979 and 1980), and then during the downturn drew down these assets and started to borrow. Finally, adjustment could no longer be postponed. The fixed exchange-rate policy was abandoned with a massive devaluation, from 1.26 SDR per naira at the end of 1984 to only 0.25 two years later. The exchange rate was defended by a severe tightening of trade restrictions. By contrast, Indonesia relied only to a limited extent on the use of reserves and on borrowing during the downturn. Instead, the exchange rate was again devalued, so that by 1984 the Indonesian rate was less than half its 1972 value, whereas the Nigerian rate was down only slightly. After the large Nigerian devaluation of 1986, the government gradually returned to a policy of severe overvaluation sustained by import rationing, which by 1994 was approaching the scale of the overvaluation of a decade earlier. Hence, Nigerian trade policy was both more variable and on average more restrictive than that in Indonesia.

Agricultural and Industrial Performance

AGRICULTURE

In both countries agriculture is significant in three respects: because some of the staple foods are nontradable, agricultural supply affects the price of key consumer items; agriculture dominates the nonoil export sector; and it is the income source for a substantial majority of the poor. A poor performance of agriculture can create a food security problem, greater vulnerability of the economy to oil prices, and a less equal distribution of income.

There is no doubt that Nigerian agriculture grew substantially less rapidly than Indonesia's. Between 1960 and 1984 the agricultural sector's value added grew by 18 percent in Nigeria and 122 percent in Indonesia, a far larger divergence than for GDP as a whole. Prima facie, this is surprising. It might be expected that agriculture, being the least dynamic sector of both economies, would have the narrowest difference in performance. Clearly, there is something sector specific to be explained. (A major difficulty in comparing agricultural performance is that, within a wide margin, the performance of Nigerian agriculture is unknown.)

There is little basis for the quantitative comparison of food production. Taking the period since 1962, for which the U.N Food and Agriculture Organization (FAO) series on total food production are available, the annual rates of change in per capita production fell in Nigeria to −0.8 percent and rose in Indonesia to 1.6 percent. According to the FAO series, this differential performance has no pronounced pattern, although the difference is somewhat narrower in the sub-period 1972–1985. This is surprising because both policy changes and exogenous technological innovations favored Indonesia post-1972. During the oil boom the Indonesian government allocated 20 percent of its budget to agriculture, while the proportion in Nigeria was markedly lower; Indonesia's green revolution in irrigated rice cultivation enhanced yields, while no such innovation emerged suitable for Nigerian conditions. Offsetting this, relative food prices rose substantially in Nigeria during the 1970s, presumably reflecting the conjunction of production failure and oil boom spending power. Policy and technology changes shifted the Indonesian supply curve relative to the Nigerian; market-clearing prices moved Nigerian production up the supply curve. It must be emphasized, however, that in dealing with Nigerian food production data we are on uncertain ground, and the FAO series for the 1972–1985 period yields implausibly high growth. Unfortunately, the only secure conclusion is that, taking the whole period since 1962, per capita food production has declined in Nigeria and risen in Indonesia.

Some of this growth differential was reflected in changing foreign trade patterns, with Nigeria becoming increasingly dependent on imports and Indonesia achieving self-sufficiency, but mostly it has been reflected in different trends in the relative price of food and in per capita consumption.

Given the large divergence in outcomes and in policies toward food production, it is tempting to attribute the former to the latter. There are two difficulties with this inference. First, according to the FAO series, the difference in performance predates the oil boom. This is not too problematic because the profood policy shifts in Indonesia date back to the late 1960s. The second difficulty is more substantial; namely, Indonesian rice production benefited from technical progress not suitable for Nigeria. Food production other than rice grew less rapidly, but this is partly explained by the diversion of land and labor into rice from other crops. Hence, it is not possible to derive a credible quantitative attribution of divergences in outcomes to differences in policies.

In food production the Indonesian government had both greater impetus to act (a political threat posed by food insecurity) and greater opportunity (because of foreign technical progress in irrigated rice). In nonfood agriculture neither of these considerations applied. For both countries nonfood agriculture was predominantly a foreign exchange earner; before the oil boom it was the dominant foreign exchange source. Technological opportunities were similar because some of the most important crops were common to both countries. Had both governments given equal weight to agriculture in aggregate, the better opportunities in the food sector in Indonesia should have induced it to concentrate more on that sector. Thus we should observe the Nigerian government being more active than the Indonesian in promoting nonfood agriculture, where opportunities were the same in absolute terms but better in relative terms. This makes the comparative performance of nonfood agriculture a better indicator of the consequences of the policy environments.

Table 10.5 compares the growth rates of four important nonfood crops. Rubber and palm oil are common to both countries. Cocoa is the major crop in Nigeria but was only recently introduced in Indonesia. A better comparator is coffee, a tree crop with similar economic characteristics that is important and long established in Indonesia. Over the whole period 1950–1985, Indonesia had faster growth rates for palm oil, coffee, and cocoa but slower for rubber. When we refer to subperiods, however, a clear picture emerges. We consider 1950–1966 and 1972–1985 as subperiods distinguishing both the new order and the oil booms. The intervening years, 1967–1972, are omitted as being disturbed by civil war in Nigeria and by a reconstruction phase in both countries.

In the first subperiod Nigeria had a faster growth rate than Indonesia for each crop. Not only was performance relatively good, but in absolute terms growth rates were high. In the second subperiod relative performance is precisely reversed: in all three crops (again comparing coffee in Indonesia with cocoa in Nigeria), Indonesia had substantially higher growth rates. This reversal of the three pairwise rankings reflects substantial absolute changes. The final row of the table shows the change in the Nigeria/Indonesia growth rate differential between the two subperiods. This ranges from a low of 9 percentage points for palm oil to a high of 19 percentage points for rubber. These large changes came about partly through an increase in the Indonesian growth rates and a decrease in the Nigerian. That the absolute growth rate in Indonesia should be higher in the second subperiod is remarkable in view of the expectations of Dutch disease. Although relative prices moved against the nonoil export sector, this resource reallocation effect was evidently more than offset by the enhanced GDP growth brought about by the New Order regime and the windfall savings from the oil boom. Nigeria offers a much clearer case of Dutch disease, with growth rates in nonfood agriculture not merely falling but becoming heavily negative. The proximate reasons for output decline were the withdrawal of labor, the reduced use of fertilizer, and failing to replace the tree stock.

Although we have confined our comparison to three crops, the extent of the divergence in performance is more marked because Indonesia diversified into new crops, whereas Nigeria became more concentrated in the three cited above. Indonesia developed its timber exports and diversified into cocoa, Nigeria's major

Table 10.5   Production of Major Nonfood Crops in Nigeria and Indonesia, 1950–1993 (in thousand metric tons)

	PALM OIL		RUBBER		COCOA		COFFEE
Year	Nigeria	Indonesia	Nigeria	Indonesia	Nigeria	Indonesia	Indonesia
1950	390	126	14	704	107		59
1951	340	121	21	828	109		51 [a]
1952	360	146	19	761	111		47
1953	390	161	22	706	102		62
1954	440	169	21	751	91		58
1955	450	169	31	749	116		65
1956	420	166	39	697	137		61
1957	460	165	40	738	90		75
1958	410	160	52	696	143		78
1959	457	148	54	705	157		90
1960	433	138	60	640	195		92
1961	541	146	56	682	194		97
1962	509	141	60	682	179		111
1963	510	148	64	582	220		144
1964	515	161	72	649	298		87
1965	530	163	69	717	184		105
1966	508	151	71	716	167		116
1967	325	174	48	695	238	1	159
1968	370	188	53	730	192	2	157
1969	425	189	57	788	223	2	177
1970	488	215	59	811	300	2	185
1971	500	225	60	820	285	2	180
1972	460	269	81	819	241	2	179
1973	430	289	91	852	214	2	163
1974	450	334	80	893	230	3	182
1974	485	339	90	855	297	3	161
1975	500	409	95	825	306	4	162
1976	510	456	85	845	250	4	168
1977	660	497	90	835	202	5	193
1978	670	525	58	885	160	5	223
1979	650	606	60	905	180	9	227
1980	675	650	60	919	175	9	240
1981	675	741	43	963	191	13	315
1982	700	824	45	880	160	15	265
1983	730	972	50	997	118	28	236
1984	700	1,132	58	1,041	150	33	331
1985	730	1,230	60	1,057	110	37	311
1986	760	1,351	60	1,113	100	39	361
1987	730	1,313	70	1,128	145	44	354

Table 10.5   (*continued*)

Year	PALM OIL		RUBBER		COCOA		COFFEE
	Nigeria	Indonesia	Nigeria	Indonesia	Nigeria	Indonesia	Indonesia
1988	834	1,833	68	1,235	165	49	405
1989	857	1,942	78	1,260	160	122	411
1990	900	1,937	80	1,300	155	150	391
1991	900	2,658	155	1,284	110	169	419
1992	940	3,162	129	1,387	135	175	421
1993	965	3,500	130	1,370	140	220	441

Annual Growth Rates (fitted time trend) (in percent)

Year	PALM OIL		RUBBER		COCOA		COFFEE
	Nigeria	Indonesia	Nigeria	Indonesia	Nigeria	Indonesia	Indonesia
1950–1993	2.1	8.0	5.3	1.6	0.6	—	4.8
1950–1966	2.4	0.5	10.2	−0.9	6.4		5.7
1972–1985	4.6	11.3	−5.6	2.1	−5.8	21.5	5.1
Growth Differential		−8.6		−18.8		−11.6	

ª Estimated from estates production.
SOURCE: *FAO Production Yearbooks.*

crop. The high Indonesian growth rate in this sector (more than 20 percent) overtook that of Nigeria in 1991.

The reasons for this radical difference in performance after 1972 are due to policy. The crops we are comparing were common to both countries, and Nigeria's record before the oil boom was superior to Indonesia's. Because of the new opportunities that emerged in food agriculture in Indonesia but not in Nigeria, the counterfactual proposition is that post-1972 Nigeria's superiority in nonfood crops should have been enhanced.

The question, therefore, is not whether the massive deterioration in Nigerian performance is attributable to policy but rather to which policies it should be attributed. The candidates are macroeconomic policies, policies in the nonfood agricultural sector, and the general equilibrium effects of policies in other sectors. The domestic price of nonfood agricultural output relative to importables and nontradables is influenced by the trade–exchange rate–monetary policy nexus. Macroeconomic policies favored the rapid growth of nonfood agriculture in Indonesia. The exchange rate was devalued earlier, import controls were less restrictive, and monetary policy was more conservative. Hence, the relative price symptoms of Dutch disease would be expected to be, and were, far less severe in

Indonesia. Policies toward the sector also diverged. The only substantial help directed to the sector by the Nigerian government was the phasing out of export taxes. In contrast, the Indonesian government directed substantial public investment into the sector and subsidized fertilizer on a large scale. Finally, the general equilibrium effects of public expenditure in Nigeria were to draw labor from agriculture, thereby hitting hardest the most labor-intensive agricultural crops, which happened to be the nonfood crops.

INDUSTRY

In Nigeria industry grew rapidly up to the civil war; between 1960 and 1967 the growth rate was 10 percent per annum. This was largely a result of foreign direct investment, which was actively encouraged by lowering tax and import duties. Much of this industrial expansion was in the area of consumer goods. In the 1970s industrial policy changed. The goverment no longer saw its role as encouraging foreign investment but rather as holding a majority stake in petroleum refining and other industries deemed to be "strategic," including petrochemicals, iron and steel, and fertilizers. Two enormous steel mills were built at a cost of $11 billion, which are probably incapable of producing at a unit cost less than three times the world price. During the first oil cycle manufacturing output increased rapidly (contrary to the prediction of Dutch disease theory) as a result of massive investment in the sector, directly by the government and by subsidized private investment. By 1980 industrial investment accounted for 20 percent of federally retained revenue.

Two aspects of the Nigerian government's involvement in manufacturing deserve to be stressed. First, part of it was based on resentment of a successful racial minority, the Lebanese and Syrians, who had shown themselves effective small-scale entrepreneurs. Second, public sector officials were fascinated by large-scale industry, of which iron and steel projects are the most dramatic examples.

The promotion of industry was thus a constant Nigerian policy; what changed was the capacity to finance it and the distribution of industry between the public and private sectors and among the regions. The oil boom enabled more to be spent, and the switch in 1979 from rule by senior civil servants to rule by regional barons of the dominant political party was probably instrumental in the increased emphasis on private ownership and regional dispersion. Like education, industry was an emotive and respectable item on which the state could spend money. Yet it had the advantage over public services that the potential rents were higher because ownership of the assets could pass to private agents, the output from these assets could be marketed, and their reliance on imported inputs gave continuing opportunities for overinvoicing.

In Indonesia, resentment (initially of the Dutch, later of the Japanese, always of the Chinese) also played a role in industrial policy. In the 1950s a series of government initiatives tried to encourage the growth of an indigenous entrepreneurial class. These attempts were considered a failure by 1957, the year in which most Dutch properties were taken over, prompting the decision to set up state enterprises.

The New Order welcomed foreign industrial investment. This attracted massive Japanese investment, for example, in the textiles sector, which later led to much resentment and contributed to a policy reversal. The direction of foreign and eventually domestic investment became an object of government policy. Investment loans were used to encourage investment in intermediate and capital goods. At the same time, members of the elite, usually in cooperation with Chinese businessmen, built up industrial conglomerates.

As in Nigeria, there was an Indonesian fascination with large, "basic" industries and with "linkages." The industrial sector became heavily protected by a combination of trade policy, licensing, investment loans, and local content requirements. The emphasis was on resource processing and on capital-intensive and technology-intensive industries.

Why Economic Policies Differed

From independence, Indonesia and Nigeria have shared a number of characteristics that placed their continuance as unitary nations in doubt. They both have large and heterogeneous populations of divergent linguistic, cultural, ethnic, and religious composition and geographic regions that share no common historical or political tradition. Furthermore they are ecologically and economically diverse, so there is nothing to guarantee even a community of self-interest. In consequence, there was little to engender any sense of a shared past, a common nationhood, or a joint future. It was to be expected that both countries would be troubled by regional revolts and attempted secession. Even so, each has survived as a single entity and has constructed a powerful central authority, with the military playing a crucial role in these achievements.

Despite these similarities, the experience and the economic record of the two countries diverge markedly, and it is important to stress the differences that underlie the similarities. First, the diversity of population was very differently constituted. The Javanese dominated Indonesia both numerically and in terms of history and culture. There was no possibility of any coalition of the Outer Islands ever wresting control of the Indonesian state from them. In contrast, the Nigerian North (the most powerful of the Nigerian regions) had a slender numerical advantage over the other regions and was the most backward of all in education. From the perspective of cohesion, Nigeria was burdened with a power structure that permitted neither outright dominance by one group nor a stable coalition of several.

Second, Indonesia won its independence in a true war of liberation with a common enemy and had an extraordinarily charismatic national leader in Sukarno. The adoption of the relatively uncomplicated language is one indicator of a genuinely national perspective. Thus what would have been naturally centrifugal forces were countered by unifying ones. In contrast, Nigerian independence was marked by evident mutual distrust among the regions, threats of secession, and an actual attempt at secession. No political leader emerged to represent the nation, nor were political parties organized along national lines. Moreover, the army was led by members of the northern elite and was not rooted, as was the Indonesian army, in the wider community.

In these important respects, the initial political conditions differed considerably. Another crucial difference emerged some time after independence. If Sukarno's political legacy was an Indonesian state more unified than could reasonably have been anticipated, his economic legacy may have been equally significant. His cheerful disdain for matters economic had cumulated into an economic disaster. This not only ushered in the New Order, but it made it impossible for any successor government to exhibit the same cavalier disregard for economic imperatives.

This had two consequences for economic management in Indonesia. One was to establish the technocrats as a powerful lobby that was respected, albeit sometimes reluctantly, in opposition to the strand of nationalistic dirigisme that had largely characterized the earlier period and remained a potent force in Indonesian thinking. The other was to enshrine a sort of policy fetishism involving self-sufficiency, a balanced budget, and currency convertibility. In some respects this simply exhibited a confusion between instruments and objectives; at the same time, it shows the potential value of rules over discretion. The centrality of these rather rigid rules paradoxically enforced flexible policy responses on the Indonesian authorities, as illustrated by their readiness to devalue the currency. The rules also provided the technocrats with the necessary leverage to make policy change effective. This stands in dramatic contrast to the Nigerian case, where the exchange rate itself became an inflexible symbol and a restriction on policy. There is, however, little evidence of a group of frustrated Nigerian technocrats willing to intervene but lacking the political or institutional muscle. Given the extent to which the military authorities abdicated from questions of economic management, it is difficult to believe that such a group would not have infiltrated the policy vacuum.

In any event, what distinguishes the two countries in the latter part of the period following independence is the greater capacity of the Indonesian authorities to respond appropriately to the turbulent conditions both countries faced. The Indonesian authorities showed a relatively thorough appreciation of the importance of sectoral relative prices, of sectoral relationships in general, and of fiscal stance. The Nigerian authorities simply followed the precept that windfall gains should be invested. At the same time, both countries tolerated high levels of corruption, waste, bureaucratic incompetence, and ill-conceived microeconomic intervention.

Thus it is certainly not true that the hugely different performance of the two economies during the oil booms can be attributed to fundamental differences of governmental intention, such as that between a platonic guardian and predatory state. On the contrary, while both governments have exhibited a high degree of corruption, it could be argued that it was the Nigerian military who early on most closely strove to fulfill the role of guardian. The difference in outcome appears to be due partly to exogenous events (the green revolution, for example) and partly by a more sophisticated understanding in Indonesia of the problems of adjustment, coupled with superior execution. These differences, in turn, may be partly attributed to the different histories of the two countries before the booms. Indonesia was still rehabilitating an economy that had suffered a long history of mismanagement associated with hyperinflation, exchange crises, and unmanageable foreign debts; it attached a high premium to maintainng economic order. Nigeria was also in the process of reconstructing after the damage caused by the civil war, but the emphasis was on the need to repair and create infrastructure. The economic problems of the previous decade had been largely associated with a lack of revenue, and the apparent removal of the revenue problem was seen as eliminating them. From this perspective, the requirements of economic management were thus reduced to the matter of project selection, an area particularly vulnerable to corruption.

Notes

1. D. L. Bevan, P. Collier, and J. W. Gunning, in *Nigeria: Policy Responses to Shocks, 1970–90* (San Francisco: International Center for Economic Growth, 1992), develop a counterfactual case. The 85 percent estimate is based on a comparison of actual investment with counterfactual investment.

2. The "New Order" is the term used to describe the Suharto era dating from 1966. We refer to the preceding Sukarno regime as the "Old Order."

3. The fitted growth rate of 2.9 percent is a full percentage point above our own estimate of the maximum growth rate of the six major food crops; that figure is based on taking whichever of four series for each crop showed the highest growth rate.

———— 11 ————————————————————

Perspectives on the Economic Experience of Two Countries of Sub-Saharan Africa

Ghana and Malawi from the 1960s to the 1980s

JAN HOGENDORN and
ROBERT CHRISTIANSEN

Introduction

Any study of the general causes of sub-Saharan Africa's economic growth must ask why that region has failed to have sustainable growth and reduce poverty. With few exceptions, the high hopes that prevailed at Africa's independence have failed to materialize, and most people are as poor today as they were three decades ago. The proximate causes of this disappointing performance are complex: poor education, infrastructure, and institutional capabilities, among others. But a fundamental factor is the quality of governance, policy formulation, and its implementation. The argument advanced below is that, without a strong political commitment to policies that provide incentives for producers, the returns to investments are likely to be small, meaning that little economic growth will take place.

We demonstrate this point by contrasting the experiences of Ghana and Malawi during the period from the 1960s to the 1980s. Certainly, the developments in these two countries are unlikely to capture fully the range of experience of the African countries during the past thirty to thirty-five years. Yet the decisions taken by Ghana and Malawi reflect the events of a broad range of African countries. At the time of independence the two nations were similar in many respects.

Yet by the 1980s their differences in policy had become pronounced, and the performance of the two economies had diverged remarkably—even though the underlying growth issues facing them were similar.

The similarities between Ghana and Malawi are apparent in table 11.1. Both were British territories (as the Gold Coast and Nyasaland) with comparable institutions; they became independent in 1957 and 1964 respectively; each had towering figures as founding fathers (Kwame Nkrumah and Hastings Banda). Ghana is geographically larger than Malawi (239,000 square kilometers versus 118,000 square kilometers), but the population density of the two countries is approximately the same (see line A, table 11.1).[1] Their rate of population increase has been high (line B) and was identical in the late 1980s (line C). Fertility rates are high (line D), and age distribution is similar (line E). Although Ghana has low plains with some hilly regions, whereas Malawi is more mountainous with high plateaus, agriculture dominates in both, employing more than 50 percent of the labor force (line F). Literacy is low (line G).

Ghana had a historical advantage in that its precolonial Ashanti kingdom was politically sophisticated and certainly unmatched in what became Malawi. Ghana's gold exports were famous and lucrative when slaves were the only export from most of West Africa. After Britain's colonial conquest Ghana's cocoa industry quickly became one of the world's foremost suppliers. Taxes from cocoa production paid for transport and education. Malawi was not so fortunate; victimized by the Arab slave trade, it had no main export to nurture economic growth. For centuries Ghana was the richer of the two, and by the early 1990s it still held that position by a substantial margin (line H). Ghana's superiority was even more evident in international purchasing power (line I) and comparing for health, mortality, and energy consumption (lines J, K, L, and M).

From independence to the late 1980s, Ghana's economic lead over Malawi rapidly eroded as confirmed in table 11.1 and the account below. The average annual growth rate in Ghana's GNP per capita from 1967 to 1987 was *negative*, whereas Malawi's was positive despite greater population growth (line N). Inflation was higher in Ghana (line O), which also experienced substantial demonetization, whereas Malawi became more monetized (line P). Gross domestic investment and saving in Ghana was first higher than in Malawi but fell well below Malawi's level (lines Q and R), with wide disparities in saving performance. Export growth in Ghana was negative but positive in Malawi (line S). Beginning in the 1960s, Ghana's leaders encouraged manufactures, but Malawi's did not. Yet Ghana's dependency on primary products *rose*, as a percent both of GDP and of exports, whereas Malawi's fell (lines T and U). Malawi, without a policy of industrialization, actually increased its industrial exports as a percentage of total exports, whereas Ghana's fell (line V). Finally, Ghana's health, education, and nutrition went into decline, whereas Malawi, which was poorer, improved in these areas, overtaking Ghana (lines W, X, Y).

Table 11.1   Comparative Data, Ghana and Malawi

	Ghana	Malawi
A. Population density per square mile, 1988 estimate	160	176
B. Population increase, average percent per year, 1980–87	3.4	3.8
C. Population increase, percent per year, 1987	3.3	3.3
D. Total fertility rate, 1987	6.4	7.6
E. Age distribution, percent aged 0–14, 1988 estimate	46.6	47.8
F. Labor force in agriculture, percent of total, 1980	56	83
G. Literacy, estimated percent of population, 1983	30	25
H. GNP per capita, 1987	$390	$160
I. GNP per capita, 1981, adjusted for purchasing power	$1,140	$540
J. Infant mortality per 1,000 live births, 1987	90	150
K. Death rates per 1,000, 1987	13	20
L. Life expectancy at birth, 1987, years	54	46
M. Energy consumption per capita, 1987, kWh	129	40
N. Per capita GNP, average annual growth, percent, 1965–1987	−1.6	1.4
O. Average annual inflation, percent, 1965–1980	22.8	7.0
1980–1987	48.3	12.4
P. Monetary holdings (broad), average, percent of GDP, 1965	20.3	17.6
1987	11.7	25.0
Q. Gross domestic investment, percent of GDP, 1965	18	14
1987	11	14
R. Gross domestic saving, percent of GDP, 1965	8	0
1987	4	12
S. Export growth, annual, percent, 1965–1980	−1.8	4.1
1980–1987	−1.6	3.4
T. GDP from agriculture, percent, 1965	44	50
1987	51	37
U. Primary product exports, as percent of all exports, 1965	85	99
1987	97	84
V. Manufactured exports, as percent of all exports, 1965	3	1
1987	2	16
W. Population per physician, 1965	13,740	47,320
1987	14,890	11,560
X. Daily calorie supply, 1965	1,950	2,244
1986	1,759	2,310
Y. Primary schools, percent of age group enrolled, 1965	69	44
1987	63	64

SOURCE: World Bank, *World Development Report*, 1988 and 1989, except line I, which is from Robert Summers and Alan Heston, "Improved International Comparisons of Real Product and Its Composition, 1950–1980," *Review of Income and Wealth* 30, no.2 (June 1984).

There differences were the result neither of natural disasters nor of external relations. Although both countries suffered a decline in their terms of trade, Malawi's fall was greater. Ghana also had a refugee problem in the early 1980s, when perhaps a million of its citizens were expelled from Nigeria. Yet Malawi was then virtually in a war zone, its transport disrupted by events in neighboring Mozambique. If anything, the outside world impinged more negatively on the better performing of the two economies.

The *policies* chosen by the two governments and their ability to implement them effectively caused their different performances. In Ghana, the state intervened in economic activity by establishing many state-operated enterprises and imposing high taxes, thereby distorting economic incentives for producers. Public sector institutions responded poorly to changing domestic and international environments. In contrast, Malawi's government intervention was less comprehensive and different: there was no public ownership of critical industries; the government supported certain private enterprises with connections to the political elite, which proved to be less damaging. This approach helped establish a small manufacturing sector where none existed before, although less competition produced concentration, inefficiency, and, ultimately, Malawi's dramatic political changes in the early 1990s. At the same time, Malawi's public institutions appeared to be more effective implementing agencies than were Ghana's institutions.

The Wreck of the Ghanaian Economy

A wreck as complete as that which had overtaken Ghana's economy by the early 1980s did not occur all at once, and it has been well documented.[2] The first country in black Africa to receive its independence from a colonial power (1957), Ghana was a showpiece of development. Later it became a much-studied model of "how not to develop."[3]

The causes of economic decline are identifiable as follows: (1) Ghana tried to industrialize by import substitution and extensive foreign exchange control and licensing of imports. (2) Financing for this policy was based on taxing agriculture and deficit financing through inflation. The consequence was a long period of widespread price controls. The financial burden fell heavily on cocoa farmers and urban workers. (3) Many new state-owned and -operated industries proved to be inefficient and unprofitable. (4) There was instability in government, with several coups. In general, economic policy was carried out by an urban power elite that rewarded its supporters and penalized its opponents.

INDUSTRIALIZATION THROUGH IMPORT SUBSTITUTION

President Nkrumah advocated that economic development was best achieved by protecting the domestic market to promote large-scale manufacturing. He wrote in 1963 that "if we import goods that we could manufacture, we continue our economic dependence."[4] W. A. Lewis had warned ten years before that the inadequate infrastructure would mean high-cost manufacturing. Moreover, the need to tax the agricultural sector to obtain investment funds would reduce the size of the already small domestic market.[5]

Industrialization via import substitution went forward in any case. In 1960, only eleven of Ghana's forty-three most important import items (those with an import value above 1 million Ghanaian cedis) were being produced in Ghana, whereas by 1970, that number had risen to thirty-three. The ratio of imported consumer goods to the consumption of those goods fell from 32.2 percent in 1960 to 21.3 percent in 1970. The share of manufacturing in GDP did indeed rise, to 9.7 percent in 1965, 11.4 percent in 1970, and 13.9 percent in 1975. Most manufacturing was, as planned, undertaken by large firms, whose production made up more than 75 percent of all manufacturing output in the late 1970s.[6]

The industrialization by import substitution was associated with extensive use of a planning mechanism, which was the centerpiece of the comprehensive seven-year plan of 1963. But the planning was weak—according to Killick, "a piece of paper, with an operational impact close to zero." Indeed, the projects attempted were considerably *larger* than adumbrated in the plans. Contractors paid commission to ministers and other officials to elicit additional projects, while ministers financed these additions by negotiating short-term suppliers credits.[7]

IMPORT LICENSING AND FOREIGN EXCHANGE CONTROL

To implement import substitution, strict import licensing and foreign exchange control were imposed in 1961. J. C. Leith found numerous cases where the effective rate of protection was as high as 1,000 percent or more (and one of 78,000 percent).[8]

Foreign exchange control involving multiple exchange rates and substantial overvaluation of the cedi was used partly to tax the agricultural sector (cocoa farmers were paid cedis for their crop at the overvalued official rate), but the control was mostly a response to the inflationary financing used to promote the industrialization. The real effective foreign exchange rate appreciated 816 percent from 1973 to 1981. Inflation was continuous, but President Nkrumah and most succeeding governments treated maintaining a fixed parity as a matter of national pride. By 1982, imported goods prices for such staples as sugar, palm oil, rice, and maize at the official rate were 10 percent or less of the domestic price.[9]

Overvaluation caused a severe decline in legal exports, not only for the new manufacturing industries that could not export but for cocoa. Export decline meant less foreign exchange, and shortages of spare parts and raw materials began to damage the economy. Consumer goods also became scarce.

The overvalued exchange rate, together with the long, easily crossed borders with hard-currency CFA franc countries to the west (Côte d'Ivoire), north (Burkina Faso), and east (Togo), made smuggling profitable.[10]

BUDGET DEFICITS AND TAXATION OF AGRICULTURE

From the outset, domestic saving was inadequate to finance the government's large investment program unless the conservative fiscal policies of the colonial period were jettisoned. Once that took place, private saving shrank because rates of interest on bank deposits were sharply negative in most years, as seen in table 11.2.

The immediately available revenue source that could be enhanced was the taxation of cocoa farmers, who had less political influence than the city dwellers. The Cocoa Marketing Board's payments to farmers as a percentage of total FOB export receipts at the official rate of exchange fell from 72 percent in 1960 to 41 percent in 1965, 37 percent in 1970, and 34 percent in 1983/84. With overvaluation of the cedi taken into account, by 1983/84 cocoa farmers were receiving just 6.0 percent of the world price, FOB, valued at the prevailing parallel exchange rate. But this revenue source eventually failed; the decline in cocoa production, together with the real fall in import duties collected and in sales tax revenues, meant that government tax revenue in real terms declined by approximately four-fifths from 1969/70 to 1982.[11]

The only other source of revenue was seigniorage and the forced saving of the "inflation tax." Money creation leading to fiscal deficits became permanent in 1960; these deficits had reached 10.9 percent of GDP by 1965. By the early 1980s, deficit financing was covering nearly 60 percent of government expenditure. The deficits were monetized by direct sales of government securities to the Bank of Ghana. Money supply growth, some 12 percent a year in the early 1960s, reached 30.9 percent in 1975, 41.7 percent in 1978, and 35 percent in 1981.[12]

INEFFICIENT STATE-OPERATED ENTERPRISES

The quality of state investment undertaken in the state-operated enterprises (SOEs) was also poor, and much of the government's spending ended up subsidizing their losses and supporting the large-scale public sector employment that these enterprises came to provide.[13]

The SOEs were mostly established in the 1960s; by 1965 there were forty producing a wide variety of products from shoes to steel. Their performance was

Table 11.2   Real Rates of Interest in Ghana, 1965–1982 (percent)

1965	−21.9	1980	−35.2
1970	1.6	1982	−11.8
1975	−21.7		

SOURCE: Bank of Ghana, *Annual Reports.*

disappointing; only two had earned profits by 1965.[14] By 1982, their combined annual operating deficits were equivalent to about 50 percent of government spending, a major contributor to inflation.[15] Many depended on unskilled labor, often from the government's political supporters, and the growth rate of SOE employment reached 9.5 percent in the late 1970s. Public employment grew larger than in any other major African country, nearly three-quarters of all formal employment and constituting more than 10 percent of the working population.[16]

Capacity utilization in Ghanaian industry appears to have been about 40 percent for long periods (34.8 percent in 1967/68), which was the estimated figure for the United States in 1933 at the trough of the Great Depression.[17] A study of efficiency among the parastatal firms carried out in the 1970s yielded revealing results concerning the domestic resource cost (DRC) of saving foreign exchange. This is the ratio of the opportunity cost of all domestic resources used directly or indirectly to produce a good compared with the net foreign exchange gained from producing domestically. (*Net* because domestic production may require foreign exchange to pay for some inputs.) William Steel calculated DRCs for forty firms in large-scale manufacturing valued at both the overvalued official exchange rate and the parallel rate. Only six firms of the sample (producing 13.5 percent of the sample's output) had a coefficient of less than one; that is, their cedi cost to gain foreign exchange by domestic manufacture was less than the foreign exchange was worth in cedis at the official rate. Thirty of the firms (with 67.3 percent of the sample's output) had coefficients *greater* than one even at the overvalued parallel rate; that is, their cedi cost to gain foreign exchange was greater than the cedi value of that foreign exchange even at the parallel rate.[18]

The state enterprise workers' value added was low—₵690 compared with ₵1,775 in private industries in 1965/66—according to Killick's calculation. At that time total wages and salaries as a percentage of total value added were 46.1 percent in the state enterprises, much higher than the 23.4 percent in private industries, leading Killick to claim that much of manufacturing had become "a high-cost way of providing what were, in effect, unemployment benefits." Even purchases of material inputs from other sectors of the economy declined as the SOEs gained in importance. It must have seemed that nothing could go right when the vaunted Volta River Project did not succeed in delivering cheap hydro-electric power, primarily because of decay in the distribution system.[19]

Another type of SOE was the system of large state farms, established in the Nkrumah administration, that received about 90 percent of the agricultural development budget in the period 1962–1966. These farms, established without the undertaking of a pilot project, reported yields of 0.5 tons a hectare in 1970, compared with 2.32 tons a hectare on peasant holdings. Their labor productivity was also low, 0.59 tons per worker on the state farms compared with 3.33 tons on the peasant holdings.[20]

INFLATION, PRICE CONTROL, AND RATIONING

Fiscal deficits, financed by rapid money supply growth, the restriction of imports, and the inefficient industrial enterprises caused great inflation.[21] Inflation averaged 40 percent in the 1970s and 70 percent in the early 1980s, with high variability. Peaks were reached in 1977 (116 percent), 1981 (117 percent), and 1983 (123 percent). Price controls were first introduced in 1962; by 1969, 5,920 price controls were being enforced on 725 goods. A Prices and Incomes Board was established in 1972, but its price control inspectors were easily bribed. After the inspectorate was abolished, a comprehensive price control followed, but it was haphazardly enforced. After the accession of the Rawlings government in December 1981, the army and police imposed strict controls on 1,900 prices.

The predictable shortages of goods that followed led to an ad hoc rationing system in which supplies were turned over to large organizations for distribution to their members. In 1981 the distribution of fifteen "essential commodities" in short supply was entrusted to the personnel and clientele of the Ghana Trades Union Congress, the Civil Servants' Association, the National Association of Teachers, the universities, the police, the Farmers' Council, the Cocoa Marketing Board, the Food Distribution Corporation, and the Ministries of Defense, Education, and Health.

Did price controls help the poor? Surveys in the early 1980s revealed that nearly two-thirds of Ghana's population simply had no access to the price-controlled goods, with the lowest availability in villages and the countryside. The effects were dampened, however, because people often did not observe the controls. It is estimated that the value of transactions in the black (underground) economy amounted to anywhere from 25 percent to 42 percent of 1981 GDP. In any case, the subsistence economy was relatively unaffected by the controls.[22]

POLITICAL INSTABILITY IN A POLITICIZED ECONOMY

President Nkrumah was overthrown in 1966. The elected government (1969) under President Busia was ousted in a 1972 coup after having devalued the cedi a month before. General Acheampong was replaced by General Akuffo in 1978. The 1979 election of President Limann was voided by Flight Lieutenant Rawlings and the Provisional National Defense Council in 1981.

However different these governments were, each learned that a controlled economy delivers short-term political advantages. The licensed imports, the selective availability of scarce, price-controlled goods, and employment on the state farms or in the parastatal industries and agencies were rewards that could be granted or withdrawn. When Robert Bates interviewed a cocoa farmer in 1978, Bates asked why he and fellow farmers did not organize politically for an increase in the cocoa price.

> He went to his strongbox and produced a packet of documents: licenses for his vehicle, import permits for spare parts, titles to his real property and improvements, and the articles of incorporation that exempted him from a major portion of his income taxes. "If I tried to organize resistance to the government's policies on farm prices," he said while exhibiting these documents, "I would be called an enemy of the state and would lose all these."[23]

The farmer did not mention the fertilizer and insecticide subsidies (which eventually reached 50 percent of the purchase price), the tractor subsidies, and the like, which would also have been lost.

THE DAMAGE TO THE ECONOMY

When the World Bank published its index of price distortions in 1983, taking into account foreign exchange pricing, factor pricing, and product pricing, Ghana was cited as the most distorted economy of a thirty-one-country list. On the list of economies less distorted than Ghana were Argentina, Bolivia, Peru, and Tanzania.[24] The damage to Ghana was severe.

Agriculture

There was an alarming rise in subsistence production and a major fall in cocoa output.[25] Ghana contributed 36.5 percent of the world's supply of cocoa in 1962/63 but only 10 percent in 1983/84. The 1964/65 crop was 566,000 tons, while that of 1983/84 was only 159,000 tons. Shadow prices for rice, maize, and cocoa (1980) showed cocoa yielding at least fifteen times more returns per acre than the two food crops. Because the price controls for cocoa were effective and those for rice and maize were not, the returns to cocoa were only about half those from food crops.[26] Along with cocoa's decline, there were shortages of insecticides and sprayers.

For many farmers, food production therefore became more profitable than cocoa production. Smallholders shifted to food and sold on the black market.

But the economic disruption was so severe that per capita food production fell from 1969/71 = 100 to 1977/79 = 82.[27]

Other Exports

The damage extended to all traditional exports (see table 11.3). Manufactured exports and other miscellaneous items (except aluminum, cocoa butter, and cocoa paste) increased at first, rising to 9 percent by value of all exports in 1970 but then shared the decline, falling to 6 percent in 1975 and just 1 percent in 1980.[28]

Wage and Salary Earners

The real wage (at 1970 prices) in the medium and large-scale industrial sector fell from ₡636 in 1967 to ₡196 in 1980 and ₡101 in 1984. The decline pushed even salaried professionals into the black-market economy to feed their families; a month's salary for a university teacher did not cover a week's supply of food.[29] Variability in access to the black-market economy probably made income distribution more unequal. During the 1970s two revealing examples of the decline in living standards included a drop of nearly 40 percent in newspaper circulation and a fall of 82 percent in cinema attendance.[30] In response, emigration mounted. By 1985, around one-half to two-thirds of Ghana's skilled and qualified managers had been lost to other countries.[31]

Infrastructure

The overall infrastructure decayed: schools were without books; street lights, without bulbs; telephones, permanently out of order; the availability of pumped water and electricity was shrinking; and highway surfaces were so broken that it was better to take a dirt track. In 1983 some 70 percent of the country's buses and trucks were idle because of no tires and batteries, and 80 percent of all railway locomotives were out of service due to the shortage of spare parts.[32]

REBUILDING THE ECONOMY

In April 1983 the ruling Provisional National Defence Council initiated reform. Waves of IMF and World Bank economists provided advice, though little that had not been said before by Ghana's academic community.

The Economic Recovery Plan's (ERP's) first phase, 1983–1986, tried to stabilize the damage by reversing the import substitution policy, adjusting the regulated foreign exchange rate toward a market-determined rate, restricting aggregate demand by cutting the government budget deficit and tightening money

Table 11.3   Export Volumes in Ghana, 1970–1982

	1970	1975	1980	1982
Logs and timber				
(in thousands of cubic meters)	842	623	185	110
Bauxite (in thousands of tons)	211	320	223	36
Manganese				
(in thousands of tons)	397	373	148	97
Industrial diamonds				
(in thousands of carats)	2,872	2,373	897	686
Gold (in kilograms)	19,762	14,593	10,820	9,386

SOURCES: World Bank, *Ghana: Policies and Program for Adjustment*, table 3.15; except manganese, 1980, from Huq, *Economy of Ghana*, p. 202.

and credit, reducing price controls over goods and services, and relying less on cocoa taxation.[33] The second phase, still ongoing, combined structural adjustment of the economy with promotion of economic development.

The Foreign Exchange Rate and Trade Restrictions

Having reduced the cedi's overvaluation from twenty-two times to about three times during 1983–1985, in February 1987 Ghana began allocating foreign exchange by means of weekly auctions, and over a period of about a year, most consumer goods imports were made eligible for financing through the auctions.[34] (Similar policies have been promoted by the bank and the IMF in Zambia, Nigeria, and elsewhere.) These auctions reduced much corruption, and the only factor keeping a parallel exchange rate market going (with a rate in 1987 and 1988 of 1.4 times the official rate) was that the move toward auctioning was gradual rather than once and for all. Private foreign exchange bureaus featuring market-determined rates were permitted from 1988, open to the public on a daily basis for trades in small amounts of currency.

The ERP managed to dismantle some trade barriers, but others remained. Import licensing, the primary protectionist tool of the former economic system, was abolished in January 1989, leaving a relatively moderate and uniform tariff structure with a maximum rate of 25 percent and a program of reductions in existing rates.[35] Offsetting this, however, barriers were still high, with numerous special import taxes and excises that raised the incidence of nominal protection to the range of 25 percent to 90 percent.

Reform of Spending

Bringing the government budget deficit under control was a priority of the ERP, and a combination of spending cuts and enhancing tax revenues was embarked on in 1983. Results were positive, with a surplus in the current budget in 1985 and an approximate balance in the overall budget (including development expenditures considered as investment) in 1986.[36] Bringing government expenditure under control was a major achievement.

A major part of deficit reduction involved cutting staff in both the government and the parastatals. The wage bill for civil servants was held to the range of 5.0 to 5.5 percent of GDP, and approximately 36,000 of Ghana's 300,000 civil servants were laid off for redundancy in 1987–1989.[37] Other spending cuts reduced the bursaries for secondary school and university students in real terms by up to 50 percent and lowered the subsidy element in the fertilizer price from 50 percent to 15 percent. Most important, the decision was taken to sell thirty-two of the forty-six SOEs, though poor accounts, a lack of trained accountants, and legal delays slowed the process substantially.

Overseas Aid

Aid from national governments and international agencies rose considerably in importance during the ERP and was instrumental in making the ERP politically possible. Whereas in 1982 little foreign financing of any kind was being received, net foreign finance reached 1.7 percent of GDP in 1984, 2.7 percent in 1986, and more than 3 percent in 1987. Grants made up about 33 percent of the total, with multilateral lenders providing about 58 percent of all assistance in 1988. The aid was useful in financing the costs of the ERP. (With the world price of cocoa in decline at the time, it is hard to see how the program could have been politically possible without it.) In the period 1986–1989, aid was equivalent to 37–40 percent of the country's total import bill. Although debt service had not been a major cause of Ghana's economic shipwreck, and although private debt continued low, repaying the official debt incurred during the ERP became a burden in itself. Total obligations reached $2.2 billion in 1987, more than 40 percent of GDP, and debt service was about 66 percent of export earnings.

Tax Reform

The implicit tax on cocoa was greatly reduced by raising the farmers' share of cocoa prices from 24 percent in 1983/84 to 46 percent in 1988/89. The income tax on salaries was lowered and the brackets changed to provide some degree of inflation proofing, while the marginal rate for high incomes was cut. The corporation tax was reduced from 55 to 45 percent, and the standard sales tax, from 25 to 22.5 percent. The resumption of economic growth brought about a major recovery in government revenues. These revenues had fallen to just 4.6 percent of GDP in 1983, but the share increased to 12.7 percent in 1987, with sales tax revenues and import duties showing the strongest rise.[38]

Eliminating Price Controls

A major factor in the ERP was reducing price controls. These had been comprehensive in 1982, but dismantling was rapid during the first year of the reforms, after which twenty-three items were still controlled. Within two more years (1985) only eight items remained on the controlled list; they were still there in 1988. The Ghana government's 1988 budget contained a statement that price controls do not work.[39]

EFFECTS OF THE REFORMS ON THE ECONOMY

Although inflation remained strong (under the ERP, usually in the range of 25–40 percent), there was substantial growth in both exports and imports (see table 11.4). Even this impressive growth did not make up the ground lost on the export side, however; exports were $1,066 million in 1979 and $1,104 million in 1980. On the import side, the 1987 figure barely exceeds that for 1981 ($1,021 million). The export figure reflected the weakness in the important cocoa sector, where receipts continued to decline because of world market conditions.

GDP Growth

Under the ERP, real GDP growth was 8.6 percent in 1984, 5.2 percent in 1985, 5.2 percent in 1986, and 4.8 percent in 1987. (These figures are not per capita; population growth was estimated to have been 3.4 percent a year during 1980 to 1987). The growth was relatively uneven across sectors, slower in agriculture, faster in services, and most rapid in industry, with strength in construction and utilities output. Investment as a proportion of GDP expanded from 6.9 percent in 1984 to 10.8 percent in 1987.

But much of this investment was funded from abroad, with low national savings as a proportion of GDP. Private saving actually fell, from 3.6 percent of GDP in 1986 to 2.7 percent in 1987.[40] A major reason for the low savings ratio was the combination of low income and the pent-up consumer demand from the period of price controls and import substitution policy. Another cause, however, was the continuation of negative real rates of interest on deposits (−4.5 percent in 1986, −13.1 percent in 1987, −9.4 percent in 1988). Why real rates were negative, even with the dismantling of most controls and the Ghana

Table 11.4   Exports and Imports, Ghana, 1983–1988 (US$million)

	1983	1984	1985	1986	1987	1988 prel.
Merchandise exports (FOB)	439	567	632	749	827	828
Cocoa, cocoa products				503	495	430
Other exports				246	332	398
Merchandise imports (CIF)	−539	−681	−729	−805	−1,025	−1,110

SOURCES: Bank of Ghana and World Bank estimates.

government's recognizing that this situation had to be altered, apparently involved the structure of the banking system.[41] Little competition existed among the three big banks, and they were not monitored by the Bank of Ghana. The banks were also burdened with many nonperforming loans, suffered foreign exchange losses, and faced high reserve requirements. By mid-1988 their net worth was negative. Facing a weakened banking system, the central bank was unwilling to tighten monetary policy and raise interest rates when needed. Unfortunately, the estimated cost of restructuring the banking system was high, $300 million, or about 6 percent of GDP, and that task was not undertaken during the period studied.[42]

All in all, the achievements under the ERP were considerable. It is understandable that the World Bank and the IMF both came to view Ghana as an affirmation of their structural adjustment programs, one to be emulated by other African countries.

GHANA: A CONCLUSION

For all the success, two decades of calamitous economic policies left Ghana with a deteriorating infrastructure, low (even by African standards) productivity in food production caused by the long-term neglect of smallholder agriculture, a downward trend in nutrition, health, and education, and high population growth.[43]

Malawi's Superior Performance

A comparison between Ghana and Malawi during the period from the 1960s to the 1980s shows that however similar these countries were at independence, their postindependence economic policies were utterly unlike. Ghana's web of macro- and microeconomic distortions put that country as the most distorted on the World Bank's list of distorted economies.[44] By contrast, Malawi was the *least* distorted on that list (which was based, we recall, on an index of price distortions that took into account the pricing of foreign exchange, factors, and products). Its economy was less distorted than Thailand's, Malaysia's, or South Korea's; only its capital pricing was graded as being moderately distorted.

Malawi's governing authorites saw commercial agriculture as offering the best prospects for rapid growth, and their hopes were to a large extent fulfilled. Government policy did discriminate among sectors in agriculture, causing damaging distortions not fully reflected in the World Bank's high ranking. But Malawi did not attempt industrialization through import substitution as Ghana did. Agriculture's importance in Malawi remained high and accounted for approximately 75 percent of employment and 40 percent of GDP at the end of the 1980s.

Malawi's economy was also characterized by comparatively good macroeconomic management, in sharp contrast with Ghana and indeed with most of Africa. During the whole of the period studied, Malawi maintained a reasonably favorable macroeconomic environment. Of equal importance, during the 1970s and most of the 1980s Malawi was characterized by a high degree of political stability.

In general, government interventions were not especially damaging. Although most agricultural prices, for example, fertilizer and food crops, were regulated, only a small number of consumer prices were controlled. Growth of the nominal money supply during the 1970s was relatively modest, with the increase amounting to about 60 percent between 1973 and 1979. Later, money supply growth increased considerably, by 227 percent between 1983 and 1989. As a result there was considerably more inflationary pressure during the 1980s than there had been in the 1970s. Between 1974 and 1979, the low-income urban price index increased by 56 percent, whereas during the 1984–1989 period the same index increased 138 percent. However, the government did not seriously resist the resulting nominal currency devaluation. Between 1982 and 1988, the nominal exchange rate was allowed to decline by about half, with Malawi's kwacha falling from 1.30 = $1 to 2.54 = $1.

For these reasons, our analysis of Malawi's economy can be undertaken within a much narrower focus than was true of our treatment of Ghana. The agricultural sector always played the central role in Malawi's development strategy. Agricultural policy was unceasingly the main area of concern, and the government decisions in this area were usually the primary focus of the debate on economic policy. The contrast with Ghana was extreme.

MALAWI'S REMARKABLE GROWTH IN AGRICULTURE

During the 1970s, Malawi's economy, and in particular its agricultural sector, displayed one of the fastest growth rates for GDP and export in sub-Saharan Africa. Between 1965 and 1980, the average annual growth of GDP was 5.8

percent, while that of exports, chiefly tobacco, tea, and sugar, was 4.1 percent.[45] The principal force behind this impressive performance was the rapid growth in "estate" production of tobacco and, to a lesser extent, tea and sugar.[46] The excellent performance of estate agriculture was in turn the result of the preferential policy treatment accorded to the estates. This estate-oriented development strategy was a successful means of generating growth, especially of exports. We shall emphasize, however, that despite its undoubted success it also possessed a major weakness in that the benefits of this growth tended to be concentrated in the estate subsector without much spillover, at least in terms of the growth of production, to the much larger smallholder subsector.[47] For example, throughout the period of estate expansion in the 1970s there was little change in smallholder productivity. This weakness was a significant fator in compounding the problems of food insecurity at the household level because productivity increases in smallholder agriculture were not sufficient to allow food production to keep pace with population growth. It also meant that the inability of estates to expand as a result of land pressures left Malawi without a source of self-sustaining growth.

The following section examines how the estate-oriented strategy affected the economy's capacity for long-term, self-sustaining growth. It is followed by an analysis of the policy reform programs that Malawi undertook during the 1980s, together with an assessment of the weaknesses of those policy reforms.

THE ERA OF RAPID GROWTH AND ESTATE DOMINANCE, 1972–1980

The estate-oriented tobacco strategy that began in the late 1960s was well established by the early 1970s. To secure Malawi's international position as a reliable supplier, tobacco production was increased by expanding cultivated area. Between 1970 and 1980 the amount of leasehold land increased from 78,996 hectares to 267,152 hectares, or approximately 240 percent. The volume of burley and flue-cured tobacco production also increased by 231 percent and 207 percent, respectively.

Several ingredients were necessary to support the expansion of estate agriculture: securing leasehold land, recruiting estate managers, and obtaining a market share in the oligopolistic international tobacco market. International sanctions against Rhodesia after UDI helped achieve the latter two aims. To finance estate agriculture, the state taxed smallholders by maintaining a gap between producer prices and international prices[48] (see table 11.5, which compares Malawi with Kenya and Tanzania). The crops most heavily taxed were tobacco, cotton, and groundnuts. (The staple food crop, maize, received a small subsidy, even though the consumer price never fell below the producer price.) The revenue from taxing cash crops went to support an estate strategy.[49]

Table 11.5   The Ratio of Smallholder Producer Prices to International Prices
              for Malawi, Kenya, and Tanzania, 1970–1979

	KENYA		MALAWI			TANZANIA	
Year	Coffee	Tea	Dark-Fired Tobacco	Groundnuts	Cotton	Tobacco	Cotton
1970	0.91	0.60	0.22	0.69	0.24	0.43	0.72
1971	0.90	0.67	0.25	0.63	0.21	0.50	0.61
1972	0.98	0.63	0.23	0.70	0.22	0.46	0.57
1973	0.96	0.60	0.22	0.51	0.13	0.44	0.35
1974	0.97	0.55	0.23	0.28	0.15	0.42	0.32
1975	1.01	0.63	0.22	0.50	0.19	0.47	0.51
1976	0.85	0.57	0.21	0.51	0.13	0.40	0.41
1977	0.92	0.70	0.26	0.41	0.16	0.42	0.45
1978	0.94	0.64	0.26	0.41	0.17	0.47	0.55
1979	0.93	0.66	0.24	0.72	0.17	0.37	0.51

SOURCE: Robert E. Christiansen and V. Roy Southworth, "Agricultural Pricing and Marketing Policy in Malawi," paper presented at the National Agricultural Symposium, Mangochi, Malawi, November 1988.

Taxation by Means of a Marketing Board

As a first step toward taxing smallholders to support estate production, the statutory responsibilities of the food marketing parastatal (the Farmers' Marketing Board, or FMB) were broadened. A newly formed corporation was created in March 1971, when the Farmers' Marketing Board was reconstituted as the Agricultural Development and Marketing Board (ADMARC).

In addition to generating a financial surplus, ADMARC was also expected to ensure national food security and some degree of price stabilization.[50] By expanding seasonal markets and pursuing a policy of panterritorial and panseasonal pricing, ADMARC fulfilled these roles and began to dominate agricultural marketing.

The restrictions imposed on Asian traders during the 1970s and the limits on illicit exports caused by the weak economies of neighboring countries enhanced ADMARC's dominance. Thus ADMARC was an attractive alternative to private traders, and it increasingly moved toward a monopoly and monopsony position.

Also, ADMARC generated substantial financial surpluses from its operations (see table 11.6), although the rates of return on the investments made with these funds were low if not negative.[51] But even though ADMARC developed an extensive marketing infrastructure that provided smallholders with a guaranteed market at a predictable price, its taxation of smallholder agriculture contributed to the subsector's poor performance during the 1970s. Between 1972 and 1980 the

Table 11.6   ADMARC Profit (Loss) on Selected Crop Accounts,
1973/74–1986/87 (in thousands of kwachas)

Year	Tobacco	Groundnuts	Total	Profit as a Share of Smallholder Payments (%)
1973/74	2,563	1,770	8,111	56.55
1974/75	4,911	1,079	11,031	64.21
1975/76	10,609	1,266	9,977	48.77
1976/77	15,760	5,995	22,685	98.45
1977/78	25,860	4,500	30,040	117.91
1978/79	4,225	2,219	4,181	13.70
1979/80	2,709	3,746	70	0.25
1980/81	3,233	4,228	326	1.09
1981/82	9,145	3,280	8,863	30.71
1982/83	18,622	783	12,219	29.14
1983/84	13,364	277	6,550	14.22
1984/85	15,734	(904)	(12,853)	17.31
1985/86	(6,974)	(4,761)	(17,799)	−20.10
1986/87	3,893	(3,476)	(16,630)	−18.36

SOURCE: ADMARC, "Annual Accounts and Report for the Year Ended 31st March," Blantyre, Ministry of Agriculture, 1972–1987.

average annual growth rate of smallholder-marketed production of cotton was 2.1 percent, tobacco, 5.2 percent, and groundnuts, −10.43 percent (see table 11.7).

THE 1980s: ERA OF AGRICULTURAL POLICY REFORM

Despite the success of estate agriculture, its production suffered from a number of structural weaknesses, primarily undercapitalization and management problems, which contributed to the financial crisis and consolidation of the estate-based strategy in 1979/80.[52]

In broad terms the structural adjustment program in Malawi focused on restoring macroeconomic balance, improving agricultural pricing policy, and increasing the efficiency of the marketing parastatal, ADMARC.

SMALLHOLDER PRICING POLICY

The price policy reforms were intended to stimulate smallholder production of export crops by paying farmers prices that were closer to export parity. The implementation of the revised pricing policy, however, yielded mixed results.

Table 11.7   Smallholder Marketed Production, 1971/72–1987/88
              (in thousands of metric tons)

Year	Tobacco	Ground-nuts	Cotton Lint	Rice Paddy	Maize	Other*
1971/72	14.6	36.7	22.2	16.9	31.9	21.5
1972/73	17.7	39.6	22.1	20.0	63.6	20.8
1973/74	15.0	29.3	16.2	17.3	60.1	10.4
1974/75	11.6	28.7	17.8	20.9	65.5	21.3
1975/76	12.2	32.8	17.9	14.7	29.2	11.9
1976/77	14.5	32.6	24.2	24.5	64.8	25.7
1977/78	23.2	18.5	22.4	23.9	89.9	15.9
1978/79	23.7	11.1	24.2	30.8	120.6	16.3
1979/80	19.5	24.3	22.4	20.5	82.2	12.3
1980/81	11.3	31.5	23.1	17.5	91.9	16.8
1981/82	12.8	19.5	21.8	14.7	136.6	9.6
1982/83	8.7	10.7	14.6	12.5	246.1	9.0
1983/84	9.3	10.2	13.4	8.5	244.9	5.2
1984/85	19.2	9.9	32.1	9.8	296.3	7.0
1985/86	20.8	18.6	32.7	11.0	271.6	18.2
1986/87	17.1	53.0	21.9	12.1	112.6	11.9
1987/88	18.1	44.8	21.4	NA	59.6	NA

* Includes wheat, coffee, pulses, sunflower, and cassava.
SOURCES: ADMARC (1972–1987) and World Bank (1986).

Beginning in 1981 smallholders received a higher share of the world price for cotton exports and a much higher price for groundnuts, though the producer's share for dark-fired tobacco was little changed. The impact of higher prices on smallholder production was mixed. For example, in 1981/82 the government raised maize prices by 60 percent in response to food shortages. Although ADMARC purchased more maize, the increased production meant that farmers shifted land away from groundnuts and tobacco (see table 11.7). Although individual crops showed considerable responsiveness to changes in relative prices, technical constraints and a shortage of arable land limited the overall response by smallholders.

    Market surpluses not only allowed ADMARC to increase its strategic grain reserve but also forced it to store at considerable cost the stocks not consumed domestically or exported. To deal with ADMARC's growing financial difficulties, the government tried to shift production toward export of crops, particularly groundnuts, between 1984 and 1987. Farmers again responded to the relative price change by increasing marketed groundnut output, from 9,900 tons in 1984/

85 to 44,800 tons in 1987/88. Meanwhile, marketed maize declined from 296,000 tons to 59,600 tons.[53]

The response of smallholders to the changed pricing policy indicates that other constraints affected agricultural production. Farmers' responses to changing prices hinged on timely access to inputs, the availability of appropriate technology, and reliable marketing arrangements. In Malawi, these nonprice factors appeared to be binding constraints on increased productivity.

The low productivity that characterized smallholder production also affected food security by limiting off-farm employment opportunities, the prodution of more food, and the generation of income from other crops. Smallholders's welfare, at least in the short run, was likely impaired by the rising producer price of maize and the corresponding increases in the consumer price because more than half of all households were in food deficit—that is, they were net purchasers of maize.

Finally, in the mid-1980s the government tried to eliminate subsidies on smallholder fertilizer. The program was suspended before completion, however, because of concerns about the impact of fertilizer prices on the ability of smallholders to produce adequate quantities of marketed maize.

Restructuring ADMARC

In response to ADMARC's deteriorating finances, the government placed the agency under the auspices of the Statutory Bodies Act and classified it as a commercial organization that was required to operate on a self-sustaining basis. The Malawi government purchased the silos and grain that constituted the strategic grain reserve and began selling off ADMARC's investment portfolio (including several estates and shares in agroprocessing firms, industrial enterprises, and financial institutions).

Private Sector Participation in Agricultural Marketing

The liberalization program was supposed to encourage private sector marketing of all smallholder crops except tobacco and cotton. Its objective was to create an environment conducive to developing a multichannel marketing system where private traders could compete with ADMARC in buying and selling smallholder crops. The government's initial steps involved clarifying the legal status of private trade in food crops. The ADMARC monopsony actually covered only cotton and tobacco, so the clarification changed nothing legally, but it did send the signal that the government was encouraging a parallel private market.

Reorienting Malawi's Agricultural Strategy

With much of the macroeconomic and structural adjustment in Malawi complete, the major issue facing policy makers came to be identifying the most promising sources of growth in the medium and long term. Despite the weaknesses characterizing the smallholder subsector, it was the most likely source of broad-based growth in the medium term.[54] The serious shortage of land required that in the longer run other sources of growth must be found. In the next short-to-medium term (three to ten years), however, the dictates of household food security and the dominance of smallholder production meant that smallholder agriculture continued to offer the most promising source of growth.[55] A strategy based on smallholder growth did not preclude a role for estates in terms of maintaining a potential for foreign exchange earnings. The growing shortage of land, however, meant that continued competition between the estates and smallholder subsectors for land was likely to be incompatible with a smallholder-oriented growth strategy. The question was, what were the components of an agricultural strategy that would increase labor productivity in smallholder agriculture and contribute to sustainable growth in the economy?

The hypothesis put forward in this chapter is that a range of factors hindered the growth of production in the smallholder subsector during the 1970s, the most notable of which was the disincentive effects of the pricing policy implemented by ADMARC. Thus, despite its ranking by the World Bank as the most distortion-free less developed country, Malawi did face some damaging price constraints in agricultre, which the policy reforms implemented during the 1980s concentrated on eliminating

Although price incentives are critical to agricultural performance, they must be regarded as necessary but not sufficient conditions for growth. The emphasis on price was accompanied by, and perhaps even led to, a neglect of several nonprice factors that are essential to the development of the smallholder sector. Even though nonprice barriers to agricultural growth were well recognized during the 1970s and did figure in the policy debates of the time, it was surely correct initially to focus the 1980s policy reforms on price, as this was the binding constraint. After the price environment had been improved to the extent that international conditions allowed, the importance of the nonprice factors once more became evident. These constraints—particularly the heavy pressure on land from population growth, the credit dearth for small farmers, the inadequacy of the internal and external transport networks, ADMARC's occasional unreliability as a supplier of inputs and as a purchaser of output, and the need further to define its role—will continue to hinder labor productivity growth in Malawi's smallholder subsector.

Lessons from the Experience of Ghana and Malawi

During the period from the 1960s to the 1980s, the policy experience of Malawi was enormously different from that of Ghana. Malawi was the least-distorted LDC economy on the World Bank's list, while Ghana was the most distorted. In a region as diverse as Africa, it was and is no doubt ill-advised to seek generalized explanations for the widespread failure of economic growth, let alone of economic development. Yet the factors affecting the long-term prospects for both countries were more similar than might be supposed, with Ghana and Malawi during these decades illustrating a number of the important weaknesses in macroeconomic and agricultural policies that have affected economic performance in numerous other African countries as well. There can be no doubt of the destructive impact of Ghana's macroeconomic and pricing policies on that country's economic performance during the period in question. Ghana became one of the world's most dramatic illustrations of the damaging consequences of a distorted economy. As such, it became a test case for judging the corrective power of the economic policy reforms and structural adjustment lending that Ghana's own economists and those from donor governments and international agencies had long called for. As evidenced in our discussion, the implementation of macroeconomic policy reforms and new pricing strategies contributed greatly to Ghana's recovery. The reforms left unanswered a basic question that still confronts Ghana, however. Once the lost ground is made up, where will the future sources of growth be and where will the productivity increases come from?

Malawi's stable macroeconomic environment in the 1970s contributed to the strong export performance that the economy experienced during that period. The investment and growth strategy that Malawi pursued was flawed in several ways, however, not the least of which were price and policy distortions in smallholder agriculture that did not harmonize with Malawi's lofty position on the World Bank list as a nondistorted economy. Malawi's growth was too narrowly focused, and as such it was unable to generate broad-based economic progress. As a result, the employment opportunities available to labor, whether on one's own holding or for wages, continued to be characterized by low productivity.

The general conclusion that follows from our analysis of the Ghanian and Malawian economic experience is widely appreciated among development economists, but it also bears repetition. Structural adjustment and macroeconomic reform are necessary, but not sufficient, conditions for growth. For most African countries, once these vital reforms are accomplished, the heart of a strategy for continued successful growth lies in a broad increase in productivity in the agricultural sector. Productivity increase in agriculture is not the only dimension, but in most countries—certainly including Ghana and Malawi—it is the most important one.

Achieving a broad increase in agricultural productivity will in turn require a well-coordinated strategy involving policy reform and investment, with investment expansively defined to include not only physical capital but education and technical change in all their forms. The constraints that hinder productivity increases, and that must be broken by broad-based investment if development is to proceed successfully, are mundane perhaps compared with the day-to-day drama of the micro and macro policy reforms undertaken in Ghana and Malawi in recent years. However encouraging the accomplishment of these reforms has been, the constraints of low agricultural productivity will remain. How to promote productivity increases through efficient physical and human investment is the overriding long-term concern. The real creation of wealth comes from investment broadly defined and the associated productivity increases derived from that investment. The concentration on macro- and microreforms in Africa, necessary as they are, will not be sufficient unless the quantity and quality of that investment rises substantially or can be made to rise.

Notes

1. Ghana's population in 1988 was estimated to be 13.8 million; Malawi's, 8.1 million.

2. Among the major works are W. Birmingham, I. Neustadt, and E. E. Omaboe, eds., *A Study of Contemporary Ghana*, vol. 1, *The Economy of Ghana* (London, 1966); Tony Killick, *Development Economics in Action: A Study of Economic Policies in Ghana* (London, 1978); M. M. Huq, *The Economy of Ghana: The First 25 Years* (New York, 1989); J. Clark Leith, *Foreign Trade Regimes and Economic Development: Ghana* (New York, 1974). Also see Simon Commander, John Howell, and Wayo Seini, "Ghana 1983–7," in Simon Commander, ed., *Structural Adjustment and Agriculture* (Portsmouth, N.H., 1989); Bjorn Beckman, *Organising the Farmers: Cocoa Politics and National Development in Ghana* (Uppsala, 1976); Bjorn Beckman, "Ghana 1951–78," in J. Heyer, P. Roberts, and G. Williams, eds., *Rural Development in Tropical Africa* (London, 1981); John C. deWilde, "Case Studies: Kenya, Tanzania, and Ghana," in Robert H. Bates and M. F. Lofchic, eds., *Agricultural Development in Africa* (New York, 1980); Michael Roemer, "Ghana, 1953–1980: Missed Opportunities," in Arnold C. Harberger, ed., *World Economic Growth* (San Francisco, 1984); Michael Roemer, "Economic Development in Africa: Performance since Independence and a Strategy for the Future," *Daedalus*, spring 1982. More general works that pay considerable attention to Ghana and have been used here are Robert H. Bates, *Markets and States in Tropical Africa* (Berkeley, 1981); Robert H. Bates, *Essays on the Political Economy of Rural Africa* (Cambridge, 1983); D. K. Fieldhouse, *Black Africa 1945–80: Economic Decolonization and Arrested Development* (London, 1986); and Douglas Rimmer, *The Economics of West Africa* (New York, 1984).

3. Roemer, "Ghana, 1953–1980," p. 202.

4. Kwame Nkrumah, *Africa Must Unite* (London, 1963), p. 112.

5. W. A. Lewis, *Report on Industrialization and the Gold Coast* (Accra, 1953).

6. For the data, see Killick, *Development Economics in Action*, p. 168 and table 5.8; and Government of Ghana, *Five-Year Development Plan 1975–76 to 1979–80* (Accra, 1977), vol. 2, p. 189. Restrictions on foreign operation of industry in certain sectors came relatively late, beginning in 1968 with extension in 1970. Foreign enterprises had to take Ghanaian partners under the Investment Policy decrees of 1976.

7. Killick, *Development Economics in Action*, pp. 140 and 143.

8. Leith, *Ghana*, pp. 68–80. The years covered were 1968–70. For other ERP calculations from this period, see W. F. Steel, "Import Substitution and Excess Capacity in Ghana," *Oxford Economic Papers*, n.s., 24, no. 2 (July 1972).

9. World Bank, *Ghana: Policies and Program for Adjustment*, p. 4; R. Jeffries, "Rawlings and the Political Economy of Underdevelopment in Ghana," *African Affairs* 81 (1982); Huq, *Economy of Ghana*, p. 21.

10. Jeffries, "Underdevelopment in Ghana," p. 314, discusses how the overvaluation not only bred corruption among the government officials entrusted with allocating foreign exchange licenses but attracted many officials even at the highest level into smuggling on their own account and rather openly at that.

11. For cocoa remuneration, see World Bank, *Ghana: Policies and Program for Adjustment*, pp. 179–81; personal communications of data from the World Bank; and Fieldhouse, "Ghana and Nigeria," in *Black Africa*, p. 145. The decline in government tax revenue is calculated from World Bank, *Ghana: Policies and Program for Adjustment*, tables 5.1 and 7.1

12. Huq, *Economy of Ghana*, pp. 13, 176, 300, and tables A.11, A.14; Bank of Ghana data and World Bank, *Ghana: Policies and Program for Adjustment*, p.149.

13. A judgment rendered by World Bank, ibid., p. xv.

14. R. E. Dowse, *Modernisation in Ghana and the USSR: A Comparative Study* (London, 1969), p. 96. The Ghana Industrial Holding Company (GIHOC) became the largest of the parastatals, operating a wide variety of enterprises.

15. World Bank, *Ghana: Policies and Program for Adjustment*, p. 5. This deficit would have been much larger if any provision had been made for payback of capital invested.

16. See World Bank, *Accelerated Development in Sub-Saharan Africa* (Washington, D.C., 1981), table 4.1.

17. The 40 percent figure is from Killick, *Development Economics in Action*, pp. 171–72 and 182.

18. William F. Steel, "Import Substitution and Excess Capacity in Ghana," *Oxford Economic Papers* 24 (1972). The data used covered 1967/68. Also see Rimmer, *Economies of West Africa*, pp. 233–34, who has a lucid discussion of the issue.

19. For the calculations, see Killick, *Development Economics in Action*, p. 239 and table 9.2. The decline in purchase of material inputs from other sectors was from 65 percent in 1960 to 46 percent in 1968, according to ibid., table 8.5. For the Volta project,

see H. Dickinson, "The Volta Dam: Energy for Industry," in M. Fransman, ed., *Industry and Accumulation in Africa* (London, 1982), p. 351. The Volta scheme also tied up much capital and, with the exception of the production of aluminum, did not result in much stimulation of new industries. Early on, some other extravagances attracted wide attention, such as the expensive embassies established overseas, the superhighway equipped with an emergency telephone system for breakdowns, monumental conference centers and hotels, modern aircraft for Ghana airways, a gold bed for a minister, and so on. See R. Dumont, *False Start in Africa* (London, 1966), p. 294.

20. For the state farms, see Killick, *Development Economics in Action,* table 4D.

21. This paragraph draws on Huq, *Economy of Ghana,* p. 3, and chapter 11, "Prices and Internal Trade"; and on Tony Killick, "Price Controls in Africa: The Ghanaian Experience," *Journal of Modern African Studies* 11 (1973): 405–26.

22. For the surveys, see Huq, *Economy of Ghana,* appendix B, citing the data. Highest availability was in the universities; next highest was in Accra. Killick estimated that, in 1970, price controls were being observed in only about 17 percent of the cases he studied. *Development Economics in Action,* p. 288. In Ghana the black-market economy is widely known as the *kalabule* (dishonest) economy. It has recently been studied by Huq, *Economy of Ghana,* appendix B.

23. Bates, *Essays,* pp. 130–31.

24. World Bank, *World Development Report, 1983* (New York, 1983), pp. 60–63.

25. For this paragraph, we utilized data from the International Cocoa Organization; Huq, *Economy of Ghana,* chapter 5 and p. 204; Ghana Council of State, *Reviving Ghana's Economy* (Accra, 1981), p. 42; World Bank, *Accelerated Development in Sub-Saharan Africa,* box A; and other World Bank information made available to us.

26. It should be noted that the comparative advantage of cocoa was so strong that the upward trend of cocoa exports was not broken until 1966 and not seriously until 1974, even though taxation of that sector dated from 1940. See Rimmer, *Economies of West Africa,* p. 243.

27. World Bank, *Sub-Saharan Africa: From Crisis to Sustainable Growth* (Washington, D.C., 1989), p.276; World Bank, *Accelerated Development in Sub-Saharan Africa,* appendix 1.

28. Some slight gains were recorded in the export of cocoa butter and cocoa paste, and aluminum exports went from virtually nil at the start of the 1970s to 10 percent of the value of all exports in 1975 and 12 percent in 1980.

29. Huq, *Economy of Ghana,* p. 231.

30. World Bank, *Ghana: Policies and Program for Adjustment,* p. xii.

31. From E. R. Rado, "Notes toward a Political Economy of Ghana Today," *African Affairs* 85, no. 341 (October 1986): 563.

32. *IMF Survey,* November 12, 1984, p. 340.

33. See the summary in *IMF Survey,* October 30, 1989. For this section of the paper we had access to various unpublished documents of the World Bank. Although many of these are for official use only, and may not be quoted, their contents have allowed us to form judgments that are not otherwise footnoted here. This paragraph also draws on World

Bank, *Accelerated Development in Sub-Saharan Africa*, p. 167, and World Bank, *World Development Report*, 1983, pp. 12–13.

34. For this paragraph, see Huq, *Economy of Ghana*, p. 197; Rimmer, *Economics of West Africa*, p. 292; and Government of Ghana and World Bank estimates.

35. The corruption at the Ministry of Trade, which administered the import licenses, was so pervasive that in 1989 the police, acting on government orders, closed down the ministry. Before it reopened, all its employees were ordered to reapply for appointment and to submit an accounting of their personal assets. The accounting requirement was also applied retroactively to all former employees of the ministry dating back to 1984. See *West Africa*, November 27, 1989. We do not recall a precedent.

36. Projects financed by foreign assistance not included.

37. In the first year of staff reductions, about a quarter of those made redundant (3,000 of 12,000) had reached retirement age and were not replaced. *West Africa*, December 4, 1989, reported that 32,542 had actually been laid off during 1987–1989. Some of these (14 percent) have been resettled in farming. In addition to restricted World Bank sources, this paragraph draws on World Bank, *Accelerated Development in Sub-Saharan Africa*, p. 167, and World Bank, *World Development Report*, 1983, pp. 12–13.

38. Large revisions have been made in this data, and considerably different figures are quoted by various authors. We have used World Bank figures available in 1989.

39. *Ghana National Program for Economic Development* (Accra, 1987), p. 24.

40. It was accepted that foreign private capital flows would not be a likely source of much assistance until economic recovery was far more advanced. The prime reliance had to be on domestic resources together with foreign aid.

41. Allocation of credit by sector was abolished except for agriculture, where a lending requirement (20 percent) still applied.

42. World Bank, *World Development Report*, 1989 (Washington, D.C., 1989), p. 71.

43. For data, see the statistical appendix to World Bank, *Sub-Saharan Africa: From Crisis to Sustainable Growth*.

44. World Bank, *World Development Report*, 1983 (New York, 1983), pp. 60–63.

45. For a more detailed account of Malawi's economic performance during the 1970s, see J. G. Kydd and R. E. Christiansen, "Structural Change in Malawi since Independence: Consequences of a Development Strategy Based on Large-Scale Agriculture," *World Development* 10, no. 5 (1982): 355–76; and R. E. Christiansen and J. G. Kydd, "The Political Economy of Agricultural Policy Formulation in Malawi: 1964–85," World Bank, MADIA Working Paper, Washington, D.C., 1990. Malawi has had the benefit of fewer comprehensive studies than has Ghana. Generally in this section of the paper we have drawn on Christopher Fyfe, ed., *Malawi: An Alternative Development Strategy* (Edinburgh, 1985); Government of Malawi, *Economic Report* (Zomba, 1970–1988); *Malawi Statistical Yearbook*; various Ministry of Agriculture reports; Uma Lele, "Structural Adjustment, Agricultural Development and the Poor: Some Lessons from the Malawian Experience," *World Development* 18, no. 9 (September 1990): 1207–20; USAID, "Malawi Economic Policy Reform Program," Lilongwe, 1985; and four studies by the World Bank.

46. In Malawi, unlike other countries, estates are defined in terms of the crops they are

permitted to grow (flue-cured and burley tobacco), rather than on the basis of size. For more details on land issues, see Lele, "Structural Adjustment."

47. See Kydd and Christiansen, "Structural Change in Malawi"; Christiansen and Kydd, "Political Economy of Agricultural Policy Formulation in Malawi"; and Lele, ibid.

48. As part of the search for sources of funding to plow into the estate sector, the government of Malawi approached donors including the World Bank in the hope that project financing could be obtained for this purpose. Donors were, however, reluctant to provide such support because of qualms concerning the equity implications for the smallholders.

49. For a more detailed account of how the revenue was acquired to finance the estate strategy, see R. E. Christiansen, "Financing Malawi's Development Strategy," in Fyfe, ed., *Malawi: An Alternative Development Strategy.*

50. ADMARC never reduced the nominal producer price of maize and typically provided a small subsidy to consumers on maize, that is to say, it usually lost money on its maize trading account.

51. See Christiansen, "Financing Malawi's Development Strategy," in Fyfe, ed., *Malawi: An Alternative Development Strategy,* for a more detailed account.

52. More detailed accounts of the factors contributing to the weaknesses of the estate sector may be found in Christiansen and Kydd, "Political Economy of Agricultural Policy Formulation in Malawi," and Lele, "Structural Adjustment."

53. The decline in ADMARC purchases of maize in 1987/88 is exaggerated because private sector trading was liberalized during that year and a considerable but undetermined amount of maize was sold through private channels.

54. See the analysis in John W. Mellor, "Emphasizing Agriculture in Economic Development—Is It a Risky Business?" paper presented to the Tenth Agricultural Symposium of the World Bank, "Risk in Agriculture," January 1990, for a compelling argument on the role of agriculture in a development strategy for countries in sub-Saharan Africa.

55. See Uma Lele and S. Stone, "Population Pressure, the Environment, and Agricultural Intensification: Variations on the Boserup Hypothesis," 1989.

12

Egypt and Syria under Socialism
A Forty-Year Perspective

VICTOR LAVY

Introduction

Since the end of the World War II the Middle East has made significant advances in economic development. Countries have experienced periods of accelerated economic growth and a notable rise in living standards. But a great deal of disparity still exists in the rates of economic growth and in levels of public well-being. Differences in natural resources, particularly oil, account for some of this disparity. Government policies are also partly responsible. During the postwar period Middle Eastern governments adopted several approaches to economic development. Some encouraged economic growth by providing incentives to the private sector; others favored a large public sector and a centrally planned economy.

This chapter evaluates the effect of government ideology and its derived policy on development by targeting the economic performance of Egypt and Syria from 1946 to 1987. During these years both countries switched their economic agendas from programs within the free enterprise system to ones in which government played a dominant role in running the economy.

This chapter first describes the similar cycles that Egypt and Syria experienced over four decades: a gradual shift in economic policy from an almost laissez-faire system to a centrally planned economy, then a reversal, and a struggle to undo the heritage of the past. In recent years, both nations have attempted to depart from their socialist legacy, to restore free market institutions, to restructure property rights, and to change the system of incentives in the economy. The second part of the chapter evaluates various development phases in terms of economic performance and correlates that performance with changes in government strategies and policies. It analyzes growth in national product, factor productivity, changes in income distribution, the incidence of poverty, and measures of well-being and development such as access to and quality of health and education.

Table 12.1 presents some comparative data for the two nations. Syria appears more developed than Egypt; it enjoys higher income per capita, has a larger industrial sector, and boasts a better-educated and healthier population. Similarities between Egypt and Syria are substantial, however. Both are former colonies (Egypt under British domination and Syria under the French); both were governed by military and nondemocratic regimes; both engaged in military conflicts that created a serious drain on scarce national resources (water and cultivable land). Of the two, Syria, has experienced more political instability and more serious fluctuations in income.

The full cycle that Egypt is about to complete—from laissez-faire through socialism, central planning, land reforms, and nationalization, then back toward a free marketplace—provides the setting and timing for an examination of how the economy has fared in the course of this journey. Because Syria has followed in Egypt's footsteps, it is a natural candidate for comparison.

Ideology, Political Instability, and Economic Doctrines: The First Years of Self-Government (1946–1957)

The decade after World War II brought political independence to Syria and a new system of government to Egypt. Syria gained full independence in 1946. Syrian politics were extremely volatile because of factional infighting. The National Party government was only the first of many to rule Syria in those early years. Four successive governments were overthrown by military coups between 1947 and 1957. There were broad political differences over issues of policy, Arab unity, and economic growth.

Disagreement over Syria's economic agenda pitted those who promoted a socialist state against those who supported a free enterprise system. The socialists advocated complete transfer of productive sectors to public ownership. They believed that a market-based system fostered economic inequity by letting profit, rather than social need, determine the direction of investment. Socialist support tended to come from the middle class—the professionals, teachers, students, and civil servants—and from the urban lower class. The Baath Party, the Commu-

Table 12.1   Basic Indicators: Egypt and Syria

	Egypt	Syria
GNP per capita (US$)		
1962	$140	250
1987	$680	1640
GNP (US$ billion)		
1960	$6.9	3.2
1987	$34.5	24.0
Population (millions)		
1987	50.1	11.2
Population growth rate		
1952	2.3	3.5
1980–1987	2.7	3.6
Labor force in agriculture		
1980	45.7	32.3
Labor force in industry		
1980	20.3	31.7
Infant mortality rate		
1952	196.6	157.0
1985	85.0	48.0
Crude death rate		
1952	23.4	20.9
1985	9.9	7.0
Total fertility rate		
1952	6.6	7.1
1985	4.8	6.8
Literacy rate		
1960	74.2	—
1985	55.5	40.0
Population per physician		
1960	2,560	4,630
1984	790	1,260
Exports (US$ billion)		
1987	$4.0	1.4
Fuel exports (US$ billion)		
1987	$2.8	0.6
Life expectancy at birth, female		
1952	44.1	47.7
1987	62.0	66.9

SOURCE: World Bank, *World Bank Development Report* (various issues).

nists, and the Arab Socialist Party (ASP) all embraced socialism. Among the socialists themselves, views differed over how fast to move toward socialism: the Baath Party advocated gradual transition, whereas the Communists and some other regionalists favored quick transformation. In opposition to the socialists, the industrialists supported economic growth fueled by the private sector. Supporters of this view included the National Party and the People's Party, whose constituency included wealthy merchants and landowners from Damascus and Aleppo.

The dispute over Syria's economic agenda was particularly bitter because of the country's relative backwardness. In 1946 Syria experienced many problems common to developing nations. Agriculture dominated the economy, accounting for 65 to 75 percent of the population and for almost half of national income when combined with husbandry (IBRD 1955, 9). Although agriculture was the largest economic sector, yields were considerably below potential output. Farm techniques remained backward, and there was little use of fertilizers. In addition, the country suffered from a severe shortage of cultivable land. Less than a third of Syria's total land area (181,337 square kilometers) was arable, and a much smaller proportion benefited from irrigation. According to the World Bank, irrigated land accounted for only 11 to 12 percent of the 3.5 million hectares under cultivation. The rest depended on rainfall, which is fairly reliable only along the coast.

Syrian industry was small, contributing no more than 7 to 8 percent of national income (Sayigh 1978, 240). The important industries were textiles, flour milling, sugar refining, vegetable oil extraction, and the manufacture of cement, glass, and tobacco products. Almost all other industrial activity took place at the handicraft level.

Despite Syria's economic backwardness, the government made few structural changes before 1958 and played a limited role in guiding the economy. This passivity can largely be explained by political instability. Military coups often disrupted policies; powerful interest groups prevented controversial programs from being carried out. The Shishakli regime (December 1949 to July 1953) made two separate attempts to foster agrarian reform; both failed because of opposition from landowners.

There were, however, a few government initiatives during Syria's first decade. Several laws were enacted encouraging economic growth through the private sector. In 1949 the government provided facilities for companies to obtain state-guaranteed, low-interest loans from the Banque de Syrie et du Liban. The following year the authorities dissolved a Syrian economic union with Lebanon so that Syria could have greater latitude in raising the effective rate of protection for industry. During 1950 and 1951, Syria increased import duties and tariffs on a wide range of goods. All the early Syrian governments believed that high duties were necessary to strengthen the country's infant industries.

The government began several projects to improve the infrastructure. These included constructing the Euphrates River Dam to bring water to Aleppo, building new roads and hospitals, expanding irrigation, and developing Latakia Harbor. Despite these investments, Syria's infrastructure remained inadequate. Throughout the 1950s the rail system consisted of only three railways, all built during the Ottoman Empire. Most roads were unpaved and often impassable in the rainy season.

The private sector invested heavily in irrigation. Indeed, between 1945 and 1960, when the area under irrigation grew by 58 percent, almost all the increase was funded by private money (Firro 1986, 47). This expansion of cultivable land was important in stimulating economic growth. Between 1945 and 1953, the Syrian economy grew by 28 percent in real terms, or roughly 5 to 6 percent a year (IBRD 1955, 21).

In sum, Syria's economic growth between 1946 and 1957 was stimulated by the private sector. Private investors channeled funds toward low value-added activities (agriculture), and this investment spurred growth throughout the economy. The government played a minor role, guiding the economy and investing in infrastructure. The political instability that plagued the early governments prevented them from amending property rights or enacting other policies opposed by powerful interest groups.

Egypt's economic situation at the end of World War II was similar to that of Syria. About 60 percent of the population lived in rural areas and engaged in agricultural activities; industry was small. The system of land ownership was inequitable and caused large disparities in income distribution. Despite irrigation, the country faced a severe shortage of cultivable land. Poverty, malnutrition, and illiteracy were widespread.

Egypt's political environment was much less volatile than that of Syria. Until 1952, Egypt was a monarchy, and King Farouk's policies were greatly influenced by British interests. This regime of government came to an end on July 23, 1952, when a military coup forced Farouk to abdicate. The young military officers who staged the coup were united against the monarchy but divided in political leanings. As Peter Mansfield noted, "They had a vague idea of the sort of society they wanted Egypt to become. But they had no time to develop any political ideas, let alone a political program" (McDermott 1989, 17). Instead, the revolutionaries made ad hoc responses to the country's pressing political problems, responses that eventually led to state socialism.

The turning point in this revolution occurred in November 1954, when Gamal Abdel Nasser took the helm. During the next seventeen years Nasser was to transform Egypt into a socialist state in which all major industry, commerce, and financial services came under government control. At first, the new regime followed a cautious economic policy in which the government collaborated with the private sector. The only policy that restricted the private sector was agrarian reform. The reform law (1952) was less a direct assault on the private sector than an attempt by the government to undermine the political power base of landowners. In 1952, "2,000 or so owners held 20 percent of the acreage, while more than two million held just 13 percent" (McDermott 1989, 21). As a result, the big landowners controlled a disproportionate amount of both wealth and political power. Agrarian reform aimed to dismantle this feudal system and redistribute income more equitably.

The reform[1] restricted the amount of land that could legally be owned.[2] The reform also set a time limit of five years for owners to sell all land in excess of the ceiling. Until the land was sold, surtaxes were placed on the excess holdings; compensation was set at seventy times the basic land tax, which averaged about half the land's market value. All beneficiaries who had acquired land through the reform were required to join cooperative societies. These societies provided seed and advice on farming techniques but were really set up so as to give the government some control over the new landowners. Finally, the reform defined the relationship between owners and tenants by spelling out the rights of the agricultural worker. Nasser's government succeeded in restructuring the system of land distribution. By 1965 no landowner owned more than two hundred feddans, and 95.05 percent of all landowners had holdings under five feddans (Sayigh 1978, 333).[3]

Land reform was only one of the government's programs to promote economic development. The new Egyptian regime also gave high priority to expanding the industrial base. Early policies emphasized both import substitution and increased private investment in industry. Under amended tax laws new companies investing in projects that promoted economic development were exempt from taxes for seven years; existing companies were exempt for five years. The government also reduced taxes on raw materials and equipment and raised those on competing manufactured goods.

Between 1952 and 1957 Nasser's regime initiated several projects to increase productivity and national income by working through the private sector. Government investment programs targeted three economic sectors: industry, infrastructure, and agriculture. In industry, the government expanded energy sources, increased the production of light manufacturing, and set up several heavy industries (iron, steel, nitrogenous fertilizers). Infrastructure investments improved the railway system, built new roads, expanded the system of canals, extended communications, and widened and deepened the Suez Canal. The government's agricultural program sought to expand cultivable areas through greater irrigation and reclamation of desert land. The Aswan High Dam became a key government project. By increasing food production and reducing demand for imported foodstuffs, the government hoped to divert foreign exchange to the importation of industrial goods.

During the 1950s Egypt suffered from a severe shortage of foreign exchange, which prevented the industrial sector from buying much of the material and equipment needed to increase production. Even so, Egypt was able to solicit significant foreign assistance to finance certain development projects. The Soviet Union and the United States both provided foreign aid. The Soviets loaned US$170 million to finance the Helwan Iron and Steel Complex, and the United States loaned US$97 million for the construction of the first stage of the Aswan High Dam (Ikram 1980, 344).

In sum, the Nasser regime first played a limited role in the economy. The government continued to invest in traditional sectors—light manufacturing, agriculture, infrastructure—while encouraging private domestic investment. Its policies fostered import substitution (particularly foodstuffs and light manufacturing) in an attempt to reallocate resources from lower value-added activities (agriculture) to those with higher value added (industry). Property rights in land were radically altered. Agrarian reform laws successfully redistributed land so that ownership became more equitable. But the government failed to balance the country's demand for imports with available foreign exchange. As a result, the industrial sector lacked many intermediate goods and raw materials necessary to increase production.

The Gradual Transition toward Socialism (1958–1961)

The period 1958 to 1961 was unique for two reasons. It witnessed the political union of Egypt and Syria, and it determined that both Egypt and Syria were dedicated to instituting state socialism. During Syria's union with Egypt, the country underwent many of the same structural changes that Egypt had already experienced. Syria was finally able to carry out a program of agrarian reform in 1958, almost replicating the process in Egypt; the Syrian reform set a limit on the amount of land that could be legally owned and outlined conditions for requisitioning the excess area.[4]

In Egypt, the government now assumed a much larger role in running the economy. By 1958 it had gained control of all foreign specialist banks through the state agency called the Economic Organization. Two years later the Egyptian authorities nationalized both the Bank Misr and the National Bank, two of the largest banks holding Egyptian assets. These nationalizations were the first to involve domestic assets. They spread alarm throughout Egypt and Syria as investors grew fearful of Nasser's expected set of industrial policies.

Socialism in Full Swing, 1961–1970

Full-scale nationalization took place in Egypt in June and July 1961. During these two months the state nationalized all remaining banks and insurance companies, plus forty-four companies engaged in basic manufacturing. In addition, it expropriated half the capital of eighty-six light manufacturing and commercial firms. The state also passed a law limiting the ownership of assets by any one person or company to 10,000 pounds and required that all shares in excess of 10,000 pounds pass into public ownership.[5]

New legislation radically altered commercial policy as well. In 1961 the government closed the Alexandria cotton futures market and assumed the exclusive right to purchase cotton by placing all companies involved in the cotton trade under state control. Virtually all import-export companies were nationalized, and foreign trade was turned into a public sector activity. During the next two years the laws became even more restrictive: in 1963 the right of private firms to import was abolished, and a year later all foreign exchange allocations were placed under state control. These measures gave the government total control over all imports. Severe shortages and bottlenecks in the supply of goods soon resulted.

The problem of resource misallocation grew worse under the system of foreign exchange allocations. In 1964 "the foreign exchange devoted each week to imports was linked to actual export earnings and payment obligations of the preceding and following weeks" (Ikram 1980, 262). Although this system was relaxed in 1965, misallocations of foreign exchange for imports continued.

The economic rationale for the nationalization measures lay in two arguments. First, nationalization was necessary to prevent the working class from being further exploited by big business, an idea that was spelled out in the 1962 National Charter under the heading of "Arab Socialism." According to this charter, the private sector could not be trusted to guide the nation toward economic development; instead, the government would ensure universal and equal access to the benefits of economic progress. This argument justified nationalization on the grounds of "mobilizing national savings." According to this theory, nationalization would increase business savings, which would then increase national savings.

Second, although the Egyptian government publicized the economic rationale for nationalization, strong political motives also prompted the public takeovers. State socialism allowed the government to expand its political base without building a comprehensive political organization. For example, the government gained the support of the middle class by placing it on the state's payroll. The government quickly absorbed white-collar workers into the public sector by nationalizing most of the country's large-scale industry.[6] Nationalization replaced the small industrial elite with a large contingent of public servants whose livelihood became dependent on the government. The government also courted the lower classes by initiating an extensive system of consumer-goods subsidies that raised the standard of living. Through these two policies, the government was able to gain support from a wide spectrum of society.

In Syria, Nasser initiated a series of nationalizations without first consulting the Baath Party, then in power. The state took control of all banks and insurance companies and partially nationalized twenty-four other companies. In addition, salaries were fixed and a progressive income tax initiated. The government made all imports conditional on licenses and the availability of foreign exchange. These actions brought Syria economic chaos and political instability.

In 1961 a Syrian military coup removed the Baath Party from power and installed a conservative government. The ruling Conservative Party immediately dissolved Syria's union with Egypt and reversed many socialist policies. All nationalized industries were returned to their former owners, with certain conditions attached. Exchange controls were abolished, as were most restrictions on trade and capital mobility. The government also raised the ceiling on the amount of land that could be legally owned. The government's efforts to liberalize the economy were cut short in 1963, when another coup reinstated the Baath Party.

The Baath Party reinstated a strong socialist agenda. The authorities lowered the upper limit on land ownership and renewed nationalization. All banks and insurance companies were nationalized. By mid-1964 the state had nationalized nine mercantile companies and taken partial control over nine other companies. Within six months the government was in control of most oil-distributing and cotton-ginning companies, as well as 70 percent of all companies involved in import and export. Nationalization proved disastrous. By October 1965 almost all Syrian private investment had stopped, and capital flight was a severe problem. The government decided to end its nationalization program and began encouraging private investment.

In 1966 a radical wing of the Baath Party staged another miliary coup. As this new government was primarily concerned with foreign affairs (the 1967 war with Israel), few economic changes took place during its three years in power. In 1970, the Syrian government once again changed hands, and Hafiz al-Assad's government brought political stability to Syria. Assad's government remained in power throughout the 1970s and 1980s and was able to make considerable economic changes.

The Damage: Distorted Economic Systems

As a result of continuous government intervention and distortionary economic policies during the 1960s, Egypt and Syria developed inefficient and uncompetitive economic systems that were incapable of supporting self-sustained, long-term economic growth. These systems featured multiple exchange rates, administered prices, and heavily subsidized consumer goods and services. The main features of the various distortions are illustrated in the following sections.

PRICE CONTROLS AND SUBSIDIES

Most prices in Egypt and Syria are determined administratively, with no regard for costs. Prices of many products provided by public authorities and enterprises are significantly lower than their cost of production or their price on the world market. This is especially true of energy, public transport, and basic food products. One objective of such policies is to provide goods and services to low-income groups at low cost. Theoretically, this can increase the real income of the poor. Controlled agricultural prices can provide cheap inputs for the food and textile industry and keep inflation down.

Such a pricing policy wastes resources, however. It also distorts the allocation of resources, reduces efficiency in production and consumption, increases the fiscal deficit, and ultimately lowers the national savings rate. The increased fiscal deficit causes larger balance-of-payments deficits, which trigger higher inflation (to the extent that part of the deficit is financed by printing new money). Subsidizing the two main exports—energy and cotton—increases their domestic consumption and therefore reduces exports.[7]

In agriculture, farmers have benefited from implicit and explicit subsidies on seeds, fertilizer, and pesticides, while themselves providing a sizable implicit subsidy by receiving low producer prices for cotton and wheat. Low producer prices for cotton have augmented the modest explicit (budget) subsidy to the textile industry and have allowed the industry to supply cloth cheaply to domestic consumers. This reduces exports.

Syria has a comprehensive system of price controls covering all major consumer goods, public and private sector imports, and goods produced by public and private enterprises. Only public agencies sell basic food products (bread, flour, rice, sugar, tea, and vegetable oil), and the Ministerial Economic Committee determines the prices of these goods. The High Council of Agriculture establishes most agricultural producer prices. All housing except recently built or luxury units are rent-controlled.

As in Egypt, not all subsidies appear in the Syrian budget; a substantial portion is borne by Syria's Stabilization Fund, which subsidizes prices of essential consumer goods and covers the subsidy by surcharges on other goods. The government occasionally assumes part of the operating losses of public sector enterprises, financed by the Commercial Bank of Syria.

The controlled producer crop prices, at levels well below international prices, have substantially distorted Syrian agriculture. As one example, the domestic procurement price for all major internationally traded crops *except cotton* has in recent years been high relative to international prices. Such high procurement prices distort resource allocation; they encourage high-cost marginal producers, give relatively efficient producers excessive rents, and divert resources from production of other profitable, but unsupported, crops.

EXCHANGE RATE POLICY AND FOREIGN TRADE

The exchange rate and trading system in Egypt and Syria are complex. The many restrictions that affect trade and external payments include multiple exchange rates, large spreads between buying and selling rates, advance import deposit requirements, and administrative controls on trade flows. Exchange rates are only partially adjusted, so that they lag well behind inflation-rate differences with trading partners and have been highly overvalued for a long time. Overvalued currencies have made domestic products increasingly noncompetitive and have encouraged the development and expansion of the nontradables sector.

The rigidity of the Syrian system is exemplified by the official exchange rate, which was fixed at 3.925 pounds to the U.S. dollar from 1976 until January 1, 1988, when it was depreciated to 11.2 pounds. Many transactions, of course, take place at unofficial rates. In 1981 the continuous decline in export competitiveness and the existence of a black market in foreign currency forced the authorities to introduce a parallel rate of 5.425 pounds per dollar. By the summer of 1986, the rate on the black market had reached 27 pounds per dollar. In early 1987 five principal and two minor exchange rates were in use. During 1987 an effective devaluation took place as various categories of exports were shifted to higher exchange rates. During 1991, the government moved from this complex system of multiple exchange rates to a two-tier system.

The exchange rate system in Egypt is equally complicated, fragmented into three pools. The Egyptian central bank handles Suez Canal dues, imports of essential food products and agricultural inputs, and exports of rice, petroleum, and raw cotton. The exchange rate applied to these transactions was fixed from 1979 until 1987. The commercial bank pool mainly handles workers' remittances, tourism receipts, and certain private sector imports. The exchange rate for these transactions, set at 0.845 pounds in August 1981, was eliminated in 1986–1987. The third pool is the free market, where rates are much lower than in the other two pools; imports through the free market, however, are subject to import licensing. The overall real exchange rate appreciated dramatically in the 1980s. The main cause of this appreciation was the unchanged nominal exchange rate in the central bank pool. The main effect was to discourage the domestic production of tradables. Egypt's industrial and agricultural sectors grew more slowly than the service sector, and nonfuel merchandise exports stagnated or declined in real terms. In recent years, as part of a macroeconomic adjustment program, the government dismantled foreign exchange controls and unified the foreign exchange system, thereby allowing unrestricted international capital mobility.

INTEREST RATES AND CAPITAL MARKETS

Real interest rates in Egypt were negative between 1976 and 1986. Determined administratively, they were not affected by inflation or the demand for credit. This policy encouraged borrowing and led to a distorted pattern of investment that was biased toward capital-intensive projects. Interest rates were kept low for such priority sectors as agriculture and industry, a policy that might have harmed rather than helped those sectors because compressing the supply of funds discouraged bank lending to those sectors. Egypt's banks were further discouraged because agricultural and industrial projects are often riskier than commercial projects, especially when interest rates are not freely determined and cannot be adjusted to reflect different risk factors for different projects. Moreover, the negative real interest rates on deposits denominated in domestic currency discouraged savings; they encouraged both consumption and accumulation of wealth in foreign currencies.

In both Syria and Egypt the structure and level of interest rates have remained unchanged since 1981, with a ceiling of 9 percent. Priority sectors—based on social and economic considerations—get preferential lending rates. Given the rapid increase in domestic prices, prevailing deposit rates are negative. A twelve-month deposit in Syria, for example, earns 8 percent a year, about one-tenth of the 1987 inflation rate.

Egyptian and Syrian control of financial markets hampers their efficient functioning and development and hinders economic recovery. It may help to finance the large fiscal deficits and public investment programs.

Attempts at Economic Liberalization, 1974–1987

Both Egypt and Syria liberalized their economies in the 1970s and 1980s. Egypt's liberalization policies were much broader than those initiated in Syria. In September 1970 Nasser died, and his vice-president, Anwar Sadat, took over leadership of the Egyptian government. As Sadat worked to strengthen his political base, his first years in power saw little economic change. The 1973 October war with Israel provided Sadat with both the popularity and the political power to make far-reaching economic moves. In 1974, his government initiated an open-door (*infitah*) economic development policy.

The cornerstone of this policy was Law 43, which sought to attract large-scale foreign investment. In 1977 Law 43 was expanded to add companies owned by Egyptian nationals to the foreign companies and joint ventures already covered by the law. *Infitah* provided clear signs that the public sector was willing to share the task of economic development with the private sector.

An evaluation of Egypt's open-door policy produces mixed results. Law 43 attracted a significant amount of foreign investment, which resulted in many new projects, but very little foreign investment was made in projects that increased the productive capacity of the country. Rather, most investment went into financial services, banking, and tourism, doing little to stimulate exports or to reduce imports.

During Sadat's second term in office the government attempted to partly dismantle the extensive system of price controls and subsidies so as to achieve greater economic efficiency. In 1977 Sadat proposed cutting the subsidies in half. This policy collapsed as people took to the streets in protest. "About 80 people were killed and another 800 injured in riots in Cairo, Alexandria and other towns" (McDermott 1989, 54). Clearly, Egyptians viewed the subsidies as necessary for maintaining their standard of living.

Since the early 1960s Egypt had maintained a system of subsidies that covered essential goods—wheat, sugar, kerosene—whose cost to the government was not substantial. During the early 1970s the number of goods and services that were subsidized increased; so did the cost. "Total subsidies rose from less than 2 percent of GDP in 1970–1971 to about 5 percent in 1973 and to 10 percent in 1978" (Ikram 1980, 315).

Throughout most of the 1970s and 1980s the system of subsidies remained intact, although certain subsidies were reduced. Between 1982 and 1987 the government increased the fixed price of many goods, bringing them closer to market prices.[8] The cost of the subsidy system still places a heavy burden on the economy.

President Hosni Mubarak, who continued the program of economic liberalization, introduced in 1982 a new investment law that gave Egyptians many of *the same* privileges as foreign investors. In addition, he relaxed the state's control over agriculture by allowing farmers more discretion in the crops they planted. Agricultural controls on many products have also been lifted; an exception is cotton, which is still completely controlled by the state. These policies have enjoyed only limited success in raising domestic investment and agricultural productivity.

In Syria, the government also initiated policies aimed at increasing the role of the private sector. One of Assad's first policies was to encourage private enterprise by assisting small manufacturers and workshops that made less than 15,000 pounds. The government encouraged these small businesses by investing in certain low-risk industrial projects. In March 1984 a law was passed that allowed private investors to take loans to promote private development projects. This law did little to stimulate investment in industrial manufacturing. During the period 1970–1978 there was some increase in light manufacturing but no real takeoff in aggregate production in private industry. Some claim that the private sector stayed away from productive outlets, choosing to remain where there was little risk. Domestic private investment went into exports and imports, real estate, construction, tourism and hotels, retail trades, trucking, and producing and making luxury items (Syed 1984, 310).

In 1974 a set of decrees opened up Syria's economy. These laws abolished restrictions on hard currency, released frozen assets, and provided tax incentives to stimulate foreign investment in the economy. "By 1975, foreign companies could collaborate with state-owned industries on an equity participation basis or could invest directly in free industrial zones" (Syed 1984, 351). Unfortunately, the government's incentives were not enough to attract large-scale investment in the Syrian economy. In part this was because of the government's reluctance to provide economic freedom to foreign investors (except in tourism and light industry).

In 1978 the government embarked on a new program to encourage foreign investment through free zones. This time it was more successful. Forty new projects were approved in 1978; half of them were in operation by 1979. Foreign investment soon poured into Syrian public utilities and infrastructure, tourism, and hotel construction. In addition, the Commercial Bank of Syria opened free-zone branches.

Syria's government was willing to set up joint companies with foreign investors, but few foreigners were willing to take the risk. One major obstacle was the country's massive bureaucracy, which made it difficult for foreigners to get projects approved. In 1975 the government departed dramatically from earlier policies by opening certain oil exploration projects to foreigners. Several oil companies, including Shell and Marathon, quickly set up operations. In 1991, the government announced a new investment law, known as "Law No. 10," which grants qualifying investors tax holiday privileges for the import of capital goods and inputs.

In sum, Egypt and Syria both made considerable progress toward social and economic development despite the obstacles facing them. The role that government played in the economy has changed considerably. At the end of World War II the role of the state was limited to providing basic social services and investing in the country's infrastructure. By the mid-1950s this situation had changed as the dominant private sector was gradually replaced by a growing public sector. The late 1950s and early 1960s witnessed a complete transformation of the Egyptian and Syrian economies along socialist lines. During the 1970s both governments partially dismantled socialist policies; they solicited foreign investors and attempted to make their economies run more efficiently.

The Performance Profile

Evaluating the economic and social performance of Egypt and Syria during the past four decades is a complicated and delicate task. The available data on the 1950s are limited and are also scant for the years preceding independence. This renders impossible any comparison with the more recent period, before the two countries socialized their economic structure and ideology. Moreover, several external shocks have directly affected both economies, which makes it difficult to disentangle the damage caused by government policy from the impact of other exogenous factors.

One external element is the Middle East conflict, which has manifested itself in an intensive military buildup, ever-increasing defense expenditures, and frequent wars that had the economic impact of natural disasters. Equally important was the diversion of the nations' total attention toward perceived security threats and away from issues such as economic progress.

The massive military buildup in Egypt and Syria since World War II has few parallels, especially among small, poor nations. By the early 1980s total military spending was 25 percent of GNP in Syria and more than 12 percent of GNP in Egypt. By way of comparison, the corresponding ratios in most other developing countries range from 2 to 4 percent and average 4.5 percent in the Organization for Economic Cooperation and Development (OECD) countries.[9] Massive military spending has been possible only by appropriating enormous domestic resources and large inputs of external aid. During the years 1955–1972, a period in which the governments of Egypt and Syria attempted to transform the structure of their economies, military real spending grew at an annual rate of 14.1 percent in Syria and 10.2 percent in Egypt, more than triple their average GDP growth (Lavy and Sheffer 1991). The resulting military burden raises questions about whether such spending contributes to economic growth and development or saps it.

The economic effects of domestic military spending are similar to those of other public outlays demanding labor and resources. There are some positive spillovers into the civilian economy in developing countries—for example, research and development, modernization, and managerial experience. But such benefits probably fail to balance out the wide range of negative factors: diverting resources from investments, imposing higher tax rates on productivity, inflationary financing of budgetary deficits, and sacrificing savings and the balance of payments. The economic implications of the Middle East conflict must therefore be taken into account to gain a fair evaluation of the economic performance of the region's countries.

The second external shock suffered by the economies was the dramatic increase in oil prices between 1973 and the early 1980s. The rags-to-riches episode of the oil-rich economies of the Middle East helped shape the fate of the economies of Egypt and Syria more than any other single factor, paving the road to a decade of unprecedented regional prosperity but also igniting the crises of the 1980s. The wealth brought to Egypt and Syria through oil exports, workers' remittances, and Arab foreign aid helped disguise the harm done to their two economies by years of central planning. Once the abundance ceased, the emperor was seen to have no clothes. Mismanagement during the years of prosperity was translated into a heavy burden imposed on future generations in the form of a large foreign debt.

A third factor complicating the evaluation of economic performance is that neither Egypt nor Syria pursued the goal of sustained growth of GDP. More equal income distribution, internal political stability, and a reduction of the economic power of the middle class and landowners appear to have had higher policy priority. As a result, an evaluation of these countries' performance leads into areas that are poor in data and empirical evidence.

Growth Acceleration or Deceleration?

The evidence presented in table 12.2 suggests that during the early years of the revolutionary government GDP growth in Egypt accelerated from 2.5 percent to more than 6 percent. The move to a fully nationalized and planned economy was accompanied by a deceleration in the growth rate, initially to 5 percent and then (according to the elaborate calculation of Ikram) to a mere 3 percent. Given a 2.5 percent population growth rate, this implies almost no growth in income per capita.

Using the growth rate of GDP as an instrument or proxy for the change in well-being of a population, the above evidence is irrelevant or even misleading. The aggregate rate, as seen from table 12.3, is a weighted average of a rapidly growing public consumption (10.3 percent in 1960–70) and a much slower growth of private consumption (4 percent). This difference culminates in a continuous decline in the share of private consumption in GDP, from 0.71 in 1960 to 0.65 in 1975 (see table 12.4). The mirror image of this change is the rapid

Table 12.2   Average Annual Growth Rate of GDP and GDP per Capita in
Egypt and Syria, 1950–1987

| | EGYPT | | |
Period	Estimates of GDP Growth [a]	Estimates of GDP Growth [b]	Estimates of per Capita Growth Rates of GDP [a]
1950–55	2.5	1.8	—
1955–60	6.2	4.6	—
1961–66	5.6	6.1	2.9
1967–73	5.2	3.3	3.2
1974–82	8.8	—	6.1
1982–87	5.0	—	2.9

| | SYRIA | | |
Period	Estimates of GDP Growth [a]	Estimates of GDP Growth [c]	Estimates of per Capita Growth Rates of GDP [a]
1950–55	—	4.2	—
1953–57	6.5	—	—
1957–60	−4.8	16.0	−9.5
1961–67	20.9	2.7	17.7
1967–71	6.7	—	3.4
1971–82	8.4	—	5.0
1982–87	−2.0	—	−5.7

[a] Estimates from International Bank for Reconstruction and Development (IRBD), *World Tables*, 1950–88

[b] Estimates from K. Ikram, *Egypt: Economic Management in a Period of Transition* (Baltimore: Johns Hopkins University Press, 1980).

[c] Estimates from B. Hansen, "Economic Development of Syria," in C. Cooper and S. Alexander, *Economic Development and Population Growth in the Middle East* (New York: American Elsevier, 1971).

increase in the share of public consumption, from 17 percent in 1960 to 23 percent in 1975.

Another disturbing aspect of low growth in the economy, as it shifted from the invisible hand of the marketplace to the drawing board of the central planner, is the diminishing role of the tradable sector and the dominance of nontradables in the growth process. The growth of services and construction sectors was much higher than that of agriculture and manufacturing. As a result the share of these two tradable sectors in GDP fell from 0.54 in 1960 to 0.40 in 1980, with

Table 12.3   Average Annual Growth Rates, Egypt and Syria, 1960–1987

			EGYPT			
Period	*GDP*	*Agriculture*	*Industry*	*Services*	*Public Consumption*	*Private Consumption*
1960–70 ᵃ	4.5	2.9	5.4	6.1	10.3	4.2
1970–80	7.4	2.7	6.8	11.0	*	5.1
1980–87	6.3	2.7	6.6	8.1	5.3	5.0
			SYRIA			
Period	*GDP*	*Agriculture*	*Industry*	*Services*	*Public Consumption*	*Private Consumption*
1960–70 ᵃ	5.7	4.4	5.9	4.7	—	—
1970–80	10.0	8.2	9.6	10.8	16.1	11.9
1980–87	0.3	−1.1	1.5	0.3	−0.6	−0.8

ᵃ 1960–70 estimates taken from 1983 *World Development Report* (WDR). 1970–80 estimates taken from 1982 WDR. 1980–87 estimates taken from 1983 WDR.
* Figures not available separately for public consumption, which is included in private consumption.

long-run implications because it meant that the economy was not laying the foundation for future sustained growth.

If there is one factor that best exemplifies this concern, it is the level and growth of industrial and agricultural exports. In 1987 Egypt had a population of 50 million and a GNP of $34 billion, but its exports totaled only 5 percent of GNP. The figure for Turkey is 15 percent; for Morocco, 12 percent; and for Tunisia, 17 percent. Egypt has obviously failed to develop a dynamic export sector, a failure that looks even worse in light of the tremendous external debt Egypt has accumulated.

The decade that witnessed attempts to open and liberalize the economy is characterized by acceleration of economic growth. This was the same decade in which windfall revenues from high oil prices brought great wealth to the oil-producing countries. Wealth radiated to the region's poorer countries through generous financial assistance, through remittances from workers abroad, and, to some extent, through trade. The increased availability of foreign exchange made a major contribution to economic growth, as incomes from oil-related sources rose sharply. As already noted, however, industrial and agricultural exports fell during this period.

Real output in Syria has been volatile. Immediately following independence, the economy expanded at a satisfying rate, at 4 to 6 percent annually. The negative growth experienced between 1958 and 1961 was largely due to severe

Table 12.4   Structure of Exports, Egypt and Syria, 1965–1987
              (in millions of current US$)

Year	Total Exports	Nonfuel Primary Exports	Fuel Exports	Manufactured Exports
		EGYPT		
1965	613.0	446.4	40.0	126.2
1970	870.0	584.8	78.6	206.6
1975	1,596.0	791.7	644.0	380.0
1980	4,759.0	786.0	3,585.0	388.0
1985	5,193.0	695.9	3,851.1	639.0
1987	4,482.0	693.0	2,767.8	1,021.2
		SYRIA		
1965	212.0	65.3	21.7	125.1
1970	350.0	123.5	28.2	198.3
1975	1,669.1	432.8	108.7	1,127.6
1980	4,118.0	736.2	1,070.0	2,311.8
1985	3,487.0	546.7	1,041.2	1,899.1
1987	2,464.8	410.6	650.6	1,403.6

SOURCE: *National Accounts Database of the World Bank*, 1950–1988.

droughts and falling agricultural output. The upward swing in growth rates in the following years resulted from agricultural output returning to its normal level and to the fact that the low GDP level of the drought years was used as a denominator in calculating the growth rate. If the growth rate of GDP for 1961–1967 is calculated after netting out the return to normal of agricultural output, as done by Hansen (1970), one observes a sharp deceleration, to 2.7 percent annually. With a 3.5 percent population growth rate, this implies that, while Syria was committing its economy to a nonmarket apparatus, per capita income declined continuously.

The problem is how to distinguish between the various influences on economic development. Political turbulence in Syria during the 1950s was often accompanied by constitutional changes. Quite apart from the impact of political turmoil on production and investment activities, political unrest can forestall the development of efficient economic institutions. At least since the mid-1950s, there has also been much uncertainty in Syria about the future ownership of means of production and about the legal status of private enterprises, distorting the volume and patterns of private investment.

The fluctuation of production and income between 1958 and 1961 seems to have had little to do with political uncertainties and change in ownership, being related, above all, to changes in annual rainfall; strong crop fluctuations have secondary effects on trade, transport, and industrial processing of agricultural products. Since 1962 there has been no sharp decline in agricultural output. One is left with a deceleration in growth, chronologically correlated with the return of the Baath Party to power and the creation of a "People's Democratic Socialist Republic" with a strong commitment to nationalization and land reform.

Syria's performance in 1958–1967 should be compared with the results achieved in the previous decade. As noted earlier, the economic regime in Syria before union with Egypt was a capitalist, laissez-faire system. Hansen's 1970 evidence suggests that in the decade from 1946 to 1956 Syria enjoyed a 6 percent annual growth rate, higher than in the following decade.

As in Egypt, several other features of Syria's economic profile indicate a deterioration in the standard of living and economic structure. Growth was biased toward nontradables, especially services and public consumption (see tables 12.5 and 12.6). The share of public consumption increased, while that of private consumption declined from 0.71 in 1960 to 0.65 in 1976 to 0.62 in 1985. The most telling negative element in the Syrian story is the total stagnation of nonoil exports. The record of an economy with a population of more than eleven million and a GNP of $24 billion that exports only $800 million in industrial and agricultural output is disappointing if not dismaying.

The decade that followed 1974 led to an impressive acceleration of growth, as the growth rate climbed to an annual 8.4 percent. The factors behind this change are identical to those behind Egypt's decade of prosperity: oil windfalls, workers' remittances, and Arab aid. The bias toward nontradables and against exports was reinforced. The government and the economy did not develop the industrial and export base to fall back on when "good times" came to an end. The crises of the 1980s are rooted in the errors of Syrian policy makers during the previous two decades.

Efficiency and Factor Productivity

Total factor productivity (TFP) measures the change in output that is not accounted for by a change in the level of inputs. In other words, TFP measures the growth or decline in an economy's technical efficiency. Any measure of TFP requires a calculation of the change in the level of inputs, capital, and labor, a difficult task in most developing countries because of the scarcity of data. In Syria, there are no data for either labor or capital inputs. Data for Egypt

Table 12.5   Structure of Demand, Egypt and Syria, 1960–1987
              (percent of GDP)

	EGYPT			
	Public Consumption	Private Consumption	Gross Domestic Investment	Gross Domestic Savings
1960	17	71	13	12
1965	19	67	18	14
1970	—	—	—	—
1976	23	65	24	12
1980	19	65	31	16
1985	23	61	25	16
1987	14	77	19	8

	SYRIA			
	Public Consumption	Private Consumption	Gross Domestic Investment	Gross Domestic Savings
1960	17	71	13	12
1965	14	76	10	10
1970	—	—	—	—
1976	25	65	30	10
1980	23	67	25	10
1985	25	62	24	14
1987	18	72	19	10

Estimates for 1960 and 1976 from *World Development Report* (WDR), 1978; estimates for 1965 and 1987 from WDR, 1989; estimates for 1980 taken from WDR, 1985.

exist, but they are often faulty. Any measurement of Egyptian TFP should be viewed as only a rough indicator of productivity growth.

Our analysis of productivity is largely drawn from the works of Mabro and Radwan (1978), Ikram (1980), and Handoussa, Nishimizu, and Page (1986). According to Mabro and Radwan, TFP growth increased continuously from 1939 until 1963/64, when it began a steady decline. Mabro and Radwan calculated TFP growth rates using two different methodologies and estimated the following rates:

1939–45	4.44	6.70 percent a year
1945–54	1.36	3.35 percent a year
1954–62	2.26	2.88 percent a year
1963/64–69/70	−1.90	−2.20 percent a year

Table 12.6   Distribution of GDP by Sector in Egypt and Syria, 1967–1987

			EGYPT			
Year	Agriculture	Industry	Manufac- turing	Services	Exports	Resource Balance
1960	30.0	24.0	—	46.0	—	—
1965	29.0	27.0	—	45.0	18	−4
1970	29.4	28.2	—	42.4	—	—
1975	29.0	26.9	17.4	44.1	—	−12*
1980	18.3	36.8	12.2	44.9	17	−15
1985	20.0	28.6	13.5	51.4	27	−9
1987	21.0	25.0	14.0	54.0	15	−11
			SYRIA			
Year	Agriculture	Industry	Manufac- turing	Services	Exports	Resource Balance
1960	25.0	21.0	—	54.0	—	—
1965	29.0	22.0	—	49.0	17	0
1970	20.2	25.7	—	54.1	—	—
1975	17.9	24.1	—	58.0	—	−20*
1980	20.2	23.3	—	56.5	18	−15
1985	21.0	22.0	—	57.0	11	−11
1987	27.2	19.0	—	53.8	15	−9

* 1976 estimates
SOURCE: National Accounts Database of the World Bank.

These estimates of productivity growth are useful because they are split into periods corresponding to shifts in economic policy. The first period reflects policies in force during the Second World War, when the Egyptian economy was cut off from the world market and had to depend on its own resources. During this period productivity grew rapidly. Mabro and Radwan do not attribute this growth to technical progress because imports of new machinery were restricted. Instead, they claim, it was the result of many elements in the economy: "improved skills, improved organization, some innovation activity at the plant level or in many workshops that sprang up to service an industry suddenly isolated from its traditional sources of supply, and economies arising from a more intensive use of capacity" (Mabro and Radwan 1978, 185).

During the second period, the private sector dominated the economy and the government played a fairly passive role in setting economic policy. Productivity growth in this period was lower than in the first period, although the rate of output growth was higher. Output continued to rise throughout the next period, when the government started to move toward more-socialist-oriented policies. Although the growth of output rose during the third period, TFP grew at a slower rate. In addition, there was a negative relationship between factor inputs and the rate of growth of TFP and output. Mabro and Radwan explain this as being the result of diminishing returns to the unspecified factors—management, entrepreneurship, innovational ability, infrastructure, and other services.

The last period for which Mabro and Radwan provide estimates covers the years of centralized economic planning and shows a negative rate of productivity, although this result should not be interpreted to mean that there was no technical progress. Instead, negative productivity was most likely a result of the employment policy initiated by the government in 1962 that guaranteed a job to every university student. The effect of this policy was to create severe overemployment throughout the public sector and a sharp rise in the number of labor hours worked without any corresponding rise in level of output. After 1962 the marginal productivity of labor was, if not close to zero, definitely less than the wage rate, which caused negative rates of growth of TFP.

Any conventional measure of Egypt's TFP for the period after 1962 is likely to produce negative growth rates because the marginal productivity of labor was near zero. This does not necessarily mean that Egypt's economy did not become technically more efficient. Handoussa, Nishimizu, and Page (1986) developed a method of measuring productivity that enables us to estimate technical efficiency when an economy is not operating on its "true" production frontier. According to them, if an economy is producing below its true production function because of technical inefficiency, there exists a "best-practice" frontier that represents the most technically efficient production process given the original inefficiency; this best-practice frontier lies somewhere below the true production frontier. Handoussa et al. estimate the change in technical efficiency that occurs as an industry moves toward or away from this best practice frontier and refer to it as the best-practice TFP change.

Handoussa et al. estimated best-practice TFP for fifteen industries in Egypt's public sector over the period 1973–1979. According to their estimates, many industries do experience high rates of best-practice TFP change, although the gap between actual and best-practice TFP change widens over time. The widening of this gap indicates that the production process is becoming more and more inefficient.

Best-practice TFP is not the only method of estimating Egyptian technical efficiency since 1962. Capacity utilization also provides a good indicator of the level of efficiency. According to Ikram, Egyptian industry experienced acute excess capacity throughout the 1970s and early 1980s. Although the government blamed underutilization on the foreign exchange constraint, that allegation was only partly true.[10] The government's mismanagement of inventories led to bottlenecks and to shortages of supplies that also created underutilization.

In sum, the Egyptian economy did experience some improvement in technical efficiency during the postwar period. Productivity rose most rapidly immediately after the war and before nationalization, although it is difficult to evaluate Egypt's economic performance after 1962 using TFP. One indicator of the level of efficiency is evidence on capacity utilization. Since the mid-1960s the economy has been running below capacity, largely as a result of government mismanagement and a cumbersome public sector.

Income Distribution and Poverty

Both Egypt and Syria committed themselves to a development process aimed primarily at guaranteeing equal distribution of income and increasing national income. Concern with equality and the social aspects of economic development have so far produced too little evidence to evaluate past policies. This section draws mainly on Abdel-Fadil (1975), Radwan (1977), and Lavy (1986) and focuses on the Egyptian experience; no data on income or expenditure distribution data are available for Syria. Two fundamental questions should be asked. First, did the three decades of socialist policies lead to a more equitable distribution of income? Second, who, as classified by income, received what share of the proceeds of economic growth?

Table 12.7 presents Gini coefficients, estimates of the incidence of poverty, and the mean annual real income of the poor and nonpoor in Egypt in 1958/59 (just before the changes in property rights and nationalizations); 1964/65 (immediately following that wave); and 1974/75 (the last year of the period of full socialism and the beginning of new economic policies). The database is a series of consumer budget surveys, and the Gini coefficients are calculated using the distribution of income by per capita household income.

The evidence suggests that there was some increase in equality in rural income distribution between 1958/59 and 1964/65 and a slight reduction during the decade ending in 1974/75. Urban income inequality rose in the first period and decreased in the second. It is surprising, however, that waves of land reforms and nationalizations, as well as policies directly intended to reduce income disparities, did not result in any change in income inequality.

The second panel of table 12.7 reveals a more dramatic story. There clearly was a large reduction in the incidence of rural poverty in the first period, with no change in the urban sector. The mean real income of the poor also increased, indicating that they gained a share from the proceeds of economic growth, as did the nonpoor. In the next decade all the gains were reversed, however, and the welfare of the poor and nonpoor deteriorated sharply. The incidence of poverty increased to 44 percent in rural areas and to 25 percent in the urban sector, a

Table 12.7   Income Distribution and the Incidence of Poverty in Egypt

	1958/59	1964/65	1974/75
	Gini Coefficient*		
Urban	0.29	0.25	0.28
Rural	0.33	0.35	0.33
	Percentage of Population below Poverty Line		
Urban	12.5	12.9	25.3
Rural	34.1	21.0	43.9
	Mean Annual Income of Poor and Nonpoor (1964/65)		
Urban	19.6 (68.0)	21.1 (72.2)	20.3 (58.7)
Rural	16.0 (44.3)	19.9 (45.7)	18.2 (40.1)

* The Gini coefficients are calculated from the income distribution of persons classified by household per capita income.
SOURCE: Lavy (1986).

significant increase even in comparison with the rates in 1958/59. Real income declined in absolute terms, to levels even lower than those of 1958/59.

To summarize this evaluation, it is apparent that Egypt's socialist policies failed to produce a more equal relative income distribution. A focus on absolute rather than relative incomes suggests that lack of growth in private consumption harmed low-income groups and increased the incidence of poverty. The government failed to protect low-income groups from the hardships that its socialist central planning policies inflicted on the economy.

Some Social Dimensions of Development

The availability of material wealth, the efficiency of its exploitation, and the equality of its distribution are all important dimensions of economic development. However, to derive a more complete picture of changes in the population's well-being, these dimensions should be amended by information that signals advancement in other aspects of quality of life—such as health and education. Changes in the level of investment in human capital, such as population per physician and per nurse or students per class and per teacher, are often used as implicit measures of advances in living conditions. Alternative measures focus on the outcomes of investment in human capital—changes in the health, nutritional, and educational status of the population. Several indicators of both inputs and outputs of investment in human capital are presented in tables 12.1 and 12.8. For Egypt and Syria, they suggest large increments in the levels of

Table 12.8   Social Indicators, Egypt and Syria, 1952–1987

	EGYPT				
	1952	1960	1970	1980	1987
Crude birth rate [a]	48.60	45.16	39.76	40.15	39.15
Crude death rate [b]	24.00	20.64	17.10	12.58	9.0
Total fertility rate [c]	65.60	7.03	5.95	5.27	4.82
Infant mortality rate [d]	200.00	178.20	158.00	108.00	85.00
Life expectancy at birth, overall [e]	42.37	46.37	51.13	57.12	60.62
Percent of population illiterate [f]	—	74.12	61.8 [g]	55.5 [h]	—
Gross primary enrollment ratio [i]	—	66.0	72.0	78.0	87.0 [h]
Gross secondary enrollment ratio [i]	—	16.0	35.0	54.0	66.0 [h]

	SYRIA				
	1952	1960	1970	1980	1987
Crude birth rate [a]	46.6	47.08	47.00	45.70	45.20
Crude death rate [b]	21.40	17.48	13.38	8.72	7.00
Total fertility rate [c]	7.09	7.31	7.73	7.28	6.76
Infant mortality rate [d]	160.00	133.00	95.60	63.40	48.00
Life expectancy at birth, overall [e]	45.97	50.00	55.79	61.56	65.00
Percent of population illiterate [f]	—	70.5	60.6	40.0	—
Gross primary enrollment ratio [i]	—	65.0	78.0	99.0	—
Gross secondary enrollment ratio [i]	—	16.0	38.0	47.0	—

[a] Per 1,000

[b] Per 100 population

[c] Birth per woman

[d] Per 1,000 live births

[e] Years

[f] Those aged 15+

[g] Percentage of school-age children

[h] Percentage of school-age children

[i] Estimate for 1975

[j] Estimate for 1985

SOURCE: *Social Indicators Database (Socind)* of the World Bank

education and health services over the past four decades in Syria and Egypt. For example, infant mortality was cut in half in Egypt and reduced even more in Syria. Crude death rates sank to below ten in both countries. The gain in life expectancy averaged more than twenty years. As in the rest of the world, the mortality rate in Egypt and Syria appeared to decline because of higher levels of education, wider access to better medical services, and the virtual elimination of famine, epidemic, and endemic disease. This came about through improved transportation systems, better food distribution, immunization campaigns, and the introduction of DDT.

Although the mortality rate has declined, serious health problems remain. The major causes of death in Egypt today are the same as they were in 1937: diseases of the digestive and respiratory systems still account for about half of all deaths; schistosomiasis, poliomyelitis, and measles continue to be major health problems. (Some progress has been made with tuberculosis, cholera is under control, and smallpox has been eradicated.) Given the high death rate from digestive and respiratory illness and the persistence of diseases that immunization could prevent, it would seem that Egypt's health service delivery system is not functioning optimally. Much more can be done, especially in preventive medicine, to improve Egyptian health conditions.

The rapid decline in Syria's mortality rate over two decades reflects both improved living conditions and better health care. Syria now exhibits a mixed pattern of morbidity and mortality—the chronic disease profile of an industrialized country increasingly superimposed on the infectious disease pattern typical of a developing country. Diarrhea and respiratory diseases are the most common causes of illness and death in children under five. It is unclear to what extent malnutrition contributes to infant and child mortality, but the nutritional status of infants and children has improved significantly in the past decade.

Two questions stand out in evaluating Egypt's and Syria's progress. First, how does it compare with that of other countries? Second, is there a performance differential between the socialist period and the latest period?

Table 12.8 presents evidence of changes in nonmaterial indicators of well-being for the periods 1952–1973 and 1973–1987. The changes are calculated as average absolute gain per decade. The third row, for example, indicates that Egypt during the first period achieved a 23.9 absolute reduction in infant mortality per decade. In the second period the gain was much higher—39.3 per decade.

Comparing the first to the second period produces mixed results. Egyptian gains in health, implied by the decline in the infant mortality rate and the overall death rate, are much larger in the second period. Similarly, in education, the enrollment ratios, especially in primary school, increased more steeply in the second period. Surprisingly, life expectancy in the second period increased by only 3.5 years per decade, compared with 4.6 in the first period. It may be that improvement in health will be reflected in the life expectancy estimates in the next decade.

For Syria, table 12.8 suggests just the opposite. The gains in the second period are much lower than in the first period. Infant mortality declined in the first period by thirty-three per decade, in the second period, by only twenty-four. Similar results appear in a comparison of any of the other health or education indicators.

We compared similar information for two neighboring countries, Morocco and Turkey, who share similar initial conditions. Morocco's performance is on average equal to that of Egypt and Syria, but Turkey is by far the best performer of the four. This comparison puts into perspective the gains achieved by Egypt and Syria.

Concluding Remarks: The Crisis of the 1980s

In 1982 the economic situation of Egypt and Syria began to deteriorate. Declining world oil consumption and an increase in oil production by non-OPEC sources held oil prices and oil exports down. The number of foreign workers in the oil-producing countries leveled off, reducing the workers' remittance contribution to the balance of payments. Egypt also experienced a slowdown in the growth of Suez Canal dues.

Domestic inflationary pressures during the boom in Egypt and Syria had been largely offset by growing imports. The decline in foreign currency inflows after 1982 took away this means of suppressing inflation. To reduce aggregate demand—including imports—both countries restricted government spending and applied direct controls on imports in order to cope with balance-of-payments difficulties. As a result of stabilization measures and the drop in export earnings, economic growth fell sharply or halted. Per capita GDP fell 4.5 percent a year in Syria between 1982 and 1987. According to World Bank estimates, by 1989, per capita income had declined from $1,780 to $980. In Egypt per capita GDP continued to grow until 1985 but stagnated in 1986 and 1987.

Egypt and Syria failed to take advantage of the boom to reduce their vulnerability to external shocks. Essential reforms to remove distortions and implement structural change—conditions essential for sustained growth—would have been easy when foreign exchange was abundant. But the two nations did not develop or expand technological bases for new exports and economic independence. Instead, price controls, distorted allocations, unrealistic exchange rates, and lack of incentives prevented the development of a diversified export sector.

The leveling and subsequent decline of foreign currency income from foreign aid, workers' remittances, and oil exports destabilized the balance of payments and forced the governments to reduce domestic demand and to limit imports. The unavoidable results were repeated balance-of-payments crises, accumulated arrears in foreign debt, slower economic growth, and declining per capita income. The momentum of development stopped and economic problems became increasingly severe.

To finance the enormous gap between imports and exports of nonoil goods, Egypt and Syria had become dependent on unstable external revenue sources. The decline in foreign currency earnings and in workers' remittances left the two countries incapable of servicing their mounting debts. International banks and foreign suppliers reacted by refusing to extend further credit, which worsened the already shaky external balance. The current account deficit reached its peak in Egypt in 1985/86 at 20 percent of GDP; it peaked in Syria at 11 percent of GDP in 1984.

Egypt's balance-of-payments deficit led to a total foreign debt of more than $40 billion by the end of 1987. Indeed, foreign debt exceeded Egypt's GNP. Egypt could not keep up with large debt service payments and ceased to honor its foreign obligations. In May 1987 representatives of eighteen of Egypt's creditor states met under the auspices of the Paris Club and agreed to spread out principal, interest, and arrears payments over ten years. As a result of debt forgiveness granted to Egypt following the gulf war, total external debt declined from $51 billion in 1990 to about $38.5 billion in mid-1993. Despite these rescheduling agreements and a large drop in Egyptian imports, the remaining foreign debt will plague Egypt's economy for some time.

The situation in Syria is unclear. Data published by Syrian authorities and by international agencies do not include Syria's (probably quite sizable) military debt to the former Soviet Union. Other components of Syria's foreign debt also seem to be omitted from the official data. According to the World Bank figures, which are underestimates, Syria's total external debt amounted to $4.7 billion— or 25 percent of GNP—at the end of 1987. With the balance of payments weakening, Syria had trouble repaying its debts to foreign countries. It was forced to reach rescheduling agreements with Iran (1984) and with Czechoslovakia and the Soviet Union (1986–1987). However, in 1990–1992 higher oil-related revenues and favorable exogenous factors (good weather) caused the real GDP to grow at an average annual rate of almost 10 percent.

Notes

1. The agrarian reform measures were spelled out in Decree No. 178 in 1952 and later were amended in 1961 and 1969.

2. Two hundred feddans per owner, plus fifty feddans per dependent (1 feddan =

1.038 acres). The total allotment per family could not exceed three hundred feddans. (This ceiling was dropped in 1961 to one hundred feddans per owner. It was reduced in 1969 to fifty feddans per owner and one hundred feddans per family.)

3. Approximately 1.25 million feddans (525,000 hectares) were expropriated between 1952 and 1969; this area equaled 11.6 percent of the total area under cultivation (Sayigh 1978, 333).

4. The ceiling on ownership was set at eighty irrigated hectares, or thirty hectares of rain-fed land (Sayigh 1978, 254). In addition, an extra ten hectares of irrigated land or forty hectares of rain-fed land could be transferred to the spouse and each child, provided that the total transfer did not exceed forty hectares of irrigated land or 160 hectares of rain-fed land. Compensation for the land requisitioned was ten times the average rent, which was estimated on the basis of the preceding three-year rotation. Both the beneficiaries and those who owned less land than the amount allotted under the land reform were required to join cooperative societies. "The total area of land that was expropriated by the end of 1952 amounted to 670,111 hectares, of which only 148,440 hectares were actually distributed" (Syed 1984, 303). Approximately 15,000 families became landowners under Syria's reform.

5. This law affected 147 firms, which were forced to relinquish most of their assets. "The nominal capital of the companies affected by the nationalization laws of 1961 was put at E258 million, about two-thirds of the total share capital of companies then registered in Egypt" (Sayigh 1978, 21).

6. According to Mark Cooper, "By concentrating on a few thousand large-scale enterprises (and leaving several thousand small-scale enterprises untouched), the government made more than half of the industrial force and almost 90 percent of the industrial technicians, foremen, administrators, etc., employees of the state" (Cooper 1982, 25).

7. The importance of the subsidy system in Egypt is underestimated because most nontax incentives are seldom explicitly identified as subsidies in the national budget and others are provided for outside the budget accounts. The subsidies for public housing and the Egyptian railway, for example, are part of the budget but are not separately identified. Implicit subsidies are provided through the pricing and exchange-rate system. The cost of five important commodities (wheat, wheat flour, edible oil, sugar, and tea) is underrated because they are imported at the overvalued central bank exchange rate, which underestimates the cost of foreign exchange as measured on the free market.

8. "Egypt has increased the price of energy, in several stages, although it is still well below world levels. The government has refused, however, to than to tinker with subsidies on foodstuffs, fearing renewed popular unrest" (EIU 1989, 20).

9. *World Military Expenditures and Arms Transfers, 1987* (Washington, D.C.: United States Arms Control and Disarmament Agency, 1988).

10. "Public sector firms, which depended on government allocation of imported raw materials and intermediate goods, sometimes ordered larger quantities than required, piling up stocks of some materials while running short of others" (Ikran 1980, 257).

References

Abdel-Fadil, M. (1975). *Income Distribution and Social Change in Rural Egypt, 1952–70.* Cambridge, Eng.: Cambridge University Press.

Cooper, Charles A., and Sidney Stuart Alexander. (1971). *Economic Development and Population Growth in the Middle East.* New York: American Elsevier.

Cooper, Mark. (1982). *The Transformation of Egypt.* Baltimore, Md.: Johns Hopkins University Press.

The Economist Intelligence Unit (EIU). (1989–90). *Egypt Country Profile.* London: EIU, Limited.

Firro, Kais. (1986). "The Syrian Economy under the Assad Regime." In Moshe Ma'Oz and Avner Yaniv, eds., *Syria under Assad.* New York: St. Martin's Press.

Ghalib, Sharif. (1967). *Development and Balance of Payments in the UAR.* Beirut, Lebanon: American University of Beirut.

Hansen, Bent. (1971). "Economic Development of Syria." In C. Cooper and S. Alexander, eds., *Economic Development and Population Growth in the Middle East.* New York: American Elsevier.

Hansen, Bent, and G. Marzouk. (1955). *Development and Policy in the UAR (Egypt).* Amsterdam: North-Holland.

Hamed, O. (1981). "Egypt's Open Door Economic Policy." *International Journal of Middle East Studies* 13: 1–9.

IBRD (International Bank for Reconstruction and Development). (1955). *The Economic Development of Syria.* Report of a mission organized by IBRD at the request of the government of Syria. Baltimore, Md.: Johns Hopkins University Press.

Ikram, Khalid. (1980). *Egypt Economic Management in a Period of Transition: The Report of a Mission Sent to the Arab Republic of Egypt by the World Bank.* Baltimore, Md.: Johns Hopkins University Press.

Lavy, Victor C. (1986). "The Distributional Impact of Economic Growth and Decline in Egypt." *Middle Eastern Studies* 22: 89–103.

———. (1983). "The Welfare and Transfer Effects of Cotton Price Policies in Egypt, 1965–78." *American Journal of Agricultural Economics,* August, pp. 576–82.

Lavy, Victor C., and Eliezer Sheffer. (1991). *Foreign Aid and Economic Development in the Middle East.* New York: Praeger Publishers.

Mabro, Robert, and Samir Radwan. (1978). *The Industrialization of Egypt, 1939–73.* Oxford, Eng.: Clarendon Press.

McDermott, Anthony. (1986). *Egypt From Nasser to Mubarak.* London: Croom Helm.

Radwan, Samir. (1977). *Agrarian Reform and Rural Poverty: Egypt, 1952–75.* Geneva: International Labour Organisation.

Richards, A. (1984). "Ten Years of Infitah." *Journal of Development Studies* 20: 323–38.

Sayigh, Yusif A. (1978). *The Economies of the Arab World: Development since 1945.* London: Croom Helm.

Sklair, Leslie. (1988). "The Costs of Foreign Investment: The Case of the Egyptian Free Zones." In E. Kedourie and S. Haim, eds., *Essays on the Economic History of the Middle East.* London: Frank Cass & Company.

Syed, Aziz-al Ahsan. (1984). "Economic Policy and Class Structure in Syria, 1958–1980." *International Journal of Middle East Studies* 16: 301–23.

World Bank. *World Development Report*. New York: Oxford University Press, various issues.

———. (1950–87). *National Accounts Database*. Washington, D.C.: World Bank.

———. (1950–87). *Social Indicators (Socind) Database*. Washington, D.C.: World Bank.

Conclusion

RAMON H. MYERS

Defining Wealth and Some Twentieth-Century Patterns of National Wealth

In almost any society one observes distinctive differences among individuals because of their wealth. La Bruyère noted several centuries ago that "if we did not see it with our own eyes, could we ever imagine the extraordinary disproportion created between men by a larger or small degree of wealth?" Indeed, wealth does matter, and just as individuals are different because of it, so are nations. Before World War II Japan towered over all other Asian nations because of its industrial wealth. The former USSR, feared and respected by the world, produced potent nuclear and conventional military arsenals. Anyone traveling the world today cannot help but notice the great gap between poor and rich countries. If we take wealth to mean the goods and services produced by a nation and valued at their market value, the output called GDP, does that measure adequately reflect a nation's wealth? Not necessarily, as A. Sen reminds us in chapter 1.

For example, deriving the market value for public goods like health, education, and social security is impossible when they are "organized outside the standard market system," Sen points out. During the 1960s and 1970s China greatly expanded medical services to its village population through "barefoot" doctors, but those activities were not included in China's GDP. Sen continues that GDP also omits another form of wealth he defines as the "real freedoms enjoyed by the people"—entitlements or capabilities—if more of them can live longer and lead valuable lives, a historical fact borne out when socialist states like China and Cuba allocated resources to reduce child mortality and malnutrition. That policy enabled more people to live longer, but that achievement was never accurately included in GDP per capita. In principle, Sen is correct about this neglected form of wealth, but will people always live more valuable lives because of it if they are not able to take advantage of what Ralf Dahrendorf calls more "life changes"?[1] It is certainly not possible if a regime mismanages as China did. China's policies spared more children to live longer, but the generation of young people who were denied their education during the Cultural Revolution lacked the necessary skills to be employable. Moreover, citizens cannot live more valuable lives even if more of them can live longer when they must compete for a limited pie of wealth.

Using GDP per capita as a measure of wealth also concedes certain economic changes that affect human welfare, as Gur Ofer demonstrates for the Soviet Union in its phase of high rate of GDP per capita growth (chapter 5). In that country, working hours still grew faster than population. High investment in human and physical capital never produced a high growth of total factor productivity and an expanding mixture of consumer goods and services to improve living standards.

As if anticipating the problems raised by Sen to estimate national wealth, the World Bank has published a new system for measuring national wealth that values natural and mineral resources as well as human and social wealth.[2] This approach debits a country's wealth according to its depletion of mineral and natural resources. (One problem with this approach is that the current extraction costs and current market prices used to value mineral wealth have proved wrong in the past.)

The difficulties raised by Sen to measure wealth do not preclude us from comparing how well countries used the market process to create wealth. Angus Maddison estimates how much GDP a nation produced through its market system by converting that value into U.S. dollars using the 1990 purchasing power parities rather than exchange rates. His results show some interesting patterns of national wealth formation, or GDP growth, in the twentieth century (chapter 2).

His estimates cover roughly four-fifths of the world's population living in forty-eight countries. They reveal that the capitalist nations of Europe, North America, and Australasia, already wealthy in 1913, expanded their GDP from 1950 until 1973 by increasing capital investment, trade, and factor productivity. Although their GDP per capita growth rates slowed down between 1973 and 1992, their average per capita product level by 1990 was still three times that of Eastern Europe and Russia as well as Latin America and ten times that of the African states.

Only Asia managed to have a growth acceleration of GDP per capita for the entire period from 1950 to 1992. The ROC on Taiwan, South Korea, Indonesia, Malaysia, Thailand, and the city-states of Hong Kong and Singapore performed better than all the other Asian countries. Their governments had somehow intervened in the economic market process to sustain GDP per capita growth and manage the random shocks that had slowed the expansion of wealth in the advanced capitalist, socialist, and poor nations.[3]

Between 1950 and 1973, most of the poor, developing countries for the first time began to increase their per capita GDP growth, so that the income gap between them and the advanced capitalist countries narrowed slightly. Even the socialist, centrally planned economies seemed to have performed well in that period, although close inspections now reveal that their economic growth was slowing down (see chapters 5 and 6). After 1973 a definite growth slowdown took place throughout most of the world economy except in East and Southeast Asia (chapter 2, tables 2.1 and 2.4). For example, by 1993 the ROC on the Taiwan had achieved the status of what the World Bank refers to as an upper-middle-income nation, having a per capita income of US$10,566, higher than that of Portugal ($9,130), Greece ($7,390), and Argentina ($7,220).[4] In that the ROC's economy grew at nearly 6 percent per year between 1990 and 1995, it will soon enter the high-income rank of nations.

The fact that some developing countries in Asia outperformed the developing world—an outcome not predicted by anyone in the 1940s and 1950s— deserves an explanation.[5] The country case studies in this volume have addressed two broad questions: first, what are the necessary salient economic processes that have enabled a nation to move from a poor- to a middle- and eventually high-income status?[6] second, what types of government policies and institutional changes have removed the impediments limiting the economic market process?

The Salient Economic Processes
Necessary for Producing Wealth

The transition from a poor- to a low-middle-income status is a difficult transition for any country. That leap requires, at a minimum, that a country double its output per capita to transform its economy from the structure and behavior of a previous epoch. The early developing countries trying to create wealth had to develop technology endogenously and by trial and error select those technologies to promote the best practices for expanding agriculture, manufacturing, and services output. It is little wonder, then, that England only doubled its output per capita between 1780 and 1838 (fifty-eight years) and that the United States did the same between 1839 and 1886 (forty-seven years). Thus both countries required roughly a half century to double their wealth on a per capita basis. Latecomers like Japan were able to borrow advanced technology from the early developers; Japan's output per capita doubled between 1885 and 1919 (only thirty-four years). Some countries after 1945 did even better: the Republic of Korea doubled its output per capita between 1966 and 1977 (eleven years), the PRC, between 1979 and 1987 (ten years), and the ROC on Taiwan, between 1952 and 1966 (fourteen years).[7] For most developing countries, however, the doubling of output per capita took longer and was achieved only with difficulty.

In the course of the post-1945 worldwide economic transition, are there some necessary, interacting economic processes that all countries must experience if they are to complete any part of the transition? The evidence in this volume as well as other research findings suggest that at least three major economic processes must interact if a nation's economy is to be transformed and create wealth. I will refer to these as ideal types that must be approximated in a determined way if a nation is to double its output per capita and repeat that performance to advance to higher-income-level stages.[8]

The three ideal types of interacting economic processes are as follows:

- A virtuous circle of four interacting economic activities: (1) a more equitable distribution of income; (2) a rise in market demand for goods and services; (3) savings as a share of GDP rise from 3–5 to 10 percent and above; and (4) more resources are invested in physical and human capital.
- Avoiding large wage increases and inflation.
- There is a long-term shift (at least within a decade) from relying on the domestic market to greater dependency on foreign markets as reflected in the integration of domestic and foreign markets.

To compare how well the countries in this volume replicated or deviated from these interacting economic processes, I rank these countries according to the above three ideal types of economic development patterns by comparing their economic performance since the mid–twentieth century.

Highly Successful Wealth Achievers
    1. Japan (1880–1937; 1950–1987)
    2. ROC on Taiwan (1950–1993)
Moderately Successful Wealth-Creating Countries
    1. South Korea (1960–1989)
    2. PRC (1978–1993)
    3. Indonesia (1965–1989)
Poor-to-Average Wealth Achievers
    1. Brazil (1950–1993)
    2. Colombia (1950–1993)

3. India (1950–1990)
4. Pakistan (1950–1990)
5. Egypt (1952–1987)
6. Syria (1952–1987)
7. PRC (1950–1978)
8. Ghana (1980–1990)
9. Malawi (1980–1990)
10. USSR (1950–1973)

Failures
1. North Korea (1960–1989)
2. USSR (1973–1986)
3. Ghana (1960s-1970s)
4. Nigeria (1965–1989)
5. Malawi (1960s-1970s)

Highly Successful Wealth Achievers

Only a few countries, such as Japan and the ROC, have performed near the optimum that their economies were capable of achieving (chapters 4 and 6). Early in the post–World War II era, Japan was singled out as the most successful non-Western wealth-producing country. The ROC's economic miracle was ignored until the 1970s, partly because of political prejudice and partly because of its growing diplomatic isolation. In recent decades international agencies have not published information about Taiwan's economy. The ROC might have performed even better had it not spent so heavily for defense, around 8–10 percent of GDP in the early decades. Japan's defense burden never exceeded 1 percent of GDP after 1945.

Both countries underwent a land reform that made for a more equal distribution of rural income and helped increase household demand for goods and services. Land reform gave both rural economies a strong family-farming foundation, which encouraged small and medium-size enterprises (SMEs) to expand employment and produce for the domestic economy. Their households prized frugality and invested in their children's education. In both economies there was a favorable interaction of more equal rural income distribution, rising household consumption, and higher savings and investment.

At the same time, their governments avoided deficit spending and inflation. Real wages continually lagged behind labor productivity. Labor unions and other interest groups never became a powerful force to increase money wages. Equally important, both economies quickly became integrated with the world economy, and their domestic and foreign trade expansion helped households increase market demand for enterprises' goods and services and encourage them to borrow new technology. Between 1990 and 1995 Japan's economy slowed down to around 1 percent a year, but only because an economic boom fueled by financial speculation in the late 1980s ended and was followed by a deep depression. Both economies have recently transferred much of their manufacturing to Southeast Asia and the China mainland, while services have become more important as a source of GDP and employment.

Moderately Successful Wealth-Creating Countries

South Korea, the PRC, and Indonesia also achieved high, sustained economic growth, but they periodically experienced some economic difficulties that were successfully avoided by Japan and the ROC (chapters 6, 7, and 10). South Korea and the PRC, for example, had excessive wage increases and inflation for brief periods during the past fifteen years. Except for the PRC, income distribution was not as equal as in Japan and Taiwan. Factor productivity and per capita income did not increase on a sustained basis as in Japan and the ROC (factor productivity slowed between 1985 and 1992 in the PRC).

But in all other respects their economic development processes were compatible with the three ideal types of interacting economic processes described above. Land reform in South Korea contributed to a more equal distribution of rural income; rural reform in the PRC made it possible for households after 1978 to produce more for the market than in the past. The Indonesian government made significant investments in agriculture to increase output and yields for food and industrial crops, which dampened inflation, expanded domestic market supply and demand, and reduced the import of food. Their rising savings and investments, along with rising domestic demand and foreign trade, nurtured a virtuous circle of interacting economic activities that helped sustain high economic growth. All these countries promoted export growth and integrated part of the domestic economy with the world market.

Poor to Average Wealth Achievers

For most countries the GDP and GDP per capita income rose steadily from 1950 to 1973 but began to slow down when inflation and unemployment gradually worsened (chapters 8, 9, 11, and 12). Countries such as Brazil, Colombia, India, Pakistan, Egypt, and Syria reveal some typical patterns of economic growth experienced by poor, developing countries after World War II. For example, these countries never had effective rural reforms that redistributed property rights to households on a scale sufficient to improve rural income distribution and provide strong incentives to increase their production for the market. Nor did their governments make significant investments in agriculture to improve rural infrastructure, make farming technology available to farmers at a cost they could afford, or promote a "green revolution" that influenced more than several crops. India and Pakistan invested more to alleviate rural poverty and reduce rural population growth than did many countries. But demand for agricultural supply was limited by the failure of their home manufacturing and services to take off. Just as domestic market demand grew slowly, the percentage of their output for export did not increase until the mid-1990s. A few rural regions benefited from government investment, but too many did not.

Household purchasing power did not increase enough to provide a strong domestic demand for manufacturing and services to expand. Small and medium enterprises never increased in large number to produce for export and expand employment and rural income as was the case in East Asia. Manufacturing enterprises mainly depended on the domestic market, and export development was slow; there was minimal competition and much monopoly in the manufacturing sector. Government mismanagement of financial and foreign exchange markets often contributed to inflation. Wages tended to rise faster than productivity. Spurts of inflation also caused growth to slow down. By failing to take advantage of foreign market opportunities and expand domestic market demand and supply, economic activity in these countries deviated from the three necessary, interacting, ideal types of economic processes that characterized the highly and moderately successful wealth-creating nations.

Failures

A final group of countries exhibited two distinctive patterns of economic development in which government intervention failed to create much wealth. The socialist countries that restructured property rights and established collective organizations in agriculture and manufacturing made income distribution more equal, but these reforms also weakened the incentives for people to work hard, strive for profit, and be innovative. These new collective and state-owned organizations performed poorly, having low productivity and wasting resources because bureaucrats overregulated and ignored their managers' recommendations, workers toiled without enthusiasm, and firms lacked the necessary information to produce efficiently. Transformation and transaction costs were extremely high. These centrally planned economies deliberately emphasized what Gur Ofer calls a strategy of haste. That strategy tended to overutilize labor and natural resources, misallocate and inefficiently use capital, devalue quality control and improvement, and produce cumulative errors and costly mistakes. Manufacturing producer goods expanded at the expense of consumer goods and services. Highly protected and badly managed, the centrally planned manufacturing sector coexisted alongside a vast, collectivized rural economy that also was badly managed, whose people experienced living standards that rose only moderately and then stagnated.

In other poor, developing countries in which the state intervened to protect and develop manufacturing in order to reduce the nation's dependency on imports, the majority of countries squandered their precious resources. Nations such as Ghana, Malawi, and Nigeria failed to take advantage of their national resources and build new economies by promoting their exports and effectively using that revenue. But the new land reform and agricultural policies, instead of assisting households in acquiring the assets and the incentives to expand their investment and savings, mainly tried to extract more resources from agriculture to support the state's inept policies elsewhere in the economy.

This brief summary of how many countries tried to create wealth after World War II shows that a wide range of national economic development performance took place and sets the stage for the following: (1) why government intervention and/or market failures caused economic growth slowdown or (2) why government intervention and/or market achievements enabled countries to replicate the three ideal types of interacting economic processes that promoted and sustained economic growth.

Government Intervention in the Economic Market Process

The resource endowments of our fourteen countries varied greatly, ranging from abundant labor and scarce land in Asia to scarce labor and abundant land in Latin America and Africa. Their economic development performance had far less to do with their resource endowment and their historical legacy, in which the benefits of colonialism were usually squandered, than with government intervention in the economic market process. The unemployment and hyperinflation that raged immediately after World War II because of civil war and delayed rehabilitation of the economy were eventually overcome only to be replaced by new challenges created by government intervention in the market process.

Part of the reason for hasty, mistaken government intervention in the economy had to do with how national leaders and elite selected another "reference society" that inspired them to transform their societies.[9] It seems that the selection of a "reference society" motivated national leaders to make wealth creation a high priority. Japan's leaders after World War II were determined to overtake the United States in economic power and living standards. The USSR wanted to surpass capitalist societies or, in Nikita Krushchev's famous words, "bury capitalism" by showing that socialism could outperform a capitalist country like the United States. Taiwan's Kuomintang leaders wanted to turn Taiwan into a powerful, prosperous society to humiliate and topple the Chinese Communists from power. Mao Tse-tung wanted China to surpass the West in iron/steel production.

Those developing nations governed by leaders adhering to Marxism and socialism eagerly embraced transformative policies to replace the market and its organizations with collective forms of economic life that were incompatible with popular economic culture and difficult to manage without markets. Many national leaders were also sensitive to what Alexander Gerschenkron has described as their nations' "relative backwardness" and wanted to accelerate economic growth by restricting consumption, using capital-intensive rather than labor-intensive methods, and promoting the expansion of producer goods industries.[10]

Whatever their motives to overcome backwardness, they were determined to double GDP per capita and create more wealth as quickly as possible. The worldwide trend after World War II was for governments to intervene everywhere in the economic market process. Historical hindsight now confirms that, except for a few nations, government intervention eventually produced more harm than the conventional wisdom of that time thought was possible.[11]

Our sample of fourteen countries shows why only a few countries succeeded in producing wealth and the majority did a poor job or failed. Consider the two important roles that markets perform: first, they facilitate the efficient allocation of resources—the more elastic the supply, the fewer the obstacles to reallocating resources; second, they provide a creative function by promoting investment and innovation to increase supply.[12] When government intervention impedes the market from performing these two interacting roles, markets can fail, adversely affecting economic activity. The authors of this volume found that the following categories of government policies and institutional reforms affected the acceleration or slowdown of economic growth.

Far too many national leaders ignored Adam Smith's first principle of allocating more capital to agriculture and then to manufacturing and foreign commerce. They preferred to develop manufacturing first and usually ended up impoverishing their countryside and the economy while not encouraging domestic and foreign trade. By so doing, they failed to transform and enrich their economies. Only a few states engaged in successful institutional reform to restructure private property rights in agriculture and create enough incentives for households and firms to produce more for the market, to improve rural income distribution, and to increase household purchasing power enough to stimulate market expansion. These policies characterized state intervention in the markets of Japan, South Korea, and Taiwan after World War II. These same countries simultaneously invested in agriculture to increase land and labor productivity. Countries such as Indonesia later invested more resources in agriculture to increase food production. Socialist countries such as China only later reversed decades of economic growth slowdown by restructuring property rights and speeding up marketization.

Those states committed to socialism and central planning had eliminated private property rights and private enterprise and established collective organizations and a centrally planned economy. The USSR, PRC, and North Korea adopted such a transformative program and ignored agricultural development, producing catastrophic results for their economies in later years.

Many states initiated the wrong kinds of rural reforms or failed to push the right kinds of reform. For example, South Asian governments carried out land reform that moderately reduced the number of tenant and laboring households but did not promote a broad-based family farm system such as that in East Asia. The Indian and Pakistani land reforms never redistributed rural resources and income sufficiently to increase market demand, invigorate the rural economy, or encourage the expansion of SMEs as had occurred in Taiwan, South Korea, and Japan.

Latin America's agricultural policies took the form of regulating the exports of rural estate products and then, when their prices fell, reverting to inflationary financing and foreign exchange–rate manipulation to revive exports (chapter 9). Government leaders seemed content to allow Latin American agriculture to remain dualistic, with rural estates employing workers and poor family farms barely having enough land, assets, and technology to eke out a subsistence living. Latin American governments did not invest heavily in agriculture, and readjusting property rights was never conceived and implemented as an institutional reform benefiting both landowners and the tenant-laboring households as in Taiwan.

In Africa below the Sahara the governments did not first invest heavily to upgrade the efficiency of rural estates and family farms. Ghana's government, for example, taxed agriculture to protect and build a manufacturing sector that proved to be inefficient and incapable of competing in the world market. That state also spent about 90 percent of its rural budget in the early 1960s to establish large state farms that performed poorly while forcing family farmers to buy licenses and pay high prices for the goods they needed to farm.

North of the Sahara, two-thirds of the people in Egypt and Syria worked in agriculture. The land reform that had forced Egypt's large landholders to sell their land below market price impoverished them, but then the new landholders had to join cooperatives controlled by the state (chapter 12). Syria and Egypt then embarked on high-cost irrigation projects that were not integrated with other rural programs to increase land and labor efficiency and expand rural marketing.

These states, by pegging low food and essential clothing prices for city consumers and subsidizing rural cooperatives, discouraged domestic farm production. Whereas Egypt once had been a great cotton-exporting country, by the late 1970s Egyptian cotton could not compete in world markets.

If too many developing countries had mismanaged agriculture by failing to readjust and protect property rights and invest more resources in agriculture, virtually all these countries invested more resources than were needed in their protected infant industries in the hope that they eventually could compete in the world market. In theory, protecting infant industry makes sense if long-run cost curves can be lowered, but the above case studies demonstrate that most countries' infant industries never became efficient and qualitatively innovative to compete in the world market. The centrally planned industries in socialist states certainly were unable to do that (except the PRC after 1978), and most developing countries' industries never succeeded in doing so until the 1990s.

Most state policies toward manufacturing again violated Adam Smith's first principle by creating more impediments in the market, thereby fostering monopoly and industrial organizational rigidity rather than facilitating market competition for enterprises to adjust to market forces and be innovative. The import substitution strategy adopted by governments allocated scarce resources to state-preferred enterprises and protected their profits even after new industrial blocks were developed.[13] The creation of these new industrial blocks was associated with government policies that benefited only a few industries and were not friendly to the market: overvaluing the exchange rate, maintaining a low interest rate, granting tax relief to protected industries, building high-cost infrastructural projects to supply and service only preferred industrial suppliers, and discouraging market competition. The interaction of these economic consequences produced inflation and restricted domestic and foreign trade, thus violating two of the key, interacting economic patterns necessary for facilitating modern economic growth and structural transformation. Consider the following examples.

The socialist, centrally planned economies such as that of the USSR before World War II had quickly eliminated markets, private property, and free enterprise. North Korea accomplished that transformation between 1945 and 1950, and the PRC, between 1950 and 1956. Both states squeezed their primary sectors to obtain the resources needed to build new industrial developmental blocks. In the 1950s the PRC government created its first manufacturing blocks in northeast and north China; in the 1960s that government launched another industrial block developmental program within the interior. These mobilization efforts proved extremely costly for the PRC in the 1970s and for North Korea in the 1980s because, as their industrial blocks aged, technology became obsolete and unit costs rose. The PRC's leaders opted for economic reform in the 1980s and 1990s, but North Korea's leaders adhered to their Soviet-style, managed economy even after the USSR had collapsed. By the mid-1990s the North Korean economy, short of energy and unable to feed its people satisfactorily, was in decline. The PRC's economy boomed in the 1990s because its leaders accepted foreign investment, tried to restructure the old state-owned enterprises, and allowed new enterprise forms to produce for the market.

Other states relied on government intervention in the market to nationalize many industries and regulate those that were privately owned and managed. After winning independence, political struggles took place in Egypt and Syria over whether to have more state interference in the economy or less. Between 1946 and 1957, free enterprise and market forces helped promote Syria's economic growth, and for Egypt, those same policies operated between 1946 and 1954. But the military leaders who came to power at that time gradually began nationalizing industries and services, controlling foreign exchange and trade, and regulating prices as well as subsidizing consumers and certain producers. These policies soon produced a distorted price structure in both economies; exports declined because producers lost their competitive edge; state deficits ballooned, the money supply rose, and inflation worsened; foreign investment dried up.

In 1974, Egypt's government under Anwar Sadat finally tried to attract foreign investment, develop free trade zones, and dismantle price controls and subsidies. But these reforms ended in 1977 when public riots erupted to protest rising living costs. In the 1980s, Syria also encouraged small business investment and tried to attract foreign investment, but these reforms could not launch a private sector takeoff because the government still allocated most of its resources to support a large military and regulated far too much of the economy. Public expenditures as a share of GDP rose, while that of private consumption declined. Exports failed to increase on a sustained basis in both countries.

This same pattern of mushrooming state interference in the marketplace occurred in Ghana and Malawi but with a major difference. Ghana's first president, Nkrumah, vowed to break his country's dependency on importing manufactured goods. Ghana's radical import substitution strategy soon created a large state-operated industrial block whose industrial capacity–use level declined to only 40 percent. By the mid-1980s the economy was in ruin, and World Bank officials were trying to help the nation's leaders repair the damage by promising loans if the government liberalized the economy, privatized state-owned enterprises, and expanded exports. In Malawi the government never tried to build an industrial block, but the agricultural sector declined because state policies hindered smallholders from expanding for export and developing SMEs.

In India and Pakistan state policies managed to increase investment as a share of GDP between the early 1950s and the 1980s, but whereas India had a higher investment share of GDP than Pakistan, the latter's GDP grew more rapidly than India's, even though the investment composition of both countries was similar (chapter 8). Despite enormous investment by both countries, the developmental industrial blocks that had formed in the 1950s and 1960s were neither innovative nor efficient. Numerous state regulations such as the Industrial Development and Regulation Act in India controlled that nation's industrial block by setting priorities for expanding capacity, locating plants, and controlling the import of capital goods. In Pakistan the state imposed fewer controls on production than did India but controlled trade more tightly to achieve higher rates of effective protection. In the 1970s Pakistan nationalized many industries, but some of these were privatized by the Zia regime during the 1980s. Finally, in the 1990s, India's government reversed course by trying to deregulate the economy, encourage foreign trade, and promote foreign investment. It is too early to see whether the state can adhere to this new strategy.

Although Latin American leaders had always promoted primary-sector exports, after the Great Depression policy makers and leaders decided to reduce their dependency on trade by intervening in the market to develop domestic industry and services. Countries such as Brazil and Colombia adopted an overvalued, multiple-exchange-rate system that made for cheap imports, which were then rationed (chapter 9). Large state spending for industrialization was commonplace, and both nations welcomed foreign capital and technology transfer. But relying on these strategies failed to promote infant industry exports, except traditional agricultural products. Government deficits invariably mounted, which fueled inflation, ultimately discouraging foreign investment. Even when the state promoted traditional export products such as coffee, these activities never produced enough savings and increased domestic demand to enable the protected domestic industries producing steel and automobiles to become profitable and export-competitive. Although this strategy helped create new developmental blocks of industries, domestic and foreign trade did not grow rapidly. New innovations and investment in those blocks never followed in the 1970s and 1980s to revitalize their economies. By the 1980s, these two states, along with other Latin American countries, were in economic recession because of failed macroeconomic policies and a worsening world market. Colombia's economy fared better than Brazil's by avoiding serious foreign debt, but it gradually became engulfed in illegal drug activities. Although Colombian and Brazilian leaders had eschewed ideology and tried a pragmatic economic approach, their stop-and-go policies to speed up and then slow down economic growth had neither produced a far-reaching transformation of the economy nor sufficiently elevated GDP per capita to lift their nations to the high-income-level status. In essence, their market interventionist policies had failed to contain inflation and failed to expand domestic and foreign market demand to build efficient, competitive industrial and services sectors.

States that avoided inflation, encouraged domestic and foreign trade, and invested in agriculture expanded employment and economic growth. The contrast between Indonesia and Nigeria, which began from equivalent economic platforms in 1966 and 1977, respectively, shows that correct government intervention in the economic marketplace counts (chapter 10). Indonesia's leaders decided at the outset to control the money supply, make the currency convertible, and never overspend the state's budget. In Nigeria the leadership shared oil revenues between the many regions, allowed government spending to soar out of control, and promoted expensive, large-scale steel and petrochemical plants that could not compete in world markets. Indonesia's leaders abolished restrictive trade and exchange control systems and eventually moved to full currency convertibility. Although Nigeria's leaders liberalized trade in the 1960s, they also established an exchange-rate control system and devalued the currency several times, thereby fueling inflation. The government also built two enormous steel mills costing US$1.1 billion that never produced any products that could be sold abroad. Officials discriminated against Lebanese and Syrian entrepreneurs and squandered scarce oil without developing domestic and foreign markets. Indonesia, by contrast, adopted policies friendly to business enterprises and encouraged foreign investment from Japan and overseas Chinese. By the 1970s Indonesia was successfully building a new industrial developmental block that produced for the home and foreign markets and was fairly competitive and efficient.

In Japan, South Korea, and Taiwan, government intervention in the market to protect infant industries meshed with promoting the expansion of both the domestic and export markets. But all three countries never relied on conventional macropolicies to protect infant industries in the long term and in less than a decade had adopted policies to promote domestic and foreign market growth while keeping inflation under control. They invested and reformed agriculture to produce food products at prices urban citizens could afford. Nonagricultural income steadily became an important source of earnings for rural households who could not have made ends meet by their income from farming alone. Their rising income then helped sustain their rising demand for domestic and foreign products. Small- and large-scale industries coexisted in all three economies and produced for both the domestic and the foreign markets. Taiwan performed best to avoid inflation and recession; South Korea experienced periodic inflation and high foreign debt; and Japan suffered severe recession in the early 1990s.

Governments and Wealth Creation

To sum up, since 1945 only a few governments have effectively interfered in the economic market process. Those few, located in East and Southeast Asia, had policies and institutional reforms that successfully nurtured three interacting, ideal types of economic processes that did not slow down after 1973. Of this group, however, the PRC is still a poor country, with around US$490 per capita GDP in 1993 because of three decades of wasteful state mismanagement. This region's remarkable economic growth is attributed to government policies and institutional change that facilitated the economic market process: improving income distribution, expanding a marketed surplus by rural households, increasing capital formation, avoiding inflation, and promoting the growth of domestic and foreign markets. Their governmental policies also managed to increase national savings, investment, and innovation within economies that became increasingly competitive and trade oriented rather than monopolistic and closed. In a word, their economies demonstrated what Douglass North has called acquiring adaptive efficiency to become productive and adjust to changing demand and supply conditions.

Our case studies also show that government policies that initially promoted agriculture through institutional reform and investing resources, while encouraging the expansion of manufacturing and expanding the domestic and foreign markets, gradually transformed their economic structures. Government policies that tended to exploit and/or neglect agriculture soon regulated the domestic market and failed to promote domestic and foreign trade. In other words, government intervention that tries to eliminate barriers to competition, remove market impediments to nurture domestic supply and demand, promote foreign trade, and prevent inflation is more likely to promote economic growth and avoid economic growth slowdown. Such government intervention encourages the market process to become more efficient and creative than if the government had left the market process alone.

The evolution of economic development theory since the 1950s seems to confirm the above conclusions. In the early decades, grand theory argued on behalf of simplistic analytic models that justified government intervention in the marketplace as the best means to overcome national economic backwardness. Such theorizing justified that government take the lead to build and protect new industrial blocks, on the assumption that these blocks would later become competitive in domestic and world markets. New research in the 1960s and 1970s argued that this kind of government intervention distorted prices in the economic marketplace. A distorted price system channeled scarce resources to wasteful activities and poorly rewarded resources except those used in state-protected activities. Distorting the market process rather than facilitating the market process to perform better made it even harder for countries to overcome their poverty and backwardness.

These findings suggested that governments should intervene differently to facilitate market forces by privatizing many nationalized enterprises, deregulating more of the economy to encourage foreign investment to supplement domestic investment, and promoting domestic and foreign trade. Debate in those years also focused on which mixture of government policies and institutional reform best modulated the economic marketplace to improve its two interacting functions. Finally, in the 1980s another approach, called the "new political economy," began examining the efforts by interest groups in both society and the state to interfere in the economy and the impact these groups had on the economy.[14]

Then in 1989 the two-volume *Handbook of Development Economics*, edited by H. Chenery and T. N. Srinivan (vol. 1, 1988, and vol. 2, 1989), appeared that surveyed different countries and their economic processes. Its empirical findings affirmed more comprehensively than previous works that three interacting ideal types of basic economic processes seem to have successfully transformed a nation's economy and repeatedly doubled GDP per capita to transit from low- to high-income status. This volume's findings confirm the validity of these three interacting ideal types of economic processes that Albert Fishlow perceptively noted in his review of the *Handbook of Development Economics*.[15]

The East Asian economic miracle countries such as Japan and Taiwan illustrate that government policies and institutional reforms can facilitate the economic marketplace to allocate and use resources more efficiently and creatively rather than impede the market process's functions. Those categories of interventionist policies boil down to the following: (1) improve first the performance of agriculture and increase that sector's contribution to manufacturing and foreign trade; (2) channel resources into new developmental industrial blocks that are competitive and can encourage domestic and foreign market demand for national output to expand; (3) avoid overregulating the economy while encouraging economic competition; and (4) restrict the expansion of the money supply and avoid deficit financing, promote currency convertibility and a stable foreign exchange rate, expand savings through market-determined interest rates, and create a fair, simple tax system that tends to limit some consumption while favoring savings and investment.

Where policies exploited agriculture, overregulated the economy, ignored trying to increase domestic and foreign demand, relied on inflationary methods, and discouraged competition by protecting monopoly and oligopoly, the nation and its people remained poor. Adam Smith's first principle of creating wealth appears to be as valid for the twentieth century as it was for the eighteenth.

This volume only partially explains why some governments successfully intervened in the market process through policies and institutional reform and why the majority failed to do so. Ideology, culture, and sociopolitical factors obviously make for a complex, multicausal explanation, beyond the scope of this study, of why a few countries initiated the correct institutional reforms and policies to promote economic growth and most did not. The following questions await further research: What historical patterns of successful institutional reforms and government policies produced the three ideal types of interacting economic processes affirmed by this study? How were those groups in society and the polity that opposed these government policies and institutional reforms persuaded or forced by reformers to accept them?

Institutions, in the words of Douglass North, are the rules that govern how organizations behave or "the framework within which human interaction takes place."[16] Many institutions or rules relate to how property rights are transferred, defined, and protected. Still other rules determine how transactions of property rights and assets are contracted and enforced. Certain organizations and socio-political groups will naturally favor the preservation of their preferred rules, and others will demand they be changed. Institutional reform involves the activities of many competing organizations and sociopolitical groups. Those historical patterns of particular organizations and groups participating in successful institutional reform, therefore, deserve close study and analysis to produce theories and explanations for why institutional change successfully promoted economic growth or failed to do so. The struggle and final outcome between groups that favor or oppose institutional reform should be high on the agenda of future research.

Notes

1. Expanding on a concept first used by Max Weber, Ralf Dahrendorf defines "life chances" as a function of human options and social bonds (ligations) that influence human action. See Ralf Dahrendorf, *Life Chances: Approaches to Social and Political Theory* (Chicago: University of Chicago Press, 1979), chap. 2. If wealth measured as GDP expands, then human life chances can multiply because individuals having more wealth can take advantage of their choices and utilize their social networks.

2. In September 1995 the World Bank published a new measure of wealth, a weighted composite of wealth based on the value of natural resources, manufactured output, and human and social capital, for the nations of the world (see Peter Passel, "The Wealth of Nations: A 'Greener' Approach Turns List Upside Down," *New York Times*, September 19, 1995, pp. B-4 and B-12). This new measurement of wealth tries to value human and natural resources in each country. The new listing of the wealth of nations places Australia and Canada at the top of the list, with Luxembourg, Switzerland, and Japan next, and China, 162d.

3. Paul Krugman argues that recent measurements of the sources of East Asian economies' total growth show only an intensification of factor input use, not any growth in total factor productivity. See Paul Krugman, "The Myth of Asia's Miracle," *Foreign Affairs* 73, no. 6 (November/December 1994): 62–78. This debate on whether total factor productivity played an important role in GDP growth has not been resolved. So far, the majority of total factor productivity studies of East Asia's economic growth conclude that total factor productivity was significant during the 1950s, 1960s, and 1970s. As growth rates for Japan, South Korea, Hong Kong, and Taiwan began to fall in the 1990s, these economies experienced structural change and the great expansion of the services sector. Factor productivity in these same countries will fall as services become the major sources of employment in the economy, and growth rates will also decline.

4. World Bank, *World Development Report, 1995: Workers in an Integrating World* (New York: Oxford University Press, 1995), ranks countries according to categories of low-income, middle- to lower-middle-income, upper-middle-income, and high-income economies.

5. In 1949 the *Far Eastern Economic Review* concluded that "China's present and near-future industrial potential is negligible and therefore she does not rank as a military power of any significance in the modern world." In the late 1940s another observer noted that "Korea can never attain a high standard of living." See John M. Leger, "Rags to Riches," *Far Eastern Economic Review*, October 12, 1995, pp. 46–47. This article goes on to point out that the four tigers of South Korea, Hong Kong, Taiwan, and Singapore contribute 28 percent of all Asia-Pacific exports to ASEAN, 33 percent of all exports from this region to Japan, and 39 percent of this region's exports to the United States (p. 47).

6. As of 1995, the World Bank denotes a poor, developing country to have a GDP per capita income of less than $700, a low- to middle-income status country to have $3,000 or less, and upper-middle-income status of below $10,000, and a high-income status country to exceed $10,000. See table 1, Basic Indicators, pp. 162–63 in *World Development Report, 1995*.

7. For all countries except the ROC, see World Bank, *World Development Report, 1991: The Challenge of Development* (New York: Oxford University Press, 1991), p. 12. For Taiwan, see Council for Economic Planning and Development, Republic of China, *Taiwan Statistical Data Book, 1995* (Taipei: Council for Economic Planning and Development, 1995), p. 32.

8. These economic development processes are described by Albert Fishlow in "Review of *Handbook of Development Economics*," *Journal of Economic Literature* 29 (December 1991): 1728–37. I refer to these processes as ideal types.

9. I have borrowed this term from Reinhard Bendix, "Tradition and Modernity Reconsidered," *Comparative Studies in Society and History* 9, no. 3 (April 1967): 334.

10. For the Gerschenkron model of late developers trying to catch up with early developers, see Albert Fishlow, "Gerschenkron, Alexander," in John Eatwell, Murray Milgate, and Peter Newman, eds., *The New Palgrave: Economic Development* (New York: W. W. Norton, 1989), pp. 145–47.

11. For a list of eleven kinds of problems caused by government intervention, see Nicholas Stern, "The Economics of Development: A Survey," *Economic Journal* 99 (September 1989): 616. Market failures include imperfect markets of monopoly or oligopoly, externalities, firms slow to adjust, poor information, shirking workers, and so on.

12. For an elaboration of these two roles, first developed by N. Kaldor (*Economic Journal*, 1972), see Heinz W. Arndt, "'Market Failures' and Underdevelopment," *World Development* 16, no. 2 (1988): 219–29.

13. Erik Dahmen first introduced the concept of "developmental block" to denote the groups of industries whose demands complemented one anothers' development by supplying the necessary inputs for the others' growth and to cover their unit cost as well as earn a profit. For definition and examples, see Erik Dahmen, *Entrepreneurial Activity and the Development of Swedish Industry, 1919–1939* (Homewood, Ill.: Richard D. Irwin, 1970), p. 65.

14. G. M. Meier, "The New Political Economy and Policy Reform," *Journal of International Development* 5, no. 4 (1993): 381–89.

15. Again, the reader is referred to Albert Fishlow's review article cited in note 4.

16. Douglass C. North, *Institutions, Institutional Change and Economic Performance* (Cambridge, Eng.: Cambridge University Press, 1990), p. 6.

Index